ENTERPRISE NETWORKING
Data Link Subnetworks

A  BOOK

ENTERPRISE NETWORKING
Data Link Subnetworks

JAMES MARTIN

with

Kathleen Kavanagh Chapman / Joe Leben

PRENTICE HALL P T R
Upper Saddle River, New Jersey 07458

For book and bookstore information

http://www.prenhall.com
gopher to gopher.prenhall.com

Library of Congress Cataloging-in-Publication Data

MARTIN, JAMES (date)
   Enterprise networking : data link subnetworks / James Martin,
Kathleen Kavanagh Chapman, Joe Leben.
     p. cm.
   "The James Martin books" —p. ii.
   Includes index.
   ISBN 0-13-507575-0
   1. Business enterprises—Communication systems. 2. Local area
networks (Computer networks) 3. Wide area networks. (Computer
networks) I. Chapman, Kathleen Kavanagh. II. Leben, Joe.
III. Title.
HD30.335.M37 1996
004.6—dc20
                                         95-38073
                                          CIP

Editorial/production supervision: *Kathryn Gollin Marshak*
Liaison: *Beth Sturla*
Jacket design: *Design Source*
Cover design director: *Jerry Votta*
Manufacturing buyer: *Alexis Heydt*
Acquisitions editor: *Paul Becker*

Published by Prentice Hall P T R
Prentice-Hall, Inc.
A Simon & Schuster Company
Upper Saddle River, New Jersey 07458

The publisher offers discounts on this book when ordered
in bulk quantities. For more information write:
        Corporate Sales Department, Prentice Hall P T R
        One Lake Street
        Upper Saddle River, New Jersey 07458
        Phone: (800) 382-3419; Fax: (201) 236-7141
        E-mail: corpsales@prenhall.com

Printed in the United States of America

10 9 8 7 6 5 4 3 2 1

ISBN 0-13-507575-0

Prentice-Hall International (UK) Limited, *London*
Prentice-Hall of Australia Pty. Limited, *Sydney*
Prentice-Hall Canada Inc., *Toronto*
Prentice-Hall Hispanoamericana, S.A., *Mexico*
Prentice-Hall of India Private Limited, *New Delhi*
Prentice-Hall of Japan, Inc., *Tokyo*
Simon & Schuster Asia Pte. Ltd., *Singapore*
Editora Prentice-Hall do Brasil, Ltda., *Rio de Janeiro*

TO CORINTHIA
—*JM*

TO JOHN AND MY PARENTS
—*KKC*

TO CAROL
—*JL*

Contents

Preface

In early computer networks communication was generally handled using the telecommunications circuits provided by common carriers. For the most part computer communication was slow and expensive. In recent years, a number of important new technologies have become available for implementing computer networks. This book examines the important technologies available for creating integrated computer networks.

Since the early 1980s, individual workgroups in organizations have begun to use local area network (LAN) technology to communicate and share resources. In many cases workgroup LANs have been interconnected, using wide area network (WAN) technologies, to form extended networks that reach throughout the organization.

A goal of computer networking is to enable *enterprise computing,* where users throughout an organization are able to communicate with each other and to access data, processing services, applications, and other resources without regard to where they are located. Enterprise computing depends on an *enterprise network* that integrates the newer departmental LANs with legacy corporate networks.

This book examines the important technologies used to implement the communication links in enterprise networks. These are divided into two groups: *wide area network (WAN)* technologies used to implement long-distance communication between different computer sites, and *local area network (LAN)* facilities used for high-speed communication between devices at a particular site. Another book, *Local Area Networks: Architectures and Implementations,* looks at local area network data link technology in more detail than this book does.

A companion book, *Enterprise Networking: Strategies and Transport Protocols,* takes a higher-level view of enterprise networking and describes the application services the network provides and the data transport technologies employed to implement end-to-end communication between users.

PLAN OF THE BOOK

The chapters of this book are divided into five parts. Part I introduces the enterprise networking environment. The chapters in Part I describe the characteristics of enterprise networks, introduce the various network architectures on which enterprise networking hardware and software products are based, present an architectural model for enterprise networks for use in organizing the material in this book, describe high-level application services provided by enterprise networks, and introduce end-to-end data transport services.

Part II describes the characteristics of data link subnetwork technologies used to build enterprise networks. The chapters in Part II introduce the types of services provided by an individual data link in an enterprise network, describe network driver software used to interface with subnetworks, examine the physical signal transmission technologies data link subnetworks employ, describe repeater and hub technology, and describe strategies and techniques for interconnecting individual data link subnetworks to form an integrated enterprise network.

Part III presents specific technologies used to implement wide area network data link subnetworks. The chapters in Part III describe analog telecommunications circuits, digital telecommunications circuits, X.25 packet-switching facilities, ISDN technology, the Frame Relay protocol, asynchronous transfer mode (ATM) technology, and technology for wireless WAN data links.

Part IV presents technologies used to implement local area network data link subnetworks. The chapters in Part IV describe the characteristics of LAN data links, introduce the IEEE Logical Link Control sublayer protocols, examine specific local area network data link technologies— including Ethernet, Token Ring, Token Bus, FDDI, and Apple LocalTalk—introduce technology for wireless LAN data links, and describe standards for Metropolitan Area Networks (MANs).

Part V consists of appendices that describe standards organizations, the OSI reference model, and the IEEE/ISO/ANSI LAN architecture. Appendix D is a glossary.

INTENDED READERS

This book is intended for a broad range of readers, including the following:

- Information systems and communications managers and technical staff members who maintain and administer computer networks and who need a thorough understanding of networking technology.

- Information systems and communications technical staff members who select, install, and support network hardware and software products and who deal with the complexities of multivendor networking.

- Users of network services who desire an understanding of the technology behind the computer communication tools used in their work environment.

- Students who are studying computer communications technologies.

James Martin
Kathleen Kavanagh Chapman
Joe Leben

List of Acronyms

AARP. AppleTalk Address Resolution Protocol.

AEP. AppleTalk Echo Protocol.

ANSI. American National Standards Institute.

API. Application Programming Interface.

APPN. Advanced Peer-to-Peer Networking.

ARP. Address Resolution Protocol.

ASC. Accredited Standards Committee.

ASN.1. Abstract Syntax Notation One.

ATM. Asynchronous Transfer Mode.

ATP. AppleTalk Transaction Protocol.

B-ISDN. Broadband ISDN.

BGP. Border Gateway Protocol.

CCB. Command control block.

CCITT. International Telegraph and Telephone Consultative Committee.

CDDI. Copper Distributed Data Interface.

CMIP. Common Management Information Protocol.

CMOT. CMIP over TCP/IP.

CSMA/CA. Carrier sense multiple access with collision avoidance.

CSMA/CD. Carrier sense multiple access with collision detection.

DAC. Dual-attachment concentrator.

DARPA. Defense Advanced Research Projects Agency.

DCE. Distributed Computing Environment.

DDP. Datagram Delivery Protocol.

DNA. Digital Network Architecture.

DNS. Domain Name System.

DQDB. Distributed Queue Dual Bus.

DRP. Digital Routing Protocol.

EGP. Exterior Gateway Protocol.

ELAP. EtherTalk Link Access Protocol.

FCS. Frame check sequence.

FDDI. Fiber Distributed Data Interface.

FOIRL. Fiber-optic inter-repeater link.

FTP. File Transfer Protocol.

HDLC. High-level Data Link Control.

ICMP. Internet Control Message Protocol.

IDP. Internetwork Datagram Protocol.

IEEE. Institute of Electrical and Electronics Engineers.

IP. Internet Protocol.

IPX. Internetwork Packet Exchange protocol.

ISDN. Integrated Services Digital Network.

ISO. International Organization for Standardization.

ITU-T. International Telecommunication Union-Telecommunications.

LAN. Local area network.

LLAP. LocalTalk Link Access Protocol.

LLC. Logical Link Control.

LLC-PDU. Logical-link-control-protocol-data-unit.

LLC-SDU. Logical-link-control-service-data-unit.

MAC. Medium Access Control.

MAC-PDU. Medium-access-control-protocol-data-unit.

MAC-SDU. Medium-access-control-service-data-unit.

MAN. Metropolitan Area Network.

MAP. Manufacturing Automation Protocol.

MAPI. Mail Application Programming Interface.

MIB. Management Information Base.

MIC. Medium interface connector.

NAC. Null-attachment concentrator.

NBP. Name Binding Protocol.

NCB. Network Control Block.

NCP. NetWare Core Protocol.

NFS. Network File System.

NIC. Network interface card or, in the Internet, the Network Information Center.

NLM. NetWare Loadable Module.

NPDU. Network-protocol-data-unit.

NSP. Network Services Protocol.

OSI. Open systems interconnection.

OSF. Open Software Foundation.

OSPF. Open Shortest Path First.

PCI. Protocol-control-information.

PCMCIA. Personal Computer Memory Card International Association.

PDU. Protocol-data-unit.

PEP. Packet Exchange Protocol.

PPP. Point-to-Point Protocol.

PTT. Postal, Telegraph, and Telephone Administration.

RARP. Reverse Address Resolution Protocol.

RFC. Request for Comments.

RIP. Routing Information Protocol.

RPC. Remote procedure call.

RTMP. Routing Table Maintenance Protocol.

SAC. Single-attachment concentrator.

SAP. Service-access-point and Service Advertising Protocol.

SAS. Single-attachment station.

SDU. Service-data-unit.

SMB. Server Message Block.

SMDS. Switched Multi-Megabit Data Service.

SMTP. Simple Mail Transfer Protocol.

SNA. Systems Network Architecture.

SNAP. Subnetwork Access Protocol.

SNMP. Simple Network Management Protocol.

SPP. Sequenced Packet Protocol.

SPX. Sequenced Packet Exchange Protocol.

TCP. Transmission Control Protocol.

TCP/IP. Transmission Control Protocol/Internet Protocol.

TFTP. Trivial File Transfer Protocol.

TLAP. TokenTalk Link Access Protocol.

TLI. Transport Layer Interface.

TOP. Technical and Office Protocols.

UDP. User Datagram Protocol.

VAP. Value Added Process.

VIM. Vendor Independent Messaging.

WAN. Wide area network.

XNS. Xerox Network System.

PART I

FUNDAMENTALS

Chapter 1

Enterprise Networks

The design, installation, and operation of computer networks is vital to the functioning of modern computerized organizations. Over the last decade, organizations have installed complex and diverse networks, tying together mainframes, minicomputers, personal computers, workstations, terminals, and other devices. This chapter introduces the types of networks that organizations use and discusses how they can be interlinked to form *enterprise networks*.

ENTERPRISE COMPUTING

Hardware and software vendors would like the term *enterprise computing* to conjure up a bold and compelling vision. They speak of an environment that includes:

- **Any-to-any Connectivity.** A person or program in an organization can reach and communicate with any other person or program, in that organization or in the organization's trading partners around the world.
- **Data Highways.** A user can have access to a myriad of data sources, both internal and external to the organization.
- **Distributed Services.** All forms of processing capabilities are accessible from any location on the network.
- **Multimedia Applications.** The organization can create applications that use image processing, digitized sound, animation, and full motion digital video.
- **Flexibility.** The user can respond rapidly to changing business requirements.
- **Economy.** Small, inexpensive processors can handle the organization's information processing and share expensive data transmission facilities.

Providing this type of computing environment is not an easy task, and no single vendor can provide what is needed to build a true enterprise computing solution.

Today, moving in the direction of enterprise computing is not just a question of installing a particular set of hardware and software systems. Typically, the move to enterprise computing involves the integration of a wide range of existing computing facilities, different types of networks, operating systems, and an array of applications. To build an enterprise computing environment, the organization must develop a framework within which each of the separate pieces can fit and effectively interoperate.

Enterprise computing requires the firm footing of an effective networking infrastructure on which to build. The networking infrastructure comprises an *enterprise network* that provides the underlying connectivity and distributability required for enterprise computing applications. In this book we examine the requirements associated with the networking infrastructure required to make an enterprise computing environment a reality.

ENTERPRISE NETWORKS

In today's environment it is a rare organization that does not already use some form of networking to interconnect the computers used by individual departments. Therefore, most organizations will not be starting from scratch in building an enterprise network. One of the first tasks that must be accomplished is to interconnect the individual networks that the organization already uses. Most organizations, except perhaps for very small ones, will not be able to accomplish this in a single step. The enterprise network is usually implemented one step at a time by tying together the separate networks that already are in place in different areas of the organization.

The various networks that an organization employs are likely to use different types of networking hardware and software and might interconnect very different types of machines. A key challenge in developing an enterprise network is to find ways of interconnecting a set of existing networks that might be quite incompatible with one another. The goal is to enable a user or an application program using a machine on one network to communicate with a user or application program using a machine on any other network in the organization. As we will see, this can be a difficult task.

We will begin our investigation of enterprise networking by looking at network technology from a very high-level perspective.

NETWORKING TECHNOLOGY

As we have already mentioned, different networks might employ different types of networking technologies. An important way in which networking technologies can differ is by the distances that the networking technology is designed to span. With this form of classification, we can identify three types of computer networking technology:

- Wide area network (WAN) technology.
- Local area network (LAN) technology.
- Metropolitan area network (MAN) technology.

Wide Area Network Technology

Many of the first networks that organizations have installed employ public telecommunications facilities that allow machines to communicate over long distances. Such networks might be used to provide all users at far-flung locations access to the resources maintained in centrally located computer complexes. Such networks might permit fast interchange of information among users. Networks that tie together users who are widely separated geographically are called *wide area networks (WANS)*.

Wide area networks have evolved over time, consisting at first of dumb terminals communicating with large mainframes. As the cost of microelectronic devices has dropped, the intelligence in the various devices attached to a WAN has increased. Today's WANS might interconnect intelligent terminals, personal computers, graphics workstations, minicomputers, and other diverse forms of programmable devices.

The chapters in Part III describe the various types of data transmission technologies used to build wide area network communication facilities.

Local Area Network Technology

As wide area networks have expanded in scope, organizations have also expanded their use of personal computers and individual workstations to support the computer needs of users throughout the organization. Today's organizations make heavy use of small computers for word processing, financial analysis, sales reporting, engineering, order processing, and almost any conceivable business function. As the use of small computers has grown, a need has also grown for these computer systems to communicate, both with each other and with the larger, centralized data processing facilities that the organization maintains.

Small computers are often initially used in a stand-alone manner to support applications local in nature. But typically, additional requirements soon arise, such as to:

- Access existing data that might be stored on a machine in some other department.
- Allow a group of computer systems to share devices too expensive to be used by a single person only.
- Give users of small machines the ability to exchange electronic messages with one another, using the computers already in place.

The type of networks that users of small computers often use for such purposes are called *local area networks (LANS)*. LANS provide a means for meeting the requirements for high-speed, relatively short-distance communication among intelligent devices. The range of distances supported by typical local area networks range from a few feet to a few miles.

The majority of LANS in use today are used to interconnect personal computers and workstations. Some of the machines in a LAN are often called *servers,* to which individual users share access.

The chapters in Part IV describe the data transmission technologies used to build local area network facilities.

Metropolitan Area Network Technology

In some cases, it is desirable to identify a form of networking that falls between wide area networking and local area networking. *Metropolitan area networks (MANs)* operate in a similar manner to LANs but over longer distances, up to about 100 miles. Metropolitan area networks can be used to bridge the gap between wide area networks and local area networks.

MAN technology has not yet become important in today's networking environment. Where MANs are employed, they are used simply as a lower-cost alternative to WANs or to extend the range of an existing LAN.

Chapter 25 discusses standards being developed to address metropolitan area networks.

CLIENT/SERVER COMPUTING

In many organizations, an important application for an enterprise network is to provide the universal connectivity required to create an enterprisewide client/server computing environment. *Client/server* computing refers to a broad computing paradigm in which application components called *clients* issue requests for services. Another set of application components, called *servers,* which may run in different computing systems from the client components, provides the requested service.

A computer network, ranging from a single departmental LAN to a global enterprise network, provides the means of transporting information back and forth between the client components and the server components. This is illustrated in Fig. 1.1. Multiple clients can share the services of a single server, and users of the client applications need not be aware that processing is not being performed locally.

The term *client/server computing* has many interpretations, and the term is often used in the personal computer environment to refer to client/server database systems. In a client/server database environment, desktop computers operating in the role of clients make requests for data maintained on another computing system operating in the role of a database server. Our definition of the client/server environment described in the foregoing section is much broader than this.

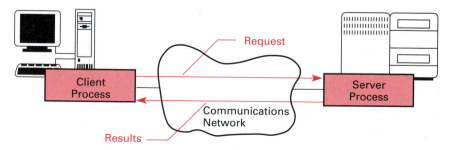

Figure 1.1   Client/server computing.

The client/server computing paradigm permits many different types of server systems to be built. The following are a few types of server systems possible in the client/server environment:

- **File Server.** Provides access to data files that reside on a separate computing system from that running the application program.

- **Print Server.** Provides access to printers attached to a separate computing system from that running the application program.

- **Communications Server.** Provides access to modems or other communications facilities that provide networked computing systems with access to specialized communication capabilities.

- **Database Server.** Provides access to databases stored on a separate computing system from that running the application program.

- **Application Server.** Provides access to application logic, allowing an application's function processing to be distributed among more than one computing system.

- **Transaction Server.** Provides facilities for coordinating the processing of distributed transactions in which entire units of work, possibly involving the updating of multiple databases, must be either executed in their entirety or not executed at all.

- **Workgroup Computing Server.** Provides access to applications, sometimes called *groupware* applications, that support the business activities of groups of end users. Such applications include compound document management, workflow processing, electronic mail, conferencing, and scheduling.

- **Object Server.** In an object-oriented computing environment, provides access to objects so that a client object can invoke a server object without having to know on which computing system the server object resides.

Client/Server Network Software

Some network software implements a client/server configuration, in which some systems on the network play the role of servers, possibly implementing file server and print server functions. Other systems directly accessed by end users play the role of clients that request services of the servers.

Most of Novell's NetWare network operating system software products implement a client/server network configuration. Microsoft's Windows NT operating system software also implements a client/server networking environment.

Peer-to-Peer Network Software

Other network software implements a *peer-to-peer* configuration, in which all systems play similar roles in the network. Each system in a peer-to-peer network can play the role of either a client or a server, and the roles can be changed from one moment to the next. Each end-user machine can act as a server that any of the other machines, playing the roles of clients, can access.

Microsoft's low-end operating system products, such as Windows for Workgroups and Windows 95, implement a peer-to-peer architecture for networking. Machines running these operating systems can also play the role of clients in a client/server configuration when they access the services of a dedicated server.

Peer-to-peer configurations are often used in small networks when communication between users is most important and when it is not cost-effective to install dedicated servers. Client/server configurations are used in networks where a greater degree of control must be exercised over shared network resources.

NETWORK COMPONENTS

Computer networks are typically implemented by a combination of hardware and software components. The components used to implement networks, shown in Fig. 1.2, include computing devices, network interface cards, physical communication links, interconnection devices, and network software.

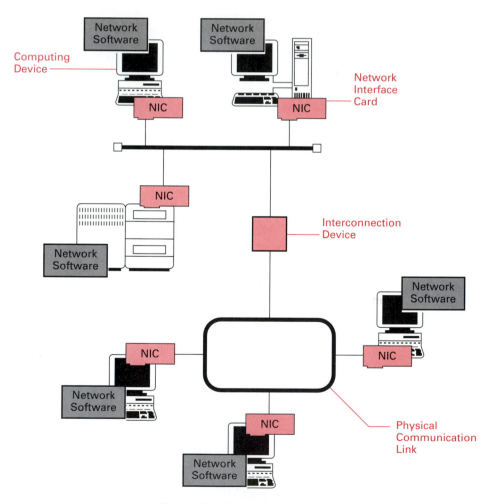

Figure 1.2 Network components.

Computing Devices

A computer network is typically used to interconnect general-purpose computing devices, such as personal computers, workstations, minicomputers, and mainframes. Simple peripheral devices, such as hard disks and simple line printers, are not typically attached to the computer network, but are instead attached to one of the networked computer systems. Peripheral devices can, however, be made accessible to other systems on the network and can be shared by all network users.

Network Interface Cards

A *network interface card (NIC)* is typically installed in each computing device directly attached to the network. A NIC performs the hardware functions required to provide a computing device with physical communications capabilities.

Some types of computing devices designed for use on specific types of networks, such as network printers or certain types of workstations, directly integrate the functions of a NIC. Other types of computing devices, such as general-purpose computing systems, typically allow various types of NICs to be installed.

In most cases, a NIC provides a computer with access to a local area network. Wide area network links are generally managed by network interconnection devices that interconnect individual LANs.

Physical Communication Links

For a local area network, the physical communication link is typically implemented by wire or cable used to interconnect the NICs installed in the networked computing devices. Various types of electrical cable or fiber-optic cable are used to implement LANs. The cabling system also typically includes *attachment units* that allow the devices to attach to the cable. For a WAN link, the physical communication link often takes the form of a circuit provided by a telecommunications provider. In some cases, the physical communication link may be provided by some form of wireless communication, such as radio, microwave, or infrared signaling.

Interconnection Devices

Some local area network implementations use devices called repeaters, access units, concentrators, or hubs that allow multiple network devices to be connected to the LAN cabling system through a central point. Individual local area networks are interconnected with network interconnection devices, such as bridges, routers, and gateways. Network interconnection devices might access both local area network cabling and wide area network circuits so the individual LANs in an enterprise network can be located anywhere in the world.

Network Software

Network interface cards perform low-level functions that allow physical communication to take place between interconnected devices. High-level functions that end users employ for doing useful work are generally handled by network software that accesses a NIC on behalf of an end user. Both client systems and server systems must run compatible network software in order for them to communicate over the network.

The systems software that runs on a server system is often called a *network operating system (NOS)*. Network operating systems augment a computer system's conventional systems software by providing basic communication facilities and implementing various types of server functions.

ENTERPRISE NETWORK BUILDING BLOCKS

The job of building an enterprise network typically consists of interconnecting different existing individual networks so they form a coherent whole. These networks generally use local area networking technology, wide area technology, or both.

In most cases, we can place an organization's existing networks into two categories: *departmental networks* and *legacy networks*. Departmental networks typically use LAN technology to interconnect systems, and legacy networks typically use WAN technology to connect mainframes or large minicomputers to groups of terminals. Most enterprise networks must incorporate the wide variety of departmental LANs that have grown up in an organization in parallel with its legacy wide area networks.

Departmental Networks

A *departmental network* typically consists of a single LAN that ties together all the computers used by a particular department. Although a departmental network typically consists of a single LAN, it is not uncommon for large departmental networks to also use WAN circuits to tie together the computers at multiple locations. A departmental network typically interconnects personal computer equipment, but it may also network other types of equipment, such as minicomputers and workstations. Some departmental networks may even incorporate mainframes. Therefore, it might sometimes be difficult to distinguish between a departmental network and a legacy network in some situations.

Legacy Networks

We use the term *legacy networks* to refer to networks that an enterprise has had installed for a relatively long period of time and are used for some specialized purpose. An important task in enterprise networking is to incorporate an organization's existing legacy networks into the enterprise network. This can be one of the most difficult tasks to accomplish in building an integrated networking environment. An organization's legacy networks might be national or international in scope, and might support connections among widely dispersed locations.

Existing legacy networks often support important, mission-critical computer applications and may cover an extensive geographic area and support a large number of users. These networks typically allow large numbers of terminals at remote locations to communicate with centrally-located mainframes or minicomputers. They typically use WAN communication links to provide connectivity among host computers that may be geographically dispersed and between host computers and terminals. However, it is not uncommon for legacy networks to also employ LAN technology in various parts of the network in conjunction with WAN links.

Legacy networks are often based on a single vendor's hardware and software. For example, many large legacy networks make extensive use of IBM equipment and software and conform to IBM's *Systems Network Architecture* (SNA) specifications.

Differences Between Departmental LANs and Legacy Networks

The equipment and software making up a departmental LAN can be purchased from any number of vendors. Therefore, it is not uncommon for different personal computer LANs within an organization to run incompatible network software. Almost always, computers on departmental LANs run software incompatible with the software used to build legacy networks. This book describes a variety of techniques that can be used to overcome such incompatibilities.

In addition to hardware and software differences, departmental LANs and legacy networks differ in their basic technology in several respects.

Relationships Between Communicating Devices

A local area network generally allows a number of independent computing systems to communicate directly with each other. A LAN typically supports *any-to-any connectivity*, where any system attached to the LAN is able to communicate directly with any other system on the LAN. This contrasts with some legacy networks that use *hierarchical* or *centrally-controlled* communication. On a typical legacy network, the central mainframe is assumed to be more capable than the remote terminals, and the mainframe (or its attached communications controller) has the primary responsibility for controlling communication.

Geographic Area

With a departmental LAN, communication ordinarily takes place within a moderately sized geographic area, often within a single building. A local area network does not ordinarily span a distance greater than a few miles. The WAN technology typically used in legacy networks may incorporate telecommunications circuits that can span thousands of miles.

Type of Transmission Facility

Communication on a departmental LAN generally takes place over private cabling that creates dedicated communications channels. This contrasts with WANs that often use public telecommunications facilities (telephone lines) for communication.

Data Rates

A typical LAN operates at a much higher data rate than the data links typically employed in a legacy network. The data rates supported by typical local area networks typically fall in the 1 megabit per second (Mbps) to 100 Mbps range. Many legacy networks use dial-up or leased telephone lines, where maximum data rates range from 2,400 bits per second (bps) to 64,000 bps.

ENTERPRISE NETWORK DEVELOPMENT

As we have already mentioned, enterprise networks typically evolve over a long period of time. Individual local area networks spring up in many different locations. Initially isolated, they are later interconnected to each other. The interconnected LANs might then be connected to legacy networks as the need arises. Specialized LANs called *backbone networks* might then be installed to provide high-speed connections between various network segments.

We can view an enterprise network as being made up of a collection of interconnected network segments, such as that shown in Fig. 1.3. Each of the individual component networks becomes one or more *subnetworks* in the full enterprise network. We can define a subnetwork as a group of computing systems that share a common transmission medium and use the same technology for exchanging signals.

The individual component networks in an enterprise network may continue to be used for their original purposes. For example, a personal computer LAN in an enterprise network may still provide support for a particular department or workgroup, and an existing legacy network might still support the specialized application for which it was originally developed.

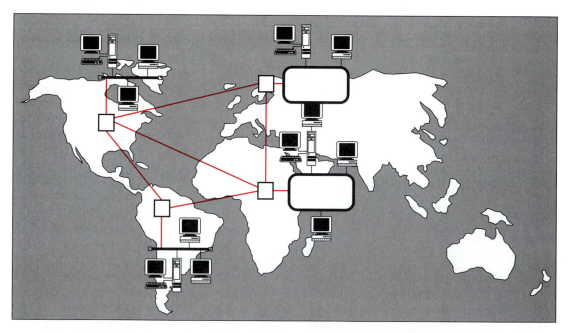

Figure 1.3 Enterprise network comprising LANs interconnected with WAN data links.

As the enterprise network becomes more integrated, the functions that any single user can perform are often greatly expanded. This often causes the distinction to blur between the original departmental LANs and the legacy networks that formed the basis of the enterprise network. LAN-based computers may be used to access the resources under the control of the legacy networks. This expands the reach of the individual departmental LAN and also expands the scope of the legacy network. Data may be downloaded from mainframes to personal computers or workstations to be processed locally. The resources accessed on a departmental LAN may no longer be stored locally.

Even with limited integration, an enterprise network is a complex entity. The various component subnetworks are likely to be based on different network specifications, use different network software, and employ different transmission technologies. Hardware and software products and transmission services used within the network may be provided by a host of different vendors. Building, operating, and managing such a network presents many challenges in terms of compatibility and interoperability.

New applications developed to take advantage of enterprise network capabilities can increase the complexity. New applications based on client/server computing technology are designed to distribute processing across the network. This can result in a requirement for connectivity among many different types of systems that can be located anywhere throughout the network.

New forms of computerized information, including computer graphics, audio, and video, may begin to be exchanged across the network, causing a dramatic increase in the volume of data that needs to be transmitted. New forms of transmission technology offer new capabilities but also require new trade-offs and generate new questions concerning compatibility and interoperability.

POLITICAL CONSIDERATIONS

This book concentrates on existing and newly emerging *technology*—network software, transmission facilities, and integration strategies—available today for building and operating enterprise networks. However, it is important to realize that mastering the technology is often not the only job that must be done in creating an integrated enterprise networking environment. The political problems that arise are often more difficult to overcome than the technical problems.

The job of creating an integrated networking environment can be approached from two different directions. The builders of the legacy networks might want to extend the reach of the legacy networks to include the functions now being performed in a decentralized way by departmental LANs. The builders of the individual LANs, on the other hand, may want to extend their own reach to include much of the processing now performed in a centralized way by the legacy networks.

One group wants to exercise more centralized control over what has become distributed and decentralized. The other group wants to continue the decentralization of the information system's function by expanding the scope of what the departmental LANs have begun to do. The differing objectives of these different groups may easily become the basis for heated political battles.

For the most part, this book leaves the political problems for the reader to overcome and concentrates on the easier technical problems that must be solved if enterprise networking is to become a reality.

SUMMARY

Enterprise computing involves the integration of different types of computing systems, networks, systems software, and application programs. Enterprise computing is based on an enterprise network that provides required connectivity and distributability. There are three types of computer networking technology: wide area networks (WANs), local area networks (LANs), and metropolitan area networks (MANs).

An important application for an enterprise network is to provide the universal connectivity required to create an enterprisewide client/server computing environment. Client/server computing refers to a broad computing paradigm in which client components issue requests for services, and server components, typically running in different machines, provide the requested service. Some network software implements a client/server configuration, in which some systems on the network play the role of servers and others act as clients. Other network software can implement a peer-to-peer configuration, in which all systems can function as both clients and servers.

Computer networks are typically implemented by a combination of hardware and software components, including computing devices, network interface cards, physical communication links, interconnection devices, and network software. The job of building an enterprise network typically consists of interconnecting different individual LANs and WAN data links to form a coherent whole. Most of an organization's existing networks consist of departmental LANs that interconnect desktop systems and legacy networks that interconnect terminals and mainframes or large minicomputers. Each of the individual building blocks of an enterprise network is called a subnetwork.

Chapter 2 continues our look at the fundamental principles of enterprise networking by examining the nature of the network architectures on which modern network hardware and software products are based.

Chapter **2**

Network Architectures

A key characteristic of the environment in which most enterprise networks operate is *diversity*. As we saw in Chapter 1, an enterprise network is ordinarily made up of a number of individual component subnetworks that may use different networking technologies. Within any of the individual subnetworks, many different types of devices may communicate. Part of the power of an enterprise network comes from its ability to allow a wide variety of different types of systems, operating in different subnetworks, to interoperate with one another.

Supporting a wide variety of systems and networking technologies can present substantial compatibility problems. For widely varying systems to be effectively linked together, the hardware and software used for communication need to be compatible, or else complex interfaces have to be built. In order to facilitate compatibility, *network architectures* have been developed to describe the various *functional software layers* necessary to allow complex networks to be built using a variety of equipment.

Before we discuss the nature of network architectures, we will introduce the functions of a computer network by using an analogy to describe the benefits of independent functional layers in complex systems.

HUMAN COMMUNICATION ANALOGY

We can make an analogy between the communication functions performed in a computer network and the functions performed in ordinary human communication. Figure 2.1 shows how we might divide the functions performed during ordinary human communication into three independent layers: a Medium layer, a Language layer, and an Ideas layer.

The Medium Layer

In the *Medium* layer, the two parties must select and use a common communications medium. A typical communication medium used in human communications might be

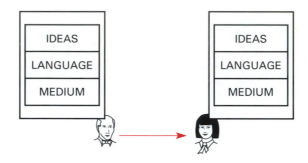

Figure 2.1   Levels of computer communication.

sound waves in air. For example, Fig. 2.2 shows the physical medium used when two parties are involved in a face-to-face conversation.

In human communications, it is important that both parties agree upon and use the same communications medium. For example, if one party is speaking, but the other party is deaf and can only read written words, no communication takes place.

The Language Layer

Once a common medium has been chosen, each party involved in a conversation must use a language understood by the other. If one party speaks only French and the other only English, little communication will take place. Figure 2.3 shows the *Language* layer when two parties are conducting a conversation using the English language.

With no common language, there is no successful dialog, even though both parties may have agreed to use the same communications medium. If I enter a Tokyo hotel and walk up to a clerk who does not speak English, I will not be able to book a room, even though we can both easily hear each other.

The Ideas Layer

We might think of the highest layer in human communication as the *Ideas* layer. In this layer, each person involved in a conversation must have some idea of what the conversa-

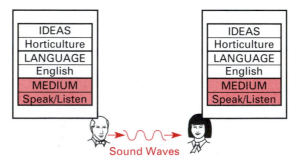

Figure 2.2   Medium level: human speech.

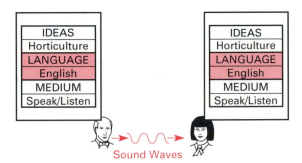

Figure 2.3   Language level: English.

tion is about and must understand the concepts being discussed. Figure 2.4 shows the Ideas layer when two parties are discussing horticulture.

     If an English-speaking gardener enters into a conversation with another English-speaking person and begins a technical discussion on horticulture, little real communication is likely to take place if the second party is a two-year-old child.

Protocols

In each layer in any communications system, a set of precisely defined *rules* must be agreed to and followed by both parties for communication to be successful. The rules governing communication at a given layer are called *protocols*. Each set of protocols can be thought of as a description of a set of *messages* and a *rule book* that specifies procedures for exchanging those messages. Each layer on one side communicates with a complementary layer on the other side using a protocol. Both parties must adhere exactly to the protocol; otherwise, communication is not possible.

Human Communication Protocols

The protocols involved in our hypothetical Medium layer of human communication are simple and involve mechanical procedures for exchanging messages in both directions. When two parties agree to use a common communication medium, they must both

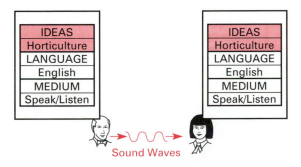

Figure 2.4   Ideas level: Horticulture.

observe the same rules in using that medium. The protocol for polite conversation using this communication medium might specify that both parties should not talk at the same time. If both people speak at once, little communication takes place.

For the Language layer, the protocols involve procedures described by the rules of grammar and syntax for the common language. The messages exchanged consist of ordinary sentences in the selected language. When two parties agree to use English, they agree to abide by the rules of grammar and syntax that govern sentence construction in the English language.

For the Ideas layer, the protocols involve procedures described by the body of knowledge concerning the subject being discussed. If two parties are discussing horticulture, the protocols might involve technical details concerning botany and agriculture.

Layer Independence

When people communicate, the protocol used for one layer is independent of the protocols used at other layers. For example, a business communication between two people might begin with an exchange of letters and then proceed to a telephone conversation. The two people may then decide that a face-to-face meeting is required to continue the discussion. The rules, or protocols, governing the Ideas and Language layers remain the same each time the discussion is resumed, even though the protocol governing the Medium layer may be different. Similarly, communication in any language—French, Russian, Chinese, Arabic—can be used in a face-to-face conversation at the Medium layer. As long as both parties agree to use the same language, the protocol used for the Language layer does not affect the protocol used at the Medium or Ideas layer.

NETWORK ARCHITECTURES AND PROTOCOLS

A network architecture is a comprehensive plan and a set of rules that govern the design and operation of the hardware and software components used to create a particular type of computer network. A network architecture is a specification that defines a set of *communications protocols* that govern how communication should take place over the network. A system for communicating in a computer network generally consists of a set of compatible hardware and software components that all conform to a particular network architecture and use a particular set of communication protocols.

A great many different network architectures and systems of communication protocols are in use today in computer networks.

Layered Approach

An important characteristic common to all network architectures is the use of a *layered approach*. In modern computer networks, data transmission functions are performed by complex hardware and software in the various devices that make up the network. In order to manage this complexity, the functions performed in network devices are divided into independent *functional layers*, analogous to the layers we described in the human communication analogy. The layered approach offers three key advantages:

- **Ease of Modification.** If a new technology becomes available for use in a particular layer, it can be incorporated without having a major impact on any of the other layers.

- **Diversity.** Two devices can be built using completely different hardware and software technologies. They will be able to communicate successfully as long as both devices employ the same communications protocols in each layer.

- **Transparency.** The layering concept allows the technical details of the lower layers to be hidden from the higher layers. At the top of the layering structure, the user perceives an easy-to-use interface to the network, even though the details of the layers below may be quite complex.

Services and Protocols

For each functional layer in a network architecture, the architecture defines a set of *services* that the layer performs and specifies a *protocol* that governs communication in that layer:

- **Service.** A layer *service* defines *what* a layer does for the layer above it. A layer service consists of the definition of a function or set of functions that a layer performs on behalf of the layer above it.

- **Protocol.** A layer *protocol* specifies *how* a layer performs its service. A layer protocol specifies the formats of messages exchanged between the layer in one machine and the same layer in another machine and rules governing the exchange of those messages.

Figure 2.5 illustrates a general model for a layered network architecture based on the idea of services and protocols.

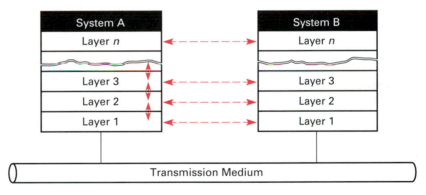

Figure 2.5 Layered model on which network architectures are based.

There is a defined *interface* between each pair of layers, and each functional layer provides a set of services to the layer above it. In the hypothetical layered architecture shown in Fig 2.6, the vertical arrows represent how Layer 2 provides its services to Layer 3.

A network architecture also defines protocols used by complementary layers in communicating systems. The horizontal arrow between complementary Layer 2 entities in Fig. 2.6 represents the protocol that governs Layer 2 of the hypothetical architecture. As we discussed earlier, a protocol defines the precise formats of the messages exchanged by complementary layers and the rules governing the exchange of those messages.

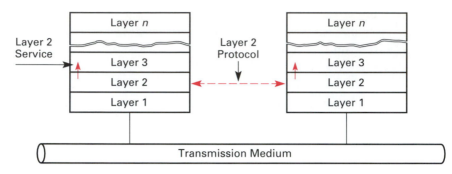

Figure 2.6   Services and protocols.

Goals of a Network Architecture

Network architectures are important to both users and vendors. An architecture must provide users with a variety of choices in the configuration of networks, and it must allow them to change a configuration with relative ease as their systems evolve. It should define the precise coordination required between network components, both hardware and software.

For providers of networking products and services, network architectures should permit mass production of hardware or software building blocks that can be used in a variety of different ways. Network architectures also provide standards and definitions that facilitate the development of new devices and software that will be compatible with existing systems. These new products can then be integrated into existing networks without the need for costly interfaces and program modifications.

The Nature of Architecture

Although network architectures provide rules for the development of new products, these rules can change. This is because the term *architecture* in the computer industry often implies an overall scheme or plan that may be evolving. An architecture defines an overall framework that allows the architecture to evolve and change to support new technologies. An architecture should also define sufficient detail to guide implementors in creating products that will fully conform to the architecture and, therefore, that will interoperate with all other implementations of the architecture. As one network architect has said:

> An architecture must be always *complete,* but it is never *finished.* It must provide a framework that permits change.

STANDARDS ORGANIZATIONS

Many of today's network architectures and computer networking mechanisms have been developed by independent hardware and software vendors. However, it is a major goal of today's network architecture development to allow diverse equipment from many different vendors to be interconnected using standard interfaces and protocols. Because of this, widely accepted standards will play an increasingly important role in network architecture development.

A number of standards organizations around the world are actively involved in developing standards and architectures for data communication and computer networking. Four important standards organizations playing important roles in the standardization of computer networking technologies are the International Organization for Standardization (ISO), the Institute of Electrical and Electronics Engineers (IEEE), the American National Standards Institute (ANSI), and the Telecommunication sector of the International Telecommunication Union (ITU-T)*. These organizations are described further in Appendix A.

THE OSI REFERENCE MODEL

During the time that today's network architectures and communication protocols were being developed, an ambitious project was underway in ISO to develop a single international standard set of communication protocols that could be used in a communication network. By 1984, ISO had defined the *Reference Model for Open Systems Interconnection*, or *OSI model* for short. The OSI model is a generalized model of system interconnection and is described in international standard ISO 7498. In some cases, both ISO and ITU-T publish the same standards. ITU-T standards are called *Recommendations*, and the OSI model is also described by ITU-T *Recommendation X.200*.

Purpose of the OSI Model

The OSI model is designed to provide a common basis for the coordination of standards development for the purpose of interconnecting *open systems*. The term *open* in this context means systems open to one another by virtue of their mutual use of applicable standards.

The OSI model describes how machines can communicate with one another in a standardized and highly flexible way by defining the functional layers that should be incorporated into each communicating machine. The OSI model does not define the networking software itself, nor does it define detailed standards for that software; it simply defines the broad categories of function each layer should perform.

The OSI Network Architecture

ISO has also developed a comprehensive set of standards for the various layers of the OSI model. These standards together make up the *OSI architecture* for computer networking.

The standards supporting the OSI architecture are not today widely implemented in commercial products for computer networking, nor does it appear that they will be widely

---

*ITU-T standards for the information technology industry were formerly referred to using the old name of the Telecommunications sector of the ITU: the International Telegraph and Telephone Consultative Committee (CCITT).

implemented in the forseeable future. However, the OSI model is still important. Many of the concepts and terminology associated with the OSI model have become generally accepted as a basis for discussing and describing network architectures of all types. The layering structure of the OSI model is also often used in categorizing the various communication protocols in common use today and in comparing one network architecture with another.

OSI MODEL FUNCTIONAL LAYERS

The OSI model defines the seven functional layers shown in Box 2.1. Each layer performs a different set of functions, and the intent was to make each layer as independent as possible from all the others. Box 2.1 also briefly describes each of the seven layers of the OSI model.

BOX 2.1   OSI model function layers.

| Application Layer |
| Presentation Layer |
| Session Layer |
| Transport Layer |
| Network Layer |
| Data Link Layer |
| Physical Layer |

- **Physical Layer.** The *Physical* layer is responsible for the actual transmission of a bit stream across a physical circuit. It allows signals, such as electrical signals, optical signals, or radio signals, to be exchanged among communicating machines. The Physical layer typically consists of hardware permanently installed in the communicating devices. The Physical layer also addresses the cables, connectors, modems, and other devices used to permit machines to physically communicate. Physical layer mechanisms in each of the communicating machines typically control the generation and detection of signals interpreted as 0 bits and 1 bits.

- **The Data Link Layer.** The *Data Link* layer is responsible for transmitting data over a single physical circuit from one system to another. Control mechanisms in the *Data Link* layer handle the transmission of data units, often called *frames,* over a physical circuit. Functions operating in the Data Link layer allow data to be transmitted, in a relatively error-free fashion, over a sometimes error-prone transmission medium. This layer is concerned with how bits are grouped into frames and performs synchronization functions with respect to failures occurring in the Physical layer. The Data Link layer implements error-detection mechanisms that identify transmission errors. With some types of data links, the Data Link layer may also perform procedures for flow control, frame sequencing, and recovering from transmission errors.

- **The Network Layer.** The *Network* layer is concerned with making routing decisions and with relaying data from one device to another through the network. The OSI model classi-

BOX 2.1   *(Continued)*

fies each system in the network as one of two types: *end systems* act as the source or the final destination of data, and *intermediate systems* perform routing and relaying functions. The facilities provided by the Network layer supply a service that higher layers employ for moving data units, often called *packets,* from one end system to another, where the packets may flow through any number of intermediate systems. End systems generally implement all seven layers of the OSI model, allowing application programs to exchange information with each other. It is possible for intermediate systems performing only routing and relaying functions to implement only the bottom three layers of the OSI model. Where the Data Link layer provides for the transmission of frames between *adjacent* systems across a single data link, the Network layer provides for the more complex task of transmitting packets between any two end systems in the network, regardless of how many data links may need to be traversed.

- **The Transport Layer.** The *Transport* layer builds on the services of the Network layer and the layers below it to form the uppermost layer of a reliable end-to-end *data transport service.* The Transport layer hides from the higher layers all the details concerning the actual moving of packets and frames from one computer to another. The lowest three layers of the OSI model implement a common physical network that many machines can share independently of one another. The functions performed in the Transport layer may include end-to-end integrity controls to recover from lost, out-of-sequence, or duplicate messages. The Transport layer is the lowest layer required only in the computers running the programs that use the network for communication. The Transport layer need not be implemented in intermediate systems that perform only routing and relaying functions.

- **The Session Layer.** There is a fundamental difference in orientation between the bottom four layers and the top three. The bottom four layers are concerned more with the network itself and provide a general data transport service useful to any application. The top three layers are more concerned with services oriented to the application programs themselves. The Session layer is the lowest of the layers associated with the application programs. It is responsible for organizing the dialog between two application programs and for managing the data exchanges between them. Session layer services also include establishing synchronization points within the dialog, allowing a dialog to be interrupted, and resuming a dialog from a synchronization point.

- **The Presentation Layer.** The five layers below the Presentation layer are all concerned with the orderly movement of a stream of bits from one program to another. The Presentation layer is the lowest layer interested in the *meaning* of those bits. It deals with preserving the *information content* of data transmitted over the network. The Presentation layer enables two communicating systems to exchange information with one another without having to be aware of the specific data formats each system uses. The Presentation layer performs the necessary conversions that allow each system to work with data in its own preferred format without having to be aware of the data formats that its partner uses.

- **The Application Layer.** The *Application* layer is the layer associated with user processes. The Application layer is concerned with high-level functions that provide support to the application programs using the network for communication. The Application layer provides a means for application programs to access the system interconnection facilities to exchange information. It provides all functions related to communication between systems not provided by the lower layers.

IEEE/ISO/ANSI LAN ARCHITECTURE

The IEEE has undertaken a major role in the development of local area network standards. IEEE Project 802 has defined a flexible architecture oriented specifically to the standardization of local area network data link technology. The approach the IEEE has taken in developing its LAN architecture is in conformance with the OSI model. However, IEEE Project 802 addresses only the lowest two layers of the OSI model, the Physical and Data Link layers.

The IEEE Project 802 LAN architecture has subsequently been accepted by ISO and ANSI to form the underlying basis for their own LAN standardization efforts. In this book, we refer to the architecture that began its development in IEEE Project 802 as the IEEE/ISO/ANSI LAN architecture.

Box 2.2 illustrates the relationships between the OSI model and the architecture that underlies IEEE, ISO, and ANSI standards for local area networks. In the IEEE/ISO/ANSI LAN architecture, the Data Link layer is divided into two sublayers: the *Logical Link Control* (LLC) sublayer and the *Medium Access Control* (MAC) sublayer.

NETWORK ARCHITECTURES AND PROTOCOL FAMILIES

Today's network software and hardware are based on a wide variety of network architectures. Some networking products, such as IBM's network hardware and software for mainframes, are based on a formal network architecture, in IBM's case *Systems Network Architecture (SNA)*. SNA consists of a formal set of specifications that exists apart from any particular hardware or software implementation of the architecture. With IBM's SNA, the architecture was developed first, and then products were designed to conform to the architecture. Both the architecture and the products based on the architecture have evolved over time as added capabilities were required.

Some network hardware and software are based on a more informal architecture. For example, the term *TCP/IP* (*Transmission Control Protocol/Internet Protocol*) refers to a *protocol family* for computer networking that has been developed one piece at a time over the years. Each protocol in the TCP/IP protocol family now has a formal specification. With TCP/IP, the network software was often developed first, and then a formal specification was written based on that working software. The complete collection of the most commonly used TCP/IP protocol standards now makes up an ad hoc network architecture for TCP/IP.

SUMMARY

This chapter began an introduction to layered architectures through an analogy showing how the functions involved in human speech can be divided into independent layers. A network architecture is a plan governing the design and operation of a particular type of computer network. A characteristic common to all network architectures is the use of a layered approach, in which network functions are divided into independent functional layers.

24

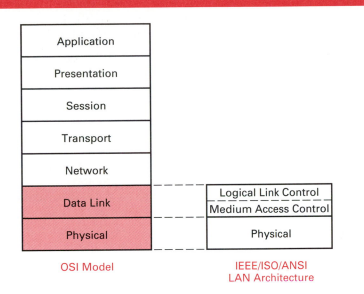

BOX 2.2   IEEE/ISO/ANSI LAN architecture functional layers.

- **Physical Layer.** The Physical layer corresponds directly to the Physical layer of the OSI model. It provides services to a user of the Physical layer, which is typically the MAC sublayer. The data units exchanged by the Physical layer consist of signals that represent individual bits. This layer defines procedures for establishing physical connections to the transmission medium and for transmitting and receiving signals over it. Physical layer specifications also include descriptions of the types of cabling, plugs, and connectors to be used and the characteristics of the signals exchanged.

- **Medium Access Control Sublayer.** A local area network typically supports multiple devices that all contend for access to a shared physical transmission medium. The Medium Access Control sublayer provides services to a user of the MAC sublayer service, which is typically the LLC sublayer. The data unit that MAC sublayer entities exchange is called the *medium-access-control-protocol-data-unit* (MAC-PDU). The MAC-PDU is often called a *MAC frame.* The purpose of the MAC frame is to carry data across a physical transmission medium from one network device, often called a *station,* to another.

- **Logical Link Control Sublayer.** The Logical Link Control sublayer is responsible for medium-independent data link functions. It allows a LAN data link user to access the services of a local area network data link without having to be concerned with the form of medium access control or physical transmission medium used. The LLC sublayer is shared by a variety of different medium access control technologies. The LLC sublayer allows different LAN technologies to present a common interface to a LAN data link user.

For each functional layer, an architecture defines services and protocols. A service defines what a layer does for the layer above it and consists of the definition of functions that a layer performs on behalf of the layer above it. A layer protocol specifies how a layer performs its service by specifying the formats of messages and rules for how those messages are exchanged.

Important organizations involved in developing standards and architectures for computer networking are the International Organization for Standardization (ISO), the Institute of Electrical and Electronic Engineers (IEEE), the American National Standards Institute (ANSI), and the Telecommunications sector of the International Telcommunication Union (ITU-T).

The Reference Model for Open Systems Interconnection (OSI model) is a generalized model of system interconnection described in international standard ISO 7498 and ITU-T Recommendation X.200. The OSI model has seven layers: Application, Presentation, Session, Transport, Network, Data Link, and Physical.

IEEE Project 802 has defined an architecture for local area networks (the IEEE/ISO/ANSI LAN architecture) that addresses the Data Link and Physical layers of the OSI model. The Data Link layer is divided into two sublayers: the Logical Link Control (LLC) sublayer and the Medium Access Control (MAC) sublayer.

Some networking products are based on a formal architecture, such as IBM's Systems Network Architecture (SNA). Other network hardware and software implement a more informal architecture, such as products that implement the TCP/IP protocol family.

Chapter 3 introduces the enterprise network model we use in this book as an organizing tool and describes important network architectures, protocol families, and data transmission technologies.

Chapter **3**

An Enterprise Network Model

This book uses as an organizing tool the general architectural model for enterprise networks shown in Fig. 3.1. The enterprise network model places the layers of the OSI model into three groups. These groups reflect functional subsets of the various services provided by network hardware and network software subsystems.

This book discusses network architectures, network software subsystems, transport network technologies, and data link subnetwork transmission facilities. We use the enterprise network model, the OSI model, and the IEEE/ISO/ANSI LAN architecture to help put these architectures and technologies into perspective and to discuss their similarities and differences.

The enterprise network model helps us to see the relationships between each of the architectures, software subsystems, and technologies described in this book and to help us compare one architecture or technology with another. The enterprise network model will also help us to visualize where standard interfaces are important in the layering structure.

The following sections introduce each of the three major components of the enterprise network model.

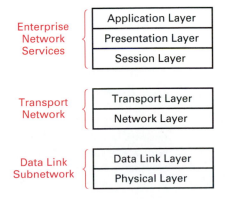

Figure 3.1 Enterprise network model.

ENTERPRISE NETWORK SERVICES

The most useful kind of network software is software that makes the network totally transparent to the user. A user should be able to access a remote file, send an electronic mail message, or print a spreadsheet on a network printer without having to know any of the details concerning the network technologies used. The software that end users employ to perform such functions implements the *enterprise network services* component of the enterprise network model. Some enterprise network services are those that application programs invoke on behalf of end users. This component is associated with the Session, Presentation, and Application layers of the OSI model.

Various enterprise network services may call on the services of the transport network in performing their functions. But enterprise network services go beyond the basic transmission-oriented services provided by the transport network.

Some enterprise network services are required for the general operation of the network. For example, directory services allow application programs and network users to locate and access network resources, and network management services allow network administration to monitor and control the network.

Other enterprise network services provide functions useful to application programs running in computers attached to the network. These might include distributed file services to access data on remote devices, and data distribution services for managing the transmission of messages and documents from one user to another. Some services may be provided directly by the networking software. For example, the network operating systems that run on servers in personal computer LANs typically provide distributed file and print services.

Enterprise network services can also be provided by application software designed specifically to use the capabilities of the network. For example, application packages are commonly used that provide electronic mail and database services in a network environment.

Chapter 4 further describes important enterprise network services useful in the enterprise network environment.

THE TRANSPORT NETWORK

Transport network functions, running below the enterprise network services, are associated with the Transport and Network layers of the OSI model. Transport network facilities provide a basic end-to-end transmission, or *data transport*, service. The transport network component of the enterprise network model calls on data link subnetwork services to provide the data transport service.

In the personal computer environment, the transport network is often implemented in the form of a network operating system that runs on server systems, along with client components that run on client systems. In other cases, software implementing the transport network is integrated directly into the operating system software. This has been common with TCP/IP support in the Unix workstation environment for many years, and this trend is continuing in the personal computer environment. For example, the Windows for Workgroups, Windows 95, and Windows NT system software from Microsoft contain integrated networking support that makes it unnecessary to install separate networking software.

Box 3.1 lists some of the most commonly used network software subsystems. Each of the network software subsystems listed conforms to its own unique network architecture and implements its own family of transport protocols. A family of transport protocols is often called a *protocol family* or a *protocol suite*.

Each software subsystem and transport protocol family provides a variety of services that also fall into the enterprise network services category as well. Chapter 5 further describes the architectures underlying the network software subsystems introduced in Box 3.1 and discusses the transport protocol families they support.

DATA LINK SUBNETWORKS

The data link subnetwork component, the main subject of this book, is the lowest level of the enterprise network model. It is associated with specific data link subnetwork transmission technologies. The data link subnetwork is responsible for managing the transmission of data over a particular subnetwork in the enterprise network.

Local area network data link transmission technologies are different from the technologies used to control data transmission over wide area network data links. Box 3.2 lists commonly used WAN subnetwork and LAN subnetwork data transmission technologies. Most of these technologies are described further in Parts III and IV.

The data link subnetwork provides for the transmission of data units, commonly called *frames*, across a specific data link between systems directly attached to that data link. Standard interfaces at the data link subnetwork level make it possible for the transport network software to support the use of many different types of data links. For example, most network operating systems or other network software subsystems for IBM-compatible personal computers allow the network administrator to use Ethernet or token ring hardware, as well as possibly allowing other choices, such as ARCnet, Apple LocalTalk, or FDDI.

NETWORKING PERSPECTIVES

Networking literature may refer to a particular type of computer network by using the name of a network software subsystem or transport protocol family. For example, we might refer to a *NetWare network*, an *AppleTalk network*, or an *SNA network*. When you see such a reference, it is important to realize that the literature is discussing the network from the viewpoint of its type of transport network facilities. Many of the chapters in the first two parts of this book view computer networks from the high-level perspective of the transport network. More details on the transport network technology can be found in this book's companion volume, *Enterprise Networking: Strategies and Transport Protocols*.

Some computer networking literature is not concerned with the high-level data transport software but instead focuses on the specific transmission technologies used to support communication between computers. When networking literature refers to a *Frame Relay network,* an *Ethernet LAN*, or a *token ring network*, you can be sure that a particular type of data link subnetwork technology is indicated. Most of this book, including all the chapters in Parts III and IV, concentrate on data link subnetwork technologies.

**BOX 3.1   Transport network software subsystems
and protocol families.**

- **TCP/IP.** *TCP/IP,* which stands for *Transmission Control Protocol/Internet Protocol,* refers to a set of communication protocols that grew out of a research project funded by the United States Department of Defense. The TCP/IP networking scheme implements a peer-to-peer network configuration. Any computing system in the network can run TCP/IP server software and can provide services to any other computing system that runs complementary TCP/IP client software.

- **NetWare IPX/SPX.** *NetWare* is a family of network operating system software marketed by Novell. The type of data transport services that NetWare uses is often referred to by the names of the two major NetWare communication protocols: the *Sequenced Packet Exchange* (SPX) protocol and the *Internetwork Packet Exchange* (IPX) protocol. Novell software is available for personal computers and Unix workstations. At the time of writing, NetWare is the most popular of all the networking software used in the personal computer environment. NetWare provides file and print sharing facilities as well as a broad range of other networking services. Many other network software systems now implement the IPX/SPX protocol family for compatibility with NetWare products.

- **Netbios.** Early IBM and Microsoft network software introduced an interface and protocol called NetBIOS for communication over a local area network. NetBIOS network software is part of the *LAN Manager* and *LAN Server* network operating systems codeveloped by Microsoft and IBM. NetBIOS has become a de facto standard for communication over LANs and is implemented by Microsoft operating systems, such as Windows for Workgroups, Windows 95, and Windows NT. NetBIOS capabilities are provided by a number of other network software subsystems as well, including the Novell networking products.

- **AppleTalk.** *AppleTalk* is Apple Computer's networking scheme that has been used for many years to network Apple Macintosh equipment and its successors. Apple system software contains integrated AppleTalk networking support that allows Apple computing systems to participate in peer-to-peer computer networks and also to access the services of dedicated AppleShare file and print servers. NICs and network software are available for a variety of other types of computing systems, including IBM-compatible personal computers and UNIX workstations, that allow them to participate in AppleTalk networks.

- **Systems Network Architecture.** *Systems Network Architecture (SNA)* is IBM's proprietary networking scheme that has been widely used in the mainframe environment. A form of SNA called *Advanced Peer-to-Peer Networking (APPN)* provides SNA communication support for smaller systems.

- **DECnet.** *DECnet* is a term that Digital Equipment Corporation uses to refer to its proprietary networking software. DECnet networking facilities are typically used in the DEC minicomputer and workstation environments.

- **PATHWORKS.** *PATHWORKS* is a family of personal computer network operating system software marketed by Digital Equipment Corporation. The original goal of PATHWORKS was to provide personal computers with access to DECnet networking capabilities. However, PATHWORKS now supports access to other forms of networking as well.

- **VINES.** *VINES* is a family of network operating system software marketed by Banyan Systems. VINES supports a client/server network configuration and provides many facilities especially well suited for large networks.

- **LANtastic.** *LANtastic* is a family of network operating systems for the personal computer environment marketed by Artisoft. LANtastic network software implements a peer-to-peer network configuration.

BOX 3.2   Data link subnetwork technologies.

WAN Data Link Subnetwork Technologies

- **Analog Telecommunications Circuits.** Analog telecommunications circuits are often used for data transmission by employing devices called *modems* (short for modulator/demodulator) on each end of the circuit. A number of protocols for the data link subnetwork have been developed to control transmission over long-distance telecommunications circuits. These protocols are described in Chapter 11.

- **Digital Telecommunications Circuits.** In addition to analog circuits, most telecommunications providers offer digital transmission facilities in which computer data can be carried directly in digital form. Analog and digital telecommunications circuits are also described further in Chapter 11.

- **X.25 Packet-Switched Data Networks (PSDN).** *X.25* is the name of an ITU Recommendation that describes standards for *Packet-Switched Public Data Networks* (PSDN). A PSDN uses data units called *packets* that can be routed individually through the PSDN. An X.25 PSDN implements *virtual circuits* that appear to end users as simple point-to-point data links. X.25 packet-switching facilities are described further in Chapter 12.

- **Integrated Services Digital Network (ISDN).** An *Integrated Services Digital Network* (ISDN) is a public telecommunications network—typically administered by a telecommunications provider—that supplies digital end-to-end data transmission services that can be used to transmit any type of information, including voice, data, graphics, image, facsimile, and video. ISDN technology is described further in Chapter 13.

- **Broadband ISDN (B-ISDN).** *Broadband ISDN* (B-ISDN) represents a probable future direction of the telephone industry based on fiber-optic communication. B-ISDN is designed to provide much higher data rates in addition to those supplied by ISDN. B-ISDN defines *interactive* services, which involve two-way transmission, and *distribution* services, where transmission occurs primarily in one direction. B-ISDN is intended for the transmission of all types of information, including text, documents, graphics, sound, and video. B-ISDN facilities are also described further in Chapter 13.

- **Frame Relay.** *Frame Relay* is a data transmission technology based on international standards for the Data Link and Physical layers of the OSI model originally defined as part of ISDN. Telecommunications providers now offer data transmission facilities based on Frame Relay standards that provide data rates higher than can ordinarily be achieved over conventional telecommunications circuits. Frame Relay technology is described further in Chapter 14.

- **Asynchronous Transfer Mode (ATM).** *Asynchronous Transfer Mode* (ATM) transmission technology was also first defined in the form of ISDN specifications for the Data Link and Physical layers of the OSI model. ATM products and services are now available as a communications technology being implemented apart from ISDN. ATM products and services support very high transmission speeds and can be used to provide both local area network and wide area network facilities. ATM is described further in Chapter 15.

- **Switched Multi-megabit Data Service (SMDS).** *Switched Multi-megabit Data Service* (SMDS) is a high-speed data transmission technology that can be used to implement high-

(Continued)

BOX 3.2 *(Continued)*

speed WAN data links that can carry data at LAN speeds. SMDS technology is based on a standard for *metropolitan area networks* (MANs) called *Distributed Queue Dual Bus* (DQDB). The SMDS and DQDB technologies are described further in Chapter 25.

- **Wireless WAN Technologies.** Telecommunications providers and other organizations have developed various technologies for implementing data transmission over relatively long distances using wireless transmission media, such as radio signals. Wireless WAN technology is described further in Chapter 16.

LAN Data Link Subnetwork Technologies

- **Ethernet.** *Ethernet* is a LAN data link technology in which systems are attached to a common transmission facility, such as a coaxial or twisted-pair cable, to form a bus- or tree-structured configuration. A system typically attempts to transmit whenever it has data to send. Ethernet is the most widely used form of LAN data link technology and is described further in Chapter 19.

- **Token Ring.** *Token Ring* is a LAN data link technology in which systems are connected to one another using point-to-point twisted-pair cable segments to form a ring structure. A system is allowed to transmit only when it has a special data unit called the *token,* which is passed from one system to another around the ring. Token Ring technology is described further in Chapter 20.

- **Token Bus.** *Token Bus* is a LAN data link technology in which systems are connected to a common transmission medium in a similar manner as an Ethernet LAN. A system is allowed to transmit only when it has the token, which is passed from one system to another. Token Bus LANs are sometimes used in factory automation environments. Token Bus technology is described in Chapter 21.

- **ARCnet.** *ARCnet* is the name of a family of LAN products that implement a relatively low-speed form of LAN data link technology in which all systems are attached to a common coaxial cable. Like the Token Bus form of LAN, a system transmits when it has the token. ARCnet technology is also described further in Chapter 21.

- **Fiber Distributed Data Interface (FDDI).** FDDI is a high-speed LAN data link technology in which systems are connected to one another using point-to-point fiber-optic cable segments to form a ring structure. A system is allowed to transmit only when it has the token. FDDI technology is described further in Chapter 22.

- **LocalTalk.** *LocalTalk* is a low-speed LAN data link technology—part of Apple Computer's AppleTalk networking scheme—in which systems are attached to a common cable. LocalTalk technology has been built into most of the computing devices Apple Computer has manufactured for many years, although Apple has been building Ethernet technology as well into much of its more recent equipment. LocalTalk technology is described further in Chapter 23.

- **Wireless LAN Technologies.** Local area network infrastructure vendors have developed various technologies for implementing LAN communication over wireless transmission media, such as radio and infrared signals. Wireless LAN technology is described further in Chapter 24.

PROTOCOL STACKS

The network software systems in common use today were all originally developed to use a particular set of transport protocols. For example, NetWare software is built around the IPX/SPX protocol family, and Microsoft networking software implements NetBIOS. However, given the demands that exist for network interconnection and interoperation, the network software provided by many vendors now supports other transport protocol families in addition to their own native protocols.

When a network software subsystem supports multiple transport protocol families, the terms *transport protocol stack*, *transport stack*, or *protocol stack* are often used to refer to a software component that implements a particular transport protocol family.

SUMMARY

The enterprise network model used to organize this book places the layers of the OSI model into three groups to reflect functional subsets of the various services provided by network hardware and network software subsystems: enterprise network services, transport network, and data link subnetwork.

The enterprise network services component of the enterprise network model is associated with the Session, Presentation, and Application layers of the OSI model. Enterprise network services are application-oriented services that end users use directly or that support application programs.

Transport network functions run below the enterprise network services and are associated with the Transport and Network layers of the OSI model. This component provides a basic end-to-end data transmission, or data transport, service. Different protocol families that implement transport network facilities include TCP/IP, NetWare IPX/SPX, NetBIOS, AppleTalk, Systems Network Architecture, and DECnet.

The lowest level component of the enterprise network model is associated with the Data Link and Physical layers of the OSI model. This component is concerned with specific data link subnetwork technologies responsible for managing the transmission of data over a particular data link. Technologies associated with the data link subnetwork component include wide area network technologies and local area network technologies. Important WAN technologies include analog and digital telecommunications circuits, X.25 packet switching, integrated services digital network (ISDN), Frame Relay, Asynchronous Transfer Mode (ATM), switched multi-megabit data service (SMDS), and wireless WAN facilities. Important LAN technologies include Ethernet, Token Ring, Token Bus, ARCnet, Fiber Distributed Data Interface (FDDI), LocalTalk, and wireless LAN facilities.

Chapter 4 introduces the application services associated with the enterprise network services component of the enterprise network model.

Chapter **4**

Enterprise Network Services

Different network software subsystems vary widely in their capabilities and in the services they provide. However, certain types of functions have now become commonplace in generally available network software. This chapter introduces some of the application-oriented services that network software provides in an enterprise networking environment. Application-oriented services are among those provided in the Enterprise Network Services portion of the enterprise network model, as shown in Fig. 4.1.

CATEGORIES OF APPLICATION SERVICES

We begin this chapter by describing some of the broad categories of services that network software provides to users of the network. Most of these represent the types of services

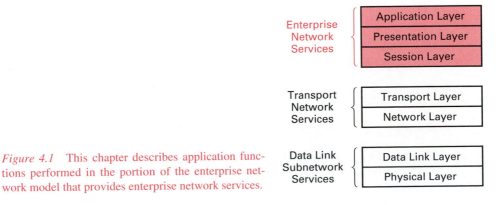

Figure 4.1   This chapter describes application functions performed in the portion of the enterprise network model that provides enterprise network services.

provided in a typical PC LAN implementation, but most are also provided by network software that operates in the mainframe and minicomputer environments as well.

Print Services

Print services allow any system on the network to use a printer attached to some other system functioning in the role of a print server. With the print services implemented by most network software, an end user on one computing system in the network can direct output to a remote printer controlled by a print server exactly as if the printer were attached directly to the user's own local system.

Remote printing software generally implements some form of queueing mechanism to allow end users to send printed output to the print server even when it is currently busy printing some other job. Remote printing software may allow print queues or individual print jobs to have different priorities, thus allowing certain print jobs to be scheduled ahead of others. Printers might be grouped in pools, with output printed by the first printer in the pool that becomes available. Print services might also allow users to start, end, cancel, or flush queued print jobs.

File Services

File services allow end users within the network to access the disk devices and files controlled by other systems functioning as file servers. Network software may implement various levels of remote file access. For example, it might be possible to control sharing at the device level, where a user can access all the files on a particular hard disk drive on the file server as if the file server's hard disk were directly attached to the user's local system. Sharing might also be controlled on a directory basis, where the user is allowed to access only particular directories on a shared disk. Sharing can also be controlled at individual file level, where users are granted the authority to access only particular files on the file server's disks. The network software configuration process may allow any or all these levels of sharing to be specified.

Electronic Mail Services

Network software often provides *electronic mail services* that allow end users to compose, send, receive, and store messages and documents. Some electronic mail implementations provide messaging facilities that operate only within a particular local network. Other electronic mail applications provide users with access to the messaging facilities provided by other networks and with messaging facilities provided by public electronic mail services as well.

Directory Services

Network users and application programs that use network software often request services based on *network names*. Network names are names used to represent resources within the network to which end users require access. Typical resources that might be given network names are other network users and the physical resources available in the network, such as print queues and collections of shared files.

A *directory service* translates a network name into a network address that specifies the exact location in the network of a given resource. With a network directory service end users can access network resources with easy-to-use names rather than needing to know specific details concerning the network addressing scheme.

Network Management Services

Network software commonly offers a variety of management and administration facilities that network administrators can use for monitoring and controlling the network. Specialized network management software is also available that runs in conjunction with commonly used network software.

EXAMPLES OF SPECIFIC APPLICATION SERVICES

Some network architectures provide detailed descriptions of the specific application services that systems implementing that architecture typically provide. Most systems that implement a network architecture provide implementations of appropriate application services defined by that network architecture.

TCP/IP Application Services

The TCP/IP network architecture provides a particularly rich assortment of application services generally implemented by systems that implement the TCP/IP protocol suite. Box 4.1 describes application services commonly provided in a network that implements the TCP/IP networking protocols to form a TCP/IP network.

OSI Application Services

The standards that have been developed to support the OSI model include some standards for the Application layer that define facilities of general applicability to users of computer networks. Although OSI networking is not today widely used, many network software subsystems implement a few specific OSI application services in the upper layers. Box 4.2 describes three key OSI Application layer standards particularly useful in an enterprise networking environment.

METHODS FOR ACCESSING APPLICATION SERVICES

The application services available on any given network will depend on the specific network software used and may vary widely from one environment to another. There are

BOX 4.1   TCP/IP application services.

- **FTP File Transfer.** The *File Transfer Protocol* (FTP) implements a file transfer service typically employed by TCP/IP end users. FTP allows the user to transfer data in both directions between the local system and a remote system. FTP implementations can be used to transfer files that contain either binary data or ASCII text. Certain versions of FTP also allow for the transfer of files containing EBCDIC data. Files can be transferred one at a time, or a single request can cause multiple files to be transferred. FTP also provides ancillary functions, such as listing the contents of remote directories, changing the current remote directory, and creating and removing remote directories.

- **TFTP File Transfer.** The *Trivial File Transfer Protocol* (TFTP) is a simple file transfer protocol that can be used to transfer data in both directions between the local system and a remote system. TFTP is generally used only by system software that performs such functions as downline loading of program code; it is not intended to be employed directly by end users.

- **NFS Remote File Service.** The *Network File System* (NFS) implements a number of high-level services that provide authorized users with access to files located on remote systems. Systems administrators generally designate one or more systems in the network to play the role of file servers. These systems run NFS server software that make certain designated directories on their disk storage devices available to other systems. A user accesses an NFS-mounted directory in the same manner as accessing a directory on a local disk.

- **SMTP Electronic Mail.** The Simple Mail Transfer Protocol (SMTP) is a protocol used for the transfer of electronic mail messages. SMTP is designed to be used by electronic mail software that provides the user with access to messaging facilities. Mail facilities allow the user to send messages and files to other users. Many types of electronic mail systems have been implemented for the TCP/IP environment, some of which can be interconnected with the electronic messaging systems of other types of networks such as PROFS and DIS-OSS in the IBM environment, and with public electronic mail services, such as MCI Mail, CompuServe, and the Internet.

- **DNS Directory Service.** Each system attached to a TCP/IP network has at least one network address assigned to it. Each system also typically has a unique name to make it possible for users to refer to the system easily without knowing its network address. Since the underlying TCP/IP protocols all refer to individual systems using their network addresses, each system must implement a name resolution function that translates between system names and network addresses. The *Domain Name System (DNS)* is a directory service that can be used to maintain the mappings between names and network addresses.

- **SNMP Network Management.** Network management services are typically provided in a TCP/IP network through software that implements the *Simple Network Management Protocol* (SNMP). SNMP defines a Management Information Base (MIB), which is a database that defines all the objects in the network that can be managed in the Internet. SNMP also defines the formats of a set of network management messages and the rules by which the messages are exchanged. The network management messages are used to make requests for performing network management functions and to report on events that occur in the network.

BOX 4.1   *(Continued)*

- **Kerberos Authentication and Authorization.** Kerberos is an encryption-based security system that provides mutual authentication between a client component and a server component in a distributed computing environment. It also provides services that can be used to control which clients are authorized to access which servers. In the Kerberos system, each client component and each server component is called a *principal* and has a unique *principal identifier* assigned to it. These principal identifiers allow clients and servers to identify themselves to each other to prevent fraudulent exchanges of information.

- **X Windows Presentation Facilities.** X Windows is a set of distributed graphical presentation services that implement a windowing system on a graphics display. It implements a client/server relationship between an application program (the client) and the windowing software in a workstation or terminal that controls a window on the graphical display (the server). The client and server can be running in different computing systems or in the same computing system. The X Window system allows a user at a graphics workstation to have multiple windows open on the screen, each of which might be controlled by a separate client application program. The X Window system defines a protocol used to transmit information between the client application program and the server windowing software.

- **PING Connectivity Testing.** *PING,* which is short for *Packet InterNet Groper,* can be used to test for connectivity between any two systems on the network. In using PING, a user typically executes a program named **ping** that sends a message to another system. When a system receives the message from PING, it sends a reply message back to the original sender. For each reply message that it receives, PING calculates the amount of time elapsed since it sent the original request message. This provides the PING user with an estimate of the round-trip delay experienced in exchanging data with the specified system.

- **Telnet Remote Login.** Telnet allows a user to log in to some other system on the network. The Telnet protocol establishes a client/server relationship between the local user (the client) and the remote Telnet application (the server). Telnet handles the data transfers required between the system implementing the client and the system implementing the server. These data transfers make it appear as if the user is logged in to the remote system directly.

- **Rlogin Remote Login.** The Rlogin service is a service related to Telnet but is typically provided only by variations of the UNIX operating systems. Telnet allows a user at any type of TCP/IP system to log in to any other type of TCP/IP system. The local system and remote system may be running entirely different operating systems. The Rlogin service is normally used when a user at a local UNIX system wants to log in to a remote UNIX system. For the UNIX user, Rlogin is somewhat easier to use than Telnet and provides a few additional services.

- **Rsh Remote Execution.** The *Rsh* remote execution service allows the user to issue, at the local system, a command to request an operating system function or to request the execution of an application program on some other system in the network. When using the Rsh service, the user enters a command at the local system, and the command is then sent to and executed on the remote system. The results of the command or the results of the application program execution are then returned to the user at the local system. A similar service to Rsh called *Rexec* is available on some TCP/IP systems as well.

BOX 4.2   OSI Application layer standards.

- **File Transfer, Access, and Management (FTAM).** FTAM defines the functions required to support a remote file system in the OSI environment. The broad aim in standardizing a file service is to allow file users on open systems to be able to transfer, access, or manage information held on any type of system that behaves as if it stores data files. Such a system is called a *virtual filestore*. The virtual filestore in FTAM describes a conceptual model of a file service that might be implemented in any desired way in an open system.

- **X.400 Message Handling System.** The main objective of the X.400 message handling system is to allow users to exchange electronic messages on a store-and-forward basis. X.400 defines a number of standard message handling services useful in creating systems that implement electronic mail services. It concentrates on aspects of message handling systems that allow one electronic mail system to interoperate with other electronic mail systems conforming to the X.400 protocol specifications.

- **X.500 Directory.** The X.500 Directory standard defines naming services for the OSI environment. An important function of the naming service is to accept a name and to pass back a set of attributes associated with that name (white pages service). The naming service can be used to store attributes for any type of named object, including network devices and application programs. Another naming service function is to accept a list of attribute values and to return a list of all the objects having those attribute values (yellow pages service).

---

also varying ways in which these services can be made available to application programs or end users of the network. The following sections describe some of the ways in which network software can make application services available to application programs and end users.

Explicit End-User Requests

The network software may make certain network services directly available to end users of the network. Network operating systems and other network software typically provide interfaces that allow network users and network administrators to invoke various network functions directly.

The end-user interface usually defines a set of commands and/or menus that users employ to select options and enter information. The system of commands and menus that make up the user's or network administrator's interface to the network software are specific to each vendor's network software product and normally conform to user interface guidelines that have been established for the particular computing platform on which the network software is run.

For example, with Microsoft network software running in the Windows computing environment, a user might be able to send an electronic mail message by preparing the mail message with any ordinary word processor and then selecting the "Send" function from the word processor's File menu. This initiates a dialog with the electronic mail software in which the user is asked to supply information about the destination of the message. In such a computing environment, the electronic mail facilities of the network software are often closely integrated into the systems software and may allow many different types of application programs to directly access the mail capabilities of the network.

By contrast, a user of network software not quite as closely integrated into the computing environment may issue messages directly to the network software to control electronic mail functions. For example, a user that employs a TCP/IP SMTP electronic mail implementation might prepare a file containing the mail message to be sent using a text editor. The user might then exit the text editing application and explicitly issue a separate Mail command to the network software. The Mail command might reference the file containing the mail message and specify the destination to which the file should be sent.

I/O Redirection

Network services might alternatively be made available to an application program in a way that it is transparent to the user and to the application program. This is done through software that automatically *redirects* I/O requests. An application program may issue an I/O request for what it thinks is a local resource, such as a printer or a disk file. The network software then intercepts the I/O request and redirects it to a server machine located somewhere in the network. The server processes the request and returns the results of the request back to the application program.

To the user at the local system, and to the application program, it appears as if the request has been processed locally. (Of course it may take a little more time for the redirected I/O operation to complete than if the I/O operation has been handled locally.) The I/O redirection approach allows organizations to use network facilities in conjunction with ordinary application programs that may not be specifically designed to operate in a networking environment. The same application programs that operate on local resources can be used unchanged to operate on remote resources. The majority of ordinary productivity applications, such as word processors and spreadsheet analysis programs, operate just as well in a networking environment using automatic I/O redirection as they do in a stand-alone environment.

Application Programming Interfaces

In some instances, an application program may need to invoke network-based application services directly. For example, client/server database software may have to make explicit requests for network application services in order to implement transaction management functions that protect the integrity of a shared database.

Generally, an application program makes explicit requests for network application services by using a set of commands or system service calls that make up an *application programming interface* (API) for networking services. When the same type of application service is provided by different network software subsystems, the API used to invoke the facilities of the service may vary from one network software implementation to another.

Network software may implement a number of application programming interfaces (APIS). Box 4.3 introduces three specific network APIS that allow programs to request network application services explicitly. All three APIS have become de facto standards and are implemented in many competing products.

APPLICATION PROTOCOLS

A wide range of application protocols specify how network software provides various types of application services. As with any type of protocol, an application protocol defines the formats of both a set of messages that the network software exchanges across the network and the rules governing how those messages are exchanged. Generally, a different application protocol governs each application service that the network software

---

BOX 4.3 Representative APIs for network application services.

IBM and Microsoft LAN APIs

The IBM and Microsoft LAN APIs were originally codeveloped by IBM and Microsoft Corporation as part of their early LAN Manager and LAN server network operating systems. Many of these same APIs have subsequently been implemented in other network software subsystems as well. The LAN APIs employ data structures called Server Message Blocks (SMBs). SMBs define the formats of the messages transported between communicating systems in providing network services. The LAN APIs and the SMB protocol support a wide range of application services, including interprocess communication, workstation operation, printer and serial device control, and various administrative and management functions.

Named Pipes

The IBM/Microsoft *Named Pipes* communication facility is not, strictly speaking, an application-oriented facility since it operates at the level of the transport network in the enterprise network model. However, application programs can use the Named Pipes facility to send messages to application programs running in the same or in some other computing system in the network. The Named Pipes facility is described further in Chapter 5.

NetWare APIs

Novell has defined various sets of NetWare APIs that application programs can use to request application services. Each NetWare API consists of a set of function calls that use IPX Request and Reply packets for sending and receiving data. The different application services typically provided by the NetWare APIs include print services, queue management services, file services, locking services, directory services, transaction tracking system services, connection and workstation services, value-added process services, service advertising services, accounting services, and diagnostic services.

provides. Therefore, the protocol governing each application service defines its own set of messages and its own set of mechanisms used to provide that service.

As with APIs, even when the same type of service is provided by two different network software subsystems, the application protocol used to provide the service may vary widely from one networking environment to another. However, a particular network architecture may standardize some of the protocols used to provide application services. For example, the File Transfer Protocol (FTP) is an application service defined by the TCP/IP network architecture, and any implementation of FTP implements the same application protocol. Therefore, any two implementations of FTP, running on any types of computing systems, should be able to successfully exchange files with one another.

On the other hand, TCP/IP's FTP defines a different file transfer application protocol than OSI's FTAM. Therefore, it is not generally possible for an implementation of FTP to interoperate with an implementation of FTAM. But one implementation of FTAM should be able to interoperate with any other implementation of FTAM.

To illustrate the nature of the application services networking software can provide, the next sections further describe two important categories of network application services: *directory services* used for locating network resources and *network management services* used to control and monitor the network. This chapter ends by introducing the *Distributed Computing Environment* (DCE) developed by the *Open Software Foundation* (OSF). The OSF DCE is a coordinated set of services being implemented in a number of computing environments to provide network application services.

DIRECTORY SERVICES

The goal of a network directory service is to provide a generally accessible mechanism for storing and accessing information about objects of interest in the network. A network directory facility typically stores the names of network objects and their associated attributes in a network database. The objects of interest in a network are typically network users, shared peripheral devices, network services, application programs, and shared data files. Each object represented in the directory has a unique name associated with it. A major function that any network directory facility must perform is to accept a name and to store or return the set of attribute values associated with that name.

Logical Directory Structures

A directory that stores and manipulates information for named objects can be structured in a number of ways. Most directory systems use a tree-structured directory organization. Trees provide a natural, hierarchical scheme for organizing names. Figure 4.2 shows an example of a directory structure organized as a tree structure.

A problem with a tree-structured directory is that each object is permitted to have only one name because each node under the root has only one parent. However, most tree-structured directory systems use augmented tree structures that support the use of additional links or pointers to implement the definition of aliases.

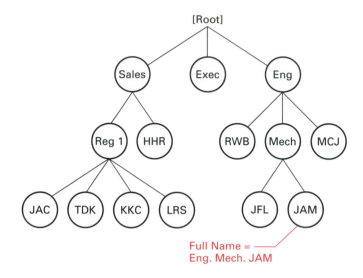

Figure 4.2   Tree structure used to implement a hierarchical naming scheme.

Physical Directory Structures

A major challenge in designing a directory service is to make the service operate in a highly distributed fashion and to make it work efficiently in a large, possibly global network. A network directory service must be highly available, highly robust, and highly distributed. To achieve the required performance and availability, it is often necessary to store directory entries in a database that is both partitioned and replicated. The term *partitioned* means that pieces of the database are stored in different physical locations on separate computing systems. The term *replicated* means that the same piece of the directory can be stored on multiple computing systems.

Directory Searches

A directory system may provide different types of search capabilities:

- **Primitive Name Searches.** A *primitive name* is a character string that uniquely identifies a network resource in the directory structure. Each primitive name refers to one and only one network object. Therefore, a primitive name can be used to either locate a particular object entry in the directory or to determine an entry with that particular name does not exist. A search capability based on primitive names provides the same search capability as a typical "white pages" telephone directory.

- **Descriptive Name Searches.** Another type of search is based on descriptive names. A *descriptive name* is a name that identifies an object by specifying information about the attributes stored for that object. A given descriptive name might refer to no objects, to a single object, or to more than one object. A search capability based on descriptive names provides a similar search capability as a typical "yellow pages" telephone directory.

Directory services that manipulate descriptive names are potentially more powerful than those that provide only primitive name searching capabilities. However, they are also the most demanding of computing resources and are difficult to implement and to distribute among multiple computer systems.

REPRESENTATIVE DIRECTORY SYSTEMS

The next sections briefly describe a few directory systems commonly used in computer networks.

TCP/IP Domain Name System (DNS)

The TCP/IP protocol suite is used in a great many enterprise networks. The *Domain Name System* (DNS) is the directory service most often used in networks that implement the TCP/IP architecture. DNS implements directory searches based on primitive names and, therefore, provides only a "white pages" directory searching capability. DNS allows users to work with easy-to-remember network names rather than actual internet addresses.

Each accessible object in a TCP/IP internet is given a unique name. DNS implements a naming service that translates these network names into the internet addresses required by TCP/IP. The process of translating a network name into an internet address in a TCP/IP network is called name resolution. In very simple TCP/IP networks, the name resolution function can be handled by each individual computer. Each computer simply maintains a table of name to address mappings, and the table is consulted each time a network name needs to be converted to an internet address.

When DNS is used for name resolution, each computing system in the network runs a DNS *resolver* process. The DNS resolver contacts another system running a *nameserver* process. The nameserver uses a directory database to perform the name translation operation and sends the results back to the resolver on the local system (see Fig. 4.3).

A DNS nameserver maintains a tree-structured directory database that contains sets of names called *domain names.* A domain name refers to a *domain,* defined by a system administrator, that consists of a collection of systems in the network or to an individual system. A domain name consists of a sequence of simple names separated by periods.

Domain names can be assigned in any desired way, but most installations follow the conventions for domain names that have been established by the Internet. A typical domain name in the Internet looks like the following:

```
www.ibm.com.
```

A domain name reads from left to right from the most local name to the most global name.

Figure 4.3   Domain Name System (DNS) resolver and nameserver processes.

The X.500 Directory Standard

One of the standards developed to support the OSI model is the *Directory* standard, documented in ISO 9594. This international standard had its roots in ITU-T Recommendation X.500, and ISO 9594 and ITU-T X.500 are essentially the same standard. Directories conforming to this standard are most often referred to using the ITU-T X.500 designation.

The names used to identify objects in the X.500 directory scheme are descriptive names that store information about an object's attributes. However, each object has one particular set of attributes that uniquely identifies that object in the network. Therefore, an X.500 directory system can implement both primitive name and descriptive name searching capabilities and can be used to implement both a "white pages" and a "yellow pages" directory service.

The collection of information for all directory entries in an X.500 directory is known as the *Directory Information Base (DIB)*. Entries in an X.500 DIB are organized hierarchically in a similar manner to a DNS naming database. The directory's hierarchical data structure is known as the *Directory Information Tree (DIT)*.

Each entry in the directory has one or more attribute values designated as "distinguished." The set of distinguished attribute values forms the entry's *relative distinguished name (RDN)*. An entry's RDN must distinguish it from all of its sibling entries in that part of the directory tree structure. However, the same RDN values may be used in different parts of the tree structure without conflict. To uniquely distinguish one directory entry from another on a global basis, a globally unique name can be constructed for each entry by concatenating all the RDN values for that entry. An entry's globally-unique name is called its *distinguished name (DN)*.

The distinguished name for an entry is constructed by successively taking the RDN for each entry along the path that starts at the root of the directory tree structure and ends at the entry in question. The example in Fig. 4.4 shows how the distinguished name for a particular

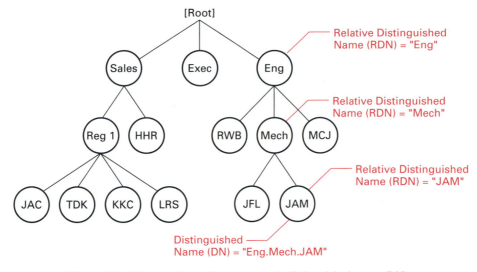

Figure 4.4   Constructing a directory entry's distinguished name (DN).

leaf node is constructed. Notice that an X.500 distinguished name begins with the most global name. This is the opposite of DNS domain names, which start with the most local name.

Novell NetWare Directory Services

Beginning with release 4.0 of the NetWare networking software, Novell has provided NetWare Directory Services (NDS), a globally distributed network directory service. The NDS Directory uses a tree-structure that has many of the characteristics of an X.500 directory. The names used to identify objects in current NDS implementations are descriptive names, as in X.500. Therefore, both "white pages" and "yellow pages" directory searches can be implemented.

NDS defines three types of directory entries (called *container objects*): *Country* objects, *Organization* objects, and *Organizational Unit* objects. *Leaf objects* identifying specific users or network resources appear below the container objects. If Country objects are used, they must appear immediately below the root. Organization objects are located immediately below Country objects, or below the root if Country objects are not used. Every Directory must contain at least one Organization object. Organizational Unit objects can be used to provide further structuring below an Organization object. Multiple levels of Organizational Unit objects can be used to any desired depth (see Fig. 4.5).

Each object is associated with a set of *properties*. The specific properties associated with an object depends on the object's type. For example, a User leaf object typically has properties, such as login name, telephone number, e-mail address, group membership, and so on. Information about an object is stored in the form of property values.

Every object in the Directory has a local name. The local name of a container object is its Country name, Organization name, or Organizational Unit name. The local name of a leaf object is called its *common name*. An object in the Directory is uniquely

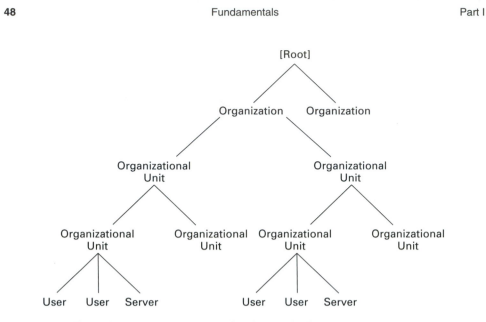

Figure 4.5   NetWare Directory Service (NDS) directory tree structure.

identified by its complete name, which is derived by concatenating all the names of all the objects that lie along the path from the root of the directory tree to the leaf object in question. The complete name consists of the local name of each object along the path. NDS syntax requires that a complete name be written in bottom-up sequence, with the lowest-level object name on the left and the highest-level object name on the right, using periods between the names:

```
JMartin.Group2.Network.CustServ
```

The NDS naming syntax also allows names to be specified using qualifiers to explicitly specify container objects. The qualifiers CN, OU, O, and C can be used as abbreviations for Common Name, Organizational Unit, Organization, and Country:

```
CN=JMartin.OU=Group2.OU=Network.O=CustServ
```

An object's local name must be unique within its particular part of the directory tree. To enable organizations to construct names that fit within a global directory context, Novell provides a registration service that assigns a unique Organization identifier to any organization that applies for one. This registration service is intended to make it possible for different organizations to interconnect their NDS directories without creating naming conflicts.

Banyan StreetTalk

Banyan Systems, Inc., provides a distributed naming service, called *StreetTalk* that is generally consistent with the X.500 standard but, like Novell's NDS, is not fully conformant with it. StreetTalk can be used with the Banyan VINES network operating system and with other types of network software as well.

A StreetTalk directory is hierarchical in structure, but is restricted to three levels below the root. The three levels, from top to bottom, are:

- Organization
- Group
- Item

Items in the directory are identified by three-part names with the following syntax:

```
item-name@group-name@org-name
```

Information about items in the directory is stored in the form of *attributes*. Standard attributes are defined as part of StreetTalk, and the network administrator can define additional attributes as needed by the organization.

StreetTalk defines different classes of items, including user, nickname, service, list, and group. Within a class, items may be further subdivided into categories. For example, the service class has categories defined for file services, and print services.

StreetTalk identifies and locates items using three-part names to implement a "white pages" directory capability. The StreetTalk Directory Assistance facility extends the search capabilities of StreetTalk to include "yellow pages" type searches based on partial names or on attribute values rather than name values.

DNA Phase V Naming Service

Phase V of the Digital Network Architecture (DNA), published by Digital Equipment Corporation, defines a distributed, global naming service implemented in DECnet Phase V network software. DECnet Phase V products are not widely used, but the DECnet naming service is important because it has been used as the basis of one of the two directory services implemented in the OSF *Distributed Computing Environment* (DCE) software, discussed later in this chapter.

The DNA Phase V directory service is based on primitive names and so is used to implement only a "white pages" directory facility in which the user must know an object's name in order to locate it. However, partial names can be used in some cases to provide limited "yellow pages" capabilities.

The main function of the DNA naming service is to accept a name and to pass back the set of attributes associated with that name. The set of names of all objects that can be referenced in the network is called a *namespace*. The naming service stores values for a set of attributes associated with each name in the namespace.

Namespace Structure

A DNS namespace is structured as a tree. Each arc of the tree is assigned a *simple name*. A complete name, called a *full name*, consists of a concatenation of all the simple names assigned to a set of arcs that begins at the root of the tree and ends with the object in question. All searching of the namespace is done on the basis of full names. The simple names in a full name are separated by periods (.). The following are examples of full names:

- `Parts.widgets.left-handed.SMOKESHIFTER`
- `ENG.NAC.JamesMartin`
- `Government.Treasury.Bills.CurrentSeries`

The tree structure is augmented by allowing a given node to have arcs from more than one parent node. These additional arcs allow a given object to have more than one name and are used to implement aliases.

Figure 4.6 shows a simple namespace in which each of the directories making up the namespace is represented by a circle. The entries stored in a directory are shown at the bottom of the circle. The simple name of the arc leading to each directory is shown at the top of the circle. Each directory has a full name made up of a concatenation of the

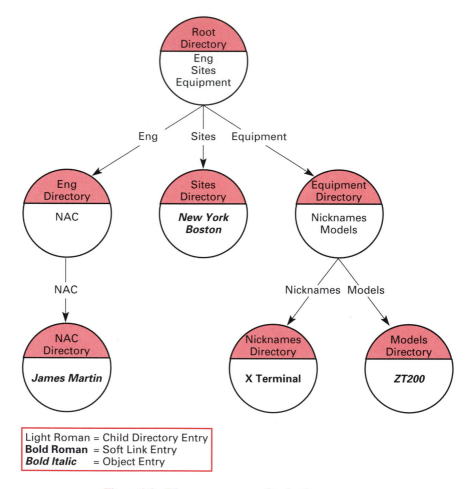

Figure 4.6   Directory structure of a simple namespace.

names of the arcs leading to it in the tree structure. The *root directory* stores the highest-level directory entries making up the namespace and is considered to be unnamed. There is a single root for the entire namespace, and all the directories are under the root.

Types of Directory Entries

Each of the entries stored in a directory has a simple name and a set of attributes. Entries stored in directories can be of three types:

- **Object Entries.** These entries form the leaves of the underlying tree structure. Object entries can store global attributes and user-defined attributes.

- **Child Pointer Entries.** These entries name the arcs of the underlying tree structure. A child pointer entry points to a child directory in the namespace tree.

- **Soft Link Entries.** These entries name the arcs that augment the underlying tree structure. A soft link entry consists of a pointer used to implement an alias name.

Naming Service Components

The namespace database is implemented in the form of repositories called *clearinghouses*. The two major functional components of the naming service are *clerks* and *nameservers*. Users request naming service operations through clerks, which communicate with nameservers. Nameservers retrieve information from and update clearinghouses on behalf of the clerks. Clearinghouses, clerks, and nameservers are distributed among all the various machines in the network. Each user computer in the network runs an implementation of a clerk.

NETWORK MANAGEMENT SERVICES

An important requirement for enterprise networking is the ability to manage large networks that consist of equipment purchased from many different vendors. This section describes some fundamental techniques and strategies used to manage the operation of enterprise networks.

ISO Specific Management Functional Areas

ISO has been active in the development of a series of standards relating to the management of all aspects of information processing systems. As part of this work, ISO has identified five *specific management functional areas (SMFAS)*. These five functional areas, as they apply to the management of communication networks, are as follows:

- **Configuration Management.** Concerned with the ability to identify the various components that make up the network configuration, to process additions, changes, or deletions to the configuration, to report on the status of components, and to start up or shut down all or any part of the network.

- **Fault Management.** Concerned with the ability to detect, isolate, and correct abnormal conditions that occur in the network environment.

- **Performance Management.** Concerned with the ability to evaluate activities of the network and to make adjustments to improve the network's performance.

- **Security Management.** Concerned with the ability to monitor and control access to network resources.

- **Accounting Management.** Concerned with the ability to identify costs and establish charges related to the use of network resources.

Network Management Functions

Network management is generally concerned with *monitoring* the operation of components in the network, *reporting* on events that occur during network operation, and *controlling* the operational characteristics of the network and its components:

- **Monitoring.** Monitoring involves determining the status and processing characteristics currently associated with different physical and logical components of the network. Depending on the type of component in question, monitoring can be done either by continuously checking the operation of the component, or it can be based on detecting the occurrence of extraordinary events that occur during network operation.

- **Reporting.** The results of monitoring activities must be reported, or made available, to either a network administrator or to network management software operating in some machine on the network.

- **Controlling.** Based on the results of monitoring and reporting functions, the network administrator or the network management software should be able to modify the operational characteristics of the network and its components. These modifications should make it possible to resolve problems, improve network performance, and continue normal operation of the network.

Approaches to the Management
of Enterprise Networks

Managing an enterprise network is not a simple task. An enterprise network may encompass a wide variety of devices from many different vendors, multiple network operating systems and transport protocols, and various types of LAN and WAN data link subnetworks. Management services should provide both a view of the entire network and the ability to manage different portions of the network on a distributed basis. Existing network management products meet enterprise network management requirements in varying degrees.

A number of different approaches to network management have been developed. Each approach provides an overall architecture that guides the development of network management software used in a computer network.

Network management software runs in two places in a network:

- In the device or devices network administrators use to monitor and control the operation of the network.

- In the devices the network administrator needs to control.

Most approaches to network management define a protocol that can be used to control the communication that must take place between the two types of devices listed above. A standardized *approach* to network management and a well-defined *protocol* for exchanging management information are both required for effective network management, especially in a multiple-vendor environment.

REPRESENTATIVE NETWORK MANAGEMENT TECHNOLOGIES

This section introduces a number of different approaches to network management and some specific technologies being used for management in the enterprise networking environment.

ISO Common Management Information Protocol (CMIP)

A comprehensive approach to the management of information systems is being developed by a subcommittee of ISO. The ISO approach to the management of information systems relates to the OSI model and includes the specification for a *Common Management Information Protocol (CMIP)*. CMIP documents the types of messages exchanged in performing management procedures and the rules governing those message exchanges. The ISO CMIP approach to management also includes the definition of a *Common Management Information Services Element (CMISE)* that documents services provided by a management component in an information system.

ISO divides network management into the five functional areas described at the beginning of this chapter. Each of these areas requires a number of supporting functions in order to meet its general requirements. A particular supporting function is often needed by more than one functional area. In CMIP, ISO has taken the approach of defining the supporting functions to be provided and allowing them to be mapped, as required, into the five functional areas. Box 4.4 lists the supporting functions, known as *system management functions,* that have been defined to date.

Structure and Identification of Management Information

The ISO Management Information Base (MIB) is a repository, or database, that stores information on network components and resources that need to be managed. Portions of the MIB are distributed among all the devices in the network—such as end systems, routers, terminal servers—that need to be managed. ISO's approach to the MIB is based on object-oriented computing technology. The information in an MIB that represents a particular element is known as a *managed object.* The ISO network management standard includes the definition of a number of generally useful object classes and attributes.

BOX 4.4   CMIP System Management Functions (SMFs).

- **Object Management.** Supports the creation and deletion of managed objects and the reading and changing of object attributes. Also specifies notifications to be generated when attribute values change.

- **State Management.** Specifies a model for how the management state of an object is to be represented and provides services to support the state management model.

- **Relationship Management.** Specifies a model for representing and managing relationships between managed objects and provides services to support the relationship management model.

- **Alarm Reporting.** Supports the definition of fault alarms and the notifications used to report them.

- **Event-Report Management.** Supports the control of event reporting, including specifying the recipients of reports, defining reports, and specifying criteria for generating and distributing reports.

- **Log Control.** Supports the creation of logs, the creation and storage of log records, and the specification of criteria for logging.

- **Security-Alarm Reporting.** Supports the definition of security alarms and the notifications used to report them.

- **Security-Audit Trail.** Specifies the types of event reports that should be placed in a log used for security evaluation.

- **Access Control.** Supports the control of access to management information and operations.

- **Accounting Meter.** Provides for accounting for the usage of system resources and procedures for enforcing accounting limits.

- **Workload Monitoring.** Supports the monitoring of attributes of managed objects that relate to the performance of a resource.

- **Test Management.** Supports the management of confidence and diagnostic test procedures.

- **Summarization.** Supports the definition of statistical measures to be applied to attributes and the reporting of summarized information.

Abstract Syntax Notation One

Managed objects are named and described using an international standard notation called *Abstract Syntax Notation One (ASN.1)*. ASN.1 defines a powerful data description notation that allows the format and meaning of data structures to be defined without specifying how those data structures are represented in a computer or how they are encoded for transmission through a network. For example, ASN.1 allows a numeric data element to be defined as an INTEGER but does not specify anything about how that integer should be represented or encoded (1's complement, 2's complement, packed-decimal, and so on). The advantage to using a notation like ASN.1 to define management information is that it can be described independently of any particular form of information processing technology.

Simple Network Management Protocol (SNMP)

The *Simple Network Management Protocol (SNMP)* was originally designed to provide an easy-to-implement, but comprehensive, approach to network management in the TCP/IP environment. However, SNMP is now being applied in networks that conform to many other network architectures. SNMP defines the formats of a set of network management messages and the rules by which those messages are exchanged.

The SNMP approach to network management was developed at a time when considerable work had already been done by ISO concerning the CMIP approach to network management. This allowed the developers of SNMP to use the same basic concepts regarding how management information should be described and defined as those being developed by ISO in the CMIP and CMISE specifications.

SNMP includes a *Structure of Management Information* document that defines the allowable data types for MIBs, the way in which MIBs can be structured, and a set of standard objects that can be used in implementing an MIB. An SNMP MIB has a tree structure. Each object has an object identifier that uniquely identifies it among its siblings. Like ISO CMIP, SNMP uses ASN.1 to define and identify objects in an MIB.

CMOT (CMIP over TCP/IP)

CMOT (CMIP over TCP/IP) is a specification that describes how ISO CMIP can be used as an approach to the management of a TCP/IP internet. CMOT works with the same Management Information Base (MIB) and Structure and Identification of Management Information (SMI) defined for SNMP. Components called managers and agents contain management information categorized according to the various TCP/IP architectural layers.

NetView

NetView is the name of IBM's network management products. It is also the name of an overall architectural approach to network management. The NetView architecture represents a proprietary view of network management. The NetView architecture is implemented in IBM's NetView products and in the products of vendors that choose to be compatible with the NetView architecture. However, many NetView specifications are closely aligned with the ISO CMIP standards for network management.

The major functions of the NetView architecture can be divided into four categories similar to the five CMIP specific management functional areas. NetView functions are briefly described in Box 4.5.

IBM offers a family of NetView products that provide network management in different environments. Some of the product categories in the NetView family include the following:

- **NetView/390.** NetView/390 products provide network management for mainframe SNA networks.

BOX 4.5   NetView major functions.

- **Problem Management.** Problem management deals with a problem from its detection through its resolution. It is concerned with problems that occur to the hardware, software, and communication links that make up the network.

- **Configuration Management.** Configuration management is concerned with the generation and maintenance of a configuration database containing information necessary to identify the physical and logical components of the network and their relationships to each other. As resources are added to or removed from the network, or the status of network resources changes, configuration information is updated.

- **Change Management.** In a network of any size, changes occur frequently to network resources, involving additions, deletions, or modifications to hardware, software, or microcode network components. These changes may be the result of problem bypass or correction procedures, or they may reflect changes to user requirements that necessitate changes to the network. Change management is involved with planning, tracking, and controlling these changes.

- **Performance and Accounting Management.** Performance and accounting management is responsible for monitoring and evaluating the operating performance of the network and for recording and tracking usage charges at the network resource level.

- **NetView/6000.** NetView/6000 provides SNMP-based network management for TCP/IP-based internets.

- **LAN NetView.** LAN NetView provides network management in the personal computer LAN environment.

OpenView

Hewlett-Packard's OpenView family of network management products conforms to the SNMP approach to network management and also includes support for OSI CMIP standards. OpenView products can be used to manage networks conforming to the TCP/IP protocols and also networks that employ the Novell NetWare IPX/SPX protocols. OpenView includes a facility that can be used to monitor SNA networks as well.

The OpenView approach to network management provides fault, configuration, and performance management functions. OpenView is becoming a de facto standard in the enterprise networking environment and has been incorporated by OSF in the Distributed Management Environment described later in this chapter. OpenView technology has been licensed by IBM for inclusion in its NetView/6000 network management products and has also been included in some of the network management products offered by Digital Equipment Corporation.

SunNet Manager

SunNet Manager network management products from Sun Microsystems provide management capabilities for TCP/IP internets. SunNet products support any manageable device that supports the SNMP specifications. Sun also provides add-on products that support the CMIP standards and handle a two-way interface with NetView products for managing SNA networks. At the time of writing, Sun had also announced support for Novell NetWare networks. There are a large number of network management add-on products available developed by other vendors, most of which have used the three SunNet-defined APIs.

Desktop Management Interface

The *Desktop Management Interface (DMI)* is a proposed network management standard being developed by the *Desktop Management Task Force,* a group of vendors in the desktop computing marketplace. DMI is designed to provide a standardized way to manage the various hardware and software components that are part of a network consisting of primarily personal computers and desktop workstations. DMI specifically addresses network management concerns of importance in the desktop computing environment.

DMI is designed to be complementary to standard network management protocols, such as CMIP and SNMP. A network management protocol concentrates on the formats of the messages concerning network management that flow over the network. DMI, on the other hand, concentrates on the functions that must be performed in the network management software that runs in end-user computing systems.

DMI is specifically concerned with the functions performed by a *desktop agent,* software that gathers and stores data relating to the various components making up the desktop computing system. The desktop agent handles network management tasks on behalf of the desktop computing system by responding to requests and directives from management stations.

Distributed Management Environment (DME)

The Open Software Foundation (OSF) has defined a set of standards for management services called the *Distributed Management Environment (DME).* DME Services are complementary to those defined by the OSF *Distributed Computing Environment (DCE).* The OSF DCE is an example of a coordinated set of network application services that is beginning to be used in a variety of computing environments. OSF DCE is described later in this chapter. OSF is developing and introducing DME in two phases: *DME Services* and the *DME Network Management Option.*

DME Services

DME Services provide a number of common services useful to management applications of all types. In a distributed computing environment, varying types of hardware and software, located in widely disparate locations, must all interoperate. To achieve efficient and effective operation, management services must be available for monitoring and controlling all the resources connected to the network. DME Services are designed to provide the tools necessary to manage network resources. DME Services include software distribution services, event services, license management services, subsystem management services, and personal computer services.

DME Network Management Option

The DME *Network Management Option (NMO)* provides a set of application programming interfaces management applications can use to access and exchange information using the SNMP or CMIP network management protocols. The DME Network Management Option provides a common set of application programming interfaces (APIS) for accessing managed network resources using the SNMP and CMIP protocols. NMO is based on the standardized *X/Open Management Protocol Application Programming Interface (XMP API)*. Important NMO components include the X/Open management protocol API, the instrumentation request broker, the event subsystem, and the name resolution subsystem.

OSF DISTRIBUTED COMPUTING ENVIRONMENT

As we introduced earlier, the Open Software Foundation (OSF) has developed an important architecture for client/server, network-based computing called the *Distributed Computing Environment (DCE)*. The OSF DCE defines services that fall into many of the application service categories introduced at the beginning of this chapter.

DCE is intended to provide a set of standardized services that can be made available across a variety of different system environments so a distributed application developed using DCE services can support different operating systems, different network software subsystems, and different transport protocols. DCE Services operate above the level of the network software and below the level of the application-oriented services specific application programs provide. DCE Services provide a high degree of scalability by defining a cell architecture in which systems that communicate frequently can be grouped together.

OSF took a unique approach to standardization when it defined DCE and DME. Instead of writing specifications from scratch for each of the services the DCE and DME define, OSF published requests for technology and invited all the members of OSF to submit working code implemented each of the services OSF was attempting to define. OSF then selected what it felt were the best technologies from among all the submissions. In this manner, each of the services DCE and DME defines is based on proven, working technology rather than compiling abstract sets of specifications.

DCE and DME are not just paper architectures; they also consist of working code available from OSF in source form. The source code is written in a portable fashion that can be adapted to run on a wide variety of UNIX-type operating systems. It can also be tailored to run on other operating systems, such as Windows and OS/2 in the personal computer environment. It is the responsibility of a particular vendor, and not OSF, to tailor the source code for a particular platform.

Box 4.6 provides brief descriptions of the six DCE Services included in DCE at the time of writing and specifies the source of the technology for each service.

SUMMARY

General categories of application services provided in most networking environments include print services, file services, electronic mail services, directory services, and net-

BOX 4.6   DCE Services.

- DCE **Remote Procedure Call Service.** The *DCE Remote Procedure Call Service (DCE RPC)* allows an application component running in one computer system to use a simple procedure call mechanism to invoke a procedure running in some other computing system in the network. This allows procedure calls to be used to hide many of the complexities of network communication from application developers. The DCE RPC Service is based on RPC technology jointly submitted to the OSF by Digital Equipment Corporation and Hewlett-Packard.

- DCE **Threads Service.** The *DCE Threads Service* provides application programmers with the ability to create independent execution threads within the same program. This gives an application the ability to carry out multiple computing tasks concurrently. The DCE Threads Service is based on the *DECthreads* implementation of the *Concert Multithread Architecture (CMA)* submitted to the OSF by Digital Equipment Corporation.

- DCE **Directory Service.** The *DCE Directory Service* implements a distributed repository that stores information about objects in the computing environment, including users, computing systems, and distributed services application programs can request. The DCE Directory Service provides facilities for submitting a name to the Directory Service and getting back a list of the attributes associated with that name. The DCE Directory Service includes the following two components available from the OSF:

  — DCE **Global Directory Service.** The *DCE Global Directory Service (DCE GDS)* is designed to handle directory operations that take place between individual cells. The DCE GDS is based on the ITU X.500 standard as implemented by the DIR-X X.500 directory service submitted to the OSF by Siemens.

  — DCE **Cell Directory Service.** The *DCE Cell Directory Service (DCE CDS)* is designed to handle directory operations that take place within a single cell. The DCE CDS is based on the *DECdns* implementation of the Distributed Name Service architecture submitted to the OSI by Digital Equipment Corporation.

  In addition to the two OSF DCE directory technologies, the DCE Directory Service also integrates the TCP/IP Domain Name System (DNS) that can be used as an alternative to the DCE GDS for performing directory operations between cells.

- DCE **Distributed File Service.** The *DCE Distributed File Service (DCE DFS)* allows users to access and share files maintained by computing systems operating in the role of *file servers* that can be located anywhere in the network. DCE DFS is based on the *Andrew File System (AFS)* technology submitted to the OSF by Transarc Corporation. It performs many of the same functions as the Network File Service (NFS) widely implemented in the TCP/IP networking environment.

- DCE **Distributed Time Service.** The *DCE Distributed Time Service* allows application programs to request services that work with date and time-of-day values in a standardized manner that is the same across all computing platforms. The Distributed Time Service also implements a set of distributed algorithms that ensure that the clocks in all the computing systems in the network are synchronized and contain correct values for the date and time of day. DCE DTS is based on the *Distributed Time Service (DTS)* technology submitted to the OSF by Digital Equipment Corporation. The DCE DTS interoperates with the *Network Time Protocol (NTP)* widely used in the TCP/IP environment.

- DCE **Security Service.** The *DCE Security Service* provides facilities for implementing secure communications in a networked environment and for controlling access to resources in the computing environment. The DCE Security Service is based on the *Kerberos* security system submitted to the OSF by Project Athena. It is augmented by a number of additional security components submitted by Hewlett-Packard.

work management services. Three major methods can be employed with network software for using network application services: issuing end user commands, using a redirection function, or invoking function calls defined by an API supported by the network software.

Application programming interfaces (APIS) are defined by network software subsystems to allow application programs to explicitly request application services. Three important APIS are the LAN APIS defined by IBM and Microsoft products, named pipes, and the NetWare APIS used with Novell NetWare products.

The goal of a network directory service is to provide a mechanism for storing and accessing information about network objects of interest, such as network users, network devices, network services, application programs, and data files. A directory service might provide searches based on primitive names that uniquely identify objects in the network in order to implement a "white pages" directory facility. It might alternatively use descriptive names that permit "yellow pages" type searches to also be implemented. Commonly used directory systems include the TCP/IP Domain Name System (DNS), the X.500 Directory standard, the Novell NetWare Directory Services (NDS), Banyan StreetTalk, and the DECnet Phase V Naming Service.

The ISO committee responsible for international standards relating to the management of information systems has identified five major functional areas management should address: configuration management, fault management, performance management, security management, and accounting management. Important approaches to network management include the ISO Common Management Information Protocol (CMIP), the TCP/IP Simple Network Management Protocol (SNMP), CMIP over TCP/IP, the Desktop Management Interface (DMI), IBM's NetView, HP's OpenView, Sun's SunNet Manager, and the OSF Distributed Management Environment (DME).

The Distributed Computing Environment (DCE) was developed by the Open Software Foundation (OSF). DCE defines application services useful in a heterogeneous, distributed computing environment. DCE Services provide a high degree of scalability by defining a cell architecture in which systems that communicate frequently can be grouped together. DCE Services include the DCE Remote Procedure Call Service (DCE RPC), the DCE Threads Service, the DCE Directory Service, the DCE Distributed File Service (DCE DFS), the DCE Distributed Time Service (DCE DTS), and the DCE Security Service.

Chapter 5 describes the services and protocols associated with the Transport Network component of the enterprise network model.

Chapter **5**

The Transport Network

This chapter presents an introduction to the *transport network* component of the enterprise network model. The transport network provides services generally associated with the Transport and Network layers of the OSI model. These layers make use of the facilities provided by one or more physical data transmission facilities. These are implemented by data link subnetworks operating below the transport network in the enterprise network model (see Fig. 5.1). Box 3.1 described the transport network software subsystems and protocol families important for enterprise networking.

    The exact details of the services provided by the transport network, and the protocols used to provide data transport services, vary from one network architecture to another and from one network software subsystem to another. However, some general services are common to almost all protocol families, and this chapter describes these general data transport services.

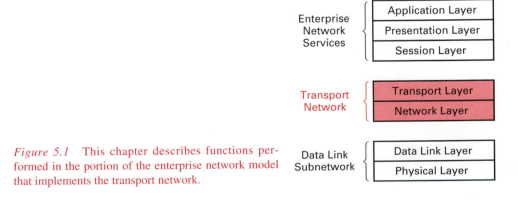

Figure 5.1 This chapter describes functions performed in the portion of the enterprise network model that implements the transport network.

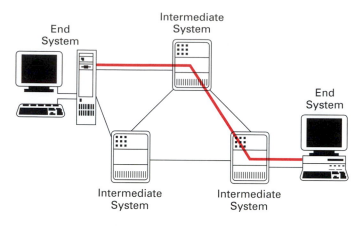

Figure 5.2   Data transport between end systems can involve inter-mediate systems.

TRANSPORT NETWORK FUNCTIONS

The primary function of the transport network is to move data from a source end system to a destination end system. The end-to-end communication function of the transport network is associated with the Transport layer of the OSI model.

The end-to-end data transport function of the transport network may involve the use of intermediate systems, as shown in Fig 5.2. Therefore, the transport network may include a *routing* function to determine the path each message should take through the network and a *relaying* function that moves each message through intermediate systems on its way to the destination end system. The routing and relaying functions of the transport network are generally associated with the Network layer of the OSI model. The routing and relaying functions are discussed later in this chapter.

NETWORK ADDRESSING MECHANISMS

The network architectures and protocol families discussed in this book all provide *addressing mechanisms* in many of their layers. With most network architectures, addressing is important in the Transport, Network, and Data Link layers.

- **Transport Layer Addressing.** Addressing in the Transport layer is intended to uniquely identify a program using data transport services within a particular computer system. Addressing in the Transport layer generally consists of a simple identifier assigned to each executing program. The identifier assigned to a program need be unique only among the programs running concurrently within a particular computer system.

- **Network Layer Addressing.** Addressing in the Network layer is intended to uniquely identify a particular computing system attached to the network. Addressing in the Network layer consists of a *network address* value assigned to each point of attachment to the network. Network address values must be unique within the entire enterprise network.

- **Data Link Layer.** Addressing in the Data Link layer is intended to uniquely identify a network interface card (NIC) installed in a particular computing system and is attached to a particular data link subnetwork. Addressing in this layer consists of a *station address* value assigned to a NIC that must be unique only among the systems attached to a given data link. (In many cases, a NIC address is also *globally* unique, but this is not a requirement for operation in many networks.)

The following sections further discuss the addressing requirements for the Transport, Network, and Data Link layers.

Transport Layer Addressing Mechanisms

Most modern computing systems allow more than one program or process at a time to be active and executing in a given computing system. Therefore, it is possible for multiple processes to manage network communication activities at the same time in the same computing system. The addressing mechanisms associated with the OSI Transport layer are designed to differentiate among multiple concurrent users of the data transport service active in the same machine.

Transport layer addressing mechanisms are generally simple and straightforward and often involve an identifier called a *port* used to control communication activities within a computing system. Each active process uses a different port, and each active port generally has a different port identifier associated with it.

In many network architectures, certain port identifiers may be reserved and associated with particular types of data transport services. For example, a file transfer service might be assigned one port identifier, an electronic mail message service might be assigned another, a remote procedure call service another, and so on. Generally, some port assignments are available for use by end-user processes, and mechanisms may be available for automatically assigning user processes to unused transport ports.

Network Layer Addressing Mechanisms

In order to be able to route and relay data to a particular destination computing system, there must be a mechanism that uniquely identifies each system in the enterprise network. This is normally done by assigning a unique *network address* to each point at which a network device is physically attached to the enterprise network. This level of addressing is normally handled by mechanisms associated with the OSI Network layer.

Network Address Assignment

A device attached to a network, such as an end-user system with a single point of attachment to the network, is generally assigned a single network address. A device, such as a network interconnection device, with multiple points of attachment to the network, is assigned multiple network addresses, one for each point of attachment.

Depending on the particular network architecture and network software subsystem in use, the network software may create network addresses automatically or it may be necessary for a network administrator to assign them manually.

Network Address Formats

Each network architecture and protocol family uses a different Network layer addressing mechanism, and each uses a different data structure for network address values. For example, each system in an enterprise network that implements TCP/IP networking software must have a unique network address that conforms to the TCP/IP network address structure. In the same manner, each system in a network that uses Novell NetWare software has a unique network address that conforms to the NetWare network address structure.

In most instances, a network address consists of two parts: a *network identifier* that identifies some subset of the entire enterprise network and a *node identifier* that identifies a specific system within the subset defined by the network identifier. Each full network address, made up of a combination of a network identifier value and node identifier value, must be unique throughout the entire enterprise network.

Data Link Layer Addressing Mechanisms

A computing system is generally attached to a transmission medium segment through a *network interface card (NIC)*. Each NIC may be assigned a *station address*. Data link station addresses are typically processed in the Data Link layer and are used to control the transmission of a frame from a sending device to a receiving device in a given data link subnetwork.

WAN Data Link Station Addressing

On a point-to-point WAN data link, station addresses are not typically used, since each frame sent has only one destination: the NIC at the other end of the data link. The specific requirements for data link station addressing and station address formats for each form of WAN data link are discussed in Part III.

LAN Data Link Station Addressing

On a local area network data link it is necessary to assign a unique *station address* to each network interface card on that data link. Station addresses are used to identify the source and destination of each frame transmitted over the LAN. A local area network NIC's station address is often called its *MAC address* because typically the Medium Access Control (MAC) sublayer of the Data Link layer processes station addresses.

Each particular form of data link subnetwork technology uses its own data link addressing scheme and defines its own specific station address format. Data link subnetwork station addressing schemes and station address formats for LAN data link technologies are described in the chapters in Part IV.

A Data Link layer station address identifies a particular NIC attached to a data link. A computing system that has multiple NICs installed can be connected to more than one data link. Each of the system's NICs has its own station address.

On local area network data links that conform to the IEEE/ISO/ANSI LAN architecture, each network interface card used to attach a system to the data link ordinarily has a 48-bit physical hardware address associated with it. This hardware address is usually permanently set at the time the network interface card is manufactured and is never changed. The NIC's physical hardware address is most often used as its station address.

Data Link layer station addresses may be globally unique. For example, the global address administration scheme defined by the IEEE/ISO/ANSI LAN architecture guarantees that no two NICs, manufactured anywhere in the world, will ever have the same station address. However, some types of LAN data links allow a network administrator to assign station addresses to NICs manually. With such types of LAN data links, it is not necessary for Data Link station addresses to be globally unique. Station addresses need only be unique within a particular data link subnetwork.

Network Address and NIC Station Address Mapping

In a particular network, there must be a one-to-one mapping between each NIC's *station* address and the *network* address assigned to that point of network attachment.

With some network architectures, a NIC's station address is used directly to form the node identifier portion of a system's network address. The Novell NetWare architecture uses such a scheme. The node identifier portion of a device's NetWare network address consists of the 48-bit NIC station address associated with the NIC installed in that device. Therefore, in a NetWare network, there is a simple one-to-one mapping between a NIC station address and the Network address associated with that station.

With some other network architectures the node address portion of a network address does not correspond directly to NIC addresses but conforms to some other data format. With a network architecture in which node identifiers values do not consist of NIC station addresses, there must be some mechanism provided to map between a station address and the node identifier portion of a network address.

For example, with the TCP/IP architecture, each network address is 32 bits in length, and some subset of those 32 bits is used as a node identifier. The TCP/IP *Address Resolution Protocol (ARP)* and *Reverse Address Resolution Protocol (RARP)* are used to translate between NIC station addresses and their corresponding internet addresses. (At the time of writing, an addressing architecture for TCP/IP that allows for larger network addresses is under development. It is likely that these larger TCP/IP network addresses will become widely used in the years ahead.)

DATA TRANSMISSION THROUGH THE TRANSPORT NETWORK

Figure 5.3 illustrates the general procedure the transport network uses to transmit user data from a source system to a destination system. The following describes the steps in the data transmission procedure:

1. A transport network user sends data to a distant transport network user by passing the data down to a process running in the Transport layer of the communication system. The user

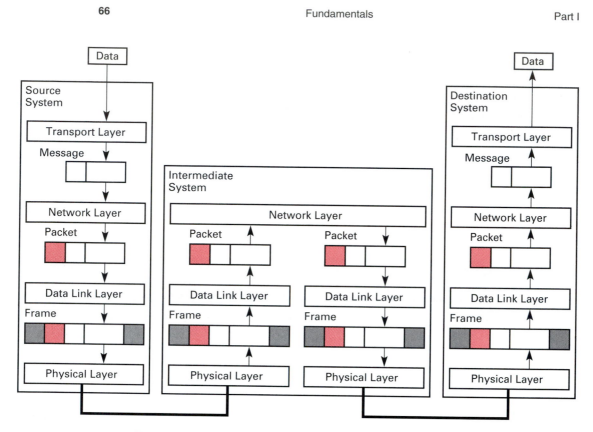

Figure 5.3   Message transmission through the Transport network.

also supplies information about the user to which the data should be sent, such as the network address of the destination user's system. The Transport layer process adds any necessary control information, such as a sequence number, checksum, and the destination network address, to the user data to create a Transport layer *message*. The Transport layer then passes the message down to a Network layer process.

2. Based on the destination network address of the system to which the message is being sent, the Network layer in the source system determines the next system to which the message should be transmitted and the particular data link to be used to reach that system. The Network layer adds additional control information to the transport message, creating a *packet*. The Network layer then passes the packet down to the Data Link layer in the source system.

3. The Data Link layer adds additional control information to the packet in the form of a header and a trailer, creating a *frame*. It then uses the services of the Physical layer to send the frame across the specified data link. The Data Link layer in the system that receives the frame removes the Data Link control information and passes the resulting packet up to the Network layer.

4. Only one intermediate system is shown in the diagram, but a packet can flow through any number of intermediate systems in reaching the destination system. The Network layer in each system that receives a packet determines a destination for the next hop, makes any modifications to the packet's control information necessary, and passes it to the Data Link

layer. The Data Link layer encloses the packet in a new frame for each data link the packet traverses in reaching the final destination system. The Data Link layer in the final destination system eventually receives the final frame and passes the enclosed packet to the Network layer.

5. The Network layer in the final destination system removes the Network control information and passes the original packet up to the Transport layer there. The Transport layer process in the destination system then removes the remaining control information from the message and passes a copy of the original data to the destination transport network user.

The transport network can implement one of two possible types of data delivery service in carrying data from a source system to a destination system: a connection-oriented service and a connectionless service. The following sections describe these two types of data delivery service.

CONNECTION-ORIENTED DATA TRANSPORT

A *connection-oriented* data transport service performs functions similar to those provided by the telephone system. A connection-oriented service consists of three distinct stages:

1. Connection establishment (dialing a call).
2. Data transfer (talking over the connection).
3. Connection release (hanging up the phone).

With a connection-oriented service, data transfer always involves a pair of transport service users. If a user wishes to transmit the same messages to two or more other transport users, it must establish a separate connection with each, and it must transmit the message to each recipient in a separate operation.

With a connection-oriented service, the full network address of the recipient is typically specified only when the connection is established. The connection-establishment process generally assigns an identifier to the connection, and subsequent data transfer operations can then refer to the connection identifier rather than to the full network address.

When data transmission is completed, the connection is released. If a serious problem occurs during data transmission, the connection is reset or released, and both users are informed of the reset or release. The connection can be reset or released at any time by either of the communicating parties or by the data transport service itself.

Sequence Checking

A connection-oriented data transport service must perform at least two functions related to error correction: sequence checking and message acknowledgment. To perform the sequence checking function, messages being sent are assigned sequence numbers. As messages are received, the sequence number of each incoming message is checked to ensure that messages have arrived in the sequence in which they were sent, that none are missing, and that none have been sent twice. If messages are received out of sequence, the data transport service may implement functions to put the messages back into their proper sequence before passing them up to the user.

Periodically, the receiving transport component sends an acknowledgment so the sending component knows the messages it has sent have been received successfully. If problems occur, and the receiving component informs the sending component that messages were not successfully received, or if an acknowledgment is not received within a specified time period, the sending component retransmits the missing or damaged messages.

Checksums and CRCs

The transport network software may perform another form of error detection through the use of *checksums* or *cyclical redundancy check (CRC)* bits. With checksums or CRCs, a calculation is performed on the bits in each message sent. The calculation results in a checksum or CRC value included as part of the message. When the message is received, the receiving component repeats the checksum or CRC calculation and the calculated value is compared to the checksum or CRC in the message. If the two values do not agree, the message is assumed to have been corrupted and is discarded.

Because of the error checking and sequence checking performed, a connection-oriented service is often described as providing *reliable* and *sequential* data transfer. As long as the connection remains established, the sender can generally assume each message sent is successfully received and that the messages are received in the same order sent.

Flow Control

Sequence numbers and acknowledgments may also be used to implement a flow control mechanism to control the flow of messages between a sender and a receiver. The flow control mechanism can be used to prevent the sender from transmitting messages faster than the receiver can accept them. Flow control is based on the use of a *window*, which defines the amount of data a sender can transmit before it must wait for an acknowledgment from the receiver. The data transport service may change the window size from time to time in order to reflect changing conditions in the network.

CONNECTIONLESS DATA TRANSPORT

A connectionless service works more like the postal system than the telephone system. The service accepts each message for transmission and tries its best to deliver it, just as the post office accepts addressed letters and attempts to deliver them to the intended recipients. The delivery of each message is independent of all others.

With a connectionless data transport service, communication takes place in a single phase. The sending user hands each message to the data transport service for delivery to a receiving user. The sending user provides the full address of the receiving data transport service user in each message it sends. The data transport service then attempts to deliver each message to its destination. Each message must contain the full address of its intended recipient, and the data transport service handles each message independently of all other messages. A connectionless data transport service may allow a group address to be used that identifies more than one recipient for a message. The data transport service then delivers the message to each receiving user identified by the group address.

Checksums or CRCs may be used by a data transport service to identify and discard messages received in error. However, no sequence checking is done to ensure that messages are received in the same sequence in which they were sent, and the receiver sends no acknowledgment that it has received a message. No flow control or error recovery is provided as part of a connectionless data transport service. When a connectionless data transport service is used at the transport network level, any flow control and error recovery services required must be provided by the user of the connectionless transport network service.

A connectionless data transport service is typically described as providing a *best-efforts* delivery service. It is also sometimes called a *datagram* service. The sender does not know for sure that a message being sent will actually be received by its intended recipient. Therefore, a connectionless data transport service cannot be considered a *reliable* service.

CONNECTION-ORIENTED VERSUS CONNECTIONLESS DATA TRANSPORT SERVICES

It is important to point out that the term *reliable* often used in the literature to describe a data transport service is perhaps not the best term that could be used. The term reliable has a "good" connotation, and it might be inferred that a connection-oriented data transport service is somehow inherently "better" than a connectionless data transport service. This is not the case. A number of factors determine when a particular layer in a communication system should provide connection-oriented delivery and when a connectionless service is more appropriate.

For example, a connection-oriented service, although considered reliable, may provide a very poor service if frequent failures cause the connection to be constantly broken, thus requiring new connections to be established to continue data transfer. On the other hand, a connectionless service may deliver 999,999 messages out of every 1,000,000 sent. However, we cannot consider it reliable because we don't know for sure whether any given message will be successfully delivered.

A connectionless data transport service can have many advantages over a connection-oriented service. For example, a connectionless service may incur less protocol overhead than a connection-oriented service, especially when small amounts of data must be transferred. The delay involved in sending small amounts of data is also often less with a connectionless service because no time is spent in setting up a connection before the user data is sent. With a connectionless service, there is no need to establish a logical connection between the sending and the receiving transport components, and each message is sent and processed independently of any other message. Also, with a connectionless service, a message can be sent to one destination or to several destinations using the same service request.

In order to use a connectionless data transport service in any particular layer on a communication system, it is only necessary to ensure that reliability controls are being provided at some higher layer in the architecture. The higher layer can then recover from errors that occur in lower layers by requesting message retransmissions.

ROUTING AND RELAYING FUNCTIONS

As we introduced early in this chapter, an important function of the transport network component of the enterprise network model is to determine the route each message should take through the network and to relay each message from system to system on its way to the destination end system. Systems capable of playing the role of intermediate systems and performing the routing function are typically called *routers*.

A router must have sufficient routing information available so it can examine the destination network address associated with a message and determine the address of a system that will bring the message closer to its final destination. A router must also have a way of updating the routing information to reflect changes that occur in the topology of the enterprise network.

Each of the major transport protocol families has its own unique routing protocols that routers use for exchanging routing information with other systems in order to update their stored routing information. But there are certain general approaches to routing applicable to all network architectures. The characteristics of five broad categories of routing protocols are summarized in Fig. 5.4. The sections that follow introduce these different categories of routing protocols.

Static Routing

With *static routing*, all routing information for each system is precomputed and is provided to each router through a management action. Static routing has the advantage that sophisticated computational methods can be used for computing routes, since routes are not computed in real time. However, with static routing techniques, routing information must be recomputed and provided to the routers each time the network topology changes. Thus, static routing techniques are generally not well suited to large networks that may be constantly changing.

Quasi-Static Routing

Quasi-static routing is similar to static routing except that the routing information computed and provided to each node includes information about alternative paths that can be used when certain types of failures occur. Quasi-static routing techniques can handle certain types of topological changes, such as links becoming unavailable, but major changes to the network topology still require routing information to be recomputed offline for the routers.

Method	Collection	Distribution	Computation	Adaptability
Static	Through network management	Through network management	Routes computed offline	None in real time
Quasi-static	Through network management	Through network management	Routes computed offline	Limited adaptability to failures
Centralized	Routers report information about the local environment to a central facility	Central facility distributes forwarding information to each router	Routes computed by central facility	Can adapt to any changes to the central facility, but routers have difficulty finding the central facility
Distributed Distance Vector	Routes computed individually by each router upon receipt of information that changes their routing domain tables	Routers accept routing information from neighbor routers and redistributes their view of the local neighborhood	Routes computed individually by each router upon receipt of information that changes their routing decisions	Adapts to any changes that are reported by neighbors
Link State	Routes computed individually by each router upon receipt of information that changes their routing domain tables	Routers globally distribute information about their local environments to all other routers	Routes computed individually by each router upon receipt of information that changes their routing domain tables	Adapts to any changes that are reported in the link state information

Figure 5.4   Characteristics of routing algorithms.

Centralized Routing

With *centralized routing*, end systems and routers report information about their local environments to a centralized facility. The centralized facility accumulates routing information from all the systems in the network, computes routes, and sends to each router the information it needs to handle routing decisions. In effect, only the centralized facility has complete knowledge of the network topology. Although, in theory, a centralized routing scheme can respond to topological changes, it has two major drawbacks. First, a way must be found for relaying the routing information to the centralized facility after a topological change occurs. This is difficult because the routing information maintained by the centralized facility cannot be reliably used for this purpose after the network topology changes. Second, the delays inherent in propagating routing information to and from the centralized facility can cause the calculated routes to be different from the routes that should be used.

Distributed Adaptive Routing

With *distributed adaptive routing*, systems dynamically sense their local environments and exchange this information with each other in a distributed fashion. Each router uses the routing messages it receives from end systems and other routers to periodically compute new routes for relaying packets from one system to the next. Distributed adaptive algorithms are robust, and they can quickly adapt to changing network topologies. Almost all modern routers use distributed adaptive algorithms and exchange routing messages with one another to maintain their routing information.

TRANSPORT INTERFACES

We next examine important *application programming interfaces (APIs)* that network software implement to allow application programs to request basic network data transport services. Each of these APIs defines services at roughly the level of the OSI Transport layer. They have each been developed for use with a particular network architecture and communication protocol family. However, some of the data transport APIs described here are being used to provide access to the Transport layer protocols in networks that implement different network architectures.

Remote Procedure Call (RPC)

A *remote procedure call (RPC)* facility can make it possible for programmers to implement a client/server application without needing to explicitly issue requests for communication services. The idea behind this facility is that procedure calls are a well understood mechanism for transferring control and data from one procedure to another in a computing application. It is very useful to extend the procedure call mechanism from a set of procedures in a single-computer environment to a set of procedures in a distributed, client/server environment.

Procedure Calls in a Client/Server Environment

An RPC facility allows the procedure call mechanism to work in a client/server computing environment where the calling procedure (the client) and the called procedure (the server) reside in different computers connected by a network. Ideally, this should be done so the calling client procedure can call a remote server procedure using exactly the same technique it would use to call a procedure residing on the local system. In other words, the mechanisms the remote procedure call facility employs should be hidden from both the client and the server procedures, although no actual RPC implementation yet provides complete transparency.

Remote Procedure Call Functional Model

A simplified functional model of a remote procedure call facility is shown in Fig. 5.5. In this functional model, a calling client procedure executes a procedure call in the

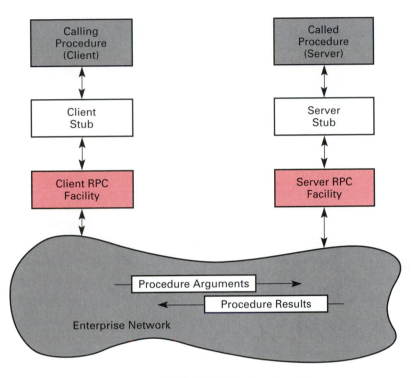

Figure 5.5   RPC facility functional model.

same manner as if it were executing a procedure call to a local procedure. The called server procedure runs as if it executed in the same system as the client procedure. A module called a *stub* in the local system mimics the presence of the actual procedure to which the calling procedure is attempting to pass control. The stub, in turn, requests the services of the remote procedure call facility.

Remote Procedure Call Implementations

The first RPC implementations to gain widespread use ran in the UNIX operating system environment with TCP/IP networking software. In the TCP/IP environment, two commonly used remote procedure call facilities are:

- **Sun RPC.** An implementation of the *Sun RPC* facility is provided in most variations of the BSD UNIX operating system developed by the University of California at Berkeley. The Sun RPC facility is also provided on a number of other UNIX and non-UNIX operating systems and is normally available with any implementation of Sun's Network File System (NFS). Source code for the Sun RPC facility is available from Sun Microsystems for a nominal charge.

- **Hewlett-Packard RPC.** The *Hewlett-Packard (HP) RPC* facility (originally developed by Apollo Computer Inc., which was subsequently acquired by Hewlett-Packard) is provided by a software subsystem called the Network Computing System (NCS). The HP NCS is a programmer toolkit that allows programmers to access the HP RPC facilities in a similar manner to Sun RPC. Like Sun RPC, the NCS software subsystem is implemented on a wide variety of UNIX and non-UNIX operating systems.

Named Pipes

The *Named Pipes* facility is a system for interprocess communication codeveloped by IBM and Microsoft for their respective network operating system products. The Named Pipes mechanism has become a de facto standard that has been implemented in other network operating systems, including Novell NetWare software.

The Named Pipes application programming interface allows a program to send data to or receive data from another program in a way similar to issuing ordinary file management commands. The data is sent and received in the same way as it would be if it were being read to or written from a file. The two programs communicating over a named pipe can be local (located on the same system) or remote (on different systems in a network). The programs are unaware of whether communication is local or remote.

A named pipe provides a two-way communication facility that operates in a similar manner as a full-duplex telecommunications circuit. The program at each end of the named pipe has a read buffer and a write buffer and can both read and write concurrently. If desired, access to a named pipe can be restricted so communication takes place in one direction at a time.

When two programs communicate using a named pipe, one program operates in the role of the server and the other in the role of the client. The server process creates the named pipe and then waits for a client process to open it. Once the client process opens the named pipe, either process can write to or read from the named pipe. Either of the processes can then close the pipe. After a named pipe is closed by a client, it can be opened again by the same or another client. A server can establish multiple *instances* of a named pipe. Each instance can be used to communicate with a different client. This allows a server to communicate with multiple clients using a single named pipe.

A named pipe can be a *message* pipe or an *octet* pipe (called a *byte* pipe in IBM and Microsoft documentation).* When an application writes data to a message pipe, it creates a header that defines the length of the message being written. When an application writes data to an octet pipe, no header is necessary. When an application reads data from a message pipe, it can be read either as a message stream or an octet stream. If it is read as a message stream, an entire message is read as a unit based on the message length in the header. If it is read as an octet stream, headers are skipped over, and data is read up to the size requested in the read function call. The Named Pipes facility defines a set of function calls. These function calls are used to create, open, and close named pipes; read and write data over them; and determine their status.

* International standards for data transmission typically use the term *octet* to refer to a collection of 8 bits. Even though the term *byte* is today more common in practice than *octet,* we will adopt the international standards terminology and use the term *octet* to refer to an arbitrary collection of 8 bits, such as when describing a communication protocol. But we will continue to use the term *byte* when referring to a collection of 8 bits in a storage system.

Sockets

The *Sockets* application programming interface was initially developed for use with TCP/IP networking software in the BSD UNIX operating system environment. By using the Sockets API, two application programs, one running in the local system and another running in the remote system, can communicate with one another in a standardized manner.

The Sockets API can be used to provide access to networking systems other than TCP/IP, including IBM SNA, systems that implement the OSI protocols, and many networking systems for the personal computer environment.

The Sockets API is typically used to implement a client/server relationship between two application programs running in different computing systems. The client and server programs each invoke functions that set up an association between them. The client and the server application then invoke functions to send and receive information over the network in a similar manner to the named pipes API described previously.

The association between the two programs is based on the use of data structures called *sockets*, which provide access to data transport services. A particular socket supplies addressing information at the levels of both the Transport layer and the Network layer of the OSI model. In a typical Sockets implementation, this addressing information consists of a port number and a network address. Multiple application programs can share the same socket.

The Sockets API can support the use of either a connectionless data transport service or a connection-oriented data transport service. The Sockets API defines a series of system calls application programs invoke to request communication services. The system calls included in the Sockets interface were originally developed for use with the C programming language. Corresponding functions have also been implemented for various other programming languages.

Windows Sockets

A variation of the Sockets application programming interface is now being widely used in networks of systems using Microsoft operating system software, such as Windows. The *Windows Sockets*, or *WinSock*, API has been developed in an effort to provide a standardized API for network communication in the Microsoft operating system environment. The WinSock API was jointly defined by Microsoft, JSB Corp., FTP Software, and SunSelect, and has been included as part of the Microsoft *Windows Open Services Architecture (WOSA)*. It is based on the BSD UNIX Sockets API and supports both a connectionless data transport service and a connection-oriented data transport service.

The WinSock API specification also includes a number of extensions to the BSD Sockets API specification. These extensions are designed to provide message-based, asynchronous access to network events. They allow applications that perform complex message-dispatching functions to be used with either nonpreemptive single-threaded or preemptive multithreaded versions of the Windows system software.

Many vendors of TCP/IP implementations and vendors of network-oriented application software have committed to WinSock compliance, and in some cases, have released compliant products.

Common Programming Interface
for Communications (CPI-C)

CPI-C is an application programming interface developed by IBM as a standard method of accessing SNA LU 6.2 communication services. CPI was developed as part of IBM's Systems Application Architecture (SAA). IBM has now reduced its commitment to the SAA effort, but CPI-C has become a widely used data transport API in the IBM computing environment.

CPI-C defines a set of callable services that a program, written in any of several supported programming languages, can issue via a standard subroutine call mechanism. Initially designed to be used with SNA protocols, IBM also supports the use of CPI-C services using TCP/IP protocols. Since the specifications of CPI-C are publicly available, other vendors may provide support for the CPI-C API in their own networking products.

CPI-C is built upon the basic idea that communication between two programs takes place using a *conversation*. In the SNA networking environment, a conversation uses an underlying session when exchanging across the network. Any given application program can be involved in multiple conversations. CPI-C assigns a different *conversation_id* value to each conversation. This conversation_id value is included as a parameter in CPI-C calls, thus allowing CPI-C to determine the conversation each call references.

The callable services that are part of the CPI-C API include services for allocating conversations, sending and receiving data, deallocating conversations, data transfer, determining conversation characteristics, setting conversation characteristics, and handling confirmations.

IPX/SPX Services

The IPX/SPX Services application programming interface is used by application programmers in the Novell NetWare networking environment to implement communication using the IPX or SPX communication protocols. The IPX/SPX Services API consists of a set of function calls. To send data using the IPX or SPX communication protocol, the application must provide a properly formatted IPX or SPX Data packet. With IPX/SPX Services API calls a data structure called an *Event Control Block (ECB)* controls data transmission.

NetBIOS Network Control Blocks (NCBs)

The NetBIOS API is based on the use of control blocks called *Network Control Blocks (NCBs)* for requesting the NetBIOS data transport services provided by a network software subsystem.

A program using the NetBIOS interface constructs an NCB data structure that specifies information about the desired data transport service. The program requests a transport service by invoking a NetBIOS communication function that references a formatted NCB. The specific mechanism used to invoke NetBIOS communication functions depends on the operating system environment.

A command code in the NCB data structure identifies the particular data transport function to be performed, and other fields in the NCB contain information associated with the service request, such as the addresses of buffer areas for incoming or outgoing messages. The NetBIOS NCB API function categories include name service commands, session service commands, datagram service commands, and status and control commands.

SUMMARY

The transport network provides services associated with the Transport and Network layers of the OSI model. These layers make use of the facilities provided by one or more data link subnetworks operating below the level of the transport network. The primary function of the transport network is to move data from a source end system to a destination end system. The transport network provides an end-to-end communication function associated with the Transport layer. It also provides Network layer routing and relaying functions that may involve intermediate systems in addition to the two end systems.

Network architectures and protocol families provide three types of addressing mechanisms. Transport layer addressing uniquely identifies programs using data transport services within a particular computer system and generally consists of identifiers assigned to each executing program. Transport layer addresses need to be unique only among the programs concurrently running within a particular computer system. Network layer addressing uniquely identifies each computing system attached to the network and consists of a unique network address value assigned to each point of attachment to the network. Data Link layer addressing consists of station address values assigned to network interface cards that uniquely identify the stations attached to a particular data link.

The transport network can implement two types of data delivery service in carrying data from a source end system to a destination end system: a connection-oriented service that provides a reliable delivery service, and a connectionless service that provides a best-efforts delivery service.

Routers are intermediate systems that perform routing and relaying functions. Each major transport protocol family has its own unique routing protocols used for exchanging routing information among end systems and intermediate systems. The five general approaches that can be taken with respect to routing are static routing, quasi-static routing, centralized routing, distance-vector distributed routing, and link-state distributed routing. Most protocol families use a distance-vector or link-state form of distributed adaptive routing.

The various application programming interfaces that network software provides for accessing data transport services include remote procedure calls, named pipes, sockets, Common Programming Interface for Communications (CPI-C), IPX/SPX Services, and Network Control Blocks (NCBs).

Chapter 6 begins Part II of this book, which discusses technologies associated with the Data Link Subnetwork component of the enterprise network model, by introducing the general characteristics of data link subnetworks.

DATA LINK SUBNETWORK TECHNOLOGY

Chapter 6

Data Link Subnetworks

This chapter introduces the functions performed by the *data link subnetwork* portion of the enterprise network model introduced in Chapter 3. Figure 6.1 reviews the enterprise network model. Data link subnetwork technology is associated with the Data Link and Physical layers of the OSI model. Most modern network architectures have layers that correspond very closely with the OSI model Data Link and Physical layers.

The exact details of how data link services are provided vary from one type of data link subnetwork to another. However, some elements are common to most types of data link subnetworks. This chapter examines some common elements of many data link subnetworks. The chapters in Parts III and IV present specific details concerning the important data link subnetwork technologies used in building enterprise networks.

DATA LINK TYPES

The primary function of a data link subnetwork is to transfer data between two systems attached to the same data link. An important way of categorizing data link subnetworks is according to how many different devices can be accommodated on the link. A *point-to-point* data link subnetwork connects exactly two devices; a *multiaccess* data link subnetwork can connect two or more devices.

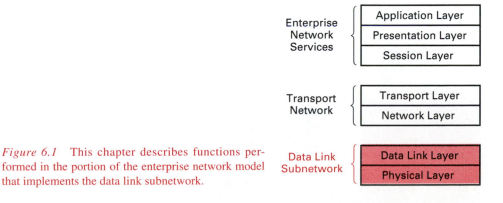

Figure 6.1 This chapter describes functions performed in the portion of the enterprise network model that implements the data link subnetwork.

Figure 6.2   Point-to-point data link.

Point-to-Point Data Links

The simplest type of data link is a *point-to-point* data link implemented through a direct connection between exactly two systems. For example, a point-to-point data link can be implemented by using a wire or cable to connect two systems directly (see Fig. 6.2). A point-to-point connection can consist alternatively of a *logical* connection, where two systems are connected using facilities a service provider implements using a complex network to provide the connection (see Fig. 6.3). A logical point-to-point link is often referred to as a *virtual circuit* or *virtual channel*. Systems connected using a virtual circuit implemented by a service provider perceive a simple direct link between them and can operate as if a wire or cable directly connected them.

Wide Area Network Data Links

Point-to-point data links are most often used to implement wide area network (WAN) data links that span long distances. The most important types of WAN data link subnetwork technologies, which we introduced in Box 3.2, are:

- Analog Telecommunications Circuits
- Digital Telecommunications Circuits
- X.25 Packet-Switched Data Networks (PSDN)
- Integrated Services Digital Network (ISDN)
- Broadband ISDN (B-ISDN)
- Frame Relay
- Asynchronous Transfer Mode (ATM)
- Switched Multi-megabit Data Service (SMDS)
- Wireless WAN Technologies

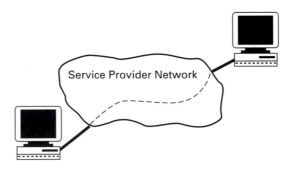

Figure 6.3   Virtual point-to-point data link implemented by a service provider.

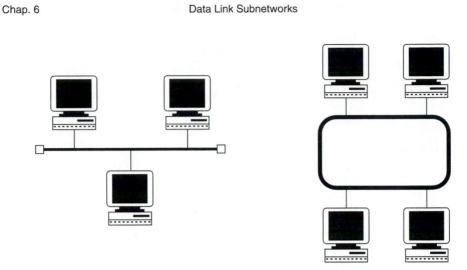

Figure 6.4   Multiaccess data links allow multiple systems to be attached to the same data link.

Multiaccess Data Links

A *multiaccess* data link permits more than two systems to be attached to it (see Fig. 6.4). On a multiaccess data link subnetwork, each system receives all transmissions from all other systems on the data link. All the systems on a multiaccess data link must share access to the data link's transmission capabilities.

Local Area Network Data Links

Multiaccess data links are most often used in subnetworks that use local area network (LAN) technology to implement short-distance communication among a collection of systems. The following is a list of the most important types of LAN data link subnetwork technologies used in building an enterprise network. These were also introduced in Box 3.2:

- Ethernet
- Token Ring
- Token Bus
- ARCnet
- Fiber Distributed Data Interface (FDDI)
- LocalTalk
- Wireless LAN Technologies

LOCAL AREA NETWORK CHARACTERISTICS

LAN data link technology is used to implement a flexible, high-speed form of multiaccess data link. A LAN data link provides a simple communication path between any source system and any destination system. Each source system can generate a message and use the facilities of a LAN data link to deliver that message to any destination system on that link.

We can view a LAN data link in the same way as we view any other type of data link, such as a data link implemented using an ordinary point-to-point telecommunications facility. However, as we have already pointed out, a major difference between a LAN data link and other forms of data links used for data communication is that a LAN data link typically implements a many-to-many communication facility. A LAN data link allows any device attached to the LAN to communicate with any other attached device.

Four characteristics have become important in describing a particular form of LAN data link technology. These characteristics allow us to compare one type of LAN data link technology with another.

- **Transmission Medium.** The cable or other physical circuit used to interconnect systems. Typical LAN transmission media are twisted-wire-pair telephone cable, coaxial cable, fiber-optic cable, and various forms of wireless transmission.

- **Transmission Technique.** The type of signals exchanged over the physical transmission medium. The most common techniques used with LAN data links are baseband and broadband transmission.

- **Network Topology.** Identifies the logical shape device interconnections take. Common LAN data link topologies are *bus, tree, ring,* and *star.*

- **Access Control Method.** Describes the technique communicating systems use to control their access to the transmission medium. Devices on a LAN data link share the cabling system that connects them and the transmission facilities the data link provides. However, many types of LAN data links allow only one system to transmit at a time. Some method must be used to control when each system can use the transmission facilities. Commonly used access control methods are *contention, token passing,* and *circuit switching.*

DATA LINK SUBNETWORK SERVICES

The primary service provided by a data link subnetwork is a data delivery service. Three basic types of data delivery services can be provided by a data link subnetwork.

Connectionless Service

With a *connectionless* data delivery service, one message at a time is exchanged between a source and destination system. A connectionless service provides a *best-efforts* delivery service in which a message might be lost, duplicated, or delivered out of sequence with respect to other messages. With a connectionless data delivery service, no two messages are related in any way, no sequence checking is performed, and no acknowledgments are sent. Any mechanisms for error handling must be implemented in the higher layers. A connectionless data delivery service is sometimes referred to as a *datagram* service.

Connection-Oriented Service

With a *connection-oriented* data delivery service, the service begins by establishing a logical association, called a *connection*, between the source and destination systems. The service then transmits one or more messages over the connection, in sequence, between the two communicating systems. A connection may be a permanent connection always available for transmission. The connection may alternatively be a temporary connection, where the connection is established when needed, is then used for transmission, and is then terminated. A connection-oriented data link service provides a reliable data delivery service, typically using sequence checking, acknowledgments, error correction, and flow control procedures.

Isochronous Service

An *isochronous* data delivery service is uniform with respect to time. This type of data delivery service guarantees the data being transmitted will arrive at regular, predefined intervals. Isochronous service is often required for the transmission of voice and video information, where delays or interruptions in the flow of data would be noticeable to the receiver.

DATA LINK PROTOCOLS

A data link subnetwork uses a *data link protocol* to provide one, two, or all three of the types of data delivery services described in the foregoing section. Data link protocols implement various functions in the Data Link layer and in the underlying Physical layer of the OSI model. Box 6.1 lists the general functions provided by these OSI model layers. Note that not all the functions listed in Box 6.1 are performed by all data link protocols for all data link subnetworks. The exact functions performed by the data link protocol for a particular data link subnetwork depend on a number of factors, such as the physical transmission medium used and the type of data delivery service offered.

SUMMARY

An important way of categorizing data link subnetworks is according to how many different devices can be accommodated on the link. A point-to-point data link subnetwork connects exactly two devices; a multiaccess data link subnetwork can connect two or more devices.

Point-to-point data links are most often used to implement wide area network (WAN) data links that span long distances. Subnetwork technologies useful in constructing enterprise networks are analog and digital telecommunications circuits, X.25 packet switching, Integrated Services Digital Network (ISDN), Broadband ISDN (B-ISDN), Frame Relay, Asynchronous Transfer Mode (ATM), Switched Multi-megabit Data Service (SMDS), and various wireless WAN technologies.

A multiaccess data link is a data link that permits more than two systems to be attached to it. Multiaccess data links are most often used in subnetworks that use local area network (LAN) technology to implement short-distance communication among a collection of systems. Important types of LAN data link subnetwork technologies used in

BOX 6.1   Data link protocol functions.

Data Link Layer Functions

- **Data Link Connection Establishment and Release.** Dynamically establishes, for a *connection-mode* service, a logical data link connection between two users of the data link service, and releases the connection when it is no longer required. These functions are not provided for a *connectionless* service, in which connections are not established or released.

- **Framing.** Creates a single Data-Link-Protocol-Data-Unit (DLPDU) from the data unit passed from a user of the Data Link layer service, marks the beginning and the end of the DLPDU when sending, and determines the beginning and ending of the DLPDU when receiving. The informal name most often used for the DLPDU exchanged between peer Data Link layer entities is *frame*.

- **Data Transfer.** Transfers frames over a physical circuit, extracts the data unit from each frame and passes it up to the user of the Data Link layer service in the receiving device.

- **Frame Synchronization.** Establishes and maintains synchronization between the sending device and the receiving device. This means the receiving device must be capable of determining where each frame begins and ends.

- **Frame Sequencing.** Uses sequence numbers to ensure that frames are delivered in the same order in which they were transmitted (does not apply to a connectionless service).

- **Error Detection.** Detects transmission errors, frame format errors, and procedural errors on the data link connection using a value carried in the frame control information.

- **Error Recovery.** Recovers from errors detected on data links using frame sequencing and acknowledgments (does not apply to a connectionless service).

- **Flow Control.** Controls the rate at which a user of a connection-mode Data Link layer service receives frames to prevent a user of the Data Link layer service from being overloaded (does not apply to a connectionless service).

- **Physical Layer Services.** Uses the services of the Physical layer to transmit and receive data and to control the operation of the physical communication link.

Physical Layer Functions

- **Circuit Establishment and Release.** Allows a physical circuit to be established dynamically when it is required and released when the circuit is no longer needed. This function is provided for a circuit implemented by a temporary facility, such as a dial-up line in the telephone network.

- **Bit Synchronization.** Establishes synchronization in a receiving device with a stream of bits coming in and clocks data in from the communication circuit at the correct rate.

- **Data Transfer and Sequencing.** Allows electrical or optical signals to be exchanged over the circuit connecting two communicating devices and allow bits to be accepted by the receiving device in the same order in which they are delivered by the sending device.

- **Fault Condition Notification.** Notifies the Physical layer user when fault conditions occur.

- **Medium Specific Control Functions.** Provides control functions for specific forms of transmission medium, such as encoding/decoding, carrier sensing, collision detection and collision announcement functions, and detection of illegal cabling topologies.

building enterprise networks are Ethernet, token ring, token bus, ARCnet, Fiber Distributed Data Interface (FDDI), LocalTalk, and various types of wireless LAN technologies.

There are three types of data delivery services provided by a data link subnetwork: connectionless service, connection-oriented service, and isochronous service. A data link subnetwork uses a data link protocol to provide one, two, or all three types of data delivery service. Some of the functions provided by a data link protocol include data link connection establishment and release, framing, data transfer, frame synchronization, frame sequencing, error detection, error recovery, and flow control.

Chapter 7 examines the functions of network driver software that serves as an interface between protocol stack software and network interface cards.

Chapter 7

Network Driver Software

The network software subsystems that provide data transport facilities for enterprise networks generally use software subsystems called *network drivers*. Network driver software interfaces with the network interface cards (NICs) used to support physical communication over the network and sits between the software that implements the transport network and the NIC hardware (see Fig. 7.1).

Figure 7.1 shows how data link subnetwork functions are typically handled in the personal computer environment. Data link subnetwork functions are handled jointly by

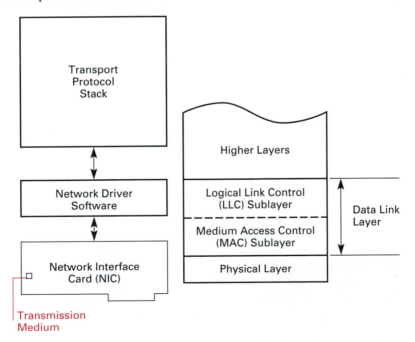

Figure 7.1   Network driver software.

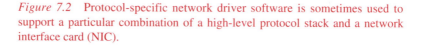

NetWare System	NetWare System	TCP/IP System
IPX/SPX Protocol Stack	IPX/SPX Protocol Stack	TCP/IP Protocol Stack
IPXTR Driver	IPXET Driver	TCPET Driver
Token Ring NIC	Ethernet NIC	Ethernet NIC

Figure 7.2   Protocol-specific network driver software is sometimes used to support a particular combination of a high-level protocol stack and a network interface card (NIC).

the network driver and the network interface card. A transport protocol stack software component then sits above the network driver software. By writing different network drivers, the same NIC can be made to operate with any transport protocol stack, and the same protocol stack can be made to work with any NIC (see Fig. 7.2).

When different network drivers are available, the network administrator chooses an appropriate network driver depending on the transport protocols supported by the network operating system installed in the system and the type of LAN to which the system is attached. The three configurations in Fig. 7.2 show three systems running network operating systems that use the NetWare IPX/SPX protocols to communicate on a Token Ring LAN, the IPX/SPX protocols over an Ethernet LAN, and the TCP/IP protocols over an Ethernet LAN. Each system uses different network driver software.

MULTIPLE TRANSPORT PROTOCOL STACKS

Many of today's network software is designed to handle multiple transport protocol stacks in the same computer system. In this environment, a network driver must be used that supports all applicable protocol families. Figure 7.3 shows a configuration in which a single system supporting three protocol stacks uses a single network driver and a single NIC.

This chapter discusses how network drivers can be used to help in handling multiple transport network protocols in the same device. Other aspects of multiple protocol networking are discussed in Chapter 10. Vendors of NICs and networking software have had to support many different combinations of transport protocol stacks, network drivers, and NICs to handle the many combinations possible, making this approach complex and expensive.

Multiple Protocol System

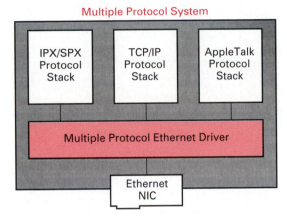

Figure 7.3   A system implementing multiple protocol stacks must use network driver software capable of handling all supported protocol stacks.

STANDARD INTERFACES

As support for multiple protocols has become more widespread, situations have arisen where a single system uses multiple transport protocols and may be connected to multiple LAN data links of different types. Providing network drivers able to support all possible combinations has become an arduous task. Because of this, *standard interfaces* are coming into more widespread use. Standard interfaces can eliminate the need for supporting large numbers of different network drivers, as illustrated in Fig. 7.4.

With this approach, standards are defined for the interface between the transport stack and the network driver. These standards define both the interface to be used by the transport protocol stack and the interface to be used by the network driver. This allows the development of transport stacks that can be used with any standard-compliant network driver, and network drivers that can be used with any standard-compliant transport stack. It is still generally necessary to have a separate network driver for the NICs associated with each different LAN technology that needs to be supported, but each network driver can be used to support any NIC that implements a given technology.

The use of standard interfaces allows a network operating system that implements the standard transport protocol stack interface to use any network driver that also implements that interface. This approach also allows any network driver that implements the standard network driver interface to be used with any NIC for a given LAN technology that also conforms to that interface. The use of standard interfaces also allows multiple protocol stacks to share a single NIC, without requiring the user to switch from one network driver to another.

Ideally, each of the two interfaces would use a single standard, thus providing maximum interoperability between network driver/NIC combinations and transport network protocol stacks. Unfortunately, competing standards have been developed. The *Open*

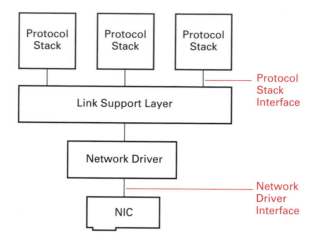

Figure 7.4   The use of standard interfaces provides a method of supporting multiple combinations of protocol stacks and network interface cards (NICs).

Data-Link Interface (ODI) was codeveloped by Novell and Apple and has been implemented in NetWare software. The *Network Driver Interface Specification (NDIS)* was codeveloped by Microsoft and 3Com and has been implemented in a variety of products, such as IBM LAN Server, Microsoft LAN Manager, Microsoft's Windows software, Banyan VINES, and DEC PATHWORKS. ODI and NDIS provide essentially the same services but define different protocol stack and network driver interfaces.

OPEN DATA-LINK INTERFACE

The *Open Data-Link Interface (ODI),* defined by Novell and Apple, is based on the architecture shown in Fig. 7.5. The two key elements that make up ODI are:

- **Link Support Layer (LSL).** A software module that implements the standard interface between the transport protocol stack and the network driver. It operates like a switchboard, passing packets between the transport stack and the network driver.

- **Multiple Link Interface Drivers (MLIDs).** Network drivers written to interface with the LSL, and thus usable by any transport stack that interfaces with the LSL.

Through the use of ODI, transport stacks can be developed independent of the frame type and LAN transmission medium being used. ODI also supports the multiplexing of different transport protocols over the same physical LAN data link. ODI's two elements are described further in the following sections.

Link Support Layer

The Link Support Layer handles communication between transport stacks and network drivers. A transport stack interfaces with the LSL using an API defined as part of the ODI

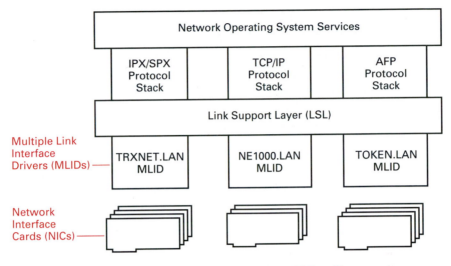

Figure 7.5   The Open Data-Link Interface (ODI) architecture.

specification. The API consists of sets of commands, listed in Box 7.1, and definitions of the data structures used with these commands.

In order to support different transport protocols on the same LAN data link, the protocol type for the packet within each frame must be identifiable. The LSL assigns a Protocol ID (PID) to each transport protocol using a LAN data link. The LSL includes the PID value when the packet is passed from the transport stack to an MLID. The MLID then includes the PID value in the frame it formats and transmits across the data link. When the frame is received, the PID value determines to which transport stack the packet is passed. Box 7.2 lists frame types and Protocol ID values used by ODI.

Frame Transmission

When a transport stack has a packet to send, it passes it to LSL, along with a board number. The board number identifies the NIC to be used to transmit the packet and the frame type to be used. (Some NICs are able to process more than one frame format. For example, a NIC may support the use of both CSMA/CD Ethernet frames and Ethernet Version 2 frames. These are described in Chapter 19.) The LSL adds the appropriate PID value and passes it to the MLID corresponding to the board number. The MLID/NIC encapsulates the packet in a frame header and trailer and transmits the frame over the data link.

Frame Reception

There are three ways in which a transport stack can receive packets:

- **Bound Protocol Stack.** A bound protocol stack has a registered PID value and receives only packets with that PID value.
- **Prescan Protocol Stack.** A prescan protocol stack receives all incoming packets received over a particular NIC before the packets are routed to a bound protocol stack. The prescan

BOX 7.1   Open Data-Link Interface (ODI) commands.

- **LSLAddProtocol ID.** Requests LSL to add a new protocol ID.

- **LSLBindStack.** Binds a protocol stack to an MLID.

- **LSLCancelAESEventRTag.** Cancels an AES event and sets the status field to an error code.

- **LSLDeFragmentECB.** Consolidates packet fragments before processing the Event Control Block (ECB).

- **LSLDeRegisterDefaultStack.** Removes the specified protocol stack with the specified MLID from the LSL's internal default stack table.

- **LSLDeRegisterPreScanStack.** Removes the specified protocol stack with the specified MLID from the LSL's internal prescan stack table.

- **LSLDeRegisterStack.** Removes the specified protocol stack with the specified MLID from the LSL's internal protocol stack tables.

- **LSLGetHeldPacketRTag.** Removes an ECB place in the hold queue.

- **LSLGetIntervalMarker.** A timing marker that can be used to determine elapsed time.

- **LSLGetLinkSupportStatistics.** Obtains a pointer to the LSL's statistics table.

- **LSLGetMaximumPacketSize.** Returns the largest physical packet size for which the LSL has been configured.

- **LSLGetMLIDControlEntry.** Returns the MLID Control Entry Point for the MLID corresponding to the specified board number.

- **LSLGetPIDFromStackIDBoard.** Returns the protocol ID that corresponds to a combination of a protocol stack ID and a board number.

- **LSLGetProtocolControl Entry.** Allows a protocol stack to communicate directly with another protocol stack.

- **LSLGetRcvECBRTag.** Obtains an ECB buffer.

- **LSLGetStackIDFromName.** Returns the stack ID for a specified stack name.

- **LSLHoldPacket.** Allows a protocol stack to queue a packet for later processing.

- **LSLRegisterDefaultStackRTag.** Binds the protocol stack to a specified MLID and allows it to receive packets unwanted by other stacks.

- **LSLRegisterPreScanStackRTag.** Binds the protocol stack to a specified MLID and allows it to receive all incoming packets before they are routed to other stacks.

- **LSLRegisterStackRTag.** Identifies an MLID from which a protocol stack wishes to receive packets.

- **LSLReturnRcvECB.** Returns an ECB buffer.

- **LSLScanPacket.** Searches the hold queue for ECBs with a specified stack ID.

- **LSLScheduleAESEventRTag.** Schedules an asynchronous event.

- **LSLSendPacket.** Sends a packet to a registered MLID.

- **LSLUnbindStack.** Unbinds a protocol stack from an MLID.

Frame ID	Frame Type String	Protocol ID on IPX/SPX	Description
		BOX 7.2 ODI frame types and PID values.	
0	VIRTUAL_LAN	0	For use where no Frame IDD/MAC envelope is necessary
1	LOCALTALK	N/A	Apple LocalTalk frame
2	ETHERNET_II	8137h	Ethernet using a DEC Ethernet II envelope
3	ETHERNET_802.2	E0h	Ethernet (802.3) using an 802.2 envelope
4	TOKEN-RING	E0h	Token Ring (802.5) using an 802.2 envelope
5	ETHERNET_802.3	00h	IPX 802.3 raw encapsulation
6	802.4	N/A	Token Bus (802.4) envelope
7	NOVEL_PCN2	1111h	Novell's IBM PC Network II envelope
8	GNET	E0h	Gateway's GNET frame envelope
9	PRONET-10	N/A	PRONET I/O frame envelope
10	ETHERNET_SNAP	8137h	Ethernet (802.3) using an 802.2 envelope with SNAP
11	TOKEN-RING_SNAP	8137h	Token Ring (802.5) using an 802.2 envelope with SNAP.
12	LANPAC_II	N/A	Racore's frame envelope
13	ISDN	N/A	Integrated Services Digital Network
14	NOVEL_RX-NET	Fah	Novell's ARCnet envelope
15	IBM_PCN2_802.2	E0h	IBM PCN2 using 802.2 envelope
16	IBM_PCN2_SNAP	8137h	IBM PCN2 using 802.2 with SNAP envelope
17	OMNINET/4	N/A	Corvus's frame envelope
18	3270_COAXA	N/A	Harris Adacom's frame envelope
19	IP	N/A	IP Tunnel frame envelope
20	FDDI_802.2	E0h	FDDI (802.7) using an 802.2 envelope
21	IVDLAN_802.9	N/A	Commtex, Inc.'s frame envelope
22	DAYACO_OSI	N/A	Dataco's frame envelope
23	FDDI_SNAP	8137h	FDDI (802.7) using 802.2 with a SNAP envelope

protocol stack may process a packet, discard it, or allow it to be passed on to another protocol stack.

- **Default Protocol Stack.** A default protocol stack receives every packet not claimed by another protocol stack.

Multiple Link Interface Driver

A Multiple Link Interface Driver (MLID), in combination with a NIC, is responsible for adding and removing frame headers and trailers and for sending and receiving frames on the LAN data link. When a frame is received, the MLID extracts the board number, PID value, and packet, and passes them up to the LSL.

The ODI specification includes a set of three software modules used to construct an MLID compliant with the ODI standard. These modules are:

- **Media Support Module (MSM).** Standardizes and manages the details of interfacing an MLID to the LSL and the operating system. It handles generic initialization and run-time issues common to all drivers.
- **Topology Specific Module (TSM).** Manages the operations unique to a specific media type, such as Ethernet or Token Ring. It implements support for multiple frames so all frame types for a given medium are supported.
- **Hardware Specific Module (HSM).** Handles all hardware interactions with a specific NIC. Its functions include adapter initialization, reset, shutdown and removal, and packet transmission and reception.

NETWORK DRIVER INTERFACE SPECIFICATION

The *Network Driver Interface Specification (NDIS),* developed by Microsoft and 3Com, is another standard for the interface between transport protocol stacks and network drivers. When protocol stacks and network drivers are written to be compliant with the NDIS standard, a transport stack can be used with any network driver, and a network driver can be used with any transport stack.

The NDIS architecture is shown in Fig. 7.6. The Protocol Manager is a software module that contains supporting routines and provides the uniform interface between the transport stack and the network driver. A binding process is used to establish an initial communication channel between a protocol stack and a network driver. A transport stack can be bound to more than one network driver, and a network driver can be bound to more than one transport stack.

NDIS Interface

The NDIS interface is specified in terms of sets of primitive operations that provide a variety of functions including transmission and reception of data and various status and control functions. Direct primitives used for the transmission and reception of data are listed in Box 7.3.

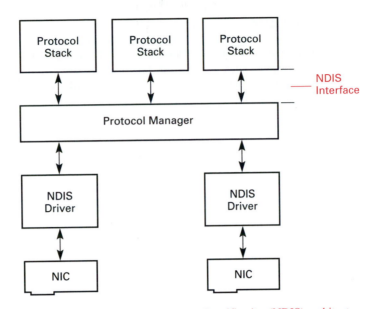

Figure 7.6   Network Driver Interface Specification (NDIS) architecture.

In addition to the direct primitives, the following groups of primitives are also defined:

- **General Requests.** Used to perform adapter management functions, such as setting the station address, running diagnostics, and changing operational parameters or modes.
- **System Requests.** Support module-independent functions, such as binding.
- **Protocol Manager Primitives.** Used to access services and information associated with the Protocol Manager software module.

BOX 7.3   NDIS direct primitives.

- **TransmitChain.** Initiates transmission of a frame.
- **TransmitConfirm.** Indicates the completion of the transmission of a frame.
- **ReceiveLookahead.** Indicates the arrival of a received frame and offers lookahead data.
- **TransferData.** Transfers received frame data from the driver to the protocol stack.
- **IndicationComplete.** Allows the protocol stack to do post-processing on indications.
- **ReceiveChain.** Indicates reception of a frame in a driver-managed buffer.
- **ReceiveRelease.** Returns frame storage to the driver that owns it.
- **IndicationOff.** Disables indications.
- **IndicationOn.** Enables indications.

Frame Transmission

When a transport stack has data to transmit, it calls the appropriate network driver for the LAN data link to be used for transmission. The network driver must previously have been bound to the transport stack. The network driver and NIC together format a frame and transmit it.

Frame Reception

When a frame is received, the network driver passes the packet in the frame to the transport stack to which it has been bound. If multiple transport stacks have been bound to the network driver, the Protocol Manager performs a demultiplexing function, sending frames to transport stacks based on the type of frames a transport stack is registered as handling. A transport stack can handle:

- Non-LLC frames.
- LLC frames with specific LLC Service Access Point (LSAP) addresses.
- LLC frames with nonspecific LLC Service Access Point (LSAP) addresses.

SUMMARY

Network software subsystems generally use network driver software to interface with network interface cards (NICs). By writing different network driver software components, the same NIC can be made to operate with any transport protocol stack, and the same protocol stack can be made to work with any NIC. The use of standard interfaces to network drivers allows a network operating system to use any network driver that also implements that interface.

The Open Data-Link Interface (ODI) architecture, defined by Novell and Apple, has two key elements: a Link Support Layer (LSL), and Multiple Link Interface Drivers (MLIDs). The Link Support Layer handles communication between transport stacks and network drivers. A Multiple Link Interface Driver (MLID), in combination with a NIC, is responsible for adding and removing frame headers and trailers and for sending and receiving frames on the LAN data link.

The Network Driver Interface Specification (NDIS), developed by Microsoft and 3Com, is specified in terms of sets of primitive operations that provide a variety of functions, including transmission and reception of data and various status and control functions. When a transport stack has data to transmit, it calls the appropriate NDIS network driver for the LAN data link used for transmission. When a frame is received, the network driver passes the packet in the frame to the transport stack to which it has been bound.

Chapter 8 examines some of the physical transmission mechanisms employed by data link subnetworks for data communication.

Physical Transmission Mechanisms

The telecommunications and information technology industries have employed a wide variety of physical media for the transmission of information. These media range from the open-wire pairs carried on poles in the early days of telecommunications to the high-speed, fiber-optic links used in high-speed LANs and to connect distant points on the globe.

TRANSMISSION MEDIA

There are four physical media commonly used in the construction of computer network data links. These are *twisted-wire-pair cable*, *coaxial cable*, *fiber-optic cable*, and *wireless transmission*. These four general types of physical media have different transmission characteristics and different costs associated with them.

Twisted-Wire-Pair Cable

A twisted-wire pair consists of two insulated strands of copper wire twisted spirally around each other. A number of twisted-wire pairs are often grouped together and enclosed within a protective sheath or jacket to form a twisted-pair cable. Figure 8.1 illustrates twisted-wire pairs.

The wiring often used within buildings for telephone systems consists of twisted-pair cable. Many conventional telecommunications circuits use twisted-pair cable, most often for the short-distance connection between individual subscribers and the switching office. It is also often used to implement local area network data links. One of the reasons this type of cable is being used to implement local area networks is that it is already installed in many locations. Many local area network products are available that use ordinary telephone wire for LAN communication, and most forms of LAN data link technology have been adapted for use over twisted-pair cable.

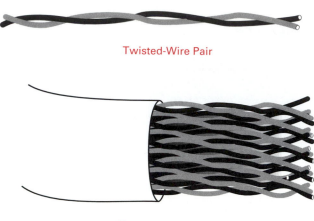

Twisted-Wire Pair

Twisted-Pair Cable

Figure 8.1   Twisted-wire pairs.

Some high-performance data link implementations that use twisted-wire pairs employ a special, higher quality form of twisted-pair cable, called *shielded-twisted-pair cable*, that uses a protective sheath. Shielded cable is less subject to electrical interference and can more reliably support high transmission rates over long distances. Twisted-pair cable remains one of the most versatile forms of transmission media, and it is often the best choice when new construction must be wired for data communication.

Coaxial Cable

Coaxial cable consists of a central conducting copper core surrounded by insulating material. The insulation is surrounded by a second conducting layer, which can consist either of a braided wire mesh or a solid sleeve. A protective jacket of nonconducting material protects the outer conductor. Figure 8.2 shows the construction of a typical coaxial cable.

Coaxial cable is less subject to interference and cross-talk than a twisted-pair cable and is more easily able to reliably support high data rates over long distances. Coaxial cable has been used for many years for television transmission. The same cable and electronic components used by the cable television industry are used in some LAN data link

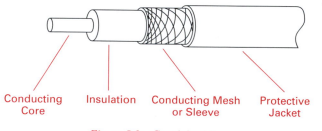

Conducting   Insulation   Conducting Mesh   Protective
Core   or Sleeve   Jacket

Figure 8.2   Coaxial cable.

implementations. In other types of LANs, a form of coaxial cable is used that has different electrical characteristics. Coaxial cable has also sometimes been employed to build long-distance telecommunications facilities.

Fiber-Optic Cable

An optical fiber can be used to carry data signals in the form of modulated light beams. An optical fiber consists of an extremely thin cylinder of glass, called the *core*, surrounded by a concentric layer of glass, called the *cladding*. The construction of a typical optical fiber is shown in Fig. 8.3.

The refractive index of the cladding is lower than that of the core, which causes light traveling down the core to be reflected back into the core when it strikes the cladding. In practice, a number of such optical fibers are often bound together into a fiber-optic cable, with all of the individual fibers surrounded by a protective sheath.

Fiber-optic cables have the potential for supporting very high transmission rates. Transmission rates of up to 565 Mbps are routinely employed in commercially available systems, and data rates of up to 200,000 Mbps have been demonstrated. Signals transmitted over fiber-optic cables are not subject to electrical interference. A fiber-optic cable is also typically smaller in size and lighter in weight than electrical cable. Optical fiber is sometimes more expensive to install than electrical cable, although the cost is dropping. Fiber optics is coming into widespread use for long-distance transmission. Cost is still a factor, though, in bringing optical fiber all the way to the desktop.

Wireless Transmission

Data link transmission that does not depend on a physical cable is becoming more prevalent in the data communications and computer networking marketplace. Wireless transmission can take various forms.

- **Microwave Transmission.** Microwave transmission involves sending a focused, narrow beam of microwave signals between antennas in fixed locations. Microwave links take the form of straight, line-of-sight links, so antennas must be positioned to avoid obstacles. Communications satellites can also be used to relay microwave signals from one ground-based station (often called an *earth station*) to another. Microwave transmission is commonly used in long-distance telephone networks and for television signal distribution. Microwave communication is used in private business networks primarily as a link between buildings or other fixed sites.

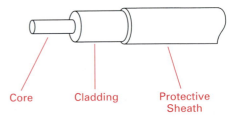

Figure 8.3   Optical fiber construction.

                                                 Core   Cladding   Protective Sheath

- **Radio Transmission.** Conventional radio transmission is typically omnidirectional, rather than focused, and thus offers greater flexibility than microwave transmission in the structure and placement of antennas. Radio transmission is the basis for several commercial computer networks that provide communications services to mobile computing devices. Conventional radio transmission has also been used as the transmission medium for certain types of local area networks. The key problem with using radio transmission is the possibility of interference. The FCC, in its administration of the airwaves, has allocated different parts of the spectrum for different uses. The frequencies used for data transmission must be shared with other commercial and scientific applications, including widely used devices such as pagers and security systems.

- **Infrared Transmission.** Infrared transmission involves the transmission of a fixed beam of infrared light between two points. Like microwave transmission, infrared transmission is line-of-sight. It is possible, however, to diffuse an infrared beam and spread it over a larger area. For example, a beam can be bounced off a ceiling to reach other areas within a room. Generally, infrared transmission is used over limited distances, generally shorter distances than are spanned by modern local area network technology. Infrared transmission is sometimes used to interconnect computer equipment, such as connecting a printer to a laptop computer, over distances that span only a few feet. Infrared transmission has also been used in some LAN implementations where the systems on the LAN are all located relatively close together.

Wireless transmission can be used in a number of different ways. One way is to interconnect individual sites where it would be difficult to physically interconnect them. For example, instead of interconnecting two buildings with a cable, a point-to-point microwave or infrared transmission link might be used. Such a point-to-point link would appear no different than a physical cable connection to other networking equipment.

Another way in which wireless transmission is sometimes used is to replace the physical cables used to interconnect systems on a LAN. Wireless forms of LAN data link transmission make it very easy to move computer systems and other types of network devices from one location to another without having to change physical wiring.

Wireless transmission has also been used to provide communication services for mobile computing. Using various wireless communication services, computing devices can be used from widely varying locations to access networks, and to perform common computing tasks, such as sending and receiving mail messages and transferring files from one system to another.

Technologies for wireless transmission are discussed further in Chapters 16 and 24.

SIGNALING TECHNIQUES

When data is sent across a physical transmission medium, it is sent in the form of an electromagnetic signal. Two basic types of transmission techniques can be used for the signal: analog transmission and digital transmission.

Analog Transmission

With analog transmission, the signals employed are continuous and nondiscrete. Signals flow across the transmission medium in the form of *electromagnetic waves,* illustrated in Fig. 8.4.

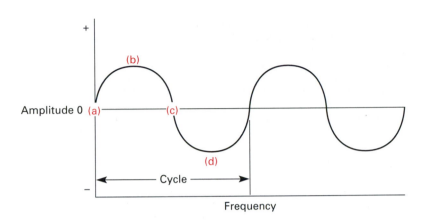

Figure 8.4   Characteristics of an electromagnetic wave.

Electromagnetic Wave Characteristics

Electromagnetic waves have three characteristics useful in telecommunications:

- **Amplitude.** With an electrical wire, a wave's *amplitude* is associated with the *level of voltage* carried on the wire; with an optical fiber, the wave's amplitude is concerned with the *intensity of the light beam.*

- **Frequency.** The *frequency* of a wave concerns the number of cycles or oscillations the wave makes per second. A frequency rate of one oscillation per second is defined as one *Hertz* (Hz).

- **Phase.** A wave's *phase* refers to the point to which the wave has advanced in its cycle. In Fig. 8.4, (a) identifies the beginning of the cycle, (b) is 1/4 of the cycle, (c) is 1/2 the cycle and (d) is 3/4 of the cycle. A wave's phase is generally described in terms of degrees, with the beginning of the cycle being 0°, 1/4 of the cycle being 90°, 1/2 of the cycle being 180°, 3/4 of the cycle being 270°, and completion of the cycle being 360°.

Modulation Techniques

With analog transmission, a data signal is superimposed on a carrier signal by varying, or *modulating*, any one of the three wave characteristics of the carrier signal. For example, a particular value of the carrier signal's amplitude, frequency, or phase might represent the value 0, and some other amplitude, frequency, or phase value might represent the value 1. In this way a data signal can be *carried* by the carrier signal.

Measurements of Channel Capacity

In general, the higher the frequency of the carrier signal, the greater is its information carrying capacity. In telecommunications literature, the term *bandwidth* is often used to refer to the capacity of a communication channel. A channel's bandwidth is the difference between the highest and the lowest frequencies carried over the channel. The higher the bandwidth, the more information can be carried. For example, a telephone channel supporting voice communication transmits frequencies ranging from about 300 Hertz

(Hz) to 3100 Hz. So the range of frequencies, or *bandwidth*, supported is 3100 – 300 = 2800 Hz, or about 3 KHz.

A channel's bandwidth has a direct relationship to its *data rate*, or the number of *bits per second (bps)* that can be carried over it. Since network data links deal mainly with data transmission, we will find bits per second to be a more useful measure of a channel's capacity than bandwidth. However, in telecommunications literature, the term bandwidth is often used synonymously with data transmission capacity.

Another term used to express channel capacity is *baud*. Baud is a measurement of the *signaling speed* of a channel; a certain communication channel is said to have a speed of so many *baud*. Signaling speed, or baud, refers to the number of times in each second the line condition changes.

Suppose we are using amplitude modulation and that one amplitude value is used to represent the binary value 0 and another amplitude binary value 1. In this particular case, the line's signaling speed in baud is the same as the line's data rate in bits per second. Suppose, however, that we use four different amplitudes to represent the binary values 00, 01, 10, or 11 (called *dibits*). In this case the data rate in bits per second will be twice the signaling speed in baud. If the signals are coded into eight possible states, then one line condition represents a *tribit* and the data rate in bits per second is three times the signaling speed in baud. Some literature mistakenly uses the term baud to mean bits per second. Since the term baud can be confusing, we will avoid using it in this book.

Signal Amplification

Another issue that concerns physical data transmission is that of *signal strength*. When an electrical signal is transmitted along a wire, it gradually decreases in strength— a process known as *attenuation*. With analog transmission, *amplifiers* may be included as part of the network. An amplifier receives a signal and then retransmits at its original strength. Placing amplifiers at appropriate points along the physical transmission medium allows devices to be more widespread geographically and still be able to detect the signals transmitted over the physical medium. However, if any noise or interference has crept into the signal along the way, the noise is typically amplified along with the signal. Thus, with analog transmission, the quality of the signal tends to deteriorate with distance even when amplifiers are used.

Frequency-Division Multiplexing

When analog transmission is used, the available bandwidth of the physical transmission medium is often divided up into multiple channels. Different transmissions can then take place simultaneously over the different channels using a technique called *frequency-division multiplexing (FDM)*.

The multiple channels may be used in entirely different ways. For example, data can be transmitted on some, video signals on others, voice telephone calls on still others, and so on. For data transmission, one channel can be used by devices for data flowing in one direction and another channel for data flowing in the opposite direction.

Digital Transmission over an Analog Channel

Although analog transmission is often used over the transmission medium used to implement a communications channel, it is important to realize that the communicating systems attached to the data link are almost always digital in nature, whether the data link uses digital or analog signaling.

When analog signaling techniques are used to implement a communications channel, the digital signals communicating systems generate must be converted to and from analog form. This conversion is often performed by devices called *modems*, short for *modulator-demodulator*. Modems are routinely employed when transmitting digital data over ordinary analog telephone channels. Special-purpose modems are also sometimes employed on local area networks when analog signaling techniques are used to transmit signals over the LAN communications medium.

Figure 8.5 shows a configuration that might be used in order for two digital devices to communicate over a physical communication medium that uses analog transmission. It is important to realize that the use of modems and analog signaling techniques is transparent to the two communicating devices. The two communicating systems send and receive digital bit streams, whether the physical transmission medium uses digital or analog techniques. The modems automatically convert these digital bit streams to and from analog form.

Digital Transmission

With digital transmission, signals are carried over the physical communications medium in the form of discrete pulses of electricity or light. With this form of transmission, a sending device sends data pulses directly over the communications channel, and the receiving device detects them.

As the pulses travel along the communications medium, they become distorted. The pulses received at the other end are far from their original shape, and if the channel is too

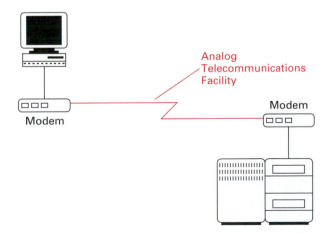

Figure 8.5   Digital transmission over an analog telecommunications facility.

long, the signals too weak, or the transmitting speed too great, the received signal may be unrecognizable and wrongly interpreted by the machine at the other end. To overcome these difficulties, *repeaters* can be used to receive the digital signals and then retransmit them at their original strength and sharpness.

Repeaters

Since a repeater totally regenerates the signal, the result of any noise that might have crept into the signal is nullified. Noise and interference are not a problem with digital transmission unless they corrupt the signal sufficiently to prevent a bit from being correctly identified as a 0 or a 1. Communicating systems attached to a network may themselves act as repeaters in some types of data links, so separate, specialized equipment is not needed for signal regeneration.

Digital Service Units

When digital transmission is used, modems are not required for data transmission. The digital bit stream used by the communicating systems can be converted directly into the pulses that make up the digital signal. Telecommunications providers who supply digital communication channels may provide devices, sometimes called *digital service units (DSUs),* for connecting computing devices to digital communication channels.

Time Division Multiplexing

With digital transmission, *time division multiplexing (TDM)* is commonly used to allow multiple users to share a communications channel. TDM divides a digital transmission medium into a series of time slots that are then allocated to different users.

With synchronous TDM, a particular slot is always allocated to the same user and is used only when that user has data to send. A user can be assigned multiple slots, in order to sustain a higher data rate.

With statistical TDM, slots are not assigned to particular users. As data arrives, it is put into available slots for transmission. Buffers are used when more data arrives than can be accommodated by the communications channel. Statistical TDM uses the communications channel more efficiently, since slots are used whenever any user has data to send. However, with statistical TDM there may be variable delays during times of heavy usage, and arrival rates may not be guaranteed.

TDM techniques can be used for multiplexing multiple digital data streams that travel over an analog communications channel. The user data streams can be multiplexed together and then passed over a modem for transmission on the analog channel.

ENCODING SCHEMES

Communicating systems can use a variety of encoding schemes to represent the binary values that make up the digital bit stream for transmission over an analog or digital communications channel. With one simple encoding scheme, used for many years over some telegraph circuits, the presence of a pulse indicates the value 1 and the absence of a pulse represents the value 0 (see Fig. 8.6).

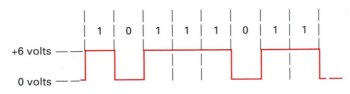

Figure 8.6   Telegraph signaling.

In order for communication to take place between two digital devices, a particular length of time is generally associated with the transmission of each bit. This is known as the *bit duration*, or *bit time*. Both the sending and receiving systems must be synchronized with one another and must be able to determine when the beginning and the ending of each bit time occurs. In order to properly interpret received data, the receiving device must be able to recognize when data is being transmitted and to identify the portion of the signal that corresponds to each bit. Communicating systems generally require periodic transitions in the signal in order to remain synchronized. Encoding schemes are often designed to ensure that, regardless of the data being sent, there will not be a long period of time without a transition.

Commonly Used Encoding Schemes

The data link subnetworks used in computer networks generally use more sophisticated encoding schemes than the one shown above for representing binary values. A number of commonly used encoding schemes are described in Box 8.1.

Code Conversion Schemes

With some data link technologies, data may undergo a process of code conversion before it is encoded for transmission. For example, the *Fiber Distributed Data Interface (FDDI)* LAN technology uses a *4b/5b* code conversion scheme. With 4b/5b code conversion, data is divided into 4-bit segments, and each 4-bit value is converted to a 5-bit value before being encoded for transmission. After transmission, the 5-bit values are converted back to the original 4-bit values.

Figure 8.7 shows the corresponding 4-bit and 5-bit values. The 5-bit values used were chosen so there are never more than three consecutive 0 bits. FDDI uses the NRZI encoding scheme for transmission, and the use of 4b/5b code conversion ensures there will never be more than three bit times without a transition in the signal.

SUMMARY

Four physical transmission media are commonly used in the construction of data links: twisted-wire-pair cable, coaxial cable, fiber-optic cable, and wireless transmission. Two basic types of transmission techniques are used for signal transmission over a physical transmission medium: analog transmission and digital transmission.

With analog transmission, the signals employed are continuous and nondiscrete and flow across the transmission medium in the form of electromagnetic waves. A data signal

BOX 8.1   Commonly used signal encoding schemes.

RS-232-D Encoding

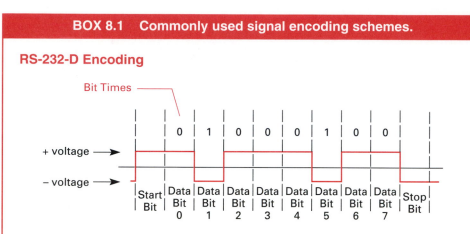

A technique often used for low-speed data communication is defined in a standard called RS-232-D, which is published by the Electrical Industries Association (EIA). With RS-232-D transmission, a negative voltage on the line for a bit time represents the value 1 and a positive voltage the value 0.

Nonreturn-to-Zero-Inverted

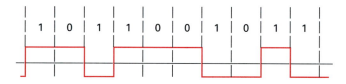

With nonreturn-to-zero-inverted (NRZI) coding, the presence or absence of a transition at the beginning of a bit time represents the bit value. The signal level then stays constant through the bit interval. With this technique, a transition on the line from negative to positive or from positive to negative at the beginning of a bit time indicates the value 1; the lack of a transition at the beginning of a bit time represents the value 0.

Manchester Encoding

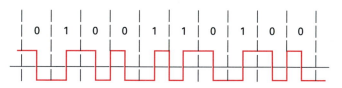

For electrical purposes, it is desirable in many data link implementations that transitions from positive to negative and from negative to positive occur often with predictable regularity. A form of encoding, called Manchester encoding, produces the desired number of transitions and is used on many types of LAN data links. With a typical implementation of Manchester encoding, a negative voltage for the first half of the bit time followed by a posi-

---

BOX 8.1 *(Continued)*

tive voltage for the second half of the bit time represents the value 1; a positive voltage followed by a transition to a negative voltage represents the value 0. Thus, with Manchester encoding, a transition from negative to positive or from positive to negative occurs every bit time.

With Manchester encoding, bit times in which the signal is held either positive or negative for the entire bit time are used to represent something other than a bit value, for example, the beginning or ending of a transmission block.

Differential Manchester Encoding

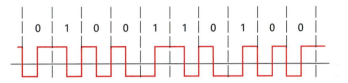

A form of Manchester encoding, called differential Manchester encoding, is used with some forms of LAN technology. With this technique, illustrated above, a transition occurs during each bit time, as with conventional Manchester encoding. However, the interpretation of the transition from positive to negative or from negative to positive depends on whether the previous bit time represented a 0 or a 1. To represent the value 1, the polarity remains the same as it was at the end of the previous bit time and then changes in polarity at the midpoint of the bit time only. To represent the value 0, the polarity changes at the beginning of the bit time and also at the midpoint of the bit time. With this form of encoding, a change from positive to negative can represent either a 0 or a 1, depending on the state of the line at the end of the previous bit time. It is the transition that occurs, or does not occur, at the beginning of the bit time that indicates the value. No transition at the beginning of the bit time indicates the value 1; a transition at the beginning of the bit time indicates the value 0.

As with conventional Manchester encoding, bit times in which no transition occurs at the midpoint of the bit time are often used for control purposes.

---

is superimposed on a carrier signal by modulating it. A digital bit stream is carried over an analog communications channel using modems to convert the digital bit stream to analog signals. The higher the frequency of the carrier signal, the greater is its information carrying capacity, or bandwidth. The available bandwidth of an analog communications circuit is often divided up into multiple channels using frequency-division multiplexing (FDM).

With digital transmission, signals are carried over the physical communication medium in the form of discrete pulses. Modems are not required for data transmission over a digital circuit. With digital transmission, time division multiplexing (TDM) is commonly used to allow multiple users to share a single communications channel.

Encoding schemes are used to carry digital information over an analog or digital communication facility. Some of the more commonly used encoding schemes include

Code Group	Symbol	Interpretation
Data		
11110	0	hex 0
01001	1	hex 1
10100	2	hex 2
10101	3	hex 3
01010	4	hex 4
01011	5	hex 5
01110	6	hex 6
01111	7	hex 7
10010	8	hex 8
10011	9	hex 9
10110	A	hex A
10111	B	hex B
11010	C	hex C
11011	D	hex D
11100	E	hex E
11101	F	hex F
Control		
00000	Q	Quiet
11111	I	Idle
00100	H	Halt
11000	J	Start Delimiter (1st symbol)
10001	K	Start Delimiter (2nd symbol)
01101	T	Ending Delimiter
00111	R	Reset
11001	S	Set

Figure 8.7   Fiber Distributed Data Interface (FDDI) 4b/5b symbol encoding.

RS-232-D encoding, nonreturn-to-zero-inverted (NRZI) encoding, Manchester encoding, and differential Manchester encoding. Some data link technologies use more complex code conversion schemes for encoding a bit stream. An example of a code conversion scheme is the 4b/5b code conversion used on a Fiber Distributed Data Interface (FDDI) data link.

Chapter 9 examines devices called repeaters, hubs, and switches that can be used in constructing local area network data links and extending their range and flexibility.

Chapter **9**

Repeaters and Hubs

Repeaters, hubs, and switches can be used in constructing LAN data link subnetworks. Repeaters are used to interconnect individual cable segments within the same LAN data link. Hubs are special repeaters that allow multiple LAN stations to be connected to a central point to form a star configuration. LAN switches, or switching hubs, are hubs that implement intelligence that allows them to act as switches to provide full network bandwidth to multiple pairs of devices connected to the same hub.

REPEATERS

A specific local area network implementation may place a limit on the physical length of any single LAN cable segment. This limit is determined by the particular LAN technology and is based on the type of physical medium and the transmission technique used. *Repeaters* allow a LAN data link to be constructed that exceeds the length limit of a single physical cable segment. A repeater receives a signal from one cable segment and retransmits it, at its original strength, over one or more other cable segments. The number of repeaters that can be used in tandem is generally limited by a particular LAN implementation.

A repeater operates in the OSI model Physical layer and is transparent to all the protocols operating in the layers above the Physical layer (see Fig. 9.1).

Using a repeater between two or more LAN cable segments requires that the same Physical layer protocols be used to send signals over all the cable segments. Repeaters are typically used to interconnect cable segments located relatively close together. Repeaters cannot be used to interconnect a LAN data link and a WAN data link.

Figure 9.2 shows some possible repeater configurations on an Ethernet LAN. Note that a repeater may be designed to support different types of LAN cabling in the same local area network, as long as the Physical layer protocols are compatible on all the cable segments.

Repeaters are generally transparent to the network software operating in the individual computers attached to a LAN. The main characteristic of a repeater is that *all* the signals generated on the cable segment on one side of the repeater are propagated to the

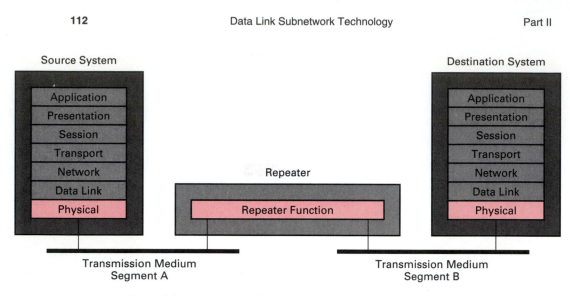

Figure 9.1   A repeater performs its function in the Physical layer.

cable segment or segments on the other side of the repeater. A repeater generally operates in both directions.

The chief advantages of repeaters are simplicity and low cost. A chief disadvantage is that repeaters provide no method for isolating the traffic generated on one cable segment from traffic generated by the others. When a repeater is used to connect cable segment A to cable segment B, all the signals generated on segment A are forwarded to segment B, whether or not a station on segment B is the destination of those signals.

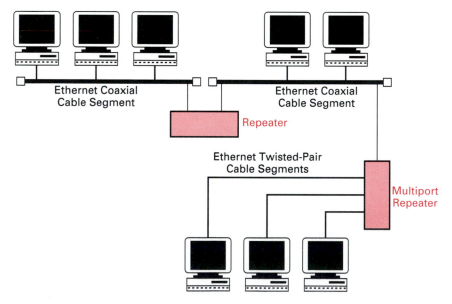

Figure 9.2   Using repeaters to interconnect LAN cable segments.

Another disadvantage of a repeater is that it generally cannot connect cable segments that support different LAN technologies. For example, a repeater generally cannot connect an Ethernet LAN cable segment to a token ring cable segment.

More intelligent network interconnection devices, such as bridges, routers, and switching hubs may be capable of interconnecting cable segments supporting different LAN technologies and performing a frame-filtering function. Frame filtering can be used to isolate the flow of some types of frames, such as broadcast frames, to certain portions of the network.

Repeaters that connect more than two cable segments are often called *hubs*. A hub is a variation of a repeater and generally performs its functions in the Physical layer. A wide variety of different types of hubs are available. The next section describes a few common hub variations.

SIMPLE HUBS

A simple hub takes the form of a multipoint repeater that can be used to create a star-structured network segment in which the hub is at the center of the star. A simple hub provides a single connection to a primary transmission medium segment and a number of *ports*, each of which can be attached to a single LAN device using a point-to-point connection. A simple hub allows a number of devices to be attached at a single point, such as in a wiring closet, as shown in Fig. 9.3.

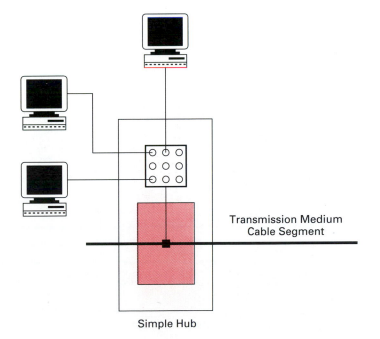

Transmission Medium
Cable Segment

Simple Hub

Figure 9.3   Simple hub.

CONFIGURABLE HUBS

A configurable hub allows the cable segments that terminate at the ports of the hub to be interconnected in different ways depending on the type of configuration desired. Configurable hubs allow groups of devices to be configured in different workgroups. A variety of configurable hubs are available, and these devices vary in the capabilities they provide.

There are three primary purposes for using configurable hubs:

- To make it easier to change LAN configurations.
- To increase the bandwidth available to individual devices on the LAN.
- To allow the traffic flowing between workgroups to be controlled.

A configurable hub generally allows the hub to be connected to two or more primary LAN transmission medium segments through a component called a *backplane*. The backplane is used to control the way in which the systems connected to the ports of the hub are connected to the cable segments attached to the backplane.

There are three primary types of configurable hubs: module assignment hubs, bank assignment hubs, and port assignment hubs.

Module Assignment Hubs

With *module assignment* hubs, shown in Fig. 9.4, each hub connects its entire set of ports to one of the LAN transmission medium segments in its backplane. When a signal is

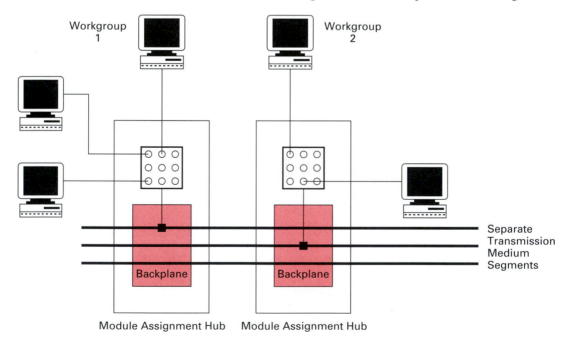

Figure 9.4   Module assignment hubs.

received over one port, it is retransmitted over all other ports in the module and over the primary transmission medium segment to which the ports are connected.

All the devices attached to the hub, and all the devices connected to the selected primary transmission medium segment, form a workgroup. With a system of module assignment hubs, the traffic generated by devices in one workgroup can be isolated from devices in other workgroups. The stations attached to a given hub can be connected to a different workgroup by changing the connection within the hub to one of the other primary transmission medium segments. A disadvantage of the module assignment hub is that all the devices attached to the hub's ports must be in the same workgroup, and all must be attached to the same primary transmission medium segment.

As we introduced earlier, one use for hubs is to increase the transmission capacity available within each workgroup. When the number of devices attached to the same LAN segment gets too large, the transmission capacity can be exceeded, especially when systems are exchanging large quantities of data. Hubs make it easy to establish multiple parallel transmission medium segments to which different groups of systems can be attached. With fewer systems attached to each segment, there should be less total traffic on each segment.

Other network interconnection devices, such as routers or bridges, can be used to interconnect the individual cable segments and thus allow some traffic to flow from one segment to another, as shown in Fig. 9.5. A router provides more traffic isolation between workgroups than a bridge.

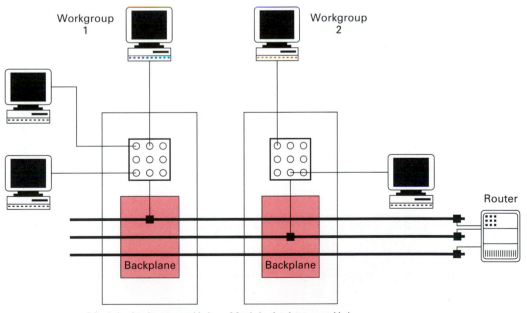

Figure 9.5 Module assignment hub with a router.

Bank Assignment Hubs

Bank assignment hubs offer more flexibility for workgroup configuration. With a *bank assignment* hub, the ports in a single hub are divided into subsets called *banks*. The hub allows each bank of ports to be connected to a different primary transmission medium segment (see Fig. 9.6). When a signal is received over a port, it is retransmitted only over all other ports in the same bank and over that bank's primary transmission medium segment. Therefore, all the devices attached to a single bank, and all the systems connected to the selected transmission medium segment, form an individual workgroup.

Port Assignment Hubs

With a *port assignment* hub, sometimes called a port-switching or configuration-switching hub, a more sophisticated backplane allows ports to be assigned to transmission medium segments on an individual basis (see Fig. 9.7). When a signal is received over a port, it is retransmitted to all other ports assigned to the selected transmission medium segment. Such hubs allow for great flexibility in workgroup assignment and for making changes in the way devices are assigned to workgroups.

Static versus Dynamic Hubs

The hubs described in the previous section are all examples of devices classified as *static hubs*. With static hubs, the assignment of ports to LAN segments is controlled by explicitly configuring the hub. With some hubs, hub configuration is controlled physically by set-

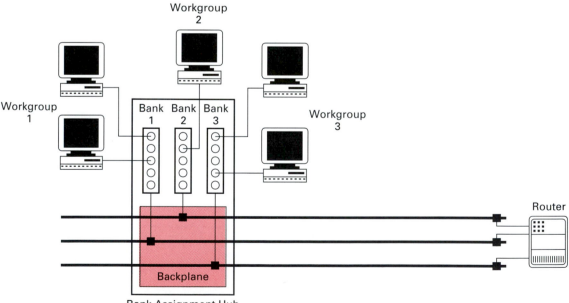

Figure 9.6   Bank assignment hub.

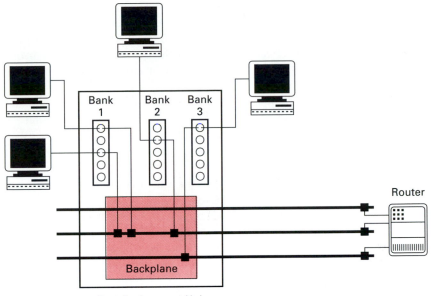

Port Assignment Hub

Figure 9.7   Port assignment hub.

ting DIP switches or jumpers in the hub. With other static hubs, the configuration can be controlled through network management software.

All such hubs are considered static hubs because an explicit network management action is required to reconfigure the hub. However, the ability to change assignments through software, particularly with port assignment hubs, makes it considerably easier for the network administrator to add and remove systems and to control the way in which workgroups are configured.

SWITCHING HUBS

The last category of hubs we discuss are *dynamic hubs* able to change configuration automatically on the fly. Dynamic hubs are generally referred to as *LAN switches* or *switching hubs*. There are two methods that a switching hub might use to establish connections and to direct frames to the appropriate destination ports:

- **Cross-Point Operation.** With *cross-point connection,* or *switching,* operation the switching hub analyzes each frame as it is received, establishes the connection as soon as it has analyzed the destination address, and immediately begins transmitting the frame while the rest of the frame is still being received.

- **Bridging Store-and-Forward Operation.** With *bridging store-and-forward* operation, the switching hub receives an entire frame and temporarily stores it. The hub then analyzes the frame's destination address, establishes the required connection, and forwards the frame to its destination.

A cross-point switch typically offers lower latency, or lag time, between receiving a frame and sending it to its destination. A bridging store-and-forward switching hub may have greater reliability than a cross-point hub, since error checking can be performed on the frame before it is forwarded. Some switching hubs support both methods of operation and allow the network administrator to choose one or the other form of operation depending on network requirements.

A switching hub implements more intelligence than a static hub and generally performs some of its functions in the Data Link layer rather than in the Physical layer. A switching hub examines the destination address of each frame it receives. When the hub receives a frame over a port, it dynamically establishes a connection with the port associated with the frame's destination and directs the frame to the appropriate destination port.

With switching hubs, connections are established across the backplane of the switch. Simultaneous connections share the backplane's total bandwidth. Switching hubs may incorporate high-bandwidth backplanes, so that each connection can be given dedicated bandwidth comparable to the full bandwidth associated with a LAN segment. For example, Ethernet LANs commonly operate at a total bandwidth of 10 Mbps. Many Ethernet switches will support multiple connections, with each connection supporting a full 10 Mbps data rate.

The following sections describe some different forms of switching hubs that network infrastructure vendors have developed.

Station Switching Hubs

A *station switching hub* allows only a single system to be attached to each of the hub's ports. Therefore, each port can have only one station address associated with it. A station switching hub can be used to replace a shared LAN transmission medium segment, creating what is commonly referred to as a switched LAN.

Figure 9.8 shows an example of a simple switched LAN using a station switching hub. Such a hub might allow any of the stations attached to the hub's ports (the stations

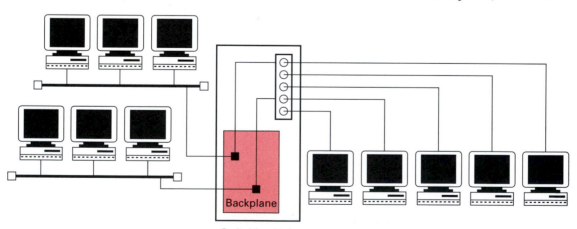

Figure 9.8　Switching hub.

on the right) to communicate with one another. At the same time, any single station on either of the two LANs attached to the backplane can communicate at full bandwidth with any of the stations attached to the hub's ports.

A switching hub has the ability to dynamically establish connections between any pair of stations on the fly and to support multiple simultaneous connections. The number of simultaneous connections the hub supports depends on the capabilities of the hub.

Segment Switching Hubs

A more complex switching hub is a *segment switching hub*. A segment switching hub allows the attachment of LAN segments, as well as individual systems, to its ports. The backplane then allows any port to communicate with any other port. This type of hub allows multiple station addresses to be associated with each port. A segment switching hub can be used to form a collapsed backbone network, as shown in Fig. 9.9. The backplane in such a hub is generally engineered to provide a maximum total bandwidth that can be used to support some maximum number of concurrent connections among the stations or LANs attached to its ports.

High-Performance Switching Hubs

Some hubs are marketed as high-performance hubs, possibly supporting a backplane with a total bandwidth of about 10 Gbps. A high-performance switching hub is sometimes called a *super hub*, an *enterprise hub*, or a *hub-of-hubs*. Such switching hubs may offer

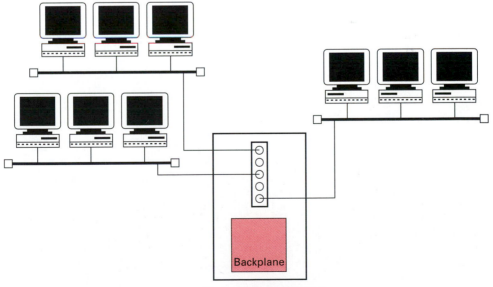

Segment Switching Hub

Figure 9.9   Segment switching hub.

additional capabilities, such as support for multiple architectures in the attached LAN segments (e.g., Ethernet and Token Ring) and hierarchical connections of hubs.

Figure 9.10 illustrates how segment switching hubs can be connected in a hierarchical arrangement. The lowest level of the hierarchy consists of switched Ethernet LANs.

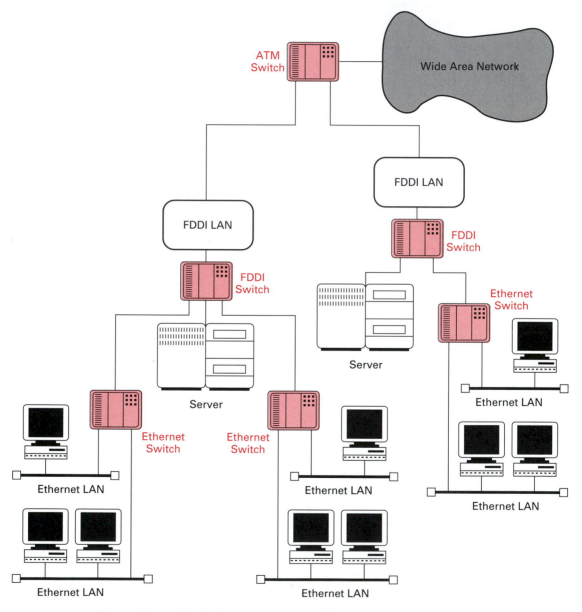

Figure 9.10   LANs implemented using switching hubs can be interconnected in a hierarchical configuration.

Switched FDDI networks provide backbone capability in the middle of the hierarchy, and an ATM switch provides high-bandwidth connectivity between the backbones as well as wide area network connectivity.

VIRTUAL NETWORKS

A capability often associated with switching hubs is *virtual networking*. Virtual networking refers to an ability to assign systems logically to two or more logical LAN subnetworks, each with full bandwidth, without physically changing the physical attachments of the systems. This is illustrated in Fig. 9.11. Some switching hubs allow logical LANs to be created and reconfigured on the fly using network management software.

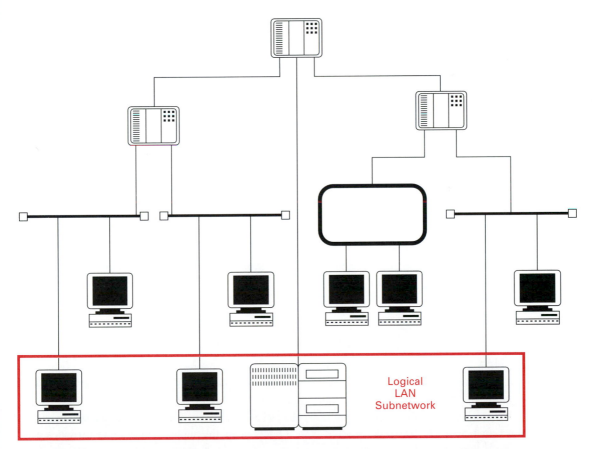

Figure 9.11   Virtual networking refers to the capability of assigning systems to different logical LAN subnetworks without respect to their physical attachment points.

BRIDGING AND ROUTING FUNCTIONS

One consideration with using switching hubs is how broadcast traffic is handled. Switching hubs that implement intelligence may operate in a similar manner to bridges or routers. A bridge generally allows broadcast traffic generated by any station on the LAN to flow across the bridge to all other stations in the LAN. (Bridges are described in Chapter 10.) A router, on the other hand, generally blocks broadcast traffic from flowing across the router and confines broadcast traffic to each individual LAN. (Routers are also discussed in Chapter 10.) Bridges and routers also allow LANs associated with different LAN technologies to be interconnected, such as connecting an Ethernet LAN to an FDDI LAN.

A switching hub can operate like a bridge and forward all broadcast frames to all attached segments. Alternatively, a switching hub may operate like a router, and not forward broadcast traffic. Some vendors are developing intelligent hubs, in which both bridging functions and routing functions are incorporated, thus giving the network administrator much flexibility in configuring the enterprise network.

If a hub supports virtual networking facility, this can be used to define the systems that make up each logical LAN. All the stations on a logical LAN can then receive only the broadcast traffic of systems on that logical LAN.

Switches can also be used in conjunction with bridges and routers. For example, switching hubs could be used to configure one section of an enterprise network, with a router used to handle traffic flowing between that section and other parts of the network.

Switching hubs generally offer increased bandwidth at a lower cost than that associated with using multiple transmission segments connected with bridges or routers. The functions of a switching hub are generally performed in hardware, using high-speed buses and specialized chips, where many of the functions of bridges and routers are performed using software. Therefore switching hubs can often provide higher performance than bridges or routers. Switches can also reduce the time and effort required to make configuration changes.

A potential problem with switches is that there are no standards underlying their design and use, and there is no consistent terminology for describing their capabilities. This can make it more difficult to identify the capabilities of a given switching device and can increase the risk of having interoperability problems.

SUMMARY

Repeaters are used to interconnect individual cable segments within the same LAN data link. A repeater receives a signal from one cable segment and retransmits it, at its original strength, over one or more other cable segments.

A simple hub is a multipoint repeater that can be used to create a star-structured network segment in which the hub is at the center of the star. A simple hub provides a single connection to a primary transmission medium segment and a number of ports, each of which can be attached to a single LAN device.

A configurable hub allows the cable segments that terminate at the ports of the hub to be interconnected in different ways, depending on the type of configuration desired. A configurable hub generally allows the hub to be connected to two or more primary LAN transmission medium segments through a component called a backplane. With module assignment hubs, each hub connects its entire set of ports to one of the LAN transmission medium segments in its backplane. With a bank assignment hub, the ports in a single hub are divided into subsets called banks. The hub allows each bank of ports to be connected to a different primary transmission medium segment. With a port assignment hub, sometimes called a port-switching or configuration-switching hub, a more sophisticated backplane allows ports to be assigned to transmission medium segments on an individual basis.

Switching hubs, or dynamic hubs, implement intelligence that allows them to act as switches to provide full network bandwidth to multiple pairs of devices. A switching hub examines the destination address of each frame it receives and dynamically establishes a connection with the port associated with the frame's destination. A station switching hub allows only a single system to be attached to each of the hub's ports. A segment switching hub allows the attachment of LAN segments, as well as individual systems, to its ports. The backplane then allows any port to communicate with any other port. A high-performance switching hub is sometimes called a super hub, an enterprise hub, or a hub-of-hubs.

Chapter 10 examines some of the strategies and techniques that can be used to interconnect individual data link subnetworks to form complex enterprise networks.

Chapter **10**

Data Link Interconnection

A very simple enterprise network (perhaps for a small organization with only one location) may consist of a single physical LAN to which all the organization's networked computers are connected. To form larger networks, network interconnection devices called *bridges* (described later in this chapter) can be used to interconnect two or more physical LAN data links to form an *extended LAN*. For an enterprise spread over a large geographic area, WAN data links may have to be used to implement some of the connections between LANs. WAN data links can be used in conjunction with bridges, or they can be used with devices called *routers* (also described in this chapter) to form a more flexible type of interconnected network, sometimes called an *internet*. The term internet literally means "network of networks." The largest internet in the world is the Worldwide Internet that links government agencies, research organizations, educational institutions, and business organizations in the United States and around the world.

This chapter examines some of the important technologies developed to support various types of interconnections a network administrator can use to create an enterprise network that may span large distances. The end result of each of the interconnection technologies we examine in this chapter is to create for network users a *single network image*. Users should perceive a single, integrated network, even though the network may consist of a complex web of different types of components. The network may be complex, but it should *appear* to end users to be simple. To two communicating end users, a complex network should appear to be nothing more than a simple point-to-point link between them.

Enterprise networks are typically constructed using three different types of components: *local area network data links*, *wide area network data links*, and *network interconnection devices*. This chapter examines in detail each of these three categories of network components.

LOCAL AREA NETWORK DATA LINKS

Local area network technology has evolved as a way to meet the requirements for high-speed, relatively short-distance communication among computing systems. As we have already discussed, LAN data links are normally used to interconnect devices that are all in the same building, or possibly within a campus of buildings. They do not ordinarily cross public thoroughfares and they normally operate over private cabling.

A LAN data link is a *multiaccess* data link. There can be a number of devices attached to the same link, and all the devices share access to the link's transmission capacity. Local area network equipment is generally used to implement *any-to-any connectivity* so any device on the data link can physically communicate with any other device on that link.

LAN Stations

A device is attached to a LAN data link via a *network interface card* (*NIC*). When we refer to the communication functions associated with the Data Link and Physical layers of the OSI model, we refer to each NIC as implementing a particular *station* attached to the LAN transmission medium. A station consists physically of a NIC and a physical point of attachment to the network. A given computer, or another intelligent device, can implement multiple stations that may be attached to the same or to different LAN data links (see Fig 10.1).

LAN Data Link Addressing

All forms of LAN data link technology use a *station addressing* scheme to uniquely identify the NICs attached to the LAN . Station addresses are used as the source and destination addresses in frames transmitted over the LAN. A station address is sometimes referred to

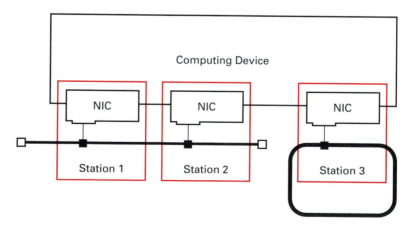

Figure 10.1   A LAN station implements a single point of attachment to a LAN transmission medium segment.

as a *MAC address*, since these addresses are processed by software or firmware operating in the Medium Access Control (MAC) sublayer. When a frame is sent out on a local area network, it is received by all systems attached to that LAN. The receiving systems use the destination address MAC address contained in each received frame to determine which of the received frames to accept and process.

Some forms of LAN data link technology use a global addressing scheme so each NIC attached to a LAN anywhere in the world has a unique station address. Other forms of LAN technology support the use of local addressing, instead of or in addition to global addressing, where the station addresses need only be unique within a given local area network. LAN addressing also usually provides for *group addresses*. The networking software can assign a group address to a set of stations, and frames sent to that address will be accepted and processed by all stations in the group. The *broadcast address* is a special group address used to send a frame to all stations on the local area network.

WIDE AREA NETWORK DATA LINKS

Wide area network data links are most often used to implement point-to-point connections between pairs of network devices in widely separated locations. Wide area networks commonly consist of a mesh of individual WAN data links interconnecting various geographic locations. WAN data links are also used to hook together local area networks too far apart to be interconnected using a LAN data link or a single network interconnection device.

WAN Data Link Addressing

Since WAN data links typically operate as point-to-point links, it is not usually necessary to use data link addresses to identify the systems connected by the link. With a point-to-point data link, there is only one possible address for each frame: the station at the other end of the data link. The most common form of addressing used at the Data Link level for WAN data links is some form of *connection identifier*, which identifies a particular WAN connection between two systems.

DATA LINK INTERCONNECTION DEVICES

To create flexible enterprise networks, it is necessary to interconnect individual local area network data links and wide area networking facilities. A number of different types of devices can be used to accomplish this. Each has its own unique uses and is appropriate for different forms of network interconnection. The types of devices available for data link interconnection can be divided into the following general categories:

- Bridges
- Routers
- Gateways
- Encapsulation facilities (portals and tunnels)

Later in this chapter, we introduce the differences among the various categories of data link interconnection devices. Note that some actual interconnection devices available from vendors combine more than one of the above data link interconnection functions in the same device.

The following sections examine some of the types of network configurations that are possible by combining LAN data links, WAN data links, and data link interconnection devices.

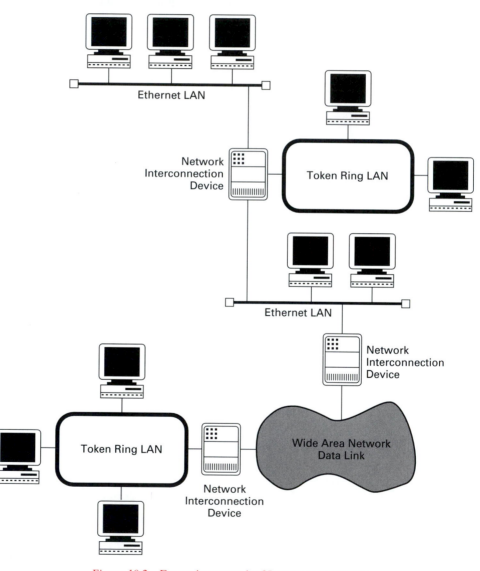

Figure 10.2   Enterprise network of Interconnected LANs.

Interconnecting LANs

Enterprise networks are most constructed using network interconnection devices, such as bridges or routers, in combination with WAN and LAN data links. A simple example of such a network is shown in Fig. 10.2. Such an enterprise network can be very extensive and complex.

Using Backbone Networks

Network interconnection devices can be used to connect two or more physical LAN data links to a *backbone LAN*. A backbone LAN often consists of a LAN to which only network interconnection devices leading to other LANs, and possibly servers, are attached. Individual end users systems are not attached directly to the backbone but to the attached LANs, as shown in Fig. 10.3. Note that for simplicity, the network interconnection devices are not shown.

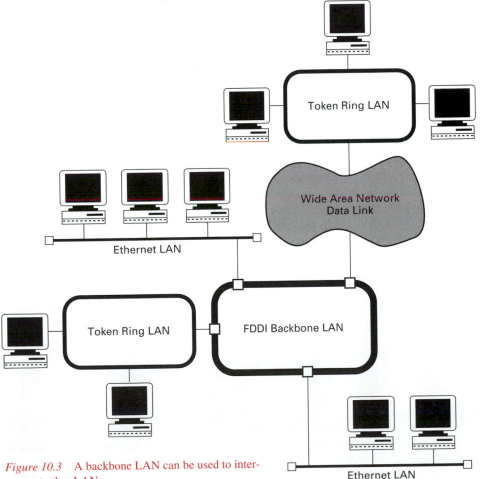

Figure 10.3 A backbone LAN can be used to inter-connect other LANs.

In many cases, the backbone LAN may support a higher transmission speed than the individual LANs attached to it. Optical fiber links are particularly well suited for use in a backbone LAN because of their ability to provide high bandwidth over relatively long distances.

The network components described in this chapter—LAN data links, WAN data links, and interconnection devices—are the building blocks for constructing an enterprise network. Like Lego building blocks, a relatively simple set of components can be combined to form very complex and varied structures. This is true even when the entire network is based on a single network architecture. When several different types of networks must be interconnected, as is often the case in an enterprise network, the challenge of designing, implementing, and maintaining the network infrastructure becomes even greater.

The next sections describe the various types of data link interconnection devices that can be used to link together LAN and WAN data links.

BRIDGES

A bridge is similar to a repeater or hub in that a bridge also forwards frames from one LAN segment to another. But bridges can be more flexible and intelligent than repeaters. A *bridge* interconnects separate LAN data links rather than just cable segments. Some bridges learn the addresses of the stations that can be reached over each data link they bridge so they can selectively relay only traffic that needs to flow across each bridge.

The bridge function operates in the Medium Access Control sublayer of the Data Link layer and is transparent to software operating in the layers above the MAC sublayer (see Fig. 10.4). A bridge can interconnect networks that use different transmission techniques and/or different medium access control methods. For example, a bridge might be used to interconnect an Ethernet LAN using coaxial cabling with an Ethernet LAN using twisted-pair cabling. A bridge might also be used to interconnect an Ethernet LAN with a Token Ring or FDDI LAN.

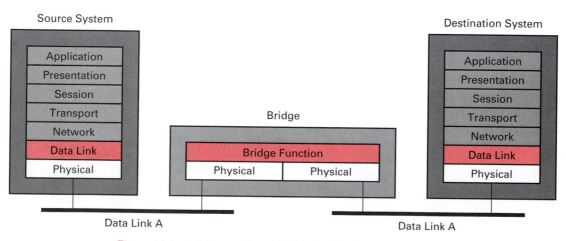

Figure 10.4   A bridge performs its function in the Data Link layer.

Bridges can be used to directly interconnect LANs, or a pair of bridges with a WAN data link between them can be used to interconnect two or more LANs in different geographical locations. Figure 10.5 shows two examples of networks implementing interconnected LANs using bridges. The mechanism implemented by a bridge is often called a *store-and-forward* facility, since frames are usually temporarily stored in the bridge and then forwarded to a station on some other LAN.

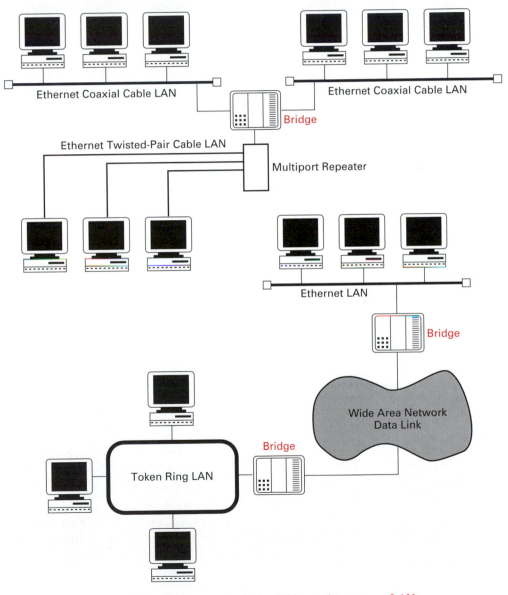

Figure 10.5   Two examples of using bridges to interconnect LANs.

Extended LANs

A collection of individual LAN data links interconnected by bridges is considered to be a single subnetwork. Each of the station addresses throughout the subnetwork must be unique and must use the same station address format. A LAN subnetwork constructed using bridges is sometimes called an *extended LAN* to differentiate it from a single physical LAN. Software operating in the layers above the MAC sublayer view the extended LAN as if it were a single LAN data link.

Frame Filtering

A bridge can implement a *frame filtering* mechanism. Such a bridge, often called a *filtering bridge*, receives all frames transmitted over each data link to which it is attached. The bridge then determines, based on each frame's destination address, whether or not the frame should be transmitted across the bridge to any of the other data links to which it is also attached. Thus, a bridge can isolate some of the network traffic generated on one LAN data link from the other LAN data links in the extended LAN.

Broadcast traffic generated on one LAN, however, is typically always transmitted across a bridge to all the other data links to which it is attached. Therefore, broadcast traffic generated by any station is received by all the stations on the extended LAN.

Bridge Types

Two types of bridges are commonly used in enterprise networks: *spanning tree* bridges and *source routing* bridges:

- **Spanning Tree Bridges.** A spanning tree bridge learns appropriate routes for frames by observing transmissions that take place on the data links to which the bridge is connected. It then forwards frames over the appropriate data links when required. Spanning tree bridges determine a tree structure to be used for an extended LAN in which only one active path connects any two stations in the extended LAN. If there is more than one physical path between two stations, only the path reflected in the tree structure is used.

- **Source Routing Bridges.** With source routing bridges, each station is expected to know the route over which to send each frame, and to include routing information as part of the frame. Source routing bridges then use the routing information in the frame to determine whether or not to forward the frame. If a station does not know the route, or if a previously known route is no longer active, the station broadcasts Route Discovery frames over the extended LAN and then determines from the responses that come back the appropriate route to use. With source routing bridges more than one path can interconnect any two LAN stations. Source routing bridges are typically used only with Token Ring LANs.

Source routing bridges are typically used when bridging individual Token Ring LANs to create a larger Token Ring extended LAN. An advantage to using source routing bridges is that multiple bridges can be installed to create parallel, active paths between individual rings. Multiple active paths allow for higher throughput and load balancing through the various bridges.

A disadvantage of the source routing technique is that source routing bridges often cannot be used to interconnect Token Ring LANs with other types of LANs. Problems can sometimes occur in extended LANs that include both source routing bridges and spanning tree bridges.

ROUTERS

This section describes the operation of routers and discusses guidelines for choosing when to use a router instead of a bridge to interconnect data link subnetworks.

Routers provide the ability to route packets from one system to another where multiple paths may exist between them. Routers typically have more intelligence than bridges and can be used to construct enterprise networks of almost arbitrary complexity. A router performs its function in the OSI model Network layer, as shown in Fig. 10.6.

A system of interconnected routers in an enterprise network all participate in a distributed algorithm to decide on the optimal path over which each packet should travel from a source system to a destination system. The algorithm used varies from one family of transport protocols to another. Routers must be aware of the protocols associated with the Network and Transport level, and can be used only with the specific transport stack or stacks for which they are designed. Unlike bridges and hubs, routers are *not* transparent to the Transport network protocols.

The Routing Function

In general, a router performs the routing function by determining the next system to which a packet should be sent. It then transmits the packet to the next system over the appropriate data link to bring the packet closer to its final destination. In an enterprise network implemented using routers, a packet may pass through a series of routers in

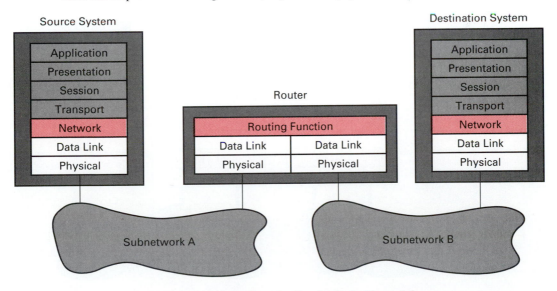

Figure 10.6   A router performs its function in the Network layer.

arriving at its final destination. And a packet might pass through more than one possible sequence of systems in traveling from the source system to the destination system.

A system of routers can implement multiple active paths between any two systems. In some network implementations, it is possible for different packets traveling from a source system to a destination system to take different routes, and a series of packets may arrive at the destination system out of sequence. Protocols operating in the layers above the Network layer in such networks must have the capability for resequencing received packets.

A router is sometimes called an *intermediate system*. By contrast, systems that originate data traffic and that serve as the source or final destination for that traffic are called *end systems* (see Fig. 10.7).

LAN Traffic Isolation

On an individual LAN subnetwork, each station on the LAN typically receives all packets transmitted. With an extended LAN implemented using bridges, the bridges can filter some of the frames, but broadcast traffic generated on one LAN is generally propagated to all the stations on the extended LAN.

Routers can be used to interconnect a number of individual LANs or extended LANs in such a way that the traffic generated on one LAN is better isolated from the traffic generated on other LANs in the network. A frame is forwarded only as required as part of its route to its destination. By using routers instead of bridges to interconnect subnetworks, broadcast traffic can be restricted to each individual LAN subnetwork.

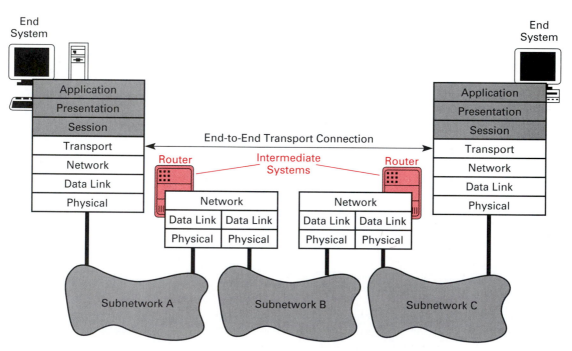

Figure 10.7   Routers act as intermediate systems between end systems.

Network Addresses

Routing is typically performed based on the values of the destination network address fields in packets flowing through the network. As we introduced in Chapter 5, a network address typically consists of two parts: a *network* identifier and a *node* identifier. The network identifier typically identifies a particular network, and the node identifier identifies a particular system within that network. The structure and format of the network address varies from one family of transport protocols to another.

Based on the destination network address, the router determines the next system along the route to the destination system and the data link to be used to bring the packet closer to that system. If two or more LANs are interconnected by routers, each of the individual LANs is considered to be a separate subnetwork. Although station addresses may be unique across the entire enterprise network, this is not a requirement. Station addresses need only be unique within each subnetwork.

Routing Algorithms

A variety of different mechanisms can be used by routers in performing routing and relaying functions. The routing function is generally performed using a routing algorithm, which is a distributed algorithm in which all the routers in the enterprise network participate. Routers use the routing algorithm to build logical maps of the network topology. These logical maps help the routers calculate optimal routes for the packets that move through the network.

As we discussed in Chapter 5, the routing algorithms that routers typically employ in an enterprise network are *distributed adaptive* algorithms that allow routers to update their routing information on the fly as the network topology changes. There are two major types of distributed adaptive routing algorithms: distance-vector algorithms and link-state algorithms. The following sections introduce the operation of each of these major types of distributed adaptive routing algorithms.

- **Distance-Vector Routing.** With a *distance-vector routing* algorithm, also sometimes called a *Bellman-Ford* algorithm, each router in the network learns about the network topology by exchanging routing information packets with its neighbors. In effect, each router learns what its neighbors think the enterprise network looks like. Each router then constructs a new description of the network topology and communicates this new picture to its neighbors. The process is repeated as many times as necessary and eventually stabilizes when all the routers learn they have the same description of the network topology.

- **Link-State Routing.** With a *link-state routing algorithm* routers also exchange routing information with one another. However, unlike with a distance-vector algorithm, each router determines only what its individual area of the enterprise network looks like and then broadcasts that information to all the other routers in the network. Each router sends out routing packets, called *Link-State Vectors,* that describe the systems it can reach on its directly attached links. The Link-State Vectors also contain metrics that represent weighted values representing the relative cost for using each data link.

A distance-vector routing algorithm is a simple algorithm that is relatively easy to design and implement. A link-state algorithm is more complex than a distance-vector algorithm and may require more router processing power. But a link-state algorithm typically scales better than a distance-vector algorithm and can support much larger networks.

BRIDGES VERSUS ROUTERS

In building enterprise network situations, the network administrator must sometimes choose between using a bridge and using a router in specific situations. Box 10.1 lists advantages and disadvantages of bridges. Box 10.2 lists some of the advantages and disadvantages of routers.

BOX 10.1   Advantages and disadvantages of bridges.

Bridge Advantages

- **Cost.** Bridges are relatively simple devices that are typically less expensive than routers.
- **Ease of Use.** Bridges tend to be easier to install and easier to maintain than routers.
- **Protocol Independence.** Bridges operate in the OSI Data Link layer and are independent of any protocol operating in the Network layer and above. This makes it relatively easy to create an internet containing systems that run networking software implementing different higher-level protocol families.
- **Performance.** Since bridges are relatively simple devices, they introduce little processing overhead into the network and tend to support higher traffic throughput than routers.

Bridge Disadvantages

- **Traffic Volume.** Bridges are best suited to networks in which the total traffic volume is relatively low and that support low numbers of total users (less than a few hundred). Problems can occur when bridging two LANs that are already experiencing high traffic volumes.
- **Flow Control.** Bridges simply pass frames from one LAN to another and do not implement flow control procedures to control the rate at which frames flow through the bridge.
- **Bridge Choking.** In a large internet, a bridge has a tendency to choke as a result of heavy traffic loads. This can result in the loss of frames.
- **Broadcast Storms.** Broadcast frames are passed over a bridge from one LAN to another. In a large internet generating a large amount of multicast traffic, broadcast storms can result in which the capacity of an individual LAN data link is exceeded by the broadcast traffic alone.
- **Loops.** Some types of bridged network configurations can result in endless loops around which frames can endlessly circulate.
- **Bottlenecks.** Bridges do not share problem information with one another, and network bottlenecks that occur can remain undetected.
- **Duplicate Addresses.** Physical station addresses must be unique within bridged networks. This can sometimes be a problem where locally administered MAC addresses are used in two or more LANs being bridged.
- **Duplicate Names.** When the same network names are employed by users on two or more bridged networks, excessive traffic can result from attempts to resolve naming conflicts.
- **Effect of Failures.** The failure of some types of bridges requires that all communication sessions using a failed bridge be terminated and restarted.

BOX 10.2   Advantages and disadvantages of routers.

Router Advantages

- **Isolation of Broadcast Traffic.** A major advantage of routers over bridges is that bridges prevent the flow of broadcast traffic from one local area network to another, thus reducing the amount of network traffic the network as a whole experiences.

- **Flexibility.** Routers can support any desired network topology. Networks that use routers are also less susceptible to time delay problems that sometimes occur in large bridged networks.

- **Priority Control.** Routers can implement priority schemes in which traffic conforming to certain protocols can be given a higher priority than traffic conforming to other protocols.

- **Configuration Control.** Routers are typically more configurable than bridges and allow network administrators to tune network performance more easily.

- **Problem Isolation.** Routers form natural barriers between individual LANs and allow problems that occur in one LAN to be isolated to that LAN. In general, large enterprise networks that use routers are easier to maintain and troubleshoot than large bridged extended LANs.

- **Path Selection.** Routers are generally more intelligent than bridges and allow optimal paths to be selected for traffic that flows across the network. Some routers also allow for load balancing over redundant paths between source and destination systems.

Router Disadvantages

- **Protocol Dependence.** Routers operate in the OSI Network layer and must be aware of the protocol or protocols they are designed to route. A router will ignore traffic associated with protocols it is not designed to handle.

- **Cost.** Routers are typically more complex devices than bridges and are generally more expensive.

- **Throughput.** The use of routers generally involves more overhead in processing each packet, and routers typically provide lower levels of throughput than bridges.

- **Address Assignment.** A bridged network consists, logically, of a single local area network. Therefore, a user device can be moved from one location to another without requiring that its network address be changed. In an enterprise network constructed using routers, moving a user machine from one LAN to another often requires that a new network address be assigned to that system.

- **Unreachable Systems.** Routing table entries must be accurate in order for a system on one LAN data link to send data to a system on another LAN data link. When using routers that do not dynamically configure their routing tables, inaccurate routing table entries can result in systems being unreachable.

- **Unroutable Protocols.** Some protocols, such as SNA subarea network traffic and NetBIOS traffic, do not lend themselves to traditional routing and must be handled using specialized techniques.

GATEWAYS

Bridges and routers can be used in various ways to form an enterprise network that supports any-to-any connectivity among all end systems. The use of any of the types of interconnection devices examined thus far assumes that the source system and the destination system both conform to the same network architecture or protocol family. For example, we have not yet shown how it might be possible for a TCP/IP end system to communicate directly with a NetBIOS end system.

Additional devices, called *gateways*, are available that perform protocol conversion functions. A gateway is a fundamentally different type of device than a bridge or a router and can be used in conjunction with them. A gateway makes it possible for an application program running on a system that conforms to one network architecture to communicate with an application program running in a system that conforms to some other network architecture. A gateway performs its function in the Application layer of the OSI model, as shown in Fig. 10.8. The function of a gateway is to convert from one set of communication protocols to some other set of communication protocols. Gateways are commonly used to allow personal computers attached to a local area network to communicate with a host that is part of a wide area network.

ENCAPSULATION FACILITIES

An *encapsulation* facility allows two systems that conform to a given network architecture to communicate using an intermediate network that conforms to some other network architecture. For example, two NetWare IPX/SPX systems might use a pair of

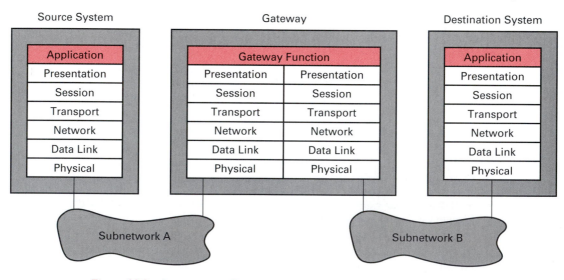

Figure 10.8 A gateway performs a protocol conversion function in the Application layer.

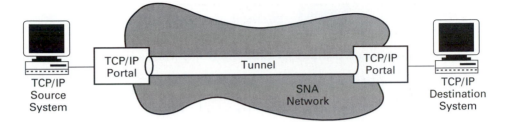

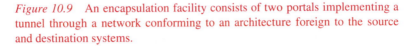

Figure 10.9   An encapsulation facility consists of two portals implementing a
tunnel through a network conforming to an architecture foreign to the source
and destination systems.

encapsulation facilities to cross a DECnet network in order to exchange messages with
each other.

   To use an encapsulation facility, there must be a compatible encapsulation facility
at each end of the foreign network that needs to be crossed. Each individual encapsulation facility is sometimes referred to as a *portal*. A pair of portals, one on each end of the
network, can be viewed as a *tunnel* through the foreign network. The tunnel transports
messages through a network conforming to a foreign network architecture.

   Figure 10.9 shows how an encapsulation facility allows two TCP/IP systems to communicate over an SNA network. Unlike a gateway, an encapsulation facility does not perform actual protocol conversions. Instead, a portal operating on behalf of the source
system encapsulates a message conforming to a source system's network architecture
within a message capable of being carried across the network. A complementary portal
operating on behalf of the destination system extracts the original message and passes it
to the destination system.

MULTIPLE-PROTOCOL NETWORKING

An organization can construct complex networks using any network architecture or data
transport protocol family. However, enterprise networks must often be able to handle network hardware and software that conform to a variety of *different* network architectures.
We next examine approaches that can be used to handle multiple transport protocol families in the same enterprise network.

Multiple-Protocol Subnetworks

Figure 10.10 illustrates a simple Ethernet local area network in which end systems on the
data link implement three different transport protocol families: TCP/IP, NetBIOS, and Net-
Ware IPX/SPX. In such a network, we can view the end systems as if they form three separate *logical networks* that all share the same physical LAN data link.

   In the Ethernet LAN subnetwork shown in Fig. 10.10, systems within each of the
three logical networks are able to communicate freely with one another. But the systems
in one logical network are unaware of the systems in the other two logical networks that

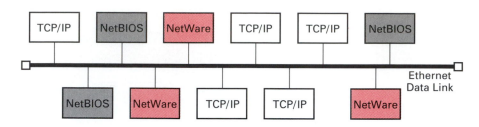

Figure 10.10   Three logical networks using different transport protocols sharing a single data link.

share the data link. For example, an end system that implements only TCP/IP communication software is not aware of the existence of end systems on the data link that implement NetWare IPX/SPX or NetBIOS communication software. In such an environment, a TCP/IP end system cannot communicate directly with a NetWare IPX/SPX system or a NetBIOS system.

A single-protocol end system implements its own network architecture, runs the data transport protocol from within its own protocol family, and sends packets over the communications medium conforming to its own Network layer specifications.

It is important to note that no special facilities are necessary at the level of the Data Link layer to handle data transport protocols from multiple protocol families. Data Link layer facilities are not aware of the protocols operating in the layers above the Data Link layer. The Ethernet data link can handle packets conforming to Network layer specifications for all three protocol families in the previous example. Packets of all three types flow over the same communications link in standard Ethernet frames, even though they may have different packet formats and Network address structures.

Multiprotocol End Systems

A general goal in enterprise networking is to provide for *any-to-any connectivity*, where a user in one system can communicate with any other computing system in the enterprise network. Many products have been developed that are designed to interconnect end systems that implement different network architectures. This chapter describes a number of approaches that such products use.

One way to move toward any-to-any connectivity is to use end systems that implement more than one data transport protocol family. An end system that implements multiple data transport protocols is called a *multiprotocol end system*.

Protocol Stacks

A multiprotocol end system typically runs a network software subsystem that supports more than one data transport protocol family. For example, an end system might run network software that provides support for the NetWare IPX/SPX data transport protocols and also the TCP/IP data transport protocols. Such an end system is said to be running network software that implements a *protocol stack* for each supported network architecture.

This term generally refers to the software within a network software subsystem that implements the functional layers of a network architecture.

Peer-to-Peer Networks

In a computer network with a peer-to-peer orientation, a multiprotocol end system can communicate with other end systems that support any of the data transport protocols the multiprotocol end system implements. For example, an end system supporting both the AppleTalk protocols and the TCP/IP protocols can communicate directly with any other end system on the network that implements the AppleTalk protocols, the TCP/IP protocols, or both.

Client/Server Networks

Many computer networks, such as a Novell NetWare network, have a client/server rather than a peer-to-peer orientation. In such a network, client end systems do not ordinarily communicate directly with one another. Rather, client systems communicate directly only with server systems on the network. Therefore, in a server-oriented computer network, it may not be necessary for individual client end systems to support multiple data transport protocols. It is generally more useful for the servers to support multiple network architectures.

Interconnecting Individual LANs

In the enterprise networking environment, it is often necessary to interconnect individual LAN subnetworks to form a larger enterprise network. When this is done, it is generally desirable for an end system on one LAN subnetwork to be able to communicate directly with end systems on the other LAN subnetwork. Supporting any-to-any connectivity in an enterprise network can be more difficult than supporting any-to-any connectivity in the single-LAN environment. To do this, it is necessary to use network interconnection equipment that can handle the various data transport protocols in use on the LAN subnetworks being interconnected.

The following sections describe a number of different subnetwork interconnection strategies that can be used in a multiple-protocol enterprise networking environment.

Bridges and Extended LANs

In a local area network environment where it is important to support end systems that implement multiple data transport protocol families, an effective way to create a larger enterprise network is to use *bridges* to interconnect individual LAN data links. A number of individual LAN data links connected by one or more bridges forms an extended LAN that appears to end systems as if it were a single LAN data link (see Fig 10.11).

As discussed earlier, a bridge operates at the level of the OSI model Data Link layer and works with any frames generated by the network interface cards (NICs) attached to the extended LAN. The frames can contain packets associated with any data transport protocol family, and the bridges will handle them correctly. When bridges are used, any two end

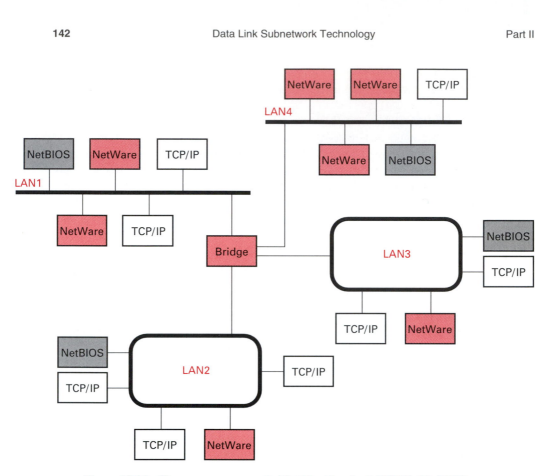

Figure 10.11   Heterogeneous extended LAN with mixed TCP/IP, NetBIOS, and NetWare systems.

systems that support common data transport protocols can communicate across the extended LAN using those protocols. The protocols operating in the layers above the Data Link layer are transparent to the bridges.

Single-Protocol Routers

In some cases it is desirable to interconnect subnetworks using routers instead of bridges. Routers provide the advantage that traffic generated on one subnetwork, especially broadcast traffic, can be better isolated from the traffic on other subnetworks. A router analyzes each packet it receives and passes only those packets that need to flow across the router based on their final destination addresses. Thus, an enterprise network constructed using routers can often support higher traffic volumes than an equivalent network constructed using bridges.

A simple router, however, works only with the packets that conform to a particular Network layer protocol. Therefore, a router must be designed to handle the packets associated with a particular data transport protocol family, such as TCP/IP or IPX/SPX. A router designed to handle only TCP/IP packets will recognize only packets that originate in TCP/IP end systems. A TCP/IP router may simply ignore all other packets it receives.

This is not a problem if all the end systems in the enterprise network support the same data transport protocol family. An enterprise network containing only TCP/IP end systems can be implemented using TCP/IP routers instead of bridges, and any end system in the enterprise network will still be able to reach any other end system.

It is possible in an enterprise network to use multiple routers, in which each routing packet is associated with a particular transport protocol family, to interconnect subnetworks. Such as strategy may be desirable in a server-oriented network that uses multiple-protocol servers. TCP/IP end systems route traffic to appropriate TCP/IP servers using the TCP/IP routers, and NetWare end systems route traffic to appropriate NetWare servers using the NetWare routers. Such an approach works well in a simple network where the servers themselves perform the routing function for the traffic they support.

Multiprotocol Routers

An alternative to installing a separate router for each protocol family that needs to be supported is to use routers capable of routing traffic for all desired protocol families. Such a router is called a *multiprotocol router* (see Fig. 10.12). A router capable of routing both TCP/IP and IPX/SPX traffic is known to both the TCP/IP and the NetWare systems and is capable of handling both IP and IPX packets.

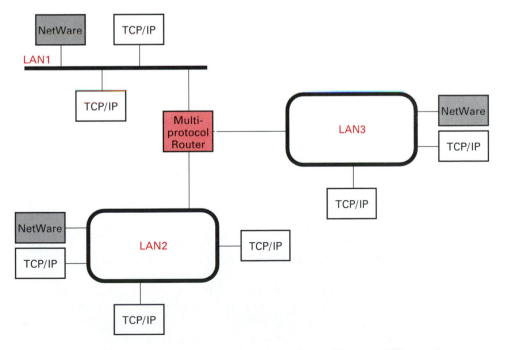

Figure 10.12   A single multiprotocol router can be used to route traffic associated with different protocol types.

A multiprotocol router must support multiple routing protocols and must maintain a different routing table for each protocol family it is designed to handle. The router accepts each packet, determines the data transport protocol family associated with the packet, and hands that packet to the appropriate routing routine. The selected routing routine uses the appropriate routing table to determine a next-hop address for each packet it receives.

A possible disadvantage to using multiprotocol routers is that they may not be able to handle as much network traffic as an equivalent set of single-protocol routers. Network designers must choose appropriate routers to handle the anticipated network traffic.

Using Encapsulation Facilities

In some enterprise networking situations it is necessary for similar end systems in two different subnetworks to communicate with one another using a system of routers that support some other network architecture. Figure 10.13 shows an enterprise network con-

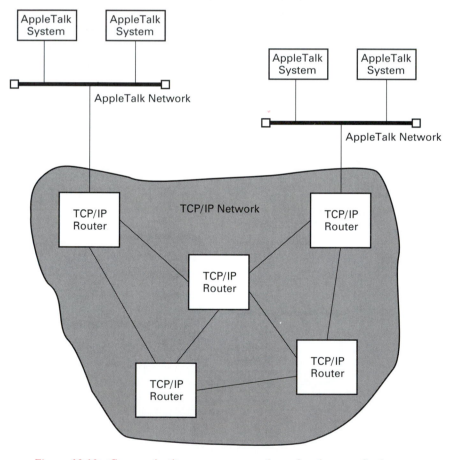

Figure 10.13 Communicating across a network conforming to a foreign network architecture.

sisting of a TCP/IP internet and two AppleTalk subnetworks. The problem here is that end systems on the two AppleTalk subnetworks generate AppleTalk packets, and the routers in the TCP/IP internet recognize only IP packets. If an end system on one of the AppleTalk subnetworks attempts to send traffic to an end system on the other AppleTalk subnetwork, the TCP/IP routers will ignore those packets.

A pair of routers that implement an encapsulation facility can be used to handle network traffic that passes over an intermediate network using a transport protocol different than that of the source and destination end systems. A possible solution to the subnetwork interconnection problem shown in Fig. 10.13 is to attach the two AppleTalk routers to the TCP/IP internet using routers that provide an AppleTalk encapsulation facility as well as a TCP/IP routing capability (see Fig. 10.14).

A router implementing an AppleTalk portal accepts AppleTalk packets and encloses each of them within an IP packet. Based on the destination address in the AppleTalk packet, the router determines the complementary router/portal in the TCP/IP network to which the packet should be relayed. The IP packet is then delivered, using TCP/IP routing,

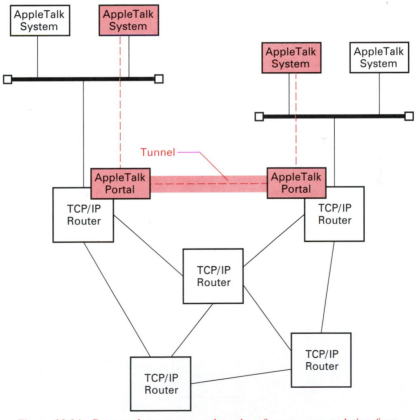

Figure 10.14   Routers that act as portals and perform an encapsulation function can be used to transport traffic of a different protocol type.

to that router/portal. The destination portal then removes the original AppleTalk packet from within the IP packet and transmits the AppleTalk packet over the destination AppleTalk subnetwork.

Using Gateway Facilities

A pair of gateways that perform appropriate protocol translations can be used as an alternative to an encapsulation facility for crossing an intermediate subnetwork. In order for two AppleTalk systems to exchange messages over a TCP/IP internet, the gateways shown in Fig. 10.15 could be used. Although the gateway functions are shown as running in separate systems, they could be run in devices that also function as routers, or the gateway functions could be performed in the two end systems themselves.

In the enterprise network shown in Fig. 10.15, the first gateway accepts an AppleTalk packet from the source AppleTalk subnetwork, extracts the user data from it, and places that information into a new IP packet. The IP packet is then relayed to a com-

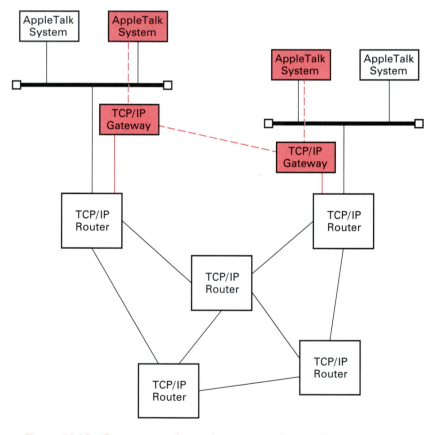

Figure 10.15   Gateways can be used to cross an intermediate network that uses a different transport protocol.

plementary gateway on the opposite side of the network. That gateway accepts the IP packet, extracts the user data from it, places it back into an AppleTalk packet, and transmits it over the destination AppleTalk subnetwork.

Handling Unroutable Protocols

Traffic associated with some network architectures cannot be handled by conventional adaptive routing techniques. Examples of these are the protocols used to implement the NetBIOS data transport protocol and the subarea network protocols defined by IBM's Systems Network Architecture (SNA). These protocol families are often characterized as *unroutable*.

Packets carrying data for unroutable protocols causes no problems when the enterprise network consists of a single extended LAN in which all connections between subnetworks are implemented using bridges. However, special techniques must be used when traffic associated with unroutable protocols must be carried through an enterprise network that uses conventional routers for subnetwork interconnection.

Using Brouters to Carry Unroutable Traffic

The simplest way to handle unroutable protocols is to use devices called *brouters* in place of conventional routers. A brouter runs a conventional adaptive routing protocol for one or more designated protocol families. However, instead of discarding packets it does not recognize, it performs a bridge function for those packets.

For example, Figure 10.16 shows how we can use a brouter that routes TCP/IP and NetWare packets and performs a bridge function for all other traffic. The brouter would allow multicast frames generated by TCP/IP and NetWare systems to be isolated to each individual LAN subnetwork but still allow all the NetBIOS multicast traffic to flow across the brouter from one LAN subnetwork to the others.

A disadvantage of a brouter is that if a high percentage of traffic is bridged instead of routed, undesirably large amounts of multicast traffic can be propagated throughout the enterprise network and can cause individual LAN subnetworks to become overloaded.

Using an Encapsulation Facility to Carry
Unroutable Traffic

Some multi-protocol routers use an encapsulation facility (portal/tunnel) instead of a bridge function to handle the routing of network traffic associated with unroutable protocols. Figure 10.17 shows routers implementing NetBIOS portals that perform an encapsulation function for carrying NetBIOS traffic over a TCP/IP internet. Such routers accept unroutable NetBIOS traffic and enclose each NetBIOS packet within a TCP/IP packet. The TCP/IP packets are then delivered, using TCP/IP routing, to a complementary router/portal on the destination LAN subnetwork. The portal there removes the TCP/IP header information from the original NetBIOS packets and transmits them over the destination NetBIOS subnetwork. As we described previously, the portals on both ends of the TCP/IP internet can be viewed as implementing a tunnel through the system of routers that run the TCP/IP routing protocol.

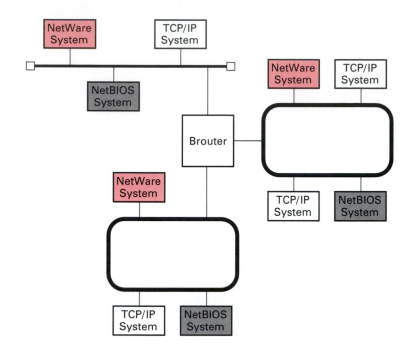

Figure 10.16 A brouter can be used to handle a combination of routable protocols and unroutable protocols.

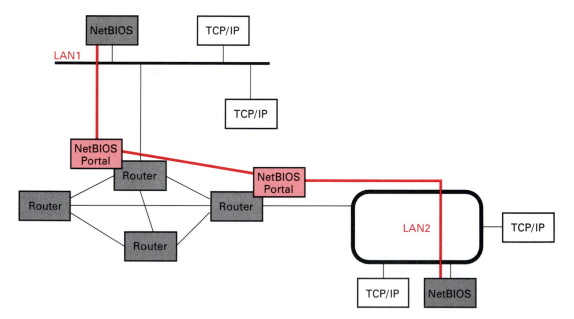

Figure 10.17 Routers that also act as portals and perform an encapsulation function can be used to transport traffic associated with an unroutable protocol.

Multiprotocol Network Software

The functions of most early network software subsystems, such as the network operating systems that ran on many servers, were based on a single network architecture and implemented the data transport protocol for a single protocol family. For example, early IBM mainframe operating systems typically supported networking by implementing the SNA data transport protocols in a telecommunications access method subsystem. UNIX operating systems for minicomputers and workstations typically had built-in support for the TCP/IP data transport protocols. Personal computers often ran a NetWare network operating system that implemented only the IPX/SPX data transport protocols.

With network software subsystems that support a single network architecture and a single data transport protocol family, it was typical for users to employ only the application protocols provided by the same protocol family that supplies that data transport protocol. For example, in the UNIX environment, users might employ the TCP/IP File Transfer Protocol (FTP) for file transfer operations, and they might access file servers that run the Network File Service (NFS) file sharing software. Both of these TCP/IP-oriented application services were then most often implemented using the underlying TCP and IP data transport protocols.

Now that network software has begun to provide support for multiple data transport protocol families, it is becoming commonplace for end systems to use application protocols associated with one protocol family and to carry that data through the network using the data transport protocols of some other protocol family. For example, a personal computer user might use NetWare client software to access a NetWare file server. But the remote file access service might be provided using TCP/IP data transport protocols.

Using a particular set of application protocols no longer automatically determines the protocols that must be used for data transport. Given the variety of networking products and product options that have been developed, determining the ideal way to configure a particular internet can become a challenge.

SUMMARY

Enterprise networks are typically constructed using WAN and LAN data links interconnected using data link interconnection devices, such as bridges, routers, gateways, and encapsulation facilities.

A bridge interconnects separate LAN data links and typically learns the addresses of stations that can be reached over each data link connected to the bridge. A bridge operates in the Medium Access Control sublayer and is transparent to software operating in the Network layer and above. A bridge can interconnect networks that use different transmission techniques and/or different medium access control methods. Two types of bridges in common use in enterprise networks are spanning tree bridges and source routing bridges.

Routers provide the ability to route packets from one system to another where there may be multiple paths between them. A router performs its function in the OSI model Network layer. A router runs a routing algorithm that determines the next system to which each packet should be sent. The major types of distributed adaptive routing algorithms used by routers are distance-vector algorithms and link-state algorithms.

A gateway performs a protocol conversion function and performs its function in the Application layer of the osi model. An encapsulation facility allows two systems that conform to a given network architecture to communicate using an intermediate network that conforms to some other network architecture. The encapsulation facility in a single system is sometimes referred to as a portal, and a pair of portals can be viewed as implementing a tunnel.

Enterprise networks must often be able to handle network hardware and software that conform to a variety of different network architectures. Supporting any-to-any connectivity in an enterprise network requires that data link interconnection equipment handle the various data transport protocols in use. Bridges are useful in multiple-protocol networks because they handle any of the protocols that operate above the Data Link layer. Routers must be designed to handle each of the protocol families used in the enterprise network. Routers that implement encapsulation facilities are useful in some types of multiple-protocol situations, and a pair of gateways can sometimes be used in place of encapsulation. Traffic associated with some network architectures, such as NetBIOS and SNA, is characterized as unroutable. Unroutable protocols can be handled by brouters that implement the functions of both bridges and routers and by using encapsulation facilities.

Chapter 11 begins Part III of this book, which examines specific technologies used in constructing wide area network data links. Chapter 11 examines data link subnetworks that employ conventional telecommunications facilities for data transmission.

WAN SUBNETWORK TECHNOLOGY

Conventional Telecommunications Subnetworks

Wide area network data transmission links are most often implemented using conventional telecommunications facilities, such as ordinary telephone circuits. In the United States, basic telecommunications services are provided by organizations called *telecommunications common carriers*. Telecommunications services are provided in many other countries by governmental postal, telephone, and telegraph (PTT) administrations. We will use the term *common carrier* in this book to refer to any service provider that offers telecommunications services to the public.

WAN data links are typically used to provide point-to-point connections between pairs of systems typically located some distance from one another. In this chapter and in the rest of this part, we look at the WAN data link services important for computer networking and the technologies on which these services are based.

ANALOG CIRCUITS

Most telecommunications facilities offered by common carriers provide an analog communication channel designed for the purpose of carrying telephone voice traffic. Telecommunication services based on conventional analog telephone circuits are sometimes referred to using the term *plain old telephone service (POTS)*.

Two types of POTS facilities are generally offered by common carriers:

- **Dial-up Circuits.** A dial-up connection requires a call to be placed, just as with voice telephone service, to establish the circuit. When data transmission is finished, the call is terminated and the connection is released.

- **Leased Line Circuits.** A leased line connection is a permanent, dedicated point-to-point telecommunications circuit leased from the common carrier. The connection is dedicated to the organization that leases it and is typically available for use 24 hours a day, seven days a week.

Most data links that employ analog telecommunications facilities use conventional telephone circuits with a relatively narrow bandwidth optimized for voice transmission.

Such circuits are used for data communication by employing a modem at each end of the data link. Commonly used modems for use with conventional dial-up voice telephone circuits provide data transmission speeds of 2400, 9600, 14,400, and 28,800 bits per second (bps).

Leased voice circuits are also available from common carriers and generally provide more reliable transmission at higher bit rates than dial-up connections. Analog telecommunications circuits of higher bandwidth than voice circuits can also be leased from common carriers. A data rate of 56 Kbps is commonly achieved using leased analog circuits with higher bandwidth than a voice channel.

DIGITAL CIRCUITS

Telecommunications common carriers now also provide specialized digital telecommunications circuits optimized for data transmission rather than for voice transmission. There are various levels of digital service available, corresponding to different data transmission rates. Some commonly available digital telecommunications circuits are listed in Box 11.1.

TELECOMMUNICATIONS INFRASTRUCTURES

The world of electronic communication currently has three fundamentally different information infrastructures: the telephone network for voice communication, the cable television and broadcasting system for video, and packet-switching technologies for computer networking. There is some overlap among these infrastructures. For example, transmission facilities intended to support voice communication are used to implement computer networks and are also used to transmit video signals. And the cable television industry

---

BOX 11.1	Common carrier digital data transmission circuits.

Type	Speed
DDS	2.4, 4.8, 9.6, 19.2, and 56 Kbps
DS0	64 Kbps
Fractional T-1	Multiples of 64 Kbps up to 1.544 Mbps
T1, DS1	1.544 Mbps
T2, DS2	6.3 Mbps
T3, DS3	44 Mbps
DS4	139 and 274 Mbps
DS5	565 Mbps

has made some inroads in allowing computer communication to coexist on the same cable used to transmit television signals. But the three infrastructures have evolved in parallel for fundamentally different purposes.

The three separate information infrastructures are all moving from analog technology to digital technology for transmission, multiplexing, and switching. At some point in the future, it will be desirable for these separate information infrastructures to merge so the same network can be used to carry any type of information. This merging is currently underway, but it will be some time before it can be completely accomplished. There are many hurdles, not all of which are technical, that will need to be overcome.

EVOLUTION OF COMPUTER COMMUNICATION

To understand some of the new telecommunications technologies that are coming into use, it is helpful to examine the way computer networking technology has evolved.

Circuit Switching

The earliest forms of electronic communication used ordinary *circuit-switching* techniques. The telephone network is essentially a circuit-switching network. With circuit switching, a fixed-capacity circuit is established between two communicating users and is dedicated to those users for the duration of the connection. Each circuit provides a fixed bandwidth for an analog circuit or a fixed data rate for a digital circuit.

The common carrier may use multiplexing facilities to carry multiple circuits over a single physical line. For analog circuits, multiplexing is typically done using frequency-division multiplexing. For digital circuits, time-division multiplexing is most often used. Multiplexing allows for more efficient use of the high-bandwidth transmission capabilities common carriers use for long-distance communication.

Circuit switching is ideal for ordinary telephone circuits because the required bandwidth is relatively low, the full bandwidth is ordinarily required during the entire duration of a call, and calls are relatively long (measured in minutes rather than milliseconds). The circuit-switching techniques used with the telephone network provide a fixed, guaranteed data rate, in that once a circuit is established, its full bandwidth is available for transmission. This type of service is well suited for isochronous traffic, where transmission is time sensitive and requires a regular arrival rate. Voice and video communication are examples of information requiring isochronous transmission, since a person receiving the transmission would be aware of delays or interruptions in the transmission. Early forms of computer communication used circuit-switching techniques to interconnect computer equipment simply because the only communication facilities available spanning long distances were ordinary telephone circuits.

Packet Switching

Computer communication does not lend itself particularly well to the type of circuit switching used in the telephone system. In a typical computer application, we would like to transmit short bursts of data very rapidly between two communicating machines, but there may be relatively long periods of time between bursts. In a typical application where a person at a user-interface device communicates with a server system, we would like a communication channel having a very high transmission speed, but we typically send information over the channel for only a very small percentage of the time.

The packet-switching techniques used today in computer networks allow a number of users to share a high-capacity transmission channel. Packet switching works well for computer data at low to moderate transmission speeds. But packet switching is not well suited for isochronous voice or video communication. The delays introduced by the packet switches are too long and too unpredictable for these types of applications.

Growth in transmission requirements for more complex forms of data, including images, animation, and digitized audio and video, has led to an increased need for higher data rates for data transmission. Data rates in the billions of bits per second may be required to support the combined traffic of users using these more complex forms of data.

It turns out that conventional packet-switching techniques, such as those in X.25 packet-switched data networks (PSDNs) do not work well for very high transmission speeds. (X.25 networks are described in Chapter 12.) With X.25 packet switching, nodes within the PSDN must all be capable of performing routing functions. Because of the quality of the physical transmission facilities used, the nodes must also perform error checking with acknowledgments and retransmission. The overhead introduced in doing all this make the nodes too slow to support very high transmission speeds.

Conventional circuit switching is also ill suited for very high-speed networking because no single user needs more than a small percentage of the total capacity of the transmission channel. Because of this, new forms of switching and transmission that combine some of the characteristics of both circuit switching and packet switching are being developed to support the use of high-bandwidth transmission facilities. Later chapters in this part examine a number of these newer forms of telecommunications switching and transmission.

CONVENTIONAL COMMON CARRIER SERVICES

Figure 11.1 illustrates the general approach used to interconnect individual systems using a conventional common carrier voice telecommunications facility. A user of the service attaches to a device that provides a point of access into the common carrier's network. The common carrier network consists of a set of nodes that act as switches with links interconnecting them. The common carrier is responsible for transporting data across the network between service users that wish to communicate. The common carrier may use a number of physical circuits to handle the data transmission, but the users on each end of the network perceive a direct logical connection, or virtual channel, over which they communicate.

When a source system has data to send, it transmits the data to its point of access to the common carrier network. The data then travels across the common carrier network to the destination system's point of access. It appears to the source and destination systems as if the data travels across a direct connection between them.

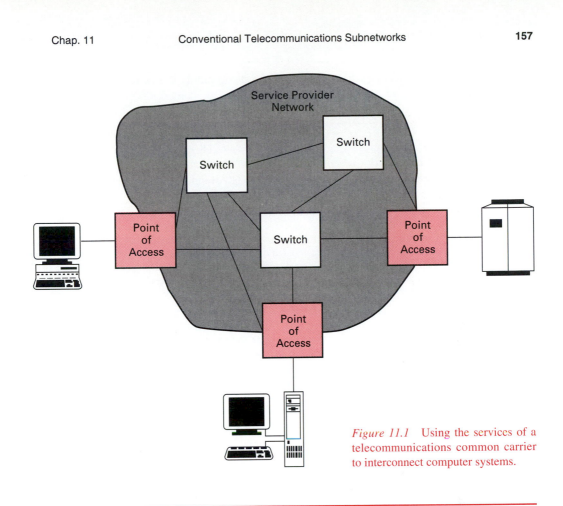

Figure 11.1 Using the services of a telecommunications common carrier to interconnect computer systems.

WAN DATA LINK PROTOCOLS

Just as in all the other layers in a network architecture, a protocol must operate in the Data Link layer to control data transmission over a WAN data link subnetwork. These protocols are called *data link protocols*. A data link protocol defines the formats of the frames carried over the data link and specifies the rules that control the exchange of frames over the data link.

The specific data link protocols commonly used when transmitting data over common carrier telephone circuits, include the following:

- **High-level Data Link Control (HDLC).** This is an ISO data link protocol defined in one of the international standards that supports the OSI model.

- **Synchronous Data Link Control (SDLC).** This is an IBM protocol often used in SNA networks. SDLC is a functional subset of HDLC and is compatible with it.

- **Point-to-Point Protocol (PPP).** This is a simplified version of HDLC developed for use with the TCP/IP protocol family to support point-to-point WAN connections between routers.

The following sections describe each of these commonly used data link protocols for WAN connections.

ISO HIGH-LEVEL DATA LINK CONTROL (HDLC)

High-level Data Link Control (HDLC) is an international standard data link protocol that has been used for many years. The specific ISO standards that define HDLC are listed in Box 11.2.

Two major types of HDLC data links can be used to connect stations:

- **Unbalanced Data Links.** An *unbalanced* HDLC data link connects two or more stations, with one of the stations designated as the *primary station* and all the others designated as *secondary stations.* Unbalanced data links are not generally used in computer networks, but they are sometimes used in a terminal-oriented network to connect a computer to a group of dumb terminals.

- **Balanced Data Links.** A *balanced* HDLC data link connects exactly two stations in a point-to-point configuration. Each station on a balanced link is called a *combined station,* either of which can originate message transmission. Point-to-point HDLC connections in computer networks are typically balanced data links.

Commands and Responses

On an unbalanced data link, messages the primary station sends are called *commands*; messages the secondary station sends in reply to commands are called *responses.* On a balanced data link, either station can originate a transmission by sending a command; the other station then replies with a response.

HDLC Operating Modes

The HDLC protocol specification defines three operational modes to support three types of protocol operation:

- **Asynchronous Balanced Mode (ABM).** Supports a balanced data link that connects two combined stations using a full-duplex physical circuit. Either station can initiate frame transmission, and frame transmission can take place in both directions at the same time. This is the mode of operation most often employed over HDLC data links in computer networks.

- **Normal Response Mode (NRM).** Used to support unbalanced data links that connect two or more stations using a half-duplex physical circuit. One of the stations on the link is the primary station and the others are secondary stations. A secondary station cannot initiate transmission without first receiving permission from the primary station. This mode of operation is often employed in networks of dumb terminals.

- **Asynchronous Response Mode (ARM).** The ISO HDLC standard also defines an asynchronous response mode, in which each station performs the function of both a primary and a secondary station. With ARM, the data link consists logically of two primary/secondary station pairs. In this mode either station can initiate transmission, but one of the stations typically retains responsibility for the data link. In practice, asynchronous response mode was found to have a number of limitations and is today considered obsolete by most authorities. It has been superseded in most cases by asynchronous balanced mode.

BOX 11.2   ISO standards documenting HDLC.

- ISO 3309   HDLC Procedures — Frame Structure
- ISO 4335   HDLC Elements of Procedures
- ISO 7776   HDLC Procedures — X.25 LAPB-compatible DTE Data Link Procedures
- ISO 7809   HDLC Procedures — Consolidation of Classes of Procedures
- ISO 8471   HDLC Data Link Address Resolution
- ISO 8885   HDLC Procedures — General Purpose XID Frame Information Field Content and Format

Nonoperational Modes

In addition to the three operational modes, HDLC defines three nonoperational modes:

- **Asynchronous Disconnected Mode (ADM).** Applies to a station on a balanced data link that is logically and/or physically disconnected from the link.
- **Normal Disconnected Mode (NDM).** Applies to a station on an unbalanced link that is logically and/or physically disconnected from the link.
- **Initialization Mode (IM).** Intended to be the mode a station is in before it actually becomes operational. One station can put another station into initialization mode when it is necessary to perform some hardware-specific initialization procedure, such as down-loading program code after a station is powered up.

Frame Format

The data unit transmitted over an HDLC data link is typically called a *frame*. Some frames are originated by HDLC itself and are used to control the operation of the data link. Other frames are used to carry the user data passed down from an HDLC user for transmission over the data link.

As shown in Box 11.3, each frame is divided into three major parts: a header, a variable-length information field, and a trailer. Protocol control information (PCI) is carried in the header and the trailer. Control frames originated by HDLC itself sometimes also use the Information field to carry protocol control information.

Frame and Control Field Formats

The HDLC standard defines three types of HDLC frames, all of which share the same general format described in Box 11.3. The following are brief descriptions of each frame type:

- **Information Frames.** The primary function of Information frames (I-frames) is to carry user data, although they sometimes also implicitly perform control functions, such as serving as positive acknowledgments to frames sent.
- **Supervisory Frames.** Supervisory frames (S-frames) are used to control the transmission of I-frames and are exchanged only when the link is in a state where it is possible to trans-

BOX 11.3 HLDC transmission frame format.

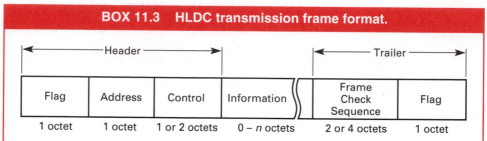

Flag	Address	Control	Information	Frame Check Sequence	Flag
1 octet	1 octet	1 or 2 octets	0 – n octets	2 or 4 octets	1 octet

- **Beginning Flag Field.** Each frame begins with a *flag field,* which consists of a single octet containing the unique bit configuration 0111 1110. A *bit stuffing* technique (described later) guarantees only that a flag field will contain six consecutive 1 bits.

- **Address Field.** The field following the flag field is a single octet in length and is interpreted as the station address. A command always contains the station address of the receiving station; a response always contains the address of the sending station. The address field is used for station identification on unbalanced data links that contain multiple secondary stations. On a balanced data link that connects only two stations, the station address field is not used. However, the address field is present in all HDLC frames for consistency of format.

- **Control Field.** The control field is one or two octets in length. The control field determines the type of frame being transmitted, conveys information necessary for the proper sequencing of frames, and carries control information.

- **Information Field.** A variable-length information field is used to carry the data portion of the frame. It consists of either control information or data passed down from a user of HDLC. The HDLC specification allows the information field to be any number of bits in length. However, most implementations of HDLC require the information field to be some multiple of eight bits. The size can be zero octets for some commands and responses. Although HDLC does not specifically define a maximum length for the information field, a particular HDLC implementation may set limits on the size of a frame based on the size of the available buffer.

- **Frame Check Sequence Field.** The frame check sequence (FCS) field contains either a 16-bit or a 32-bit cyclic redundancy check (CRC) value used for error detection.

- **Ending Flag Field.** The end of a frame is marked by another flag field containing the same bit configuration as the beginning flag field (0111 1110).

mit and receive I-frames. They carry information necessary for supervisory control functions, which include requesting transmission, requesting a temporary suspension of transmission, acknowledging the receipt of I-frames, and reporting on status. Normal, routine data transmission over an HDLC data link involves only I-frames and S-frames.

- **Unnumbered Frames.** Unnumbered frames (U-frames) are used to carry data and to perform control functions, such as performing initialization procedures, controlling the data link, and invoking diagnostic sequences.

One-Octet and Two-Octet Control Fields

I-frames and S-frames transmitted during HDLC operation can contain control fields that are either one octet or two octets in length; U-frames always contain one-octet control fields. When an HDLC data link is initialized, the two stations may exchange U-frame commands and responses to determine whether one-octet or two-octet control fields are to be used during data link operation.

A data link that uses two-octet control fields is referred to as using *modulo-128 operation*. A data link using one-octet control fields uses *modulo-8 operation*.

- **Modulo-8 Operation.** When stations operate using single-octet control fields, three bits are used for frame sequence numbers. Three-bit sequence number values allow frame sequence numbers to range from 0 through 7. Modulo-8 operation allows a sending station to transmit up to seven frames in sequence before it must request an acknowledgment.

- **Modulo-128 Operation.** When stations operate using two-octet control fields, frame sequence numbers consist of seven-bit values, allowing values from 0 through 127. Modulo-128 operation allows a sending station to transmit up to 127 frames in sequence before an acknowledgment is required.

The following sections describe the formats of I-frames, S-frames, and U-frames.

I-Frame Format

Box 11.4 illustrates the format of I-frames and shows how the control field bits are interpreted for two-octet control fields. A 0 in bit position 1 in the first control field octet identifies the frame as an I-frame. The remainder of the bits in the two-octet I-frame control field are used to contain a send count [N(S)], a receive count [N(R)], and a poll/final (P/F) bit. The count fields are used to control frame sequencing. The poll/final bit is used

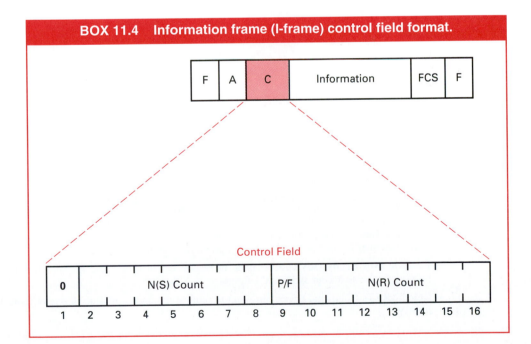

BOX 11.4   Information frame (I-frame) control field format.

to request acknowledgments. For an unbalanced data link, the poll/final bit is also used by the primary station to poll the secondary stations.

S-Frame Format

Each of the control frames used to implement the HDLC protocol has a *full name* and a shorthand *mnemonic*. For example, one of the S-frames employed in the HDLC protocol is the *Receiver Ready (RR)* S-frame. Its full name is *Receiver Ready*, and its mnemonic is *RR*.

Box 11.5 illustrates the frame format for S-frames, showing the control field layout for a two-octet control field. Box 11.5 also lists the names, mnemonics, and functions of the three most commonly implemented HDLC S-frame commands and responses.

The two bits provided for the function code allow for up to four different S-frame commands and four different S-frame responses. S-frames do not carry information fields. When bit position 1 of the first control field octet is 1, bit position 2 further identifies the frame as being either an S-frame or a U-frame. A 10 in bit positions 1 and 2 identifies the frame as an S-frame. The remainder of the bits in the S-frame control octet are interpreted

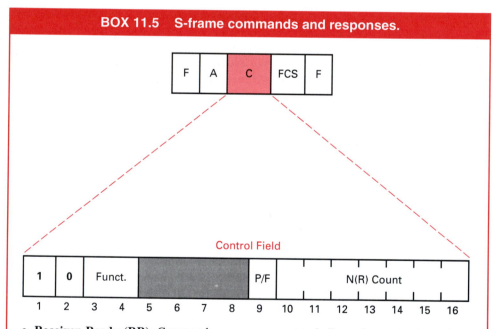

BOX 11.5   S-frame commands and responses.

- **Receiver Ready (RR).** Command or response sent to indicate the station is ready to receive another I-frame or to acknowledge previously received I-frames.

- **Receiver Not Ready (RNR).** Command or response sent to indicate the station is temporarily unable to accept additional I-frames.

- **Reject (REJ).** Command or response sent to request the retransmission of one or more I-frames.

as containing a two-bit function code, a receive count [N(R)], and a poll/final (P/F) bit. The function code bits identify the type of command or response the frame represents.

U-Frame Format

Box 11.6 illustrates the format of U-frames. It shows details for the control field and lists the most commonly used commands and responses.

U-frames always have one-octet control fields. Some U-frame commands and responses have information fields; others do not. An 11-bit configuration in bit positions 1 and 2 of the first control field octet identifies the frame as a U-frame. The remainder of the bits are interpreted as a poll/final bit and function code bits. The function code bits in a U-frame identify the type of command the frame represents. The five function code bits allow for up to 32 different commands and 32 different responses, only some of which are actually used in an implementation of HDLC.

We next describe some of the procedures defined by the ISO HDLC standard.

Bit Stuffing

An HDLC data link always operates in *transparent mode*, meaning that any desired bit configurations can be carried in the octets in a frame's Information field. A requirement for achieving transparency is to ensure that flag octets, which contain six consecutive 1 bits, are not transmitted in any part of the frame other than in the Beginning and Ending Flag field positions. If a flag field appeared anywhere else in the frame, stations would have no way of knowing where a frame begins and ends. If the protocol is to be transparent, however, frames must be capable of containing bit sequences of any desired bit configuration, including octets containing the flag configuration (0111 1110). A technique called *bit stuffing* handles this apparent contradiction.

In transmitting the data between a beginning and an ending flag, the transmitting station inserts an extra 0 bit into the data stream each time it detects a sequence of five 1 bits. The transmitter turns off the bit-stuffing mechanism when it transmits an actual beginning or ending flag. In this way, no consecutive sequence of six 1 bits is ever transmitted except when an actual flag is sent over the link. A complementary technique is used by the receiver in removing the extra 0 bits. Whenever the receiver detects five 1 bits followed by a 0 bit, it discards the 0 bit, thus restoring the bit stream to its original value. The bit stuffing technique ensures that six 1 bits in a row will never occur except in a flag field. When the receiver detects six consecutive 1 bits, it knows it has received a genuine flag field.

Error Detection

The Frame Check Sequence (FCS) field in an HDLC frame carries a cyclical redundancy check (CRC) value for detecting transmission errors. A CRC calculation is performed for each frame by the sender based on the contents of the frame. The result of the calculation is placed in the frame's FCS field. A complementary CRC calculation is then performed for each frame by the receiver. If the receiver's CRC calculation results in a different value

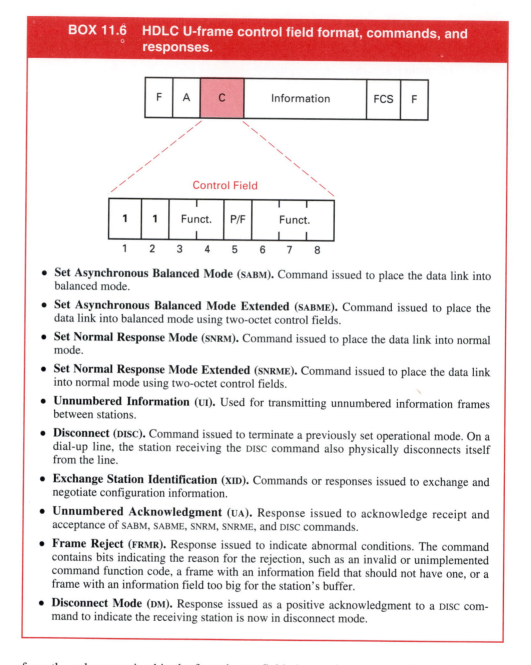

BOX 11.6 HDLC U-frame control field format, commands, and responses.

Control Field

- **Set Asynchronous Balanced Mode (SABM).** Command issued to place the data link into balanced mode.

- **Set Asynchronous Balanced Mode Extended (SABME).** Command issued to place the data link into balanced mode using two-octet control fields.

- **Set Normal Response Mode (SNRM).** Command issued to place the data link into normal mode.

- **Set Normal Response Mode Extended (SNRME).** Command issued to place the data link into normal mode using two-octet control fields.

- **Unnumbered Information (UI).** Used for transmitting unnumbered information frames between stations.

- **Disconnect (DISC).** Command issued to terminate a previously set operational mode. On a dial-up line, the station receiving the DISC command also physically disconnects itself from the line.

- **Exchange Station Identification (XID).** Commands or responses issued to exchange and negotiate configuration information.

- **Unnumbered Acknowledgment (UA).** Response issued to acknowledge receipt and acceptance of SABM, SABME, SNRM, SNRME, and DISC commands.

- **Frame Reject (FRMR).** Response issued to indicate abnormal conditions. The command contains bits indicating the reason for the rejection, such as an invalid or unimplemented command function code, a frame with an information field that should not have one, or a frame with an information field too big for the station's buffer.

- **Disconnect Mode (DM).** Response issued as a positive acknowledgment to a DISC command to indicate the receiving station is now in disconnect mode.

from the value contained in the frame's FCS field, the receiver assumes that the frame has been corrupted and discards it. The pipelining and acknowledgment mechanisms described next then cause any missing frames to be retransmitted.

Acknowledgment and Pipelining

HDLC includes an *acknowledgment* mechanism to detect lost frames and to cause them to be retransmitted. To achieve this, *each set* of one or more transmitted frames requires acknowledgment from the receiving station indicating whether frames were received correctly. A technique called *pipelining* is used in which multiple I-frames can be sent before the sending station requires an acknowledgment. As discussed earlier, with two-octet control fields, up to 127 I-frames can be transmitted between acknowledgments.

To ensure that no frames are lost and that all frames are properly acknowledged, the sequence numbers contained in I-frames and S-frames are employed to control I-frame transmission. All stations maintain counters that keep track of a *send count* value and a *receive count* value. These two counters are used to set the count fields in the control octets of the I-frames and S-frames the station transmits. The transmitter always keeps track of how many I-frames it has sent, and the receiver keeps track of how many I-frames it has received. When a station receives an acknowledgment, that acknowledgment contains the sequence number of the next I-frame the other station expects to receive. This implicitly acknowledges all I-frames up to, but not including, the frame having the specified sequence number. In this way a frame can acknowledge several previously transmitted I-frames. This process is illustrated in Box 11.7.

To ensure acknowledgments are received in a timely manner, the HDLC specification allows a limit to be set on the number of frames the Physical layer can queue up for transmission at any time. This allows the Physical layer to maintain continuous transmission while ensuring that an up-to-date acknowledgment can be sent with minimum delay.

Flow Control

HDLC defines a simple flow control procedure a station can use when it is temporarily unable to receive additional I-frames, possibly due to lack of buffers. A station indicates that the other station is to stop sending I-frames by transmitting a Receiver Not Ready (RNR) S-frame. This causes the opposite station to stop sending I-frames until it receives a Receiver Ready (RR) frame.

High-Level Protocol Identification

A limitation of HDLC in modern computer networks is that HDLC provides no mechanism to differentiate frames carrying data conforming to one Network layer protocol from frames associated with some other Network layer protocol. Therefore, HDLC is most useful in computer networks that conform to a single network architecture and carry traffic for a single high-level protocol suite.

Some types of networks have added compatible extensions to the HDLC standard in order to carry over an HDLC data link traffic conforming to multiple protocol suites. For example, DECnet Phase V networks use HDLC data links to carry ISO standard Network layer packets as well as Network layer packets conforming to other high-level protocol suites, such as DECnet Phase IV and TCP/IP.

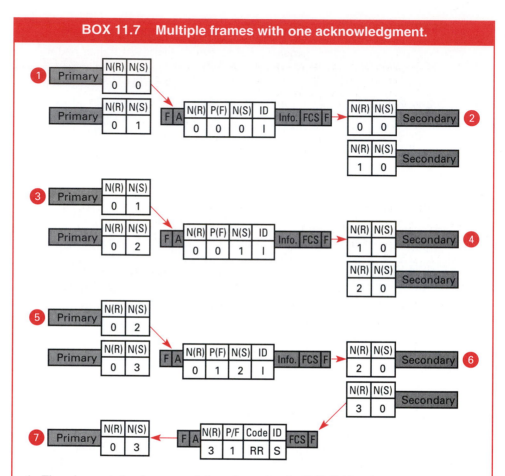

BOX 11.7 Multiple frames with one acknowledgment.

1. The primary station formats an I-frame by setting the N(S) field to the current value of its N(S) counter and setting the poll/final bit to 0. It then transmits frame 0 to the secondary station and updates its N(S) count.

2. The secondary station receives the I-frame and compares the N(S) field value to its N(R) count. Since they are both 0, frame sequencing is correct. Since the poll/final bit was set to 0, the secondary station simply updates its internal N(R) counter and waits for the next frame.

3. The primary station formats frame 1 and sends it, again with the poll/final bit set to 0, and updates its N(S) count.

4. The secondary station receives frame 1 and compares the N(S) field value with its internal N(R) counter value. Since they are now both 1, frame sequencing is again correct. The poll/final bit was set to 0, so the secondary station updates its N(R) counter and waits for the next frame.

5. The primary station formats frame 2, sends it, and updates its N(S) count. This time it sets the poll/final bit to 1, requesting a response from the secondary station.

BOX 11.7 *(Continued)*

---

6. The secondary station receives frame 2, verifies the N(S) field value, updates its N(R) counter, and examines the poll/final bit. Since the poll/final bit is set to 1, the secondary station sends an S-frame acknowledgment to the primary station.

7. The primary station receives the S-frame acknowledgment and compares the received S-frame N(R) field value with the value contained in its internal N(S) count. Since they both contain the value 3, the primary station assumes that frame sequencing is correct and that the three frames it sent were all successfully received by the secondary station.

DECnet defines an extension to the HDLC standard that adds a protocol multiplexing facility to HDLC. DECnet HDLC assigns a *protocol identifier* to each Network layer protocol that can use the services of an HDLC data link. DEC maintains a registry of valid protocol identifier values.

With HDLC, user data can be carried in I-frames by only one protocol at a time; thus only one user at a time can exchange I-frames over an HDLC data link. The identifier of the primary Network layer protocol, whose packets are to be carried by I-frames, is established using a DECnet-defined station initialization procedure.

DECnet HDLC then uses U-frames to carry data conforming to Network layer protocols other than the primary protocol. Each DECnet HDLC U-frame carries a protocol identifier field as well as user data. Therefore, DECnet HDLC can distinguish between HDLC users that employ different high-level protocol families based on the protocol identifier field values in U-frames.

Some other network architectures use similar protocol multiplexing schemes to allow HDLC to carry data conforming to multiple high-level protocol suites. However, with any of these schemes the HDLC protocol will generally be most efficient when carrying traffic associated with the primary Network layer protocol. Each U-frame must ordinarily be individually acknowledged. Therefore, frame transmission is less efficient for traffic carried in I-frames.

Because of the limitations of HDLC with respect to the implementation of multiple-protocol networks, many computer networks use other protocols for WAN data links, such as the *Point-to-Point* protocol (described later in this chapter).

IBM SYNCHRONOUS DATA LINK CONTROL (SDLC)

The HDLC protocol has its roots in the *Synchronous Data Link Control (SDLC)* protocol developed by IBM in the early 1970s for use in SNA. IBM's SDLC is a functional subset of HDLC and is compatible with the normal response mode (NRM) of HDLC for an unbalanced data link. An HDLC station operating in normal response mode can successfully communicate with a station conforming to IBM's SDLC specification.

At the time IBM developed SDLC, the predominant data link configuration consisted of a single primary station (typically a host computer or communications controller) connected to multiple secondary stations (typically terminals), using a multipoint, half-duplex physical circuit. SDLC requires one station to take the role of the primary station and the others to take the role of secondary stations. A management parameter must be set to designate one of the stations as the primary station.

SDLC Data Link Configurations

The SDLC protocol allows a primary station and one or more secondary stations to be connected in four different configurations. The following are brief descriptions of the configurations, which are illustrated in Fig. 11.2 .

- **Point-to-Point.** A single primary station is connected by a point-to-point link to a single secondary station. Each station in this configuration can send information to the other.
- **Multipoint.** A single primary station is connected to two or more secondary stations. The primary station can send information addressed to one or more of the secondary stations. A secondary station can send information only to the primary station; one secondary station cannot send information to one of the other secondary stations.
- **Loop.** The primary station is directly connected only to the first and last secondary stations on the loop. The primary station passes information to the first secondary station, it in turn passes it to the next secondary station, and so on, until the information arrives back at the primary station. Like the multipoint configuration, the primary station can send information to one or more of the secondary stations; a secondary station can send information only to the primary station. (Loop operation is not defined by HDLC.)
- **Hub Go-Ahead.** In this little-used configuration used by some older specialized equipment, two channels are used: an *inbound* channel and an *outbound* channel. The primary station communicates with any and all of the secondary stations via the outbound channel. A secondary station can communicate only with the primary station via the inbound channel; the inbound channel is daisy-chained from one secondary station to the next. (The hub go-ahead configuration is not defined by HDLC.)

Most modern SDLC equipment operates over point-to-point or multipoint data links. The SDLC loop or hub go-ahead configurations are little used today.

SDLC Frame Format and Protocol Operation

SDLC uses the same frame format as is defined by HDLC and uses a 16-bit CRC field. Like HDLC, SDLC supports the use of either one- or two-octet control fields. SDLC uses I-frames, S-frames and U-frames, and uses the same connection establishment and release, bit stuffing, pipelining, and flow control procedures defined by HDLC.

Since SDLC is designed for use on an unbalanced data link, it uses the poll/final bit for polling as well as for requesting acknowledgments. With RR-polling, the primary station sends a Receiver Ready (RR) S-frame with the poll/final bit on to each secondary station, asking if it has data to send. If the secondary station does not have data to send, it replies with a negative acknowledgment; if it has data to send, it sends the data in an I-frame.

SDLC uses the same types of I-frames and S-frames defined by HDLC. The U-frames defined by SDLC are listed in Box 11.8.

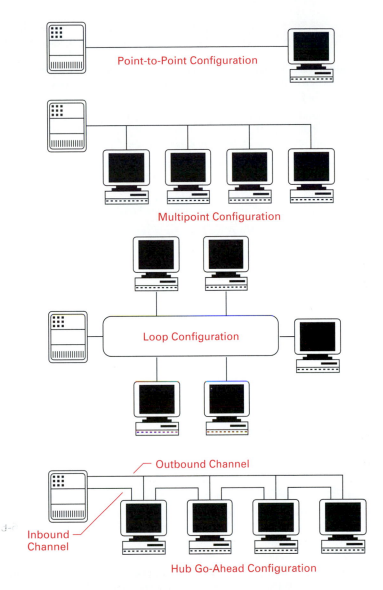

Figure 11.2   SDLC data link configurations.

SDLC Operating Modes

SDLC uses U-frames to initially set the operating mode of a secondary station. The following are brief descriptions of secondary station operating modes:

- **Initialization Mode.** The primary station places a secondary station into Initialization Mode when it is necessary to perform some hardware-specific initialization procedure, such as downloading program code to the secondary station after powering up.

BOX 11.8   SDLC U-frame commands and responses.

- **Unnumbered Information (UI).** A UI U-frame is used as a command or a response as a vehicle for transmitting unnumbered information frames between stations under certain circumstances.

- **Set Normal Response Mode (SNRM).** An SNRM U-frame is sent from the primary station to a secondary station to place the secondary station into the normal SDLC operating mode. Operating modes are discussed in a later section.

- **Request Disconnect (RD).** An RD U-frame is sent from a secondary station to the primary station to request that the secondary station be disconnected.

- **Disconnect (DISC).** A DISC U-frame is sent from the primary station to a secondary station to place the secondary station in disconnected mode.

- **Disconnect Mode (DM).** A DM U-frame is sent from the secondary station to the primary station as a positive acknowledgment to a DISC command to indicate the secondary station is now in Disconnect Mode.

- **Request Initialization Mode (RIM).** A RIM U-frame is sent to the secondary station from the primary station to request initialization. A typical Initialization procedure may consist of the downloading of a program from the primary station to the secondary station.

- **Set Initialization Mode (SIM).** A SIM U-frame command is sent from the primary station to the secondary station to begin initialization procedures.

- **Unnumbered Acknowledgment (UA).** A UA U-frame is sent from a secondary station to the primary station as a positive acknowledgment to an SNRM, DISC, or SIM command.

- **Frame Reject (FRMR).** Normal flows use the REJ and RR S-frames to indicate problems with frame sequencing and CRC errors. The FRMR command and response are used to indicate abnormal conditions. The command contains bits that indicate the reason for the rejection, such as an invalid or unimplemented command function code, a frame with an information field that should not have one, or a frame with an information field too big for the station's buffer.

- **Test (TEST).** TEST U-frames are exchanged as commands and responses in performing diagnostic procedures.

- **Exchange Station Identification (XID).** XID U-frames are sent as commands and responses in exchanging identification sequences between primary and secondary stations. XID U-frames are most often used on switched lines to identify secondary stations requesting connection to the data link.

- **Unnumbered Poll (UP).** A UP U-frame is a poll command sent by the primary station to any or all secondary stations on a loop. Loop operations are described in a later section.

- **Configure (CFGR).** The Configure U-frame is used as both commands and responses to perform loop diagnostic functions. A number of Configure subcommands are defined to define loop test functions.

- **Beacon (BCN).** A secondary station on a loop begins transmitting a sequence of Beacon U-frame responses when it detects loss of signal at its input. This allows the primary station to locate the source of the problem on the loop.

- **Normal Disconnected Mode.** A secondary station is in Normal Disconnected Mode when it is logically and/or physically removed from the data link. A secondary station assumes Normal Disconnected Mode at the following times:
  - — When the station is first powered on or is first enabled for data link operation.
  - — Following certain types of failures, such as when a power failure occurs.
  - — When a secondary station is first connected to the primary station on a switched line.
  - — After a secondary station receives a Disconnect (DISC) command from the primary station.
- **Normal Response Mode.** A primary station places a secondary station into Normal Response Mode. This is typically done immediately after a secondary station has been powered up or attached to a switched data link. When a secondary station is operating in Normal Response Mode, the secondary station transmits data only after receiving a poll from the primary station. A poll consists of a frame from the primary station that has the poll/final bit set to 1.

POINT-TO-POINT PROTOCOL (PPP)

The Point-to-Point protocol is an adaptation of HDLC that grew out of work done by the Internet Engineering Task Force (IETF). The Point-to-Point protocol improves on HDLC by adding a Network layer protocol identification mechanism useful for the efficient implementation of multiple-protocol networks. The Point-to-Point protocol allows a point-to-point connection to be established between two network devices and allows frames associated with multiple Network layer protocols to efficiently flow over the data link without interfering with one another.

Frame Format

The Point-to-Point protocol frame format is based on the generic HDLC transmission frame and is generally conformant with it. Box 11.9 shows the format of the Point-to-Point protocol transmission frame and describes its fields.

Station Identification

On a data link that uses the Point-to-Point protocol, no station identification function is necessary. Each Point-to-Point protocol frame contains an Address field for compatibility with the HDLC standard, but the Address field's value is always hex 'FF'. Each frame sent has only one possible destination: the station at the other end of the data link.

Network Layer Protocol Identification

The Network layer protocol identification function is provided by the Protocol field that has been added to the HDLC frame between the Control field and the Information field. The documentation of the Point-to-Point protocol lists the identifier values to be used for each Network layer protocol supported by the standard. Although the Point-to-Point pro-

---

BOX 11.9   Point-to-Point protocol frame.

Flag	Address (X'FF')	Control (X'03')	Protocol	Information	))	Frame Check Sequence	Flag
1 octet	1 octet	1 octet	2 octets	0 – *n* octets		2 octets	1 octet

- **Beginning Flag.** Consists of a single octet containing the unique bit configuration 0111 1110 and identifies the beginning of the field.

- **Address.** Contains the value hex 'FF'.

- **Control Field.** Contains the value hex '03'.

- **Protocol Field.** Identifies the Network layer protocol with which the packet in the Information field is associated.

- **Information.** Carries the user data portion of the frame.

- **Frame Check Sequence.** Contains a 16-bit cyclic redundancy check (CRC) value used for error detection.

- **Ending Flag.** Contains the same bit configuration as the Beginning Flag field (0111 1110) and identifies the end of the frame.

---

tocol was designed primarily for use in TCP/IP internets, protocol identifiers have been assigned to the Network layer protocols supporting the major protocol families in use today.

SUMMARY

WAN data links typically provide point-to-point connections between pairs of systems located some distance from one another. Two types of analog telecommunications facilities offered by common carriers are dial-up circuits and leased-line circuits. Telecommunications common carriers also provide digital circuits optimized for data transmission.

The world of electronic communication currently has three information infrastructures: the telephone network for voice communication, the cable television and broadcasting systems for video, and packet-switching technologies for computer networking. There is some overlap among them, and they may merge at some point in the future. The facilities used for computer communication have evolved from circuit-switching techniques to packet-switching techniques and are now moving toward a very fast type of switching that combines some of the characteristics of both circuit switching and packet switching.

To allow a common carrier telecommunications facility to be used for data transmission, a data link protocol operates in the Data Link layer. Among the data link protocols used when transmitting data over ordinary telephone facilities are High Level Data Link Control (HDLC), Synchronous Data Link Control (SDLC), and the Point-to-Point Protocol (PPP).

HDLC is an international standard data link protocol defined by ISO. HDLC supports unbalanced data links connecting two or more stations and balanced data links connecting a pair of stations. Data units carried over an HDLC link are called frames and are of three types: Information frames (I-frames), Supervisory frames (S-frames), and Unnumbered frames (U-frames). Among the procedures defined by HDLC to control frame transmission are bit stuffing, error detection, acknowledgment, pipelining, and flow control. Some implementations of HDLC also include a simple protocol identification function.

The HDLC protocol has its roots in the Synchronous Data Link Control (SDLC) protocol developed by IBM and used today in SNA. An HDLC station operating in normal response mode can successfully communicate with a station conforming to IBM's SDLC specification.

The Point-to-Point Protocol (PPP) is an adaptation of HDLC that adds an efficient Network layer protocol identification mechanism useful in multiple-protocol networks. The Point-to-Point protocol frame format is based on the HDLC transmission frame and includes a Protocol Identification field carried between the Control field and the Information field.

Chapter 12 examines the characteristics of data link subnetworks that employ X.25 packet-switching techniques for data transmission.

Chapter **12**

X.25 Subnetworks

One alternative to using conventional common carrier telecommunications circuits as a WAN data link is to use the virtual circuits provided by a public *packet-switched data network (PSDN)*. Many of today's public data networks, especially outside the United States, use packet-switching techniques and conform to ITU-T *Recommendation X.25*. Recommendation X.25 defines a standard way for attaching a computer or other intelligent device to a PSDN.

X.25 PSDNs are generally operated by a common carrier or some other private telecommunications service provider. To use an X.25 service, an organization generally contracts with a PSDN service provider to implement one or more point-to-point connections between the organization's computers. Each computer has a single point of connection into the PSDN but can make logical point-to-point connections with any number of other user machines.

PACKET SWITCHING

In a PSDN, users are provided with *virtual circuits* that appear to the end user to be identical to ordinary telecommunications connection. A virtual circuit behaves the same as a direct connection between the source and destination systems (see Fig. 12.1).

With a PSDN, a virtual circuit is generally provided by the PSDN using a technique called *packet switching*. Each packet a user generates enters the PSDN and travels from node to node within the PSDN until it reaches its destination. Each PSDN node determines the next node to which the packet should be transmitted, based on its destination address and other traffic on the network. A routing algorithm is generally used to handle the exchange of packets within the PSDN , but the specific routing algorithm used by the packet switches is not specified in the X.25 standard.

Multiple virtual circuits can be multiplexed on a single physical connection by interspersing packets. Allocation of transmission capacity is generally determined at the time each packet arrives at a node, which means that a PSDN generally provides band-

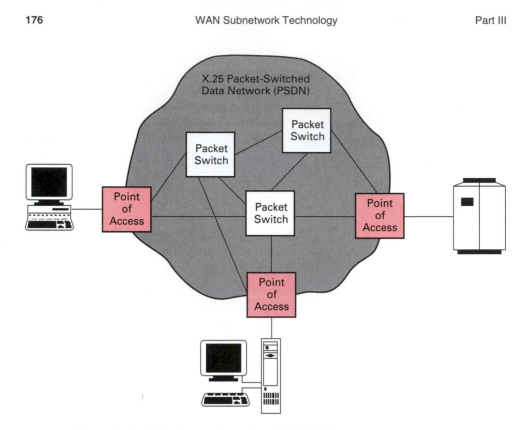

Figure 12.1   Using the services of an X.25 PSDN to interconnect computer systems.

width on demand. This is different from a typical circuit-switching network in which a fixed allocation of some portion of the transmission bandwidth is assigned to each circuit.

X.25 PSDN ARCHITECTURE

Figure 12.2 illustrates the basic architecture used for a PSDN that conforms to Recommendation X.25. A system that uses PSDN services accesses them using a *data terminal equipment (DTE)* function. The PSDN device to which the DTE connects implements a complementary *data circuit-terminating equipment (DCE)* function. Recommendation X.25 defines the interface between the DTE and DCE functions.

When the user has data to send, the user's DTE sends a packet to its DCE. That packet is then routed across the PSDN to a DCE associated with the destination system. The destination DCE then passes the packet to the DTE in the destination system.

As packets travel through the PSDN, they may be stored in queues maintained by the packet switches along their route and may wait for transmission capacity to become available. Also, different packets sent over the same virtual circuit may end up taking different routes through the PSDN. This can result in variable delays in the rate at which

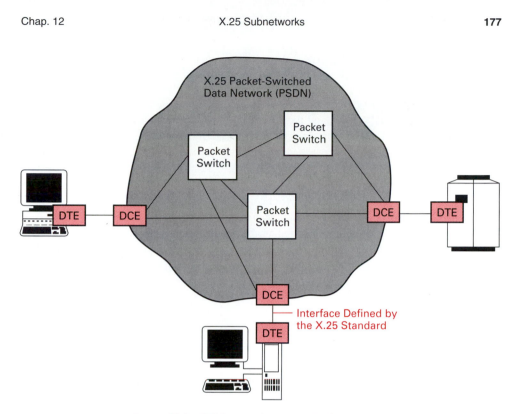

Figure 12.2   X.25 network physical implementation.

packets are delivered and possible out-of-sequence packets. The destination DTE must implement a function that places the packets back into their proper sequence. This function is often called a *packet assembly/disassembly (PAD)* function.

X.25 VIRTUAL CIRCUITS

A PSDN conforming to X.25 typically offers to its users two major types of virtual circuits: *permanent virtual circuits (PVCs)* and *switched virtual circuits (SVCs)*. A switched virtual circuit is sometimes referred to as a *virtual call (VC)*.

Permanent Virtual Circuits

A user of a PSDN may wish to be permanently connected with another network user in much the same way as two users are connected using a leased telephone connection. A permanent virtual circuit provides this facility. The users are permanently connected to their respective X.25 DCEs. They use the communications facilities of the network and consume network resources only when they are actually transmitting data; however, they remain logically connected permanently as though an actual physical circuit always exists between them. Typically, the users of a permanent virtual circuit pay a monthly connect charge plus possibly a charge based on total data transmitted over the virtual circuit.

Switched Virtual Circuits

When an X.25 DTE requests the establishment of a switched virtual circuit, the network establishes a virtual circuit with another user, the two DTEs exchange messages for a time over the virtual circuit, and then one of the two DTEs requests disconnection of the virtual circuit. A DTE requests an SVC by sending a control packet, called a Call Request packet, to the DCE. When the DCE receives the Call Request packet from a DTE, it sends another control packet, called an Incoming Call packet, across the network to the destination DTE. If the destination DTE accepts the call, the two DTEs can then begin exchanging data packets with each other over the switched virtual circuit. The various types of control packets defined by X.25 are described later in this chapter.

Users employing switched virtual circuits are generally charged based on connect time, quantity of data transmitted, or both. In requesting a switched virtual circuit, the user typically perceives no difference between using a PSDN and using ordinary dial-up telephone facilities. All the complexities of routing through a packet-switched data network are hidden from the two communicating DTEs.

THE X.25 INTERFACE

As we have already described, ITU-T Recommendation X.25 defines the *interface* between an X.25 DTE and an X.25 DCE. It is important to note that X.25 defines only this interface—the way a computer plugs into the network and exchanges packets with it—and does not specify how the network is implemented internally. Recommendation X.25 contains specifications for the interface between a DTE and a DCE at three levels (see Fig. 12.3):

- **X.25 Level 1.** This is the interface defining the characteristics of the physical link between a DTE and a DCE. This part of Recommendation X.25 corresponds to the Physical layer of the OSI model. X.25 defines Level 1 through reference to other standards, such as X.21, X.21bis, and the V series of modem standards.

- **X.25 Level 2.** This is the interface defining the protocol used to reliably pass frames of data between a DTE and a DCE. It corresponds to the Data Link layer of the OSI model and is defined by the *Link Access Protocol—Balanced (LAPB)* data link protocol. LAPB is a functional subset of ISO's HDLC data link protocol and is described later in this chapter.

- **X.25 Level 3.** This is the interface defining the format and meaning of the data portion of the frames defined in Level 2 and is often called the *X.25 packet level*. It corresponds to part of the Network layer of the OSI model and specifies the procedures by which X.25 packets are passed between a DTE and a DCE. This same interface is defined in ISO 8208 — *Packet-Level Protocol for Data Terminal Equipment.* X.25 Level 3 and ISO 8208 are essentially identical.

As we discussed earlier, a PSDN might be constructed using a great many DCEs and a number of packet switches, to construct networks having a mesh topology. However, an X.25 DTE connected to an X.25 DCE perceives any other DTE on the network as being only one hop away. In this respect, a PSDN can be viewed as a data link subnetwork in the same manner as a conventional telecommunications data link, such as an HDLC point-to-point data link.

A PSDN implementing the X.25 interface is often represented in network diagrams as a cloud. The complexities of the PSDN implementation are hidden from the user, and an

Recommendation X.25	OSI Model

	Application
	Presentation
	Session
	Transport
	Subnetwork Independent
X.25 Level 3	Subnetwork Dependent	Network
X.25 Level 2	Data Link
X.25 Level 1	Physical

Figure 12.3 ITU Recommendation X.25 comparison with the OSI model.

X.25 DTE at one end of the network perceives only a point-to-point *virtual circuit* between itself and an X.25 DTE at the other end (see Fig. 12.4).

Location of the X.25 Interface

The X.25 interface exists at the connection between the computer that implements the X.25 DTE and the network device that implements the X.25 DCE. This connection can be implemented in various ways. If the network DCE is located on the premises of a user's computer, the X.25 interface is implemented as shown in Fig. 12.5. If the user machine is

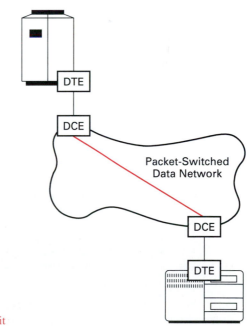

Packet-Switched
Data Network

Figure 12.4 X.25 virtual circuit

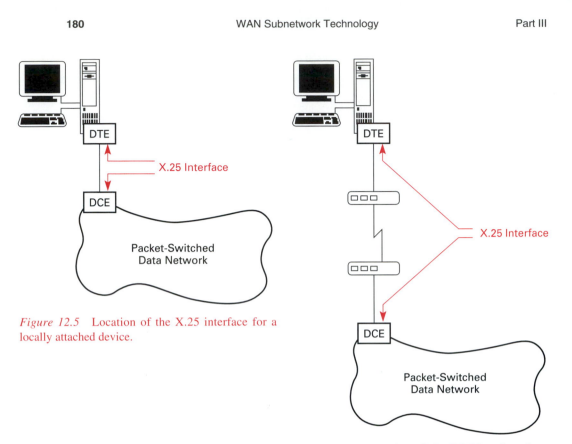

Figure 12.5 Location of the X.25 interface for a
locally attached device.

Figure 12.6 Location of the X.25 interface for a
remotely attached device.

located remote from the network DCE, the X.25 interface can be implemented using a pair
of modems and a telecommunications facility, as shown in Fig. 12.6.

PAD-Related ITU-T Recommendations

An X.25 DTE is normally implemented in a network interface card (NIC) that is designed
to be attached to an X.25 PSDN. It is possible however, to attach simple terminals to a
PSDN that do not themselves implement the X.25 DTE function. This is done through a
specialized device that implements the X.25 packet assembly and disassembly (PAD)
function. When a PAD facility is used, the X.25 interface resides as shown in Fig. 12.7.

The use of a PAD facility in conjunction with a PSDN is described by three additional
ITU recommendations. These are illustrated in Fig. 12.8 and are described below:

- **Recommendation X.3.** This ITU-T recommendation describes the functions performed by
  the PAD facility and defines the various parameters that can be used to specify its mode of
  operation.
- **Recommendation X.28.** This ITU-T recommendation describes the interface between a
  non-packet mode device and the device that implements the PAD function. X.28 describes
  the way an asynchronous terminal connects to and controls the PAD facility.

- **Recommendation X.29.** This ITU-T recommendation describes the interface between the device that implements the X.3 PAD function and a machine that implements the X.25 DTE function. X.29 describes the way in which the X.3 PAD facility communicates with an X.25 device, such as a computing system.

X.25 PACKETS

The X.25 DTE/DCE packet-level interface consists of definitions of the formats of packets passed between a DTE and a DCE. Packets contain both user data and control packets used to control the operation of the X.25 protocol.

X.25 Data Packet

Box 12.1 describes the format used for X.25 data packets. The control information in each packet is used by the packet switches in the PSDN to determine how to relay the packet through the network.

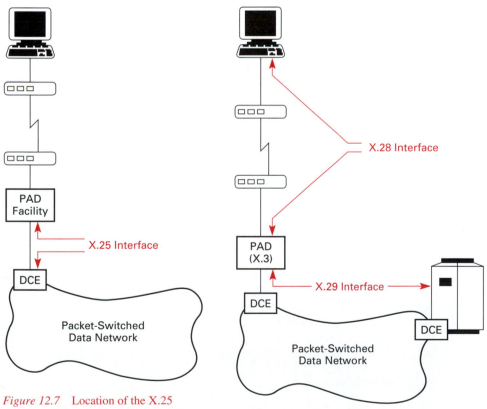

Figure 12.7   Location of the X.25 interface when a PAD facility is used.

Figure 12.8   ITU PAD-related recommendations.

BOX 12.1   X.25 Data packet format.

Octet 0	Q	D	0	1	Logical Channel Group Number (LCGN)

(diagram of X.25 Data packet format)

- **Q (Qualified Data).** Distinguishes between user data and device control data.
- **D.** Indicates whether flow control and acknowledgments have local or end-to-end significance.
- **Logical Channel Group Number (LCGN).** Combined with the logical channel number, provides the virtual circuit identifier.
- **Logical Channel Number (LCN).** Combined with the logical channel group number, provides the virtual circuit identifier.
- **Receive Sequence Number [P(R)].** Indicates the sequence number of the next packet expected to be received.
- **M (More Data).** Chains a series of packets together as one message.
- **Send Sequence Number [P(S)].** Indicates the sequence number of the current packet.

Each computer attached to an X.25 PSDN is assigned a network address used to identify the computer in the network when a connection, or virtual circuit, is being established. When a virtual circuit is established between two DTEs, a *virtual circuit identifier (VCI)* is assigned to each DTE to identify that connection. The virtual circuit identifier consists of a *logical channel group number (LCGN)* and a *logical channel number (LCN)*. For a particular connection, each DTE has its own VCI value that it uses locally. The PSDN maps between VCI values when a packet is transmitted from the source DTE to the destination DTE.

X.25 Control Packets

The PSDN uses X.25 control packets to handle such functions as connection establishment, management, connection termination, flow control, and diagnostic and restart functions.

BOX 12.2   X.25 control packets.

- **Call Request.** A DTE sends a Call Request packet to request the establishment of a switched virtual circuit.

- **Incoming Call.** A DCE accepts the Call Request packet and generates an Incoming Call packet, which it sends to the destination DTE. This asks the destination DTE if it can accept the request for the establishment of a switched virtual circuit.

- **Call Accepted.** The destination DTE transmits a Call Accepted packet as a positive response to an Incoming Call packet.

- **Call Connected.** The originating DTE accepts the Call Accepted packet and transmits a Call Connected packet as the final step in establishing a switched virtual circuit.

- **Clear Indication.** A Clear Indication packet is transmitted when a destination DTE is not able to accept an Incoming Call packet. It gives the reason for refusing to accept the call.

- **Clear Request.** A Clear Request packet is transmitted when a DTE wants to request the release of a switched virtual circuit.

- **Clear Confirmation.** A DTE transmits a Clear Confirmation packet as a positive acknowledgment to a Clear Request packet as the final step in releasing a switched virtual circuit.

The format of a control packet is similar to that of a data packet; the exact format varies with the control packet type. Box 12.2 contains brief descriptions of commonly used control packets defined by X.25.

X.25 FACILITIES

In addition to the switched virtual circuits and permanent virtual circuits used to transmit data across a PSDN, Recommendation X.25 provides a number of additional facilities to PSDN users. The following sections describe some of these facilities.

Logical Channels

A given DTE is allowed to concurrently establish up to 4095 different *logical channels* to other DTEs attached to the network by assigning a different 12-bit *virtual circuit number* to each. (Specific implementations may limit a DTE to fewer than 4095 logical channels.) For example, a DTE might be implemented in a computing system that supports many users (both people and programs), many of whom may need to use the PSDN for communication at any given time.

A virtual circuit number consists of a 4-bit *logical channel group* and an 8-bit *logical channel number*. Each user would be assigned a separate logical channel with its own virtual circuit number. Virtual circuit numbers are assigned to both permanent virtual circuits and to switched virtual circuits. Logical channel number 0 in group 0 is not a valid virtual circuit number; this value is reserved. Each message that a DTE transmits on behalf of a user contains the virtual circuit number to which the message is associated to distinguish it from message traffic generated by other users.

Flow Control

An X.25 PSDN implements flow control mechanisms to control the rate at which it accepts packets from each DTE. Flow control is implemented independently in each direction on a logical channel through the use of a windowing mechanism. The window size represents the maximum number of sequentially numbered data packets that may be outstanding at any given time.

Interrupt Packets

A DTE can use Interrupt packets to send data that bypasses the normal packet sequence. Interrupt packets can be delivered even when the destination DTE is not accepting normal data packets. A DTE sending Interrupt packets receives an Interrupt Confirmation packet for every interrupt packet it sends. A DTE must wait until it receives a confirmation before sending the next Interrupt packet.

Reset Packets

A DTE or the PSDN itself can send a Reset packet across the DTE/DCE interface to reinitialize a virtual circuit. A reset causes all Data and Interrupt packets in transit to be discarded.

Call Clearing

A DTE receives an Incoming Call packet from its DCE when some other DTE is requesting that a switched virtual circuit be established with it. When a DTE receives an Incoming Call packet, it has the option of accepting or rejecting the request. A DTE rejects a request for a virtual circuit by sending a Clear Request packet. Either of the DTEs connected by an SVC can release the SVC by issuing a Clear Request packet. The DCE responds by sending a Clear Indication packet to the opposite DTE. That DTE then responds by sending a Clear Confirmation to its DCE. That DCE then sends a Clear Confirmation packet to the DTE originally requesting release of the SVC.

Restart Facility

Either a DTE or a DCE can issue a Restart Indication packet to clear all virtual circuits at the DTE/DCE interface. A DTE sends a Restart Indication packet to the DCE as part of its initialization procedure.

Closed User Groups

This is an optional facility of X.25 allowing network managers to form logical groups of X.25 DTEs. If a user requests the use of a closed user group, and the destination DTE is in it, the destination DTE is informed that the user requested the closed user group. This provides a method for determining if the caller is your "friend" without the destination DTE needing to manage a list of DTE addresses.

Call Redirection

This is an optional facility of X.25 allowing an incoming request for a virtual circuit to be redirected to some other DTE. Capabilities of this facility include specifying a list of alternative DTEs to try and specifying a logical chain of DTEs for continued redirection.

Network User Identification

This is an optional facility of X.25 allowing a DTE to provide information to the PSDN, on a per-call basis, for such purposes as security, network management, or billing.

Call Charging

This is an optional facility of X.25 that includes mechanisms for determining who is charged for a virtual circuit and for providing information for calculating charges.

LINK ACCESS PROTOCOL—BALANCED

At the level of the OSI model Data Link layer, X.25 uses the LAPB protocol for frames flowing between the DTE and DCE. LAPB is a functional subset of HDLC and uses the asynchronous balanced mode (ABM) defined by HDLC (see Chapter 11). The LAPB frame uses a 16-bit CRC value and can use either one- or two-octet control fields. The address field is used to identify a frame as a command or a response. LAPB uses I-frames, S-frames, and U-frames in the same way as in HDLC. The U-frames used in LAPB to support the asynchronous balanced mode of HDLC operation are listed in Box 12.3.

BOX 12.3   Link Access Protocol—Balanced (LAPB) U-frame commands and responses.

- **Set Asynchronous Balanced Mode (SABM).** Command issued to place the data link into balanced mode.
- **Set Asynchronous Balanced Mode Extended (SABME).** Command issued to place the data link into balanced mode using two-octet control fields.
- **Disconnect (DISC).** Command issued to terminate a previously set operational mode. On a dial-up line, the station receiving the DISC command also physically disconnects itself from the line.
- **Unnumbered Acknowledgment (UA).** Response issued to acknowledge receipt and acceptance of SABM, SABME, and DISC commands.
- **Frame Reject (FRMR).** Response issued to indicate abnormal conditions. The command contains bits indicating the reason for the rejection, such as an invalid or unimplemented command function code, a frame with an information field that should not have one, or a frame with an information field too big for the station's buffer.
- **Disconnect Mode (DM).** Response issued as a positive acknowledgment to a DISC command to indicate the receiving station is now in disconnect mode.

LAPB Sequence Checking

LAPB uses sequence numbers and acknowledgments to perform error detection and correction and flow control. With X.25, error detection and correction can be performed at both the frame level and the packet level for the flow between the DTE and DCE.

SUMMARY

Many of today's public data networks use packet-switching techniques and conform to ITU-T Recommendation X.25. With packet switching, each packet travels from node to node within the network until it reaches its destination. X.25 defines a standard way for attaching a computer to a packet-switched data network (PSDN) and defines both permanent virtual circuits (PVCs) and switched virtual circuits (SVCs).

A system that uses PSDN services accesses them using a data terminal equipment (DTE) function. The device to which the DTE connects implements a complementary data circuit-terminating equipment (DCE) function. Recommendation X.25 defines the interface between the DTE and DCE functions. The destination DTE must implement a packet assembly/disassembly (PAD) function to place received packets into their proper sequence.

X.25 contains specifications at three levels for the interface between a DTE and a DCE. X.25 Level 1 defines the characteristics of a physical link and corresponds to the Physical layer of the OSI model. X.25 Level 2 defines the protocol used to reliably pass frames of data between a DTE and a DCE and corresponds to the OSI model Data Link layer. X.25 Level 3, the packet level, defines the format and meaning of the data portion of Level-2 frames and corresponds to part of the OSI model Network layer. The data link protocol used in an X.25 network is Link Access Protocol—Balanced (LAPB), a subset of ISO HDLC.

Facilities provided by an X.25 network in addition to virtual circuits might include logical channels, flow control, interrupt packets, reset packets, call clearing, restart facilities, closed user groups, call redirection, user identification, and call charging.

Chapter 13 describes Integrated Services Digital Network (ISDN) technology that telecommunications service providers are beginning to implement to provide digital communication links to end users.

Chapter **13**

ISDN Subnetworks

This chapter and the two chapters that follow describe three related digital telecommunications technologies particularly useful in constructing computer networks. This chapter describes the Integrated Services Digital Network (ISDN) technology; Chapter 14 covers Frame Relay technology, and Chapter 15 discusses Asynchronous Transfer Mode.

An *Integrated Services Digital Network (ISDN)* is a public telecommunications network—typically administered by a telecommunications provider—that supplies digital end-to-end communications services that can be used for any purpose, including the transmission of voice, data, graphics, image, and facsimile information.

ISDN SERVICES

ISDN defines three general types of services:

- **Bearer Services.** Bearer services provide for the basic transfer of information between users. ISDN standards define both packet-mode services and circuit-mode services. Packet-mode ISDN services offer services similar to those provided by an X.25 PSDN (see Chapter 12). Circuit-mode services can be used as replacements for conventional telephone circuits.

- **Teleservices.** Teleservices provide both basic information transfer and higher-level functions. Examples of teleservices are facsimile, videotext, teletext, and telex services.

- **Supplementary Services.** Supplementary services are additional functions that can be used with bearer services or teleservices. Examples of these are call waiting, conference calling, and caller identification.

NARROWBAND AND BROADBAND ISDN

The initial definition of ISDN, sometimes now called *narrowband ISDN (N-ISDN),* includes a broad range of services, with data rates ranging from 64 Kbps to 1.92 Mbps. A second version of ISDN, still in the process of being defined at the time of writing, addresses the need for higher data rates, in the range of hundreds of megabits per second. This version is referred to as *broadband ISDN (B-ISDN).*

NARROWBAND ISDN

The specific service offerings provided by N-ISDN technology are based on the use of 64-Kbps channels packaged into two different interfaces:

- **Basic Rate Interface (BRI).** This interface defines a bit rate of 144 Kbps, which is divided into two 64-Kbps bearer (B) channels for data transfer and one 16-Kbps data link (D) channel for signaling.
- **Primary Rate Interface (PRI).** The primary rate interface level of service consists of 23 64-Kbps B channels for data transfer and one 64-Kbps D channel for signaling, providing a bit rate to the user of 1.544 Mbps.

ISDN standards define frame formats, signal encoding, and physical transmission characteristics for using each of these interfaces for communication between a user and an ISDN point of access.

B Channels

Bearer channels (B channels) are used for user data transfer. Three types of connections can be set up over a B channel:

- **Circuit-switched Connection.** With a circuit-switched connection, a user places a call and the connection is established. The user is provided with the channel's full bit rate as long as the connection remains in effect. When transmission is complete, the connection is released.
- **Packet-switched Connection.** A packet-switched connection connects a user to a packet-switching facility, which could be a separate PSDN or a facility integrated within the ISDN itself.
- **Semipermanent Connection.** A semipermanent connection is one that is established and remains available for a relatively long period of time (perhaps days, weeks, or months). A semipermanent connection is equivalent to a conventional leased line.

D Channels

A data link channel (D channel) is primarily used for control purposes, including the establishment, management, and termination of connections. A D channel can also sometimes be used for data transfer.

If a single user requires a higher data rate than 64 Kbps, this can be provided using a technique called *multirate ISDN*. With multirate ISDN, multiple B channels are synchronized, and their combined data rate is made available to the user as if it were a single channel. For example, the two 64-Kbps B channels defined by the Basic Rate Interface are sometimes combined to implement a single 128-Kbps data link.

The User/Network Interface

Figure 13.1 illustrates key protocols used to access N-ISDN services. The protocols used depend on the type of connection requested.

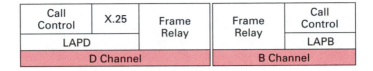

Figure 13.1   ISDN protocols for user access.

Semipermanent Connections

With a semipermanent connection, data transfer occurs on the B channel. Since there is no need to establish or terminate the connection during ordinary operation, the D channel is not used. ISDN standards do not specify a particular data link protocol to be used over a semipermanent connection. The choice of data link protocol is left to the user.

Circuit-Switched Connection

With a circuit-switched connection, the D channel is used to establish and manage the connection. The Call Control protocol defines the messages used to establish, control, and terminate a connection, or call. *Link Access Protocol-D (LAPD)* is used as the data link protocol on a D channel for a circuit-switched connection. LAPD is similar to Link Access Protocol-Balanced (LAPB) and is briefly described later in this chapter.

User data transfer over a circuit-switched connection occurs on a B channel. As with a semipermanent connection, the data link protocol to be used for user data transfer over the B channel of a circuit-switched connection is not specified by ISDN.

Packet-Switched Connection

A packet-switched connection can be established on either a B channel or a D channel. The user can employ either the X.25 protocols (described in Chapter 12), or the Frame Relay protocols (described in Chapter 14). When X.25 protocols are used on the B channel, LAPB is used as the data link protocol. When X.25 is used on the D channel, LAPD is used as the data link protocol.

LAPD Services

Link Access Protocol-D (LAPD) is a synchronous data link protocol based on ISO HDLC (see Chapter 11). LAPD offers two types of service:

- **Acknowledged Information Transfer.** Similar to the service provided by LAPB. This mode of data transfer uses Information frames (I-frames) and Supervisory frames (S-frames) to control transmission with sequence numbers and acknowledgments used for error detection and correction and for flow control.
- **Unacknowledged Information Transfer.** Uses Unnumbered frames (U-frames) and employs no acknowledgment, error correction, or flow control mechanisms.

The LAPD frame format, shown in Box 13.1, is generally consistent with the HDLC specification.

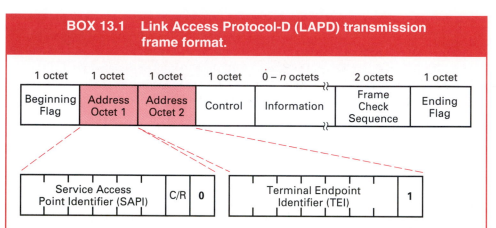

BOX 13.1   Link Access Protocol-D (LAPD) transmission frame format.

- **Beginning Flag Field.** Each frame begins with a *flag field,* which consists of a single octet containing the unique bit configuration 0111 1110. A *bit-stuffing* technique guarantees that only a flag field will contain six consecutive 1 bits.

- **Service Access Point Identifier (SAPI).** A six-bit service access point identifier value identifies a particular type of LAPD user within a system.

- **Command/Response (C/R).** The C/R bit identifies a frame as a command or a response.

- **Terminal Endpoint Identifier (TEI).** A seven-bit terminal end-point identifier value identifies a particular user system or device.

- **Control Field.** The control field determines the type of frame being transmitted, conveys information necessary for the proper sequencing of frames, and carries control information.

- **Information Field.** A variable-length information field is used to carry the data portion of the frame. It consists of either control information or user data passed down from the LAPD user.

- **Frame Check Sequence Field.** The Frame Check Sequence (FCS) field contains a 16-bit cyclic redundancy check (CRC) value used for error detection.

- **Ending Flag Field.** The end of a frame is marked by another flag field containing the same bit configuration as the beginning flag field (0111 1110).

Instead of a one-octet address field, LAPD uses two address octets for the SAPI and TEI values. Within a single system, LAPD can be used as part of some other data link function, such as call control, X.25 data transfer, frame relay data transfer, or management information transfer. Each function is identified using a different service access point (SAP) value. The SAPI value identifies the particular service access point through which LAPD is being accessed. A given service access point can be involved in multiple connections. A different TEI value is assigned to each connection using a particular service access point. When a connection is established, the user at each end of the connection will have SAPI and TEI values assigned that uniquely identify the connection. These values are used when data is sent across the connection.

For acknowledged operation, data is transferred in I-frames, and LAPD uses the same error detection, acknowledgment, pipelining, and data flow control procedures defined for HDLC. For unacknowledged operation, data is transferred in U-frames. When each frame is received, CRC-based error detection is performed and corrupted frames are discarded. Data in good frames is passed up to the user of the data transfer service. No acknowledgments or error notifications are returned to the service user.

ISDN USER INTERFACE

In order to make it easy to connect all manner of different devices to an ISDN line, a limited number of standardized connection points have been defined. Figure 13.2 shows the interface points the ISDN standards define. The boxes in the diagram represent the groupings of functions identified for the equipment used to connect to an ISDN line. These functional groupings are as follows:

- **Network Termination 1 (NT1).** The NT1 functional grouping is typically implemented in a device maintained by the common carrier. It is typically installed at the end of the local loop that provides ISDN service to an individual subscriber. The NT1 grouping performs functions associated with the Physical layer of the OSI model.

- **Network Termination 2 (NT2).** The NT2 functional grouping is typically implemented in a device owned by the ISDN subscriber. It allows a number of ISDN devices to be connected to a single ISDN connection. The NT2 grouping performs functions associated with the Physical, Data Link, and Network layers of the OSI model.

- **Network Termination 12 (NT12).** The NT12 functional grouping is typically used in regulatory environments different from that of the United States. The NT12 grouping combines the functions of NT1 and NT2. The NT12 functional grouping is used by some European telecommunications administrations, where more of the telecommunications equipment is under the control of the telecommunications administration rather than the individual subscriber.

- **Terminal Adapter (TA).** The TA functional grouping is typically implemented in a device that allows a non-ISDN device to be attached to an ISDN line.

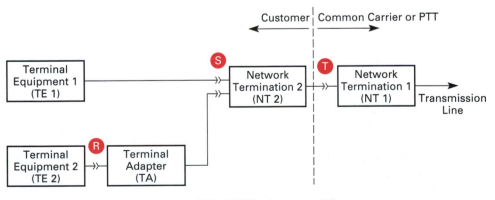

Figure 13.2   ISDN reference model.

- **Terminal Equipment 1 (TE1).** The TE1 functional grouping is implemented in an end-user device that conforms to ISDN standards. Examples of devices that implement the TE1 functional grouping are digital telephones, ISDN network interface cards (NICs) installed in computers, and ISDN-compatible fax machines.
- **Terminal Equipment 2 (TE2).** The TE2 functional grouping is typically implemented in a device not compatible with ISDN standards, such as a NIC that implements the X.21 or RS-232-D interface.

The simplest way for an end user to connect a computer to an ISDN line is to install an ISDN NIC into the computer and then to attach the NIC to the ISDN line via a TE2 device at point T. This is shown in Fig. 13.3. In this case, the NT2 grouping is implemented by a set of wires directly connecting the ISDN NIC to the ISDN line at interface point T. In a regulatory environment such as the one in the United States, point T is typically the dividing line between the equipment supplied by the common carrier and the equipment supplied by the end user.

Figure 13.4 shows a more complex arrangement in which the user plugs a device that implements the NT2 function into an ISDN line at point T. Each individual device is then connected to the NT2 device at interface point S. The NT2 device might provide any number of S-type connection points into which users can plug ISDN-compatible devices. The component implementing the NT2 function might take the form physically of a digital PBX, a terminal controller, or even an entire local area network.

As shown in Fig. 13.5, a non-ISDN device might also be connected to the NT2 device via a terminal adapter that connects to the ISDN adapter at point S. The ISDN adapter implements the TA functional grouping, and the non-ISDN terminal is connected to the TS device at interface point R.

BROADBAND ISDN

Broadband ISDN (B-ISDN) represents a probable future direction of the telephone industry and will require that the conventional copper-wire local loops that now go into subscriber premises be replaced by optical fiber cables. B-ISDN is designed to continue providing the services defined by the basic rate and primary rate interfaces of N-ISDN and to offer additional services based on much higher data rates. B-ISDN defines two types of services: *interactive* services, which involve two-way transmission, and *distribution* services,

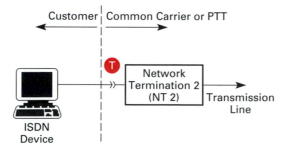

Figure 13.3 Connecting an ISDN-compatible device at point T.

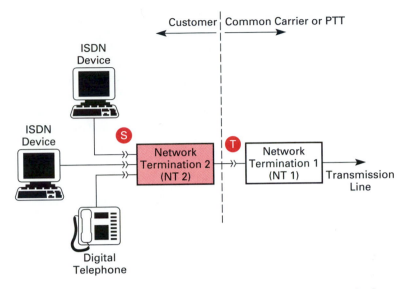

Figure 13.4　Connecting multiple ISDN-compatible devices at point S.

where transmission occurs primarily in one direction. B-ISDN services are intended to support all types of data, including text, documents, graphics, sound, and full-motion video. B-ISDN has the potential to provide wide area network connections with extremely high data rates. In order to achieve these higher data rates, B-ISDN assumes the use of certain data link subnetwork technologies for data transfer and physical transmission.

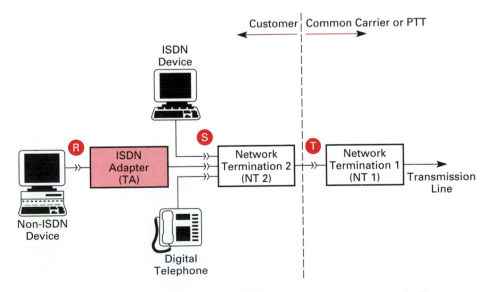

Figure 13.5　Connecting a non-ISDN device to an ISDN adapter at point R.

Data Link Technology

B-ISDN uses the *Asynchronous Transfer Mode (ATM)* technology for transferring data at the level of the OSI model Data Link layer. ATM technology is designed to meet the needs of heterogeneous, high-speed networking. ATM transmission combines some of the characteristics of both circuit switching and packet switching by implementing a form of very fast packet switching in which data is carried in small, fixed-length units called *cells*. ATM is designed to provide support for various classes of applications, including emulation of circuits based on standard telephone lines, emulation of X.25 packet-switched networks, teleconferencing transmission, and connectionless data transmission.

ATM is described further in Chapter 15.

Physical Transmission — SONET

At the physical transmission level, B-ISDN is built on top of *Synchronous Optical NETwork (SONET)* transmission services. SONET transmission services are based on an optical fiber transmission medium and incorporate both synchronous and asynchronous transmission modes. Data rates defined by various SONET physical transmission services are listed in Box 13.2. Most of the defined SONET services provide higher bit rates than an FDDI LAN and could be used in creating enterprise networks that operate over large geographic areas at speeds greater than those of most of today's local area networks.

SUMMARY

An Integrated Services Digital Network (ISDN) is a public telecommunications network that supplies three types of digital end-to-end communication services: bearer services, teleservices, and supplementary services. The initial definition of ISDN is often now called narrowband ISDN (N-ISDN) to differentiate it from broadband ISDN (B-ISDN), which defines telecommunications channels offering very high bit rates.

BOX 13.2	Data rates of SONET physical transmission services.		
Level	*Bit Rate (Mbps)*	*Level*	*Bit Rate (Mbps)*
OC1	51.84	OC24	1,244.16
OC3	155.52	OC36	1,866.24
OC6	311.04	OC48	2,488.32
OC9	466.56	OC96	4,976.00
OC12	622.08	OC255*	13,219.20
OC18	933.12		

*Theoretical maximum speed

N-ISDN services offerings include a Basic Rate Interface (BRI), which provides two 64-Kbps B channels for data transfer and one 16-Kbps D channel for signaling, and a Primary Rate Interface (PRI), which provides 23 64-Kbps B channels for data transfer and one 64-Kbps D channel for signaling. Bearer channels (B channels) provide for circuit-switched connections, packet-switched connections, and semipermanent connections. A data link channel (D channel) is used for control purposes. ISDN standards define frame formats, signal encoding, and physical transmission characteristics. A multirate ISDN service can be used to provide channels of higher capacity than a single B channel.

Broadband ISDN (B-ISDN) defines services that operate over optical fiber transmission facilities. B-ISDN defines both interactive services (two-way transmission) and distribution services (one-way transmission). B-ISDN services are provided using Asynchronous Transfer Mode (ATM) transmission technology at the level of the OSI model Data Link layer. ATM operates on top of SONET transmission facilities that provide data rates of hundreds of megabits per second.

Chapter 14 examines the Frame Relay technology that grew out of ISDN development that common carriers are using to implement high-speed digital communication circuits.

Frame Relay Subnetworks

Frame Relay data link subnetworks are based on international standards for the Data Link and Physical layers originally defined by the telecommunications industry as part of ISDN. There are now networks, typically run by common carriers or other telecommunications service providers, based on the Frame Relay standards.

USING A FRAME RELAY DATA LINK

To use a Frame Relay data link subnetwork, an organization generally contracts with a Frame Relay service provider to implement one or more point-to-point connections via the provider's Frame Relay network. Each of the organization's user machines that needs to access the Frame Relay network has its own point of connection into the Frame Relay network and can make a logical point-to-point connection with any other user machine that has a point of connection to that provider's network.

FRAME RELAY DATA LINK SERVICES

Frame Relay networks supply services similar to those provided by X.25 packet-switching networks (see Chapter 12). A Frame Relay service provider generally offers permanent virtual circuits (PVCs) and switched virtual circuits (SVCs).

DIFFERENCES BETWEEN FRAME RELAY AND X.25

Routing decisions in a Frame Relay network are relatively simple and are made based on identifiers associated with the Data Link layer rather than on a conventional network address. Another major difference between Frame Relay networks and X.25 networks is that Frame Relay networks do not provide the error correction facilities that are provided by X.25 networks. With an X.25 network, sequence checking and acknowledgments are used for each link across which packets travel. Frame Relay data link technology assumes a reliable transmission medium is used, such as optical fiber. Therefore, Frame Relay networks supply only a connectionless Data Link service and perform no sequence checking or sending of acknowledgments. If a frame is damaged and fails a CRC check at the destination device, the Frame Relay Data Link layer function simply discards the corrupted frame. Error detection and correction mechanisms must be used in a higher layer if reliable communication is required.

By eliminating the overhead associated with routing and error correction functions, Frame Relay networks are able to provide much higher data rates than X.25 networks. X.25 PSDNs typically offer the user data rates of up to about 64 Kbps. Many Frame Relay networks offer user data rates of up to 2 Mbps, and higher in some cases.

FRAME FORMAT

The Frame Relay transmission frame is similar to the frame used by HDLC, LAPB, and LAPD (see Chapters 11, 12, and 13). Box 14.1 shows the format of the Frame Relay frame and describes its fields. The key difference between the Frame Relay frame and those used in HDLC, LAPB, and LAPD is that the Frame Relay frame does not contain a Control field. Consequently, the Frame Relay transmission frame contains no provisions for sequence numbers that might be used to implement error recovery in the Data Link layer.

The DCLI provides the identification mechanism that identifies a particular virtual circuit and a particular station at the other end of the virtual circuit. A computer connected to a Frame Relay network can communicate with any number of other computers by placing an appropriate data link connection identifier value in each frame it transmits. Each end of a virtual circuit will have its own DCLI value. The Frame Relay network is responsible for mapping from the source user's DCLI to the destination user's DCLI.

The DCLI value can be 10, 17, or 24 bits long. Box 14.1 shows the format used for a 10-bit DCLI. Correspondingly, the Address field can be 2, 3, or 4 octets long. For transmission over an ISDN D channel, a 2-octet Address field is used. The DCLI values used are consistent with the SAPI and TEI values used in LAPD. This allows LAPD and Frame Relay frames to be multiplexed on the ISDN D channel. (See Chapter 13 for a discussion of ISDN D channels.)

CONGESTION CONTROL

Since no sequence numbers and acknowledgments are used with a Frame Relay data link, the Frame Relay protocol does not support the same forms of flow control associated with HDLC, LAPD, and LAPB data links. However, as with error correction mechanisms, flow control facilities can be implemented in a higher layer.

The Frame Relay standard does define an optional method of congestion control based on the use of bits in the Address field. However, few Frame Relay implementors have chosen to implement this function.

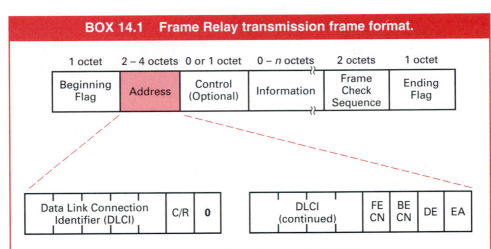

BOX 14.1   Frame Relay transmission frame format.

- **Beginning Flag.** Contains the unique bit configuration 0111 1110.
- **Address.** The Address field is at least two octets in length and sometimes longer. It contains a data link connection identifier (DLCI) that identifies the specific virtual circuit with which the frame is associated. The Address field also contains bits that can be used to implement congestion control functions and includes the following fields:
  — C/R—Command/Response
  — FECN—Forward Explicit Congestion Notification field
  — BECN—Backward Explicit Congestion Notification field
  — DE—Discard Eligibility bit
  — EA—Address Extension bit
- **Control Field.** The HDLC Control Field is treated as part of the Information field by the Frame Relay protocol.
- **Information.** Carries the user data portion of the frame.
- **Frame Check Sequence.** Contains a 16-bit cyclic redundancy check (CRC) value used for error detection.
- **Ending Flag.** Contains the same bit configuration as the Beginning Flag field (0111 1110) and identifies the end of the frame.

SUMMARY

Frame Relay data link technology is based on international standards for the Data Link and Physical layers defined as part of ISDN. Frame Relay networks supply services similar to those provided by X.25 packet-switching networks and provide permanent virtual circuits (PVCs) and switched virtual circuits (SVCs). Routing decisions in a Frame Relay network are relatively simple and are made based on identifiers associated with the Data Link layer. Frame Relay networks do not provide the error correction facilities provided by X.25 networks and supply only a connectionless Data Link service. Frame Relay networks typically provide data rates up to 2 Mbps and sometimes higher.

Chapter 15 describes the Asynchronous Transfer Mode technology that grew out of ISDN development and has the promise of integrating WAN and LAN data links.

ATM Subnetworks

As with the Frame Relay protocol, Asynchronous Transfer Mode (ATM) transmission technology was first defined as an ISDN specification for the Data Link layer. Also as with Frame Relay technology, ATM products and services are now becoming directly available as a communications technology implemented apart from ISDN. ATM products and services take the form of network interface cards (NICs), network infrastructure devices, and data transmission services.

The ATM technology, also sometimes called *cell relay*, is a form of packet-switched data transmission that uses fixed-sized packets called *cells,* each 53 octets in length.

ATM DATA LINK SERVICES

Four classes of service are defined in the ATM specifications. An ATM service provider may choose to implement one or more of these classes of service:

- **Class A.** Class A ATM service is connection-oriented and maintains a constant bit rate and a timing relationship between the source and the destination systems. Class A service can be used to replace a standard circuit-switched telecommunications facility and is useful for high-bandwidth isochronous applications such as the transmission of full-motion video signals.

- **Class B.** Class B ATM service is also connection-oriented. However, Class B service provides a variable bit rate while still maintaining a timing relationship between the source and the destination systems. Class B service is intended for audio and video applications, such as teleconferencing, where a variable bit rate can be tolerated as long as delays are within defined boundaries.

- **Class C.** Class C ATM service is also connection-oriented with a variable bit rate, but it maintains no timing relationship between the source and destination systems. Class C service is intended to be used by data transmission applications and provides a service similar to that provided by an X.25 or Frame Relay virtual circuit.

- **Class D.** Class D ATM service is connectionless, supports a variable bit rate, and maintains no timing relationship between the source and destination systems. This service provides a datagram data transmission facility where no error correction or flow control mechanisms are required in the Data Link layer.

ATM OPERATION

As with other forms of packet switching, an ATM network supports multiple logical connections multiplexed over the same physical links. And, as with Frame Relay, ATM assumes the use of reliable digital transmission facilities, such as that provided by an optical fiber link. The ATM protocol does not perform error correction or flow control functions but leaves these functions to a higher layer.

By using a fixed cell size, as opposed to the variable-length frames used by the Frame Relay protocol, transmission overhead in an ATM network is very low. Many ATM networks are able to support data rates into the tens and hundreds of megabits per second. The small, fixed cell size allows the ATM protocol to be efficient enough to provide a constant data rate for virtual circuits, so ATM is suitable for applications that require an isochronous data transmission service.

FRAME FORMAT

The ATM transmission cell format is shown in Box 15.1.

VIRTUAL CHANNELS AND VIRTUAL PATHS

The ATM specification uses the term *virtual channel connection* (VCC) to refer to a logical connection or virtual circuit. A VCC provides for the end-to-end transfer of ATM cells between two ATM service users. Each user has a *virtual channel identifier* (VCI) that it associates with a particular VCC. A sending system places its VCI in the cell header for each cell it transmits. The ATM network is responsible for mapping a sending system's VCI value to the VCI value associated with the destination system. It may be necessary to use multiple physical circuits within the ATM network to implement a given virtual channel connection, and a given virtual channel connection may pass over several links on the path from the source system to the destination system.

The ATM specifications define a *virtual path connection* (VPC) as a set of two or more VCCs flowing across the same physical circuit or series of physical circuits. By allowing a number of VCCs to be combined into a single VPC, the ATM network can switch all the VCCs in a VPC as a unit, thus reducing network management overhead. The use of VPCs also helps to improve network performance and reduce network implementation cost.

A given VCC may belong to different VPCs along different portions of its route (see Fig. 15.1). The VPI value contained in a cell's header indicates the VPC to which the cell belongs at any given time.

BOX 15.1   Asynchronous Transfer Mode (ATM) cell format.

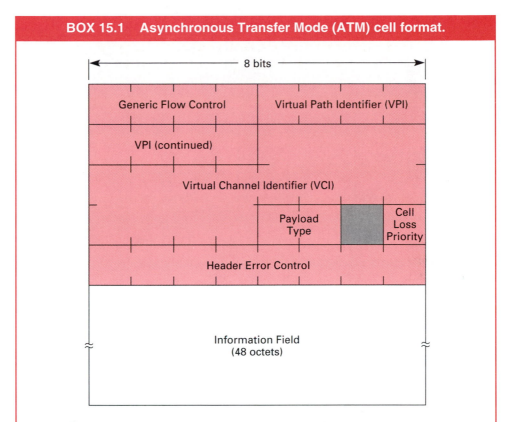

- **Generic Flow Control.** The 4-bit generic flow control field is used at the user/network interface to control the flow of cells between the user and the network. Within the network, this field is treated as part of the virtual path identifier.

- **Virtual Path Identifier (VPI).** The 8-bit virtual path identifier is used to group virtual channels for routing.

- **Virtual Channel Identifier (VCI).** The 16-bit virtual channel identifier identifies a particular virtual circuit.

- **Payload Type.** The 2-bit payload type field identifies the type of information in the Information field.

- **Cell Loss Priority (CLP).** The cell-loss priority bit provides guidance to the network for discarding cells in case of congestion.

- **Header-Error Control.** The header-error control field contains a check value used to detect errors in the header portion of the cell.

- **Information Field.** The Information field contains 48 octets (384 bits) of user data.

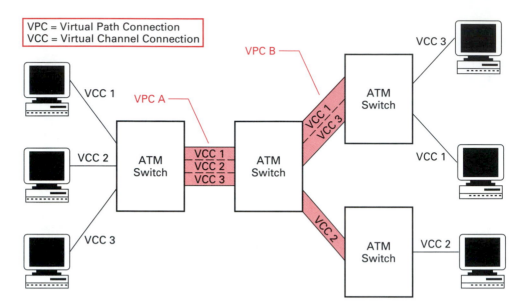

Figure 15.1   A virtual path connection (VPC) consists of a set of virtual channel connections (VCCs) sharing the same route.

END-TO-END PROTOCOLS

All ATM cells contain a 5-octet header and a 48-octet Information field, as shown in Box
15.1. The control information contained in the 5-octet header is used by the ATM switches
in relaying a cell through the ATM network. All 48 bits of the Information field are treated
as data by intermediate switches as cells are relayed through the network.

Type 1, 2, and 3/4 Information Fields

The devices at the source and destination access points implement a number of end-to-
end protocols in addition to the protocols used to carry cells through the ATM network.
These end-to-end protocols use some of the bits of the Information field for control purposes and use four different Information field formats. Information field formats of types
1 through 4 are described in Box 15.2.

Type 5 Information Field

The three Information field formats described in Box 15.2 can be used to implement the
four classes of service described in Box 15.1. However, with these formats, some of the
control information is not needed when providing the simpler class C or class D services.
Up to 9 octets out of the full 53 octets of each cell, on average, will be used for control
information when types 1 through 4 Information fields are used to implement class C or
class D service.

Type 1 Information Field

1 octet		47 octets
Seq No	Seq No Protection	User Data

- **Sequence Number.** A 4-bit value used to perform sequence checking to detect lost or out-of-sequence cells.
- **Sequence-Number Protection.** A 4-bit value used for error detection.
- **User Data.** Data being sent from the source user to the destination user.

Type 2 Information Field

1 octet		45 octets	2 octets	
Seq No	Info Type	User Data	Length Indicator	Cyclic Redundancy Check

- **Sequence Number.** A 4-bit value used to perform sequence checking to detect lost or out-of-sequence cells.
- **Information Type.** A 4-bit value that indicates the beginning, middle, or end of a message. This field is used for message segmentation and reassembly.
- **User Data.** Data being sent from the source user to the destination user.
- **Length Indicator.** A 6-bit value that indicates how much of the User Data field contains user data.
- **Cyclic Redundancy Check.** A 10-bit cyclic redundancy check value used for error detection and correction of the User Data field.

Types 3/4 Information Fields

2 octets			44 octets	2 octets	
S T	Seq No	Multiplex Identifier	User Data	Length Indicator	Cyclic Redundancy Check

- **Segment Type (ST).** A 2-bit value indicating the beginning, middle or end of a message, or a single-segment message. This field is used for message segmentation and reassembly.
- **Sequence Number.** A 4-bit value used to perform sequence checking to detect lost or out-of-sequence cells.
- **Multiplexer ID.** A 4-bit value used to multiplex multiple user connections over a single physical ATM connection.
- **User Data.** Data being sent from the source user to the destination user.
- **Length Indicator.** A 6-bit value that indicates how much of the User Data field contains user data.
- **Cyclic Redundancy Check.** A 10-bit cyclic redundancy check value used for error detection and correction of the User Data field.

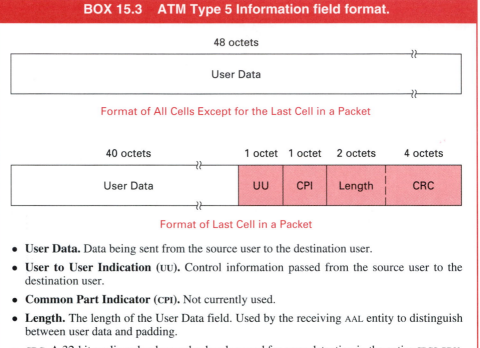

BOX 15.3   ATM Type 5 Information field format.

48 octets

User Data

Format of All Cells Except for the Last Cell in a Packet

40 octets	1 octet	1 octet	2 octets	4 octets
User Data	UU	CPI	Length	CRC

Format of Last Cell in a Packet

- **User Data.** Data being sent from the source user to the destination user.
- **User to User Indication** (UU). Control information passed from the source user to the destination user.
- **Common Part Indicator** (CPI). Not currently used.
- **Length.** The length of the User Data field. Used by the receiving AAL entity to distinguish between user data and padding.
- CRC. A 32-bit cyclic redundancy check value used for error detection in the entire CPCS-PDU.

The ATM specification defines an alternative end-to-end protocol more efficient than the protocol that uses the type 3/4 Information fields. The alternative end-to-end protocol uses a type 5 Information field to provide class C and class D services. The type 5 Information field format is shown in Box 15.3.

The protocol used to implement class C and class D service using the type 5 Information field format assumes that each user packet may be segmented and carried in multiple cells. A bit in the 5-octet cell header is used to distinguish between the final cell of a packet and all those cells that precede the final cell. All cells of a packet, other than the final cell, use all 48 octets of the Information field for user data. The final cell of a packet uses 8 octets of the Information field, in the form of a trailer, as control information to implement an error detection mechanism. The error detection mechanism is applied to the entire reassembled packet.

ATM APPLICATIONS

ATM technology provides many of the advantages of circuit switching, such as being able to guarantee a certain transmission capacity and level of service between two users. At the same time, ATM allows a very high-speed transmission facility to be shared among a number of users on an as-needed basis, in a similar manner to packet switching. The following sections describe some of the ways in which ATM technology is being used in actual products and services.

ATM LANs

A number of network infrastructure vendors are supplying ATM NICs and ATM switches that can be used in a conventional local area network environment. A system of ATM NICs and switches might be used to interconnect end-user systems and servers to create a high-speed local area network (see Fig. 15.2).

ATM Backbone Networks

An ATM switch could also be used to implement a backbone network, interconnecting a number of LANs (see Fig. 15.3).

Common Carrier ATM Services

Public ATM services provided by a common carrier can be used to implement WAN links between systems or between individual data link subnetworks. Common carrier ATM services can be used to interconnect LANs, or they can be used to interconnect ATM switches being used locally (see Fig. 15.4).

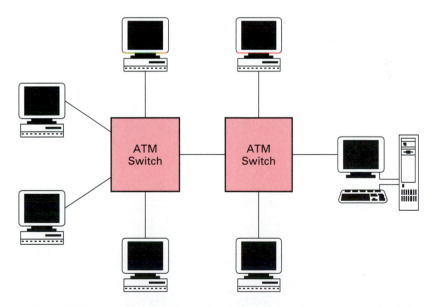

Figure 15.2   An ATM switch can be used in place of a conventional LAN transmission medium to interconnect intelligent devices.

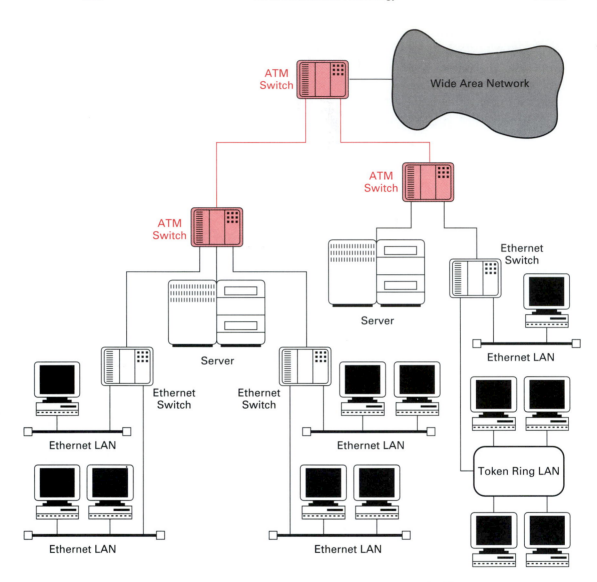

Figure 15.3   One or more ATM switches can be used to form a backbone network used to interconnect LANs.

THE FUTURE OF ATM

The proponents of ATM claim that ATM technology will be the grand unifier of voice, video, and data transmission. For the data user, ATM has the potential of removing today's distinction between local area networking technology and wide area networking technology. ATM

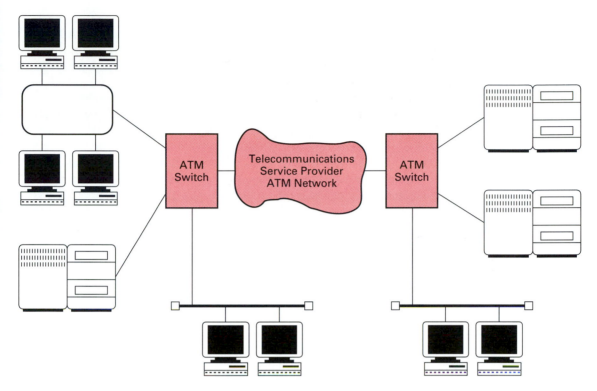

Figure 15.4 ATM services provided by a telecommunications service provider can be used to implement a wide area network data link in an enterprise network.

technology will allow the same transmission and switching technologies to be used over short-distance dedicated cabling and over long-distance common-carrier circuits.

With the high transmission speeds ATM technology is designed to support, it may eventually be possible to make the distance between two communicating devices truly transparent to application programs and end users. With such technology, it will be possible to build applications that work in an identical manner whether the two communicating systems are in the same room or across the globe.

SUMMARY

Asynchronous Transfer Mode (ATM) transmission technology was first defined as an ISDN specification for the Data Link layer and uses fixed-sized packets called cells each 53 octets in length. ATM products and services take the form of network interface cards (NICs), network infrastructure devices, and data transmission services.

Four classes of service, classes A, B, C, and D, are defined in the ATM specifications. Each provides a data transmission service having different characteristics. An ATM network supports multiple logical connections multiplexed over the same physical links. The ATM protocol does not perform error correction or flow control functions. An ATM virtual channel connection (VCC) is a logical connection or virtual circuit, and a virtual path connection (VPC) is a set of two or more VCCs flowing across the same physical circuit or series of physical circuits.

The devices at the source and destination access points implement a number of end-to-end protocols in addition to the protocols used to carry cells through the ATM network. Four different types of Information fields, types 1, 2, 3/4, and 5, can be used to provide the four classes of service defined by ATM.

ATM technology provides many of the advantages of circuit switching and allows a very high-speed transmission facility to be shared among a number of users on an as-needed basis. ATM technology can be used in a variety of ways, such as creating ATM LANs, using an ATM network as a high-speed backbone, and using common-carrier ATM services to interconnect subnetworks.

Chapter 16 introduces some of the strategies and technologies employed for implementing wireless communication over long distances.

Wireless WAN Subnetworks

It is becoming increasingly popular to interconnect computer equipment and to transmit data over wireless links rather than over conventional telecommunications circuits. Wireless transmission can be used to implement either long-distance WAN links or short-distance LAN links. In this chapter we examine wireless wide area networking. Chapter 24 examines the use of wireless transmission in local area networks.

A wireless data link can be used to provide end-to-end communication between a pair of end-user systems, or it can be used in conjunction with conventional telephone circuits. Wireless WAN data transmission is most often handled using some form of radio transmission.

Wireless data links are particularly useful for implementing mobile computing applications in which it would be difficult or impossible to connect systems using conventional land-based telecommunications lines. There are three principal technologies used to implement wireless WAN data transmission:

- Packet Radio Networks
- Cellular Telephone Networks
- Cellular Digital Packet Data

PACKET RADIO NETWORKS

Packet radio networks provide digital data transmission services in a way similar to X.25 networks. Each mobile computing device used with a packet radio network must include, or be attached to, an appropriate radio transceiver. Figure 16.1 illustrates a typical packet radio network. When data is to be sent from stationary user A to mobile user B, it travels from user A's network to a packet radio switching facility, which sends it to the appropriate broadcasting facility, or base station. The base station then uses radio transmission to forward the data to user B. For data transmitted from user B to user A, the process is reversed.

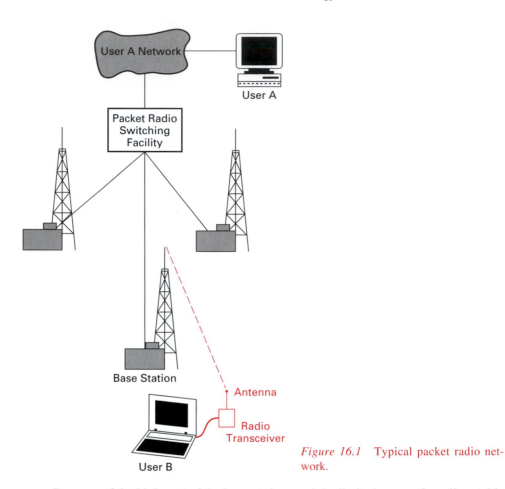

Figure 16.1 Typical packet radio network.

Because of the high cost of the base stations and the limited range of small portable transceivers, packet radio networks typically serve only selected geographic areas, such as large cities.

With a packet radio network, data is formatted in the form of individual packets, and packet-switching techniques, similar to those used in an X.25 PSDN, are used to move data through the packet radio network. Collision detection techniques similar to those used with Ethernet LANs are often used to prevent simultaneous transmissions from interfering with each other. Typical packet radio network equipment support data rates of 2400 bps through 19.2 Kbps.

CELLULAR TELEPHONE NETWORKS

Cellular networks were originally developed, and have come into widespread use, for voice communication using portable telephones. These networks are also being used for data transmission. Figure 16.2 shows a typical cellular network.

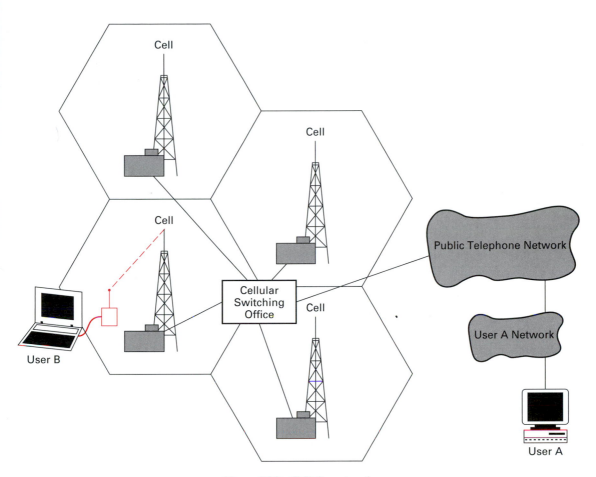

Figure 16.2　Cellular network.

Many cellular networks use analog transmission between the mobile device and a local tower that serves a particular area, or cell. Data is transmitted between the towers and a switching facility connected to the common carrier telephone network. Connections between users are established using a combination of wireless transmission and standard telephone circuits. For data transmission over a cellular network using analog technology, the computing device uses a cellular modem to access the service, and a standard voice telephone circuit is allocated for the duration of the transmission. A typical range of data rates supported by cellular networks is 2400 bps through 28.8 Kbps.

CELLULAR DIGITAL PACKET DATA NETWORKS

A newer form of cellular transmission, called *Cellular Digital Packet Data (CDPD),* is currently being implemented in conjunction with conventional cellular telephone service in certain market areas. With CDPD, no dedicated circuit is allocated by the cellular network to the data transmission. With CDPD, packets of data are carried in digital form over the existing cellular telephone network using the idle time not being used by voice calls.

USING RADIO NETWORKS

Wireless WAN services using radio transmission technology are most commonly used to provide a data communication channel to computer users who move frequently from one location to another. As long as they are within range of the radio network, they are able to communicate with the enterprise network from any location.

There are currently several limitations to wireless WAN communication given today's technology:

- **Security.** Radio transmission, because of its broadcast nature, is more easily intercepted, and more susceptible to eavesdropping.

- **Coverage.** Radio networks cover most major metropolitan areas, but do not yet have the ubiquitous reach of the global telephone network.

- **Interoperability.** There have been few standards developed for radio networks. and most devices used with radio networks, such as transceivers and radio modems, will work only with a specific vendor's network. It may be difficult for a computer system using one radio network service to interoperate with a computer system using some other service.

SUMMARY

The three principal technologies used to implement wireless WAN data transmission are packet radio networks, cellular telephone networks, and Cellular Digital Packet Data. Packet radio networks provide digital data transmission services in a way similar to X.25 networks. Packet radio networks typically serve only selected geographic areas, such as large cities. Cellular networks, originally developed for voice communication using portable telephones, are also used for data transmission. For data transmission over a cellular network, the computing device uses a cellular modem to access the service, and a standard voice telephone circuit is allocated for the duration of the transmission. Cellular Digital Packet Data (CDPD) technology is sometimes used in conjunction with conventional cellular telephone service. With CDPD, packets of data are carried in digital form over the existing cellular telephone network using the idle time not being used by voice calls.

Limitations often associated with wireless WAN data links include lack of security, insufficient range of coverage, and lack of standards for interoperability.

Chapter 17 begins Part IV of this book, which examines specific technologies used to implement local area network data links. Chapter 17 discusses the general characteristics of LAN data link subnetworks.

PART IV

LAN SUBNETWORK TECHNOLOGY

Local Area Network Technology

As we have seen, the basic building blocks of most enterprise networks are the individual local area networks serving various departments and workgroups in the enterprise. Each of these individual LANs makes up one of the *LAN data links*, or *LAN data link subnetworks*, making up the full enterprise network.

A workgroup LAN can be used on a stand-alone basis to serve the needs of a particular group of individuals, or it can be interconnected with other subnetworks of various types to form a larger enterprise network. This chapter describes the fundamental technology used to implement individual LAN subnetworks.

APPLICATIONS FOR LOCAL AREA NETWORKS

A great many of the local area networks installed today are used for the purpose of interconnecting the desktop personal computers and workstations used by individuals and allowing them to access the facilities of shared server systems. However, local area network data links are used in other ways as well.

The following sections describe a few of the many ways in which LANs are used.

Resource Sharing

Figure 17.1 illustrates a typical local area network connecting desktop systems. Such LANs are commonly used to provide computer users with shared access to resources, such as data files stored on other personal computers operating in the role of *servers*. Depending on how the local area network is implemented, it may be possible for several users to access the same resources concurrently.

Local area networks also allow network users to share expensive devices on the network, such as high-speed printers. Print jobs created on a desktop computer for printing can be sent to a computer operating in the role of a print server. A print server may maintain print queues so that multiple print jobs from different desktop systems can be queued up until it is their turn to be printed.

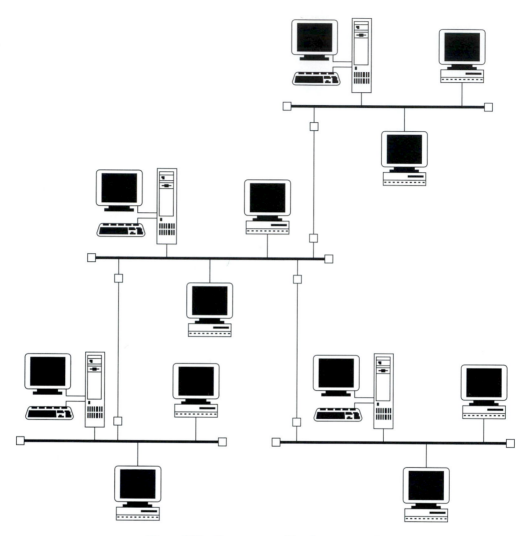

Figure 17.1 Tree-structured local area network.

Electronic Mail

Local area networks can also allow desktop computer users to send electronic mail messages to each other. Electronic mail software may provide editing and formatting aids, group addressing capabilities, and message notification and storing facilities.

Processor Complexes

Local area networks are also used outside of the personal computer environment for a variety of uses. For example, LAN data links are sometimes used to interconnect individual processors to form processor complexes. DEC VAX clusters provide an example of such

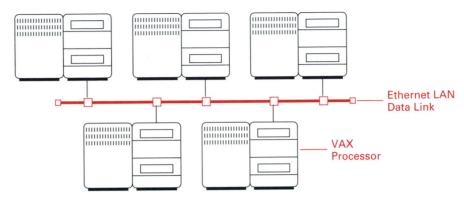

Figure 17.2   VAX cluster using Ethernet LAN data link technology.

a LAN data link application. In a VAX cluster, an Ethernet LAN is used to interconnect a number of separate VAX systems. The networked VAX processors provide computing system users with the image of a single processor that has the combined power of the clustered VAX processors (see Fig. 17.2).

Computer Room Interconnection

LAN data links are often used in the computer room to provide a simplified method of interconnecting computing devices. For example, in the IBM mainframe environment, a Token Ring LAN might be used to connect a number of terminal cluster controllers to a communications controller to avoid the need for a separate high-speed point-to-point connection for each cluster controller (see Fig. 17.3).

Other Uses

LAN data links have been used to support alarm and security systems. They are also sometimes used in the factory environment for process control and monitoring applications. The many uses of high-speed local area networking technology are limited only by the ingenuity of system designers.

LOCAL AREA NETWORK COMPONENTS

An individual local area network data link is made up of a combination of hardware and software components. The major components used to construct a LAN data link subnetwork are shown in Fig. 17.4.

The basic components of an individual LAN subnetwork are similar to the components used to form the enterprise network as a whole. A LAN consists of network interface cards (NICs) installed in computing devices that play the roles of client systems and server systems. The network interface cards are attached to a cabling system that may include various types of interconnection devices, such as repeaters, hubs, and concentrators.

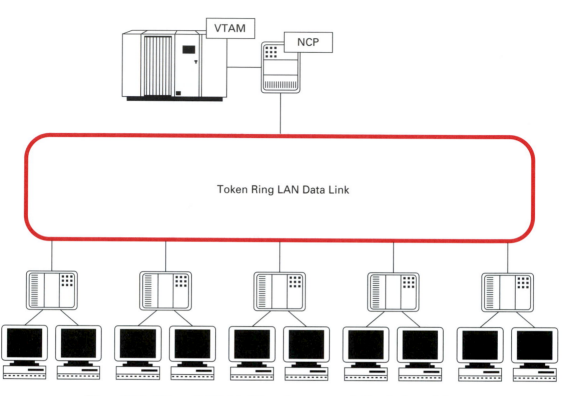

Figure 17.3   Using a LAN data link to interconnect devices in the mainframe environment.

Some type of network software subsystems may then run on top of the operating system software in each of the computing systems attached to the LAN.

The following sections discuss each of the five categories of LAN components.

Computing Devices

A LAN subnetwork is typically used to interconnect general-purpose computing devices, such as personal computers or workstations, which may be of the same or of different types. Special-purpose devices, such as intelligent printers, and devices used to interconnect individual LAN data links, such as bridges and routers, may also be directly attached to a LAN link.

Computing devices with little intelligence, such as disk drives, dumb terminals, and simple printers, are not generally directly attached to a LAN subnetwork unless they are specifically designed for LAN connection. But such devices may be attached to one or more of the computing systems that *are* attached to the LAN data link. The LAN network software running in the computing system to which such a device is attached may make it possible for that device to be shared by other users on the LAN.

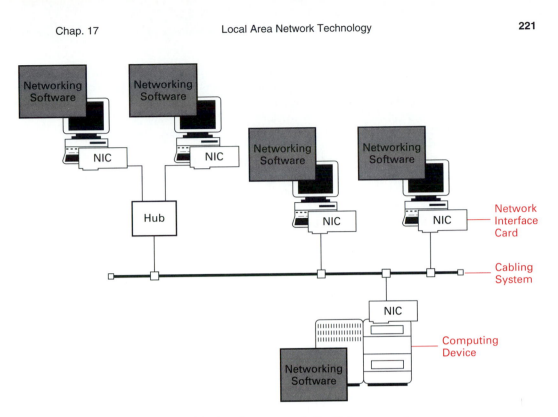

Figure 17.4   Local area network data link components.

Network Interface Cards

A *network interface card (NIC)* is typically installed in each computing device directly attached to the LAN. A NIC is sometimes called a *network adapter* or *LAN adapter*. A NIC performs the hardware functions required to provide a computing device with physical communication capabilities. Each type of LAN technology requires its own type of NIC. For example, an Ethernet NIC cannot be attached to the cabling system of a token ring LAN subnetwork.

Some types of computing devices designed for use on specific types of networks, such as a network printer, may have the functions of a NIC integrated directly into them. Other types of computing devices, such as many general-purpose computers, personal computers, and graphics workstations, may allow various types of NICs to be installed in them.

Cabling Systems

A LAN cabling system includes the cable used to interconnect the NICs installed in the networked computing devices. Various types of electrical cable or fiber-optic cable can be used to implement the cabling system in a LAN subnetwork. Each type of LAN technology defines the types of transmission media that can be used on that type of LAN data link. A cabling system may include *attachment units* used to attach the NICs to the cable. In some cases, the cabling system may be replaced with some form of wireless communication, perhaps using radio, microwave, or infrared signaling.

Interconnection Devices

Many types of LAN technology include interconnection devices called *access units*, *repeaters*, *concentrators*, or *hubs*. Such devices can often be used to simplify the wiring topology by allowing multiple network devices to be attached to the LAN wiring system from a central point. Attaching devices through central concentrators often simplifies the installation and maintenance of the local area network.

Network Software

Network interface cards perform low-level functions that support the exchange of electrical, radio, or optical signals over the LAN transmission medium. The network software that runs in a computing system implements higher-level communication functions that determine how physical signals are interpreted as information and data.

Relationship to the OSI Model

In the context of the OSI model, a NIC generally implements functions associated with the Physical layer functions and the lower half of the Data Link layer. Network software generally implements functions operating at the level of the top half of the Data Link layer through the Application layer of the OSI model (see Fig. 17.5).

Relationship to the IEEE/ISO/ANSI LAN Architecture

In the context of the IEEE/ISO/ANSI LAN architecture, the NIC typically implements the Medium Access Control (MAC) sublayer of the Data Link layer, and the network software typically implements the Logical Link Control (LLC) sublayer of the Data Link layer (see Fig 17.6).

Network Software Implementations

The network software may have different characteristics depending on the computing environment and the particular network implementation. In the mainframe environment, communication functions may be performed by telecommunications access

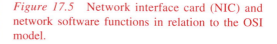

Figure 17.5 Network interface card (NIC) and network software functions in relation to the OSI model.

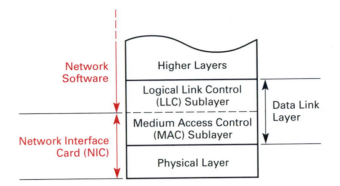

Figure 17.6   Network interface card (NIC) and network software functions in relation to the IEEE/ISO/ANSI LAN architecture.

methods running in mainframes, network control programs running in communication controllers, and specialized firmware running in terminal controllers. In the UNIX minicomputer and workstation environment, the network software may be integrated into the computer's operating system. In the personal computer environment, the network software may either be integrated into the operating system or it may take the form of a specialized *network operating system.*

Network Driver Software

As we introduced in Chapter 7, in many cases there may be specialized *network driver* software that provides low-level functions associated with a particular type of NIC. The network software may provide an interface to the driver to allow the same network software to operate with many different types of NICs or the same NIC to operate with many different network software systems (see Fig. 17.7).

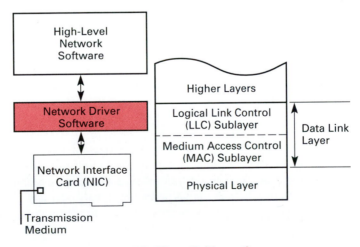

Figure 17.7   Network driver software.

LAN DATA LINK TECHNOLOGIES

As we introduced in Part I, a number of different LAN data link technologies can be used to construct LAN subnetworks. There are four important characteristics in classifying different forms of LAN data link technology and in allowing us to compare one type of technology with another:

- **Transmission Medium.** The cable or other physical circuit used to interconnect systems. Typical LAN transmission media are twisted-wire-pair telephone wire, coaxial cable, fiber-optic cable, and various forms of wireless transmission.

- **Signaling Technique.** The type of signals exchanged over the physical transmission medium. The most common signaling techniques used with LAN data links are *baseband* signaling and *broadband* signaling.

- **Network Topology.** Identifies the logical shape that device interconnections take. Common LAN data link topologies are the *bus,* the *ring,* and the *star.*

- **Medium Access Control Method.** The method by which communicating systems control their access to the transmission medium. Devices on a LAN data link share the cabling system that connects them and the transmission facilities it provides. However, a LAN data link generally allows only one system to transmit at a time. Some method must be used to control when each system can use the transmission facilities.

The remainder of this chapter discusses each of the above LAN data link technology classifications.

TRANSMISSION MEDIUM

Local area networks can use a variety of different physical media for signal transmission. Most of the transmission media described in Chapter 8 have been used to implement local area networks.

Today, most types of LAN technologies can use twisted-pair cables for signal transmission, and this is by far the most widely used LAN transmission medium. However, many modern LAN technologies may alternatively use coaxial cable, fiber-optic cable, or wireless transmission.

SIGNALING TECHNIQUES

There are two general techniques used with LAN data links for transmitting signals over a physical communication medium: *baseband* and *broadband.* Baseband transmission uses *digital* signaling while broadband transmission uses *analog* techniques. Equipment can be designed to transmit either digital or analog signals over any of the types of physical transmission media. The following sections discuss the differences between baseband and broadband transmission.

Baseband Transmission

With baseband transmission, the entire channel capacity is used to transmit a single digital data signal. The signal flow is typically bidirectional, and the signal travels away from the sending device in both directions on the physical medium. This is illustrated in Fig. 17.8. When device B transmits data, the signal goes out in both directions, eventually reaching all other devices along the cable. When the signal reaches either end of the cable, terminators employed at the ends of the cable absorb the signal and prevent reflections. Most commonly used LAN data link technologies use baseband signaling with bidirectional signal flow.

Broadband Transmission

Broadband transmission typically employs analog transmission using a wider range of frequencies than baseband transmission. With broadband transmission, frequency-division multiplexing can be used to divide the available bandwidth into different channels, with different transmissions taking place simultaneously over different channels. A limited form of broadband transmission, known as *single-channel broadband,* is also possible, where the entire bandwidth is used to make up a single channel. This form provides a relatively inexpensive way to construct a network initially that can later be converted to multichannel broadband without requiring rewiring.

With broadband signaling, the signal flow is typically unidirectional; the signal moves in one direction along the cable. In order for a signal to reach all devices on the network, there must be two paths for data flow. Figure 17.9 shows the two most common approaches used to provide the two paths.

The configuration shown in the top of Fig. 17.9 is called *midsplit broadband.* Here the bandwidth of the cable is divided into two channels, each using a different range of frequencies. One channel is used to transmit signals and the other is used to receive. When a signal is transmitted, it travels to one end of the cable, called the *head end.* At the head end, a frequency converter changes the frequency of the signal from the send channel range to the receive channel range and retransmits it in the opposite direction along the cable. The signal is then eventually received by all devices on the cable.

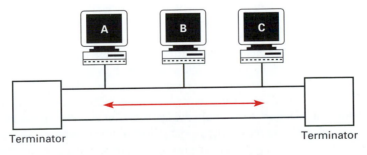

Figure 17.8   Bidirectional signal flow.

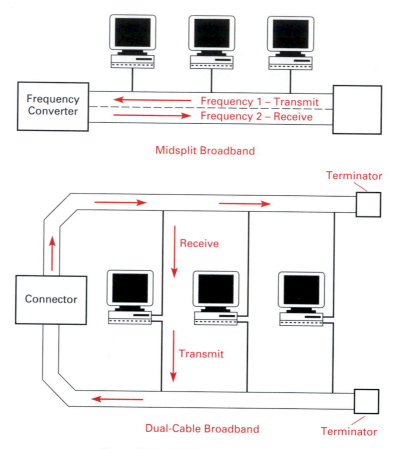

Figure 17.9   Unidirectional signal flow.

The second configuration is called *dual-cable broadband*. In this configuration, each device is attached to two cables. One cable is used to send and the other to receive. When a signal is transmitted, it reaches the head end and is passed on via a connector to the other cable, without any change in the frequency of the signal. The signal can then be received by any of the devices as it passes along the second cable.

Broadband transmission is not as commonly used in LAN implementations as baseband transmission. Since broadband transmission uses analog signaling, modems must be used on a broadband LAN data link to convert between digital data and analog signals. With broadband transmission, the carrier frequencies employed are very high-frequency radio waves. Thus, radio frequency (RF) modems must be used to attach devices to the transmission medium. Commonly available equipment used for cable television, including coaxial cable, amplifiers, and signal distribution equipment, are used for constructing some types of broadband data networks. The use of existing technology can help to keep down the cost of network components.

NETWORK TOPOLOGY

The topology of a LAN data link subnetwork concerns both the *physical* configuration of the cabling used to interconnect communicating systems and the *logical* way in which systems view the structure of the LAN. It is important to note that the way signals flow on the LAN wiring may be different from the way in which the wiring is installed physically. We will discuss these differences later in this section.

There are three principal topologies employed by LAN data link technology: star, bus, and ring.

Star Topology

In a *star* configuration, shown in Fig. 17.10, there is a central point to which each system in a group is directly connected. With the star topology, all transmissions from one system to another pass through the central point, which may consist of a device that plays a role in managing and controlling communication. The device at the center of the star may be a switching hub that establishes connections between ports in order to forward frames from one system to another.

The star topology has been employed for many years in dial-up telephone systems, in which individual telephone sets are the communicating systems and a *private branch exchange (PBX)* acts as the central controller. When one system wishes to communicate with another system, the PBX establishes a *circuit*, or dedicated path, between the two sys-

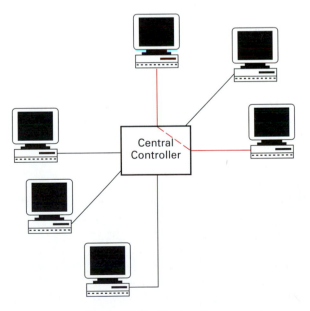

Figure 17.10   Star topology.

227

tems that wish to communicate. One such path is represented by the dashed line in Fig. 17.10. Once a circuit is established, data can be exchanged between the two systems as if they were linked by a dedicated point-to-point link. Although it is not common, a LAN data link can be implemented using PBX-type technology.

Figure 17.11 illustrates a more complex version of the star topology, often called a *snowflake* configuration. Hierarchies of switching hubs typically use this configuration. Most modern LAN technologies permit the wiring to be physically laid out in the form of a star structure.

Bus Topology

With the *bus* topology, shown in Fig. 17.12, each system is directly attached to a common communications channel, and frames are transmitted over the channel. As each frame passes along the channel, each system receives it. Each system then examines a destination address contained in the frame. If the destination address tells a particular system that the frame is addressed to it, that system accepts and processes the frame. If the

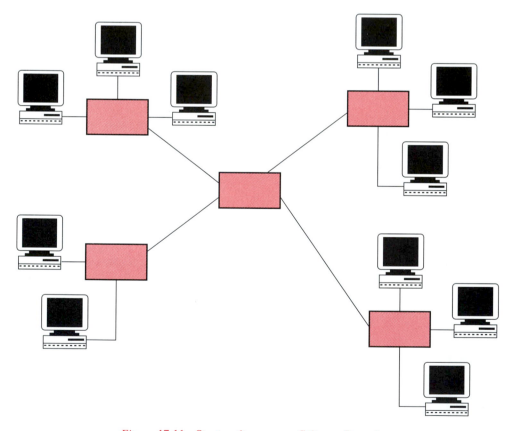

Figure 17.11   Star topology—snowflake configuration.

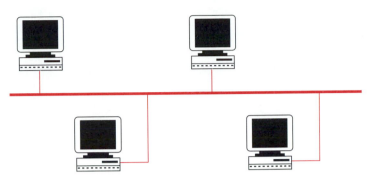

Figure 17.12   Bus topology.

destination address tells a system the frame is intended for some other system, that system ignores the frame.

An extension of the bus topology is the tree structure, shown in Fig. 17.13. With the tree topology, the common communications channel takes the form of a cable with multiple branches, and the systems are attached like leaves to the branches. As with a simple bus topology, all systems in the tree structure receive all transmissions.

Local area networks that employ Ethernet or LocalTalk technology use a bus-structured or tree-structured logical topology. However, as we will see, the wiring can often be physically laid out to form a star-structured network for ease of installation and maintenance.

Ring Topology

The *ring* topology is illustrated in Fig. 17.14. Here the cabling forms a loop, with a simple, point-to-point connection attaching each system to the next around the ring. Each system acts as a repeater for all signals it receives and retransmits them to the next system in the ring at their original signal strength.

All frames transmitted by any system are received by all other systems, but not simultaneously; frames are received by each system in turn. As with the bus topology, a system determines, based on a destination address contained in each frame, whether to copy and process a given frame. The system that originates a frame is generally responsible for determining that a frame has made its way all the way around the ring and then not repeating that frame, thus removing it from the ring. Figure 17.15 shows a more complex form of ring topology, where multiple rings are interconnected.

The Token Ring and FDDI forms of LAN technology use a ring topology. However, as with Ethernet and LocalTalk LANs, the physical wiring for a Token Ring or FDDI LAN often takes the form of a star configuration.

Different Physical and Logical Topologies

As we have already mentioned, many LAN technologies employ network topologies in which the physical layout of the cabling can be different from the logical topology of the network as perceived by systems on the LAN.

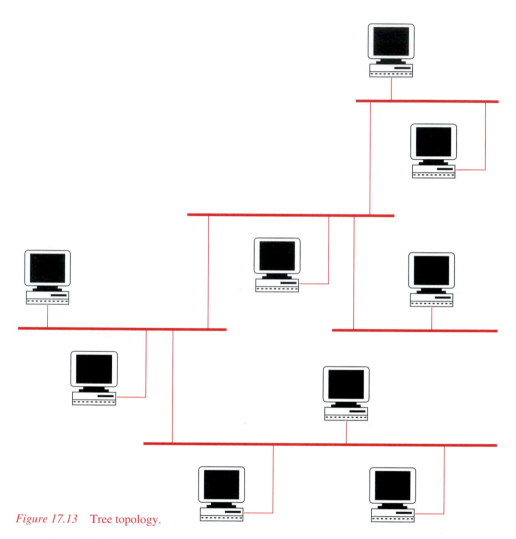

Figure 17.13   Tree topology.

Star-Wired Tree Structures

LAN technology that employs a bus- or-tree-structured logical topology, such as Ethernet and LocalTalk, often employs hubs or switches that allow individual systems to be attached to centrally located points. Each hub and its attached systems form an individual star structure. Each hub can be located in a wiring closet or equipment room, and the hubs can be interconnected to create a larger tree structure. A simple star-wired tree structure is shown in Fig 17.16.

Star-Wired Ring Structures

LAN technology that employs a ring-structured logical topology, such as Token Ring and FDDI, also often employs centrally located access units that allow individual sys-

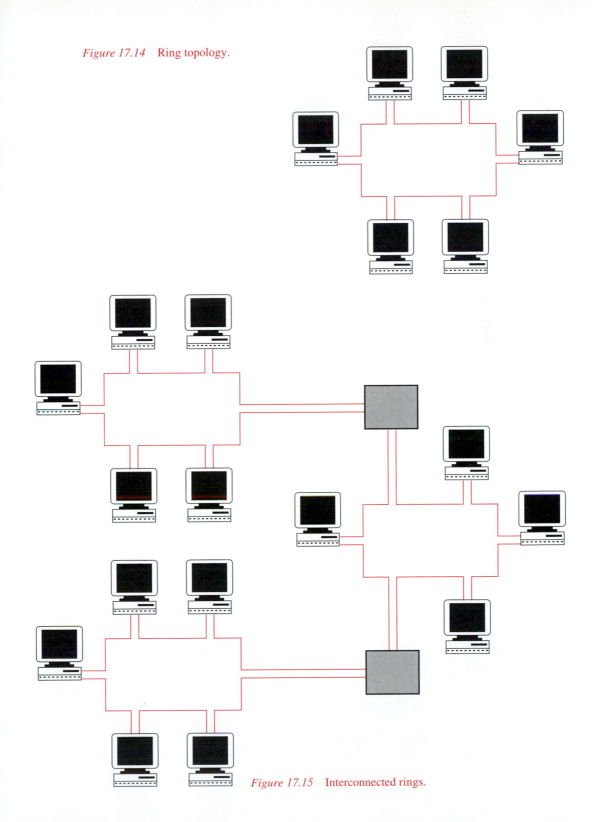

Figure 17.14 Ring topology.

Figure 17.15 Interconnected rings.

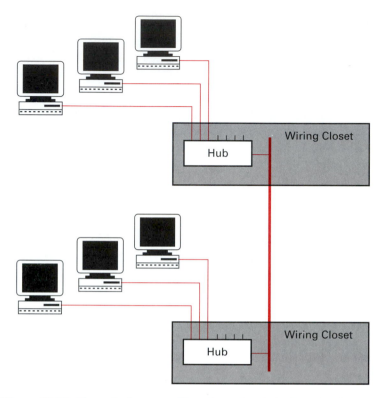

Figure 17.16   Star-wired tree configuration using hubs installed in wiring closets.

tems to be wired using a star configuration. With ring-structured LANs, a single cable supporting two communications paths is generally used to connect each system to the central access unit (see Fig. 17.17). The cabling is interconnected so the systems on the LAN perceive a ring structure, but the physical wiring appears as though there is a simple point-to-point connection between each system and the central access unit. Individual access units can be interconnected to extend the ring structure, as shown in Fig. 17.18.

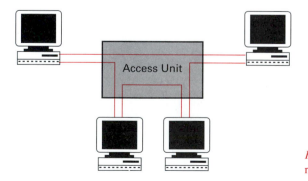

Figure 17.17   Star-wired ring configuration using a central access unit.

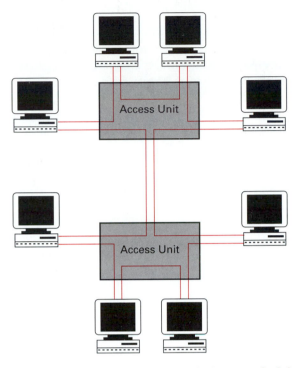

Figure 17.18   Interconnecting access units in a star-wired ring.

MEDIUM ACCESS CONTROL METHOD

Each LAN technology employs a specific technique for controlling each device's access to the transmission medium. The following *medium access control methods* are those employed by the mainstream LAN technologies:

- **Carrier Sense Multiple Access with Collision Detection (CSMA/CD).** This is the medium access control method used with Ethernet LAN data link technology (see Chapter 19).

- **Token Passing Ring.** This is the medium access control method used with Token Ring and Fiber Distributed Data Interface (FDDI) LAN data link technologies (see Chapters 20 and 22).

- **Token Passing Bus.** This is the medium access control method used with Token Bus and ARCnet LAN data link technologies (see Chapter 21).

- **Carrier Sense Multiple Access with Collision Avoidance (CSMA/CA).** This is the medium access control method used with Apple LocalTalk LAN data link technology (see Chapter 23).

Much mathematical analysis has been done of the various possible types of access control to determine which are the most efficient. The optimum choice varies depending on such factors as the number of systems served, the length and distribution of lengths of the frames, the speed of the channel, and the ratio of propagation time to frame transmission time.

It was once fashionable to compare one LAN data link technology against another based on the type of medium access control the technology employed. Ethernet supporters claimed that CSMA/CD was "better" than token ring, and the token ring and FDDI vendors made the opposite claim. Today, it is clear that all the forms of LAN data link technology that have come into widespread use have proven themselves in actual operation, and that the various forms of medium access control they employ, although different, are all efficient and reliable.

We next briefly describe each of the commonly used access control methods.

Carrier Sense Multiple Access with Collision Detection

The *Carrier Sense Multiple Access with Collision Detection (CSMA/CD)* access method has been in use in Ethernet technology for many years and is the most commonly used access method for local area networks. Access to the transmission medium is managed on an Ethernet LAN data link in a random, distributed fashion, and any system is allowed to transmit whenever the transmission medium is available.

The basic principle involved with CSMA/CD is that before a system transmits, it first "listens" to the transmission medium to determine whether or not another system is currently transmitting a frame. The term *carrier sense* indicates that a system listens before it transmits. If the transmission medium is "quiet," meaning that no other system is transmitting, the system then sends its frame.

When a frame is transmitted, the frame travels to all other systems on the network. As the frame arrives at each receiving system, that system examines the frame's destination address. If the destination address indicates that the frame applies to that system, the system receives and processes the frame.

With CSMA/CD, it occasionally happens that two (or more) systems send their frames close to simultaneously, resulting in a garbled transmission called a *collision*. All systems on the network, including the transmitting systems, continually listen to the transmission medium and are able to detect that a collision has occurred. The transmitting systems immediately stop transmitting as soon as they detect the collision and send out *jamming signals* on the transmission medium. Receiving systems ignore the garbled transmission that results from the collision followed by one or more jamming signals. Following a collision, each transmitting system waits for a varying period of time and then attempts to transmit again.

A key advantage of the CSMA/CD method is that access to the physical medium is typically very fast as long as traffic is not heavy, since a system can usually transmit as soon as it detects that the transmission medium is idle. Under heavier traffic loads, the number of collisions increases, and the time spent responding to collisions and retransmitting may cause performance to degrade. However, collisions do not typically cause a significant problem unless traffic is very heavy. Up to about 90% utilization of the channel capacity is possible with the CSMA/CD technique.

The technical details concerning the CSMA/CD form of medium access control, as it is used in conjunction with CSMA/CD and Ethernet technology, are described further in Chapter 19.

Carrier Sense Multiple Access with Collision Avoidance

A form of medium access control similar to CSMA/CD is called *Carrier Sense Multiple Access with Collision Avoidance (CSMA/CA)*. This is the form of medium access control used with LocalTalk LAN data link technology. With CSMA/CA, each system "listens" to the carrier while each transmission is in progress. After the transmission ends, each system waits for a specified period of time, based on its relative position in a logical list of systems. If no other system has started transmitting by the time a particular system's waiting time has elapsed, it may begin sending.

Different methods can be used to handle the situation that can occur when the end of the allotted time is reached and no system has a frame to send. In one approach, the highest priority system (highest in the list) sends a dummy frame, which then triggers another time period where systems have an opportunity to transmit. Another approach allows the systems to enter a free-for-all mode, where any system can transmit, and collision detection techniques are employed to handle conflicting transmissions.

There are also variations related to prioritization. With one variation, the first transmission slot is reserved for the system that has just received a frame. This allows the system to send a response and the two systems to maintain an efficient dialog. In another variation, a system that has just transmitted must wait until all the other systems have had an opportunity to transmit before it can transmit again. This ensures that the systems lower in the list have an opportunity to transmit.

The particular form of CSMA/CA medium access control used with LocalTalk LAN technology is described further in Chapter 23.

Token-Passing Ring

With networks that employ a ring topology, the most commonly used access method is *token passing*. The Token Ring and FDDI forms of LAN data link technology both use variations of the token-passing ring form of medium access control.

With a typical token ring access method, a short frame, called the *token*, is passed from one system to the next around the ring. If the token is marked as free, a system that receives the token can transmit a frame. It then marks the token as busy, appends the token to the frame, and transmits the frame along with the busy token. The frame, with the attached busy token, circulates around the ring, passing from system to system.

Each system that receives the frame checks the destination address in the frame to see if it should copy and process the frame. Whether or not the system copies the frame, it transmits the frame and the busy token to the next system on the ring. When the frame finally reaches the system that originally sent it, the originating system removes the frame from the ring, changes the token back to a free token, and transmits only the free token to the next system on the ring. The free token then circulates around the ring again until another system wishes to transmit.

Error conditions might prevent a sending system from recognizing and being able to remove its frame when the frame comes back around to the originating system. To handle this, one of the systems on the ring may be designated as a *monitor*. The monitor is responsible for detecting a busy token that is not being reset properly, removing it from the ring, and transmitting a new free token.

With the token ring approach, each system is always guaranteed a chance to transmit a frame within some predetermined period of time. The method allows for different priorities to be assigned to systems on the ring. High-priority systems can be given the opportunity to transmit before lower priority systems. A system may also be allowed to send multiple frames while it has the token. In this case, there is usually a time limit on how long a system can continue transmitting new frames. The principal disadvantages of the token ring technique are the complexity of the algorithm and the overhead involved in token processing and monitoring.

The variations of the token ring form of medium access control used with Token Ring LAN technology and with FDDI LAN technology are described further in Chapters 20 and 22.

Token-Passing Bus

Token passing is also used in the access control method used by the Token Bus and ARC-net forms of LAN technology. With the token-passing bus access method, a token is logically transmitted from one system to the next. When a system receives the token, it is allowed to transmit frames until a maximum amount of time has been reached. It then transmits the token to the next system. If a system has no frames to transmit, it immediately passes the token to the next system.

With token bus, systems are physically connected using a *physical* bus or tree topology. However, the systems use a *logical* ring topology for determining how to pass the token. This is illustrated in Fig. 17.19. The logical ring is generally implemented

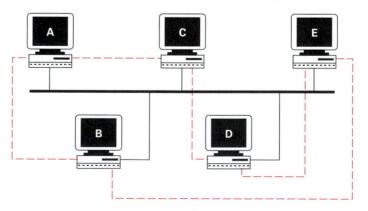

Figure 17.19   Token bus.

based on descending system address values. Physically, the systems are attached to the transmission medium in a linear sequence of A, B, C, D, and E. The token, however, may be passed in the sequence shown by the dashed line. It may go from A, to C, to D, to E, to B, and back to A, forming a logical ring. The ring is always passed to the system with the next lowest address until the system with the lowest address on the network receives the token. The token is then passed to the system with the highest network address, and the cycle begins again.

As with the token ring technique, the token bus method can provide for a high degree of control over each system's access to the transmission medium. Also, as with token ring, there is additional complexity. Removing frames from the network is not a problem because frames do not circulate from system to system as they do in a physical ring. However, provision must be made for detecting problems with the token, including loss of the token, duplication of the token, or monopolization of the token by one system. Also, as systems are added to or removed from the network, adjustments must be made to the logical sequence of the token passing to include or remove these systems.

Further details concerning the token bus forms of medium access control used with the Token Bus and ARCnet LAN technologies are included in Chapter 21.

SUMMARY

The building blocks of most enterprise networks are individual local area networks. Some of the uses to which LANs arc put in enterprise networks include resource sharing, electronic mail, implementing processor complexes, interconnection of mainframe computing equipment, building alarm and security systems, and implementing process control and monitoring functions.

An individual local area network data link is made up of a combination of hardware and software components that include computing devices, network interface cards (NICs), cabling systems, interconnection devices, and network software.

The four characteristics important in classifying different forms of LAN data link technology are transmission medium, signaling technique, network topology, and medium access control technique.

Twisted-pair cable is the most commonly used LAN transmission medium, but many LANs use coaxial cable, fiber-optic cable, or wireless transmission.

The two techniques used with LAN data links for transmitting signals over a physical communications medium are baseband signaling and broadband signaling.

The topology of a LAN data link subnetwork concerns both the physical configuration of the cabling and the logical way in which systems view the structure of the LAN. The three principal topologies employed by LAN data link technology are the star, the bus, and the ring. The physical layout of the cabling can be different from the logical topology of the network, and star-wired tree and ring structures are commonly used.

The medium access control technique refers to the method used for controlling access to the transmission medium. The four techniques used by mainstream LAN technology are carrier sense multiple access with collision detection (CSMA/CD), used by Ethernet

LAN technology, token passing ring, used by Token Ring and Fiber Distributed Data Interface (FDDI), token passing bus, used by Token Bus and ARCnet, and carrier sense multiple access with collision avoidance (CSMA/CA), used by Apple LocalTalk LAN data link equipment.

Chapter 18 examines the international standards developed for the protocols used to control frame transmission over LAN data link subnetworks.

Chapter 18

LAN Subnetwork Standards

Most of the data link protocols used to control transmission over LAN subnetworks conform to the basic layering structure defined by the IEEE/ISO/ANSI LAN architecture introduced in Chapter 2. As shown in Fig. 18.1, the LAN architecture is based on the OSI model and divides the Data Link layer into a Logical Link Control sublayer and a Medium Access Control sublayer.

Early in its work on the development of local area network standards, IEEE Project 802 determined that it would not be able to develop a single local area network standard to meet the needs of all users. In recognition of this, the project developed a *family* of LAN

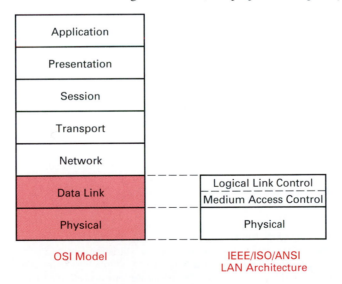

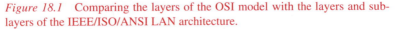

Figure 18.1 Comparing the layers of the OSI model with the layers and sublayers of the IEEE/ISO/ANSI LAN architecture.

standards. This family initially included a single standard for the Logical Link Control (LLC) sublayer of the Data Link layer and three standards for the Medium Access Control (MAC) sublayer and Physical layer: CSMA/CD, Token Bus, and Token Ring.

The IEEE standards for local area networking technology were subsequently accepted by ISO as international standards and are now also described by ISO standards. ANSI then later developed the Fiber Distributed Data Interface (FDDI) form of medium access control that has also been accepted as a MAC sublayer and Physical layer standard by ISO.

Box 18.1 briefly introduces each of the LAN standards described in this chapter and in the chapters that follow in this part of the book.

We next look at the addressing mechanisms used in conjunction with LAN data links to identify users of the data link and to identify individual network devices.

BOX 18.1   IEEE/ISO/ANSI LAN standards.

- **Logical Link Control (LLC).** This standard describes the functions of the LLC sublayer of the IEEE/ISO/ANSI LAN architecture. It is defined by the IEEE 802.2 and ISO 8802-2 standards. The Logical Link Control standard describes the function of the LLC sublayer for all three forms of medium access control defined by the IEEE and can be used in conjunction with the FDDI standard as well. The Logical Link Control sublayer standard is described in this chapter.

- **Carrier Sense Multiple Access with Collision Detection (CSMA/CD).** This standard describes the MAC sublayer and Physical layer functions for a bus- or tree-structured LAN using CSMA/CD as an access protocol. It is defined by the IEEE 802.3 and ISO 8802-3 CSMA/CD standards. Implementations conforming to this standard are most often called *Ethernet* LANs. The standard has its roots in the *Ethernet Version 2 Specification* for local area networking technology jointly developed by Digital Equipment Corporation, Xerox, and Intel. The IEEE 802.3/ISO 8802-3 CSMA/CD standard and the older *Ethernet Version 2 Specification* are described in Chapter 19.

- **Token Ring.** This standard describes the MAC sublayer and Physical layer functions for a ring-structured LAN using a token-passing access protocol. It is defined by the IEEE 802.5 and ISO 8802-5 standards. The Token Ring standard is an outgrowth of the development work IBM did for its *Token-Ring Network* family of LAN products. The standard is described in Chapter 20.

- **Token Bus.** This standard describes the MAC sublayer and Physical layer functions for a bus-structured LAN using token passing as an access protocol. It is defined by the IEEE 802.4 and ISO 8802-4 standards. The Token Bus form of LAN was designed to meet the needs of factory automation applications. The Token Bus standard is described in Chapter 21.

- **Fiber Distributed Data Interface (FDDI).** This standard defines a high-speed form of LAN standardized by a subcommittee of ANSI. It is defined by the ANSI X3T9.5 and ISO 9314 standards. FDDI uses a logical ring-structured topology using a timed token-passing access protocol different from the token-passing protocol defined by the Token Ring standard. The FDDI standard is described in Chapter 22.

LOCAL AREA NETWORK ADDRESSING

An important aspect of the IEEE/ISO/ANSI LAN architecture concerns the addressing mechanisms implemented by a LAN data link. This architecture provides for two levels of addressing: service-access-point (SAP) and Medium Access Control (MAC) addressing:

- **SAP Addressing.** A *service-access-point (SAP) address* identifies an individual service-access-point into the LLC sublayer. It represents a particular mechanism, process, or protocol operating in the layer above the LLC layer that is requesting LLC sublayer services through the associated SAP. Each mechanism, process, or protocol concurrently using the services of the LLC sublayer must use a different SAP address.

- **MAC Addressing.** A *Medium Access Control (MAC) address,* or station address, uniquely identifies an individual station that implements a single point of physical attachment to a LAN data link. MAC addressing is the concern of the Medium Access Control sublayer. Each station attached to a LAN data link must have a unique MAC address on that LAN data link.

The MAC addressing mechanism is used by the MAC sublayer to deliver each MAC frame to the appropriate station or stations on the LAN data link. The SAP addressing mechanism is used by the LLC sublayer to deliver logical-link-control-protocol-data-units (LLC-PDUS) to the appropriate user or users of the LLC sublayer service within a particular destination station. It will be easier to see how these two separate addressing mechanisms work together if we examine them one by one, from the bottom up.

MAC ADDRESSING

The main role of MAC addressing is to make it possible to move a MAC frame from the station that originates it to the correct destination station or stations. MAC address fields in the MAC frame are used to make this happen. Each of the forms of medium access control we examine in this book defines its own MAC frame format, although they are generally the same.

The general format of the MAC frame is shown in Fig. 18.2. Each type of MAC frame carries a header and a trailer that contains, among other things, destination and source

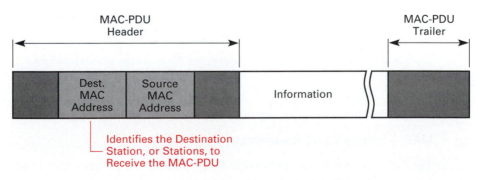

Figure 18.2 MAC sublayer frame format.

MAC address fields. Specific MAC frame formats for the different MAC sublayer technologies are examined in subsequent chapters in this part.

As shown in Fig. 18.2, the *destination MAC address* field in a MAC frame identifies the station or stations intended to receive the frame. The destination MAC address can refer to an individual station or to a group of stations. The *source MAC address* refers to the station that transmitted the frame and always refers to an individual station.

MAC Address Formats

The IEEE/ISO/ANSI LAN standards allow MAC addresses to be either 16 bits or 48 bits in length. The formats of destination and source MAC address fields are shown in Fig. 18.3 and are described below:

- **Destination MAC Address.** Identifies the destination station, or stations, to receive the MAC frame. If the first bit of a destination MAC address is 0, the address identifies an individual station; if the first bit is 1, the address refers to a group of stations. A destination address value of all 1 bits is the broadcast address and refers to all active stations on the LAN data link. A station that sends MAC frames containing group destination MAC addresses implements a multicasting function that allows it to deliver each frame to more than one destination station in a single transmission. In a 48-bit destination MAC address, the second bit indicates whether the address is a locally administered address or a globally administered address.

- **Source MAC Address.** Identifies the station that originated the MAC frame. The first bit of a source MAC address is always 0. In a 48-bit MAC address, the second bit indicates whether the address is a locally administered address or a globally administered address.

For a given LAN data link, the source and destination address fields must be the same size in all MAC frames generated on that data link.

MAC Address Administration

The IEEE/ISO/ANSI LAN standards define both locally administered MAC addressing and globally administered MAC addressing. All 16-bit addresses are locally administered. For 48-bit addressing, if the second bit is 0, addressing is globally administered; if the second bit is 1, addressing is locally administered.

- **Locally Administered MAC Addressing.** It is the responsibility of the organization installing the LAN to assign a unique MAC address to each network station. This is often done by setting DIP switches on the NIC, or it might be done using a management software function.

- **Globally Administered MAC Addressing.** Each LAN manufacturer assigns a unique address to each NIC it manufactures, thus guaranteeing that no two stations in the world have the same address, as long as they use globally administered MAC addressing. With globally administered MAC addressing, each NIC has a permanent address, and DIP switches or software functions are not required to set the NIC's MAC address.

MAC Address Value Assignment

The IEEE is the organization responsible for coordinating the assignment of address values for globally administered MAC addresses. The IEEE, upon request and upon payment of a small fee, assigns a value for the 24 high-order MAC address bits to any organization that manufac-

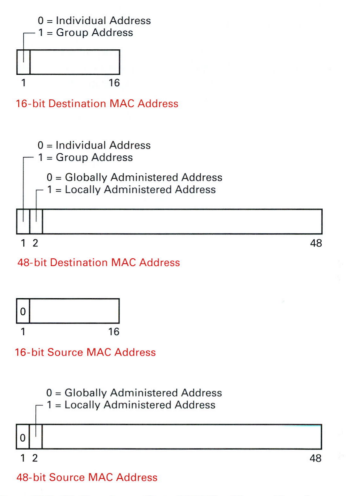

Figure 18.3   Medium Access Control (MAC) sublayer address formats.

tures networking equipment. The IEEE maintains a registry so no two organizations are ever give the same value for the 24 high-order address bits. The manufacturer receiving an address value assignment then uses that value in assigning MAC addresses to the NICs it manufactures, and assigns a unique address value to the 24 low-order address bits of each NIC.

The use of globally administered addresses simplifies address management for networks; but it does increase transmission overhead, since more addressing bits must be sent in each frame. The majority of LAN product vendors today use globally administered addresses in the NICs they manufacture. However, vendors of network products can choose whether to support one or both forms of addressing as part of their NIC products. For example, some NICs have a factory-set, globally administered MAC address but allow the preset address to be overridden by a software function should the organization installing the LAN decide to use its own locally administered address values.

MAC Address Filtering

The LLC sublayer in a computing system attached to a LAN always receives the LLC-PDUs carried in MAC frames that have that station's own destination MAC address. However, many implementations of the LLC sublayer standard often provide a *MAC address filtering mechanism*. Such a mechanism allows the LLC sublayer to request that MAC frames with other destination MAC addresses also be delivered to it.

For example, a MAC address filtering mechanism may implement a multicasting capability by allowing an LLC user to specify a list of group destination MAC addresses. The station will then accept all MAC frames that have those group destination MAC addresses. A MAC address filtering mechanism is often used in conjunction with a SAP address filtering mechanism, which we describe later in this chapter.

SAP ADDRESSING

The LLC sublayer has the overall responsibility of controlling the exchange of messages between individual users of the LLC sublayer service. Once a MAC frame carrying an LLC-PDU arrives at an appropriate destination station, the Logical Link Control sublayer in that station uses SAP addressing to ensure that the LLC-PDU is delivered to the appropriate LAN data link user or users.

SAP Addresses

Figure 18.4 shows the format of the LLC-PDU and illustrates how the LLC-PDU is carried within a MAC frame. The Information field of the LLC-PDU carries the data unit passed

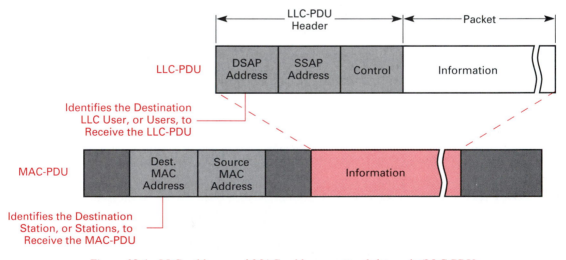

Figure 18.4   LLC sublayer and MAC sublayer protocol-data-unit (LLC-PDU and MAC-PDU) formats.

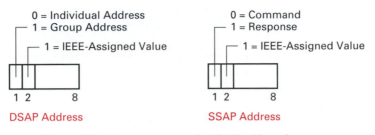

Figure 18.5   Service-access-point (SAP) address formats.

down from a user of the LAN data link. This data unit is often called a *packet*. The header of the LLC-PDU contains two 1-octet SAP address values: the destination-service-access-point (DSAP) address and source-service-access-point (SSAP) address. The formats of DSAP and SSAP address fields are shown in Fig. 18.5 and are described below:

- **DSAP Address.** The *destination-service-access-point (DSAP) address* identifies the LLC sublayer user, or users, to receive the LLC-PDU. The DSAP address can be either an *individual* address, which identifies a single SAP; or it can be a *group* address, which identifies a set of SAPs. If the first bit of a DSAP address contains a 0, the address refers to an individual SAP; if the first bit contains a 1, the address is a group address. The group address consisting of all 1 bits is the *global SAP address* that specifies all active SAPs in the station.

- **SSAP Address.** The *source-service-access-point (SSAP) address* is always an individual address that identifies a single SAP—the one responsible for originating the LLC-PDU. If the first bit of a SSAP address contains a 0, the LLC-PDU is a *command;* if the first bit contains a 1, the LLC-PDU is a *response.* A command is sent by an LLC sublayer entity initiating a data transfer operation; a response is sent by the opposite LLC sublayer entity in reply to a command. Commands and responses are discussed further later in this chapter.

As we have seen, SAP address values are used to distinguish one user of the LAN data link from another user of the same LAN data link that might be active at the same time in the same station. As we have already mentioned, it is possible for an implementation of the Logical Link Control sublayer standard to allow more than one user to concurrently request LAN data link services, each through a separate service-access-point into the LLC sublayer.

Each user of the LLC sublayer is normally associated with a particular data transport protocol family. Therefore, SAP addresses are often used to identify the specific protocols being used by the layer above the LLC sublayer. However, it is important to realize that the LLC standard itself allows specific implementations of Logical Link Control to use SAP address values for any desired purpose. As far as the LLC sublayer is concerned, SAP address values can be used to identify users of the LLC sublayer service in any way the implementor chooses.

SAP Address Filtering

A SAP address filtering mechanism may implement a multicasting capability by allowing a LAN data link user to specify a list of the group DSAP addresses in which that user is

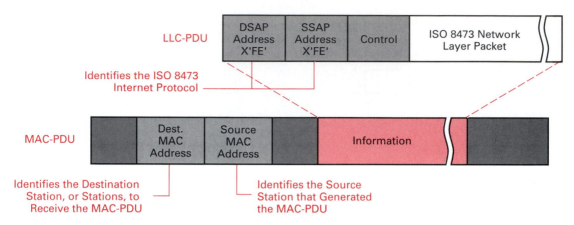

Figure 18.6   LLC-PDU carrying an ISO 8473 Internet protocol packet.

interested. Then, for all MAC frames the station accepts, the LLC sublayer will pass to a user the packets carried in all LLC-PDUs with DSAP addresses that correspond to that user's SAP address list. A SAP address filtering mechanism is often used in conjunction with a MAC address filtering mechanism, which we described earlier.

An LLC implementation typically allows only one LLC user in a particular station to receive the packets carried in LLC-PDUs with a particular *individual* DSAP address. But multiple LLC users in the same station can typically receive the packets carried in LLC-PDUs with a particular *group* DSAP address.

SAP Address Assigned Values

All SAP address values that have the second bit position set to 1 are reserved for definition by the IEEE, and specific meanings have been assigned to a number of these reserved SAP values. For example, the SAP address value X'FE' has been assigned by the IEEE to the ISO 8473 Internet protocol that operates in the OSI Network layer. Figure 18.6 shows an LLC-PDU carrying an ISO 8473 Internet protocol packet. Notice that both the DSAP and SSAP address fields carry a value of X'FE'.

SUBNETWORK ACCESS PROTOCOL

Very little of the traffic on today's LAN data links carries packets that conform to international standard protocols, such as the ISO 8473 Internet protocol. The IEEE has defined a protocol called the *Subnetwork Access Protocol (SNAP)* that many networking products use to carry traffic that does not conform to international standards, such as TCP/IP traffic or NetWare IPX/SPX traffic. The SNAP protocol implements another mechanism that can be used for the purpose of distinguishing LLC-PDUs carrying packets associated with one transport protocol from LLC-PDUs carrying packets associated with some other transport protocol.

Private Protocols

The SNAP mechanism is intended for use with *private* protocols that do not conform to international standards. Examples of such protocols are the TCP/IP protocol suite and IPX/SPX. Such protocols do not have IEEE-assigned SAP address values. Therefore, a mechanism is needed that goes beyond SAP addressing to distinguish one private protocol from another. This is especially important when packets associated with one private protocol are carried over a LAN data link that may be carrying other types of network traffic at the same time.

SNAP LLC-PDU Format

Figure 18.7 shows the format of the PDUs defined by the SNAP mechanism. The data unit carried inside the LLC-PDU when the SNAP mechanism is used is often called a *SNAP PDU*. Notice that LLC-PDUs carrying SNAP PDUs have SSAP and DSAP address values of hex 'AA'.

The SNAP mechanism provides a level of multiplexing over and above that provided by SAP addressing to differentiate one private protocol from other private protocols. The first five octets of a SNAP PDU contain a SNAP identifier value that uniquely identifies the protocol associated with the packet the SNAP PDU is carrying. The first three octets of the

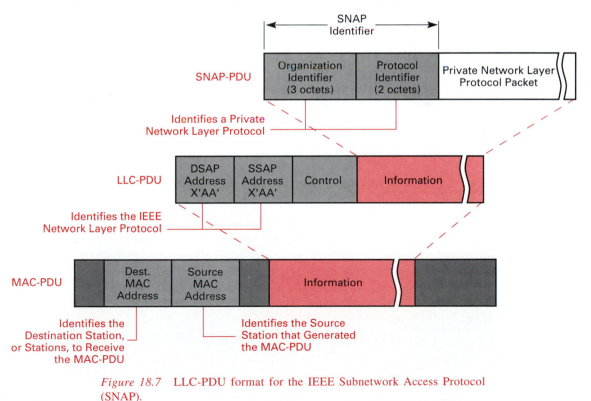

Figure 18.7   LLC-PDU format for the IEEE Subnetwork Access Protocol (SNAP).

SNAP identifier contain a value assigned to a particular organization; the remaining two octets identify a specific protocol defined by that organization.

Protocol Coexistence

Any organization that defines one or more private protocols, and chooses to implement the IEEE SNAP mechanism, can apply to the IEEE for an organization identifier it can use to distinguish its private protocols from the private protocols defined by other organizations. For example, private protocols associated with the TCP/IP protocol suite all have 5-octet protocol identifiers that begin with the TCP/IP 3-octet organization identifier, and all Novell protocols use Novell's 3-octet organization identifier. Computing equipment vendors, such as IBM and DEC, that have defined proprietary network architectures, also have unique values that distinguish their private Network layer protocols from those of other organizations.

SNAP PDUs that carry traffic for different private protocols and LLC-PDUs that carry traffic conforming to international standard protocols can all coexist on the same LAN data link without interfering with one another. The SAP address values carried in all LLC-PDUs and the SNAP identifier values carried in SNAP PDUs allow LLC-PDUs carrying packets associated with one protocol to be easily distinguished from LLC-PDUs carrying packets associated with other protocols.

SNAP Protocol Identifier Filtering

An implementation of the LLC sublayer that provides the SNAP mechanism may provide a *SNAP protocol identifier filtering* mechanism similar to the MAC address and SAP address filtering mechanisms described earlier. For example, a LAN data link user might be able to supply LLC with a list of SNAP identifier values. Then the user will only see the packets carried by SNAP PDUs with the SNAP protocol identifier values in that user's list. A SNAP protocol filtering mechanism is often used in conjunction with SAP address and MAC address filtering mechanisms.

LAN ARCHITECTURE SERVICES AND PROTOCOLS

The standards making up the IEEE/ISO/ANSI LAN architecture, like all standards based on the OSI model, define two aspects of the operation of each layer and sublayer: a service definition and a protocol specification. In the next sections, we examine the services offered by the LLC sublayer and protocol specification for providing those services.

LOGICAL LINK CONTROL SUBLAYER SERVICES

The Logical Link Control sublayer service definition specifies two general types of LAN data link service:

- Connectionless service.
- Connection-oriented service.

There is also a third type of data link service under consideration for possible addition to the Logical Link Control standard:

- Acknowledged connectionless service

A particular implementation of the LLC standard might provide only one of the above services, two of them, or all three. All LAN implementations must provide the connectionless service, and many provide only the connectionless service.

Connectionless Service

The *connectionless LLC service* incurs the least amount of protocol overhead. With this service, often called a datagram service, there is no need to establish a prior association between a source and destination system before data transmission can take place. Each LLC-PDU sent using the connectionless LLC service is processed independently of any other LLC-PDU. No sequence checking is done to ensure that LLC-PDUs are received in the same sequence in which they were sent, and the receiving system sends no acknowledgment that it has received an LLC-PDU. No flow control or error recovery is provided as part of connectionless service. When the connectionless service is used, all necessary flow control and error recovery services required must be provided in the layers above the Logical Link Control sublayer.

The connectionless service is the most commonly used LLC service in LAN implementations. With the connectionless LLC service, LLC-PDUs can be sent either to individual or group SAP addresses. The connectionless LLC sublayer service uses group SAP addresses to provide a multicasting capability a source user can employ to send an LLC-PDU to more than one destination user in a single transmission.

Connection-Oriented Service

With the *connection-oriented LLC service*, delivery of LLC-PDUs is guaranteed by the LLC service as a long as an *LLC connection* is maintained between a source LLC service-access-point and a destination LLC service-access-point. The connection-oriented LLC sublayer service is similar to the service provided on an HDLC data link (see Chapter 11).

An LLC connection consists of a logical association between a pair of LLC sublayer entities. With the connection-oriented LLC service, a connection between the source and destination LLC sublayer entities must be established before data transfer can begin, the connection must be maintained while data transfer proceeds, and the connection can be terminated when data transfer is no longer required.

The connection-oriented LLC service supports two functions related to error correction: sequence checking and message acknowledgment. LLC-PDUs being sent are assigned sequence numbers. As each LLC-PDU is received, its sequence number is checked to ensure that all LLC-PDUs have arrived in the sequence sent and that none are missing or duplicated. Periodically, the receiving LLC sublayer entity sends an acknowledgment so the source LLC sublayer entity knows that the LLC-PDUs have arrived successfully. If problems occur, and the destination LLC sublayer entity informs the source LLC sublayer entity that LLC-PDUs were not successfully received, the source LLC sublayer entity retransmits them. The protocol mechanisms associated with sequence checking and acknowledgments are described later in this chapter.

Since the connection-oriented LLC service always involves a pair of LLC sublayer entities, there is no provision for delivering an LLC-PDU to more than one destination service-access-point. Therefore, the connection-oriented LLC service does not provide a multicasting mechanism. If the source user of the LAN data link wishes to send an LLC-PDU to more than one destination user, a separate connection must be established with each destination SAP, and a copy of the LLC-PDU must be sent in a separate transmission to each destination user.

Acknowledged Connectionless Service

The *acknowledged connectionless LLC service* is somewhat of a compromise between the completely unacknowledged connectionless service and the connection-oriented service. At the time of writing, it is being considered for incorporation into the LLC standard to support certain types of process control applications. Few of today's LAN implementations provide the acknowledged connectionless service. Many authorities doubt whether it is really necessary, since it is quite complex and incurs almost as much protocol overhead as using the full connection-oriented service to provide the same capability.

With the acknowledged connectionless LLC service, no connection is established between the source and destination stations, and there is no relationship between one LLC-PDU transmitted by a source station and any other LLC-PDU. But each LLC-PDU transmitted by a source station is acknowledged by the destination station. The acknowledged connectionless service is considered to be a guaranteed delivery service because the entity that requests a data transmission service is informed if the LLC-PDU fails to be delivered.

LLC-PROTOCOL-DATA-UNIT

Box 18.2 shows the format of the LLC-PDU and describes its fields. Note that the DSAP field can contain either an individual address value or a group address value. A group DSAP value allows an LLC-PDU to be delivered to a group of service-access-points in a destination station.

Commands and Responses

An LLC-PDU can take the form of either a *command* or a *response*. A command is sent by an LLC sublayer entity initiating a data transfer operation; a response is sent by the distant LLC sublayer entity in reply to a command. The first bit of the SSAP value indicates whether the LLC-PDU is a command or a response: a 0 bit indicates a command and a 1 bit indicates a response.

BOX 18.2   Logical-Link-Control-Protocol-Data-Unit (LLC-PDU).

DSAP Address	SSAP Address	Control	Information
1 octet	1 octet	1 or 2 octets	0 – *n* octets

- **Source and Destination Service Access Point Address Fields.** A one-octet destination service-access-point (DSAP) address followed by a one-octet source service-access-point (SSAP) address. The formats of DSAP and SSAP addresses are described earlier in this chapter.

- **Control Field.** A one- or two-octet field that describes the LLC-PDU's type and contains control information. The formats of LLC-PDU control fields are described later in this chapter.

- **Information Field.** A variable-length field that typically contains the packet passed down from the layer above the LLC sublayer. The Information field is supplied by the LLC sublayer itself for LLC-PDUs that are generated by the LLC sublayer. It can consist of zero octets for some LLC-PDU types.

LLC-PDU Types

There are three general types of LLC-PDUs. The following are brief descriptions of each of them:

- **Information LLC-PDUs.** The primary function of an *Information LLC-PDU (I-format LLC-PDU)* is to carry user data. However, I-format LLC-PDUs sometimes also perform control functions.

- **Supervisory LLC-PDUs.** *Supervisory LLC-PDUs (S-format LLC-PDUs)* are used to carry information necessary to control the operation of the LLC sublayer protocol.

- **Unnumbered LLC-PDUs.** *Unnumbered LLC-PDUs (U-format LLC-PDUs)* are sometimes used to carry data and are sometimes used for special functions, such as performing initialization procedures and invoking diagnostic sequences.

I-format LLC-PDUs and S-format LLC-PDUs carry two-octet control fields; U-format LLC-PDUs carry one-octet control fields. Each of the three types of LLC protocol operation uses a different set of LLC-PDUs to carry out its functions. The specific LLC-PDUs used for each type of protocol operation are described later in this chapter.

LLC-PDU Names and Mnemonics

Each of the LLC-PDUs used to provide the LLC sublayer service has a *full name* and a shorthand *mnemonic*. For example, one of the LLC-PDUs employed in the protocol for supplying the connectionless LLC service is the Exchange Identification LLC-PDU. Its full name is *Exchange Identification*, and its mnemonic is *XID*.

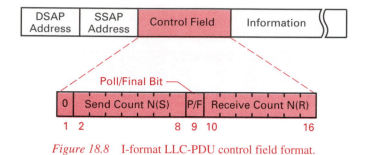

Figure 18.8 I-format LLC-PDU control field format.

I-Format LLC-PDU Control Field Format

Figure 18.8 illustrates the format of the I-format LLC-PDU control field. Bit positions 1 and 2 in the first control field octet identify the LLC-PDU's type. An I-format LLC-PDU always has a 0 in bit position 1. The remainder of the bits in the I-format LLC-PDU control field are used to contain a receive count [N(R)], a send count [N(S)], and a poll/final (P/F) bit. The count fields and the Poll/Final bit are used in implementing error-detection mechanisms described later in this chapter.

S-Format LLC-PDU Control Field Format

Figure 18.9 shows the format of the S-format LLC-PDU control field. When bit position 1 of the first control field octet is 1, bit position 2 further identifies the LLC-PDU as being either an S-format LLC-PDU or a U-format LLC-PDU. A 10 in bit positions 1 and 2 identifies the LLC-PDU as an S-format LLC-PDU. The remainder of the bits in the S-format LLC-PDU control octet are interpreted as containing a receive count [N(R)], a Poll/Final bit, and a

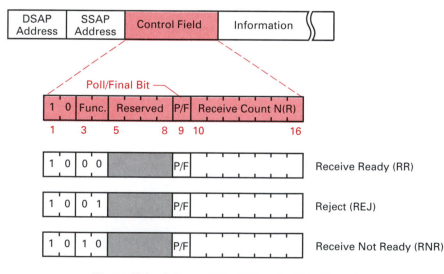

Figure 18.9 S-format LLC-PDU control field format.

2-bit function code. The function code bits identify the type of command or response the LLC-PDU represents.

U-Format LLC-PDU Control Field Format

Figure 18.10 shows the format of the U-format LLC-PDU control field. A 1-1-bit configuration in bit positions 1 and 2 of the first control field octet identifies the LLC-PDU as a U-format LLC-PDU and indicates that the control field is only one octet in length. The

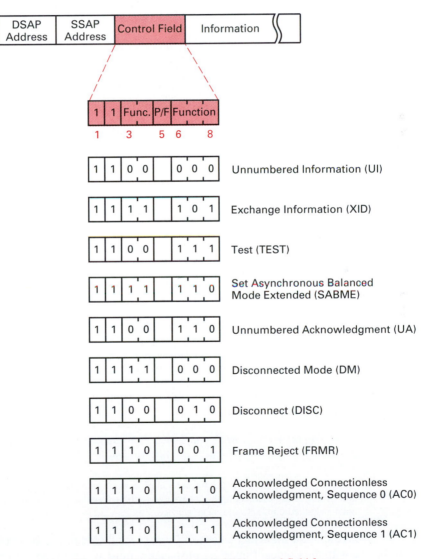

Figure 18.10   U-format LLC-PDU control field format.

remainder of the bits are interpreted as a Poll/Final bit and function code bits. The function code bits in a U-format LLC-PDU identify the type of command or response the LLC-PDU represents. Some U-format LLC-PDU commands and responses have information fields; others do not.

LLC PROTOCOL OPERATIONAL MODES

The three forms of LLC service are provided by different types of LLC protocol operation.

Types of LLC Protocol Operation

The Logical Link Control standard describes two types of LLC protocol operation that correspond to the first two forms of LLC service:

- **Type 1 Operation.** The LLC protocol provides the connectionless LLC service.
- **Type 2 Operation.** The LLC protocol provides the connection-oriented LLC service.

A third type of LLC protocol operation has been proposed for addition to the Logical Link Control standard:

- **Type 3 Operation.** The LLC protocol provides the acknowledged connectionless LLC service.

Implementation Classes

Implementations of the Logical Link Control standard are classified according to the types of LLC protocol operation they support. The Logical Link Control standard defines two LLC implementation classes:

- **Class I LLC.** A *Class I LLC* implementation supports only type 1 operation and provides only the connectionless LLC service.
- **Class II LLC.** A *Class II LLC* implementation supports type 1 and type 2 operation and provides both the connectionless LLC service and the connection-oriented LLC service.

Two additional LLC implementation classes have been proposed as possible additions to the Logical Link Control standard:

- **Class III LLC.** A *Class III LLC* implementation supports type 1 and type 3 operation and provides both the connectionless LLC service and the acknowledged connectionless LLC service.
- **Class IV LLC.** A *Class IV LLC* implementation supports type 1, type 2, and type 3 service and provides the connectionless LLC service, the connection-oriented LLC service, and the acknowledged connectionless LLC service.

Notice that all implementations of Logical Link Control, to be considered in conformance with the Logical Link Control standard, must support type 1 operation at a minimum and must provide the connectionless LLC service. Most implementations of LLC on today's LANs are Class I LLC implementations and provide only the connectionless LLC service.

We next examine the specific LLC-PDUs and the protocol mechanisms that apply to each of the three types of LLC operation.

PROTOCOL FOR TYPE 1 CONNECTIONLESS OPERATION

The protocol for type 1 operation provides the connectionless LLC service. Three U-format LLC-PDUs are used to support type 1 operation. These are listed in Box 18.3.

The protocol mechanisms for type 1 operation provide for a data transfer service and simple station identification and loopback testing procedures. The following are descriptions of each of the procedures used during type 1 LLC operation.

Data Transfer

An LLC sublayer entity carries out a request for a data transfer operation by encapsulating the data unit passed to it in an Unnumbered Information (UI) LLC-PDU command and then uses the MAC sublayer service to transmit the UI command over the transmission medium. An LLC sublayer entity receiving a UI command passes it up, in the form of an *LLC service-data-unit (LLC-SDU)*, to the appropriate LAN data link user or users in the layer above. When a UI command is received by an LLC sublayer entity in the destination station, no sequence checking is done, and the LLC sublayer entity in the destination station sends no acknowledgment.

Error Detection

Error detection is implemented by the MAC sublayer on behalf of the LLC sublayer. The error detection mechanism the MAC sublayer uses is described here, since a similar error detection mechanism is used for the various medium access control technologies described in subsequent chapters.

BOX 18.3　LLC-PDUs for type 1 operation.

- **Unnumbered Information (UI).** UI commands and responses are used to convey user data between a pair of LLC entities.
- **Exchange Identification (XID).** XID commands and responses are used to exchange identification information between a source and a destination LLC entity.
- **Test (TEST).** TEST commands and responses can be used to conduct a loopback test of the transmission path between two LLC entities.

When the MAC sublayer receives an LLC-PDU from the LLC sublayer in the form of a *MAC service-data-unit (MAC-SDU)*, the MAC sublayer encapsulates the MAC-SDU in a MAC frame. As part of the encapsulation process, the MAC sublayer places the frame through an algorithm that calculates a cyclical redundancy check (CRC) value. This CRC value becomes part of the MAC frame the MAC sublayer sends over the transmission medium. When the MAC sublayer in a destination system accepts a frame, it places the frame through an identical algorithm to calculate its own CRC value. The destination system then compares the calculated CRC value with the received value. If the values match, the MAC sublayer assumes that no errors have occurred. If the values do not match, the MAC sublayer assumes that the MAC frame was corrupted during transmission.

When the MAC sublayer detects a transmission error, it discards the corrupted frame. The MAC sublayer that detects a corrupted frame need not notify either the source or destination LLC sublayer entity of the error. The LLC sublayer receives only error-free LLC-PDUs and does not receive LLC-PDUs that were corrupted by transmission errors. An error-correction mechanism operating in a higher layer typically detects missing frames discarded by the MAC sublayer and requests their retransmission.

Exchanging Identification Information

Any LLC sublayer entity that receives an Exchange Identification (XID) LLC-PDU command is required to generate an XID LLC-PDU response specifying the class of service it can support.

The exact way in which the XID command is used is left as an implementation option. However, the Logical Link Control standard suggests possible uses for exchanging identification information using XID commands and responses. These include the following:

- Determining if a particular station is available on the network.
- Announcing the presence of a station on the network.
- Determining the stations assigned to a particular group address.
- Checking for duplicate addresses.
- Determining the implementation class an LLC implementation supports and choosing a type of protocol operation to use.
- For LLC entities supporting type 2 operation, exchanging information concerning window sizes to implement error detection and flow control procedures.

Loopback Testing

When an LLC sublayer entity receives a TEST LLC-PDU command, it is required to send a TEST LLC-PDU response back to the user that sent the TEST command. An optional Information field can be included in the TEST command. If one is included, the TEST response must echo the Information field back. Exchanges of TEST commands and responses can be used to perform a basic test of the presence of a transmission path between LLC sublayer entities.

PROTOCOL FOR TYPE 2 CONNECTION-ORIENTED OPERATION

The protocol for type 2 LLC operation provides the connection-oriented LLC service and is similar to the protocol used in HDLC. I-format, S-format, and U-format LLC-PDUs are used to support type 2 operation. These are shown in Box 18.4.

BOX 18.4   LLC-PDUs for type 2 operation.

I-Format LLC-PDU

- **Information (I).** I-format LLC-PDU commands and responses are used to transfer user data between two communicating LLC entities.

S-Format LLC-PDUs

- **Receive Ready.** A Receive Ready (RR) response is used as an acknowledgment to Information LLC-PDUs when there is no reverse traffic to send. An RR command can also be used to indicate that the LLC sublayer entity is able to receive additional LLC-PDUs after LLC-PDU transmission has been halted.

- **Receive Not Ready.** A Receive Not Ready (RNR) response is used to acknowledge receipt of an LLC-PDU and also to ask the sending LLC sublayer entity to stop transmitting I-format LLC-PDUs. The RNR response is used to handle possible internal constraints, such as a temporary lack of buffer space.

- **Reject.** A Reject (REJ) response is used to reject an LLC-PDU and to ask that it and any other LLC-PDUs transmitted after it be retransmitted.

U-Format LLC-PDUs

- **Set Asynchronous Balanced Mode Extended.** A Set Asynchronous Balanced Mode Extended (SABME) command is used to request the establishment of a connection between a pair of LLC entities.

- **Disconnected Mode.** A Disconnected Mode (DM) response is used to reject a request for an establishment of an LLC connection.

- **Disconnect.** A Disconnect (DISC) command is used to request the release of a connection previously established using the SABME command.

- **Frame Reject.** A Frame Reject (FRMR) response is sent by a destination LLC sublayer entity to indicate that it has received an LLC-PDU it is unable to handle, such as one that is invalid or unimplemented, has an invalid sequence number, or has an Information field that exceeds the maximum size.

- **Unnumbered Acknowledgment.** An Unnumbered Acknowledgment (UA) response is sent by a destination LLC sublayer entity as a positive acknowledgment. It is sent in response to an SABME LLC-PDU that requests a connection or to a DISC LLC-PDU that requests a connection release.

The protocol mechanisms for type 2 operation provide for a data transfer service and for performing LLC-PDU acknowledgments and sequence checking. The following are descriptions of the major protocol mechanisms used during type 2 operation.

Sequence Checking

Transmission errors are detected using the error detection mechanism described for type 1 operation, and erroneous frames are discarded by the MAC sublayer. The I-format and S-format commands and responses sent during type 2 operation contain sequence numbers. These sequence numbers are used to detect the missing frames that result from discarded LLC-PDUs, to ensure that LLC-PDUs are received in the order in which they were sent, and to ensure that LLC-PDUs are not duplicated.

The *send count* [N(S)] field contains the sequence number of the LLC-PDU the LLC sublayer entity is sending, and the *receive count* [N(R)] field contains the sequence number the LLC sublayer entity expects to find in the next LLC-PDU it receives. Each LLC sublayer maintains a send counter and a receive counter. After an LLC sublayer entity sends each I-format LLC-PDU, the LLC entity updates its send counter. When an LLC sublayer entity receives an I-format command, it compares the send count [N(S)] value in the LLC-PDU with its own receive counter. If the LLC-PDU's N(S) field value matches the value in the LLC entity's own receive counter, it accepts the LLC-PDU and adds 1 to its receive counter. If the counter values do not match, the LLC entity assumes that there may be one or more missing frames, and it rejects the LLC-PDU.

Box 18.5 illustrates a data flow that shows how LLC sublayer entity send and receive counter values and the N(S) and N(R) count values in LLC-PDUs are used to detect missing frames.

Acknowledgments

Several factors determine when acknowledgments are required during the operation of the connection-oriented LLC sublayer service. One is the Poll/Final bit carried in each LLC-PDU's control field. When an LLC sublayer entity sends an I-format LLC-PDU that has its Poll/Final bit set to 1, the destination LLC sublayer entity must send back an acknowledgment immediately. If the destination LLC sublayer entity does not have an Information LLC-PDU ready to send at that time, it responds by sending an S-format Receive Ready (RR) response.

If an LLC sublayer entity receives an Information LLC-PDU that does not have the Poll/Final bit set to 1, the action taken by the LLC sublayer entity depends on several factors. If the LLC sublayer entity has already received a number of LLC-PDUs equal to a value called the *window size*, the LLC sublayer entity sends an acknowledgment; otherwise, the LLC sublayer entity waits for additional LLC-PDUs to arrive. If no additional LLC-PDUs arrive immediately, the LLC sublayer entity waits a period of time before sending an acknowledgment. The length of time is based on an *acknowledgment timer* the LLC sublayer entity starts each time it receives a new I-format LLC-PDU.

BOX 18.5   LLC data transfer data flow.

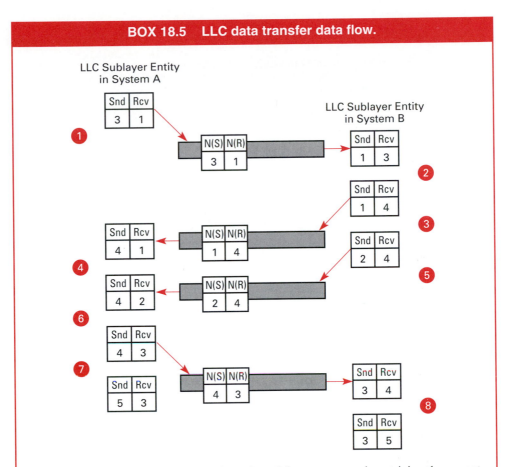

LLC Sublayer Entity
in System A

LLC Sublayer Entity
in System B

1. The LLC sublayer entity in system A sends an I-format command containing the current values of its send counter [N(S) = 3] and receive counter [N(R) = 1]. The LLC sublayer entity in system A adds 1 to the current value of its send counter, making its new send counter value 4.

2. The LLC sublayer entity in system B receives the I-format LLC-PDU and checks that the N(S) field value in the received LLC-PDU matches its receive counter value. Since the two values match, the LLC entity in system B accepts the LLC-PDU and adds 1 to its receive counter. The value of 1 in the N(R) field in the LLC-PDU indicates that the LLC sublayer entity in system A expects the next LLC-PDU it receives from system B to have an N(S) field value of 1. This LLC-PDU acknowledges receipt of the LLC-PDU with an N(S) field value of 0.

3. The LLC sublayer entity in system B formats an LLC-PDU with an N(S) field value equal to its own send counter (1) and an N(R) field value equal to its own receive counter (4) and sends it. The LLC sublayer entity in system B then adds 1 to its send counter.

(Continued)

BOX 18.5   *(Continued)*

4. The LLC sublayer entity in system A receives the LLC-PDU, sequence checks it, and adds 1 to its receive counter. This LLC-PDU acknowledges receipt of the LLC-PDU sent by the LLC sublayer entity in system A with the N(S) value of 3.

5. The LLC sublayer entity in system B sends another LLC-PDU. This one has an [N(S)] field value of 2. The LLC sublayer entity in system B adds 1 to its send counter.

6. The LLC sublayer entity in system A receives the LLC-PDU, sequence checks it, and adds 1 to its receive counter.

7. The LLC sublayer entity in system A sends an LLC-PDU with N(S) = 4 and adds 1 to its send counter.

8. The LLC sublayer entity in system B receives the LLC-PDU, sequence checks it, and updates its receive counter. This LLC-PDU acknowledges receipt of LLC-PDUs with N(S) = 1 and N(S) = 2 sent by the LLC sublayer entity in system B.

When the LLC sublayer entity starts sending LLC-PDUs, it also starts an acknowledgment timer. If no acknowledgment is received before the acknowledgment timer runs out, it sends an S-format LLC-PDU with the Poll/Final bit set to 1 to request an immediate acknowledgment. Depending on the response received, the LLC sublayer entity may resume sending, retransmit previously sent LLC-PDUs, or perform a reset procedure.

Flow Control

The window size maintained by an LLC entity places a limit on the number of LLC-PDUs an LLC sublayer entity can send before it must wait for an acknowledgment. The window size value that source and destination LLC entities maintain acts as a flow control mechanism.

The window size has a maximum value of 127, reflecting the 7-bit size of the N(S) and N(R) count fields in an I-format LLC-PDU's control field. Window sizes can be set smaller than this. In some implementations of the Logical Link Control standard, LLC entities exchange XID commands and responses prior to establishing a connection to negotiate window size values. When an LLC sublayer entity sends the number of LLC-PDUs specified by the window size without receiving an acknowledgment, it stops sending until it receives an acknowledgment.

The window size limits the number of LLC-PDUs the source LLC sublayer entity transmits and thus prevents the destination LLC sublayer entity from being overloaded. If the LLC sublayer entity in the destination system waits for multiple LLC-PDUs to arrive, the number of LLC-PDUs allowed to accumulate before a response is sent depends on the window size. The destination LLC sublayer entity can also use acknowledgments and Receive Not Ready (RNR) commands to control the rate at which it receives LLC-PDUs. In this way the destination LLC sublayer entity can ensure it does not receive more data than it has the resources to handle.

PROTOCOL FOR TYPE 3 ACKNOWLEDGED CONNECTIONLESS OPERATION

The protocol for type 3 operation provides the acknowledged connectionless LLC service. The two U-format LLC-PDUs used to support type 3 operation are shown in Box 18.6. Type 3 operation is a proposed addition to the Logical Link Control standard and is implemented very rarely. Specific protocol mechanisms used in controlling type 3 operation are beyond the scope of this book.

SUMMARY

The IEEE/ISO/ANSI LAN architecture is based on the OSI model and divides the Data Link layer into a Logical Link Control (LLC) sublayer and a Medium Access Control (MAC) sublayer. Commonly used international standards for LAN technology include a single standard for the LLC sublayer and four separate standards for the MAC sublayer and Physical layer: CSMA/CD, Token Bus, Token Ring, and FDDI.

The functions of the LLC sublayer are defined by the IEEE 802.2 and ISO 8802-2 standards. The LLC standard describes the function of the LLC sublayer for all three forms of medium access control defined by IEEE/ISO standards and can be used in conjunction with the ANSI FDDI standard as well.

LAN standards provide for two levels of addressing: A service-access-point (SAP) address identifies an individual service-access-point into the LLC sublayer and represents a particular mechanism, process, or protocol operating in the layer above the LLC layer. A Medium Access Control (MAC) address, or station address, uniquely identifies an individual station that implements a single point of physical attachment to a LAN data link.

With the connectionless LLC service there is no need to establish a prior association between a source and destination system before data transmission can take place. Each LLC-PDU sent using the connectionless LLC service is processed independently of any other LLC-PDU.

With the connection-oriented LLC service, delivery of LLC-PDUs is guaranteed by the LLC service as a long as an LLC connection is maintained between a source LLC service-access-point and a destination LLC service-access-point.

BOX 18.6   LLC-PDUs for type 3 operation.

- **Acknowledged Connectionless Information, Sequence 0 (AC0).** Used to send user data in either direction between a pair of LLC entities.

- **Acknowledged Connectionless Information, Sequence 1 (AC1).** Also used to send user data in either direction between a pair of LLC entities. Each sender alternates the use of AC0 and AC1 LLC-PDUs. A receiver acknowledges an AC0 with an AC1 and acknowledges an AC1 with an AC0.

With the acknowledged connectionless LLC service, no connection is established between the source and destination stations, but each LLC-PDU transmitted by a source station is acknowledged by the destination station.

The three types of LLC-PDUs are Information LLC-PDUs, used to carry user data; Supervisory LLC-PDUs, used to carry control information; and Unnumbered LLC-PDUs, used to carry user data and to perform special functions.

The LLC standard defines a type 1 LLC operation that provides the connectionless LLC service and type 2 LLC operation that provides the connection-oriented LLC service. A proposed type 3 LLC operation provides the acknowledged connectionless LLC service.

The LLC standard defines a Class I LLC implementation that supports only type 1 operation and a Class II LLC implementation that supports type 1 and type 2 operation. A proposed Class III LLC implementation supports type 1 and type 3 operation, and a proposed Class IV LLC implementation supports type 1, type 2, and type 3 service.

Chapter 19 describes Ethernet technology used to implement bus- or tree-structured LAN data link subnetworks.

Chapter **19**

Ethernet Subnetworks

This chapter describes the LAN technology called *Carrier Sense Multiple Access with Collision Detection (CSMA/CD),* defined by international standards IEEE 802.3 and ISO 8802-3. CSMA/CD is a term associated with the medium access control method used with the Ethernet form of LAN technology. A LAN data link conforming to the CSMA/CD standard is often called an *Ethernet* LAN because the CSMA/CD standard is based on the older Ethernet Version 2 Specification jointly developed by DEC, Intel, and Xerox. At the time of writing, the Ethernet CSMA/CD technology is the most commonly used LAN data link technology.

An Ethernet LAN uses building blocks of individual cable segments to which one or more end-user stations are attached to form a bus- or tree-structured topology. Various types of cabling are supported, and an individual cable segment has a limited length, which depends on the cable's type. *Repeaters* or *hubs* can be used to propagate the signal from one cable segment to another, thus creating a branching, nonrooted tree topology, an example of which is shown in Fig. 19.1. The CSMA/CD standard places a number of restrictions on the types of tree structures that can be formed. An important restriction is that there can be no more than one physical path between any two stations.

An Ethernet LAN implements a multiaccess form of data link in which all stations on the LAN receive the transmissions of all other stations. All MAC frames broadcast over the transmission medium reach every station, and each station is responsible for interpreting the destination MAC address contained in a frame and for accepting frames addressed to it.

MAC SUBLAYER PROTOCOL SPECIFICATION

The data unit the MAC sublayer receives from the LLC sublayer is the *medium-access-control-service-data-unit (MAC-SDU).* The MAC-SDU contains the LLC-PDU the two LLC sublayer entities are exchanging.

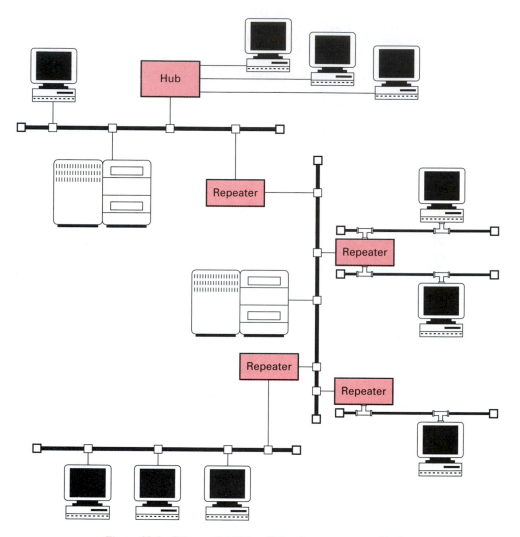

Figure 19.1 Ethernet LAN data link using repeaters and hubs.

MAC Sublayer Functions

During MAC frame transmission, the Medium Access Control sublayer entities in all sta-tions on the LAN data link perform the following functions:

- **Source Station MAC Sublayer Functions.** The MAC sublayer in a source station accepts each LLC-PDU from the LLC sublayer entity in the form of a MAC-SDU. A data encapsulation function in the source MAC sublayer entity adds protocol-control-information (PCI) to the MAC-SDU to form a *medium-access-control-protocol-data-unit (MAC-PDU)* or *MAC frame.* The MAC sublayer then uses the services of the Physical layer to broadcast the MAC frame onto the transmission medium.

- **Receiving Station MAC Sublayer Functions.** The MAC sublayer in a receiving station uses the Physical layer to receive MAC frames from the transmission medium. It interprets the destination MAC address in each frame it receives and accepts only frames addressed to that station. For each frame it accepts, the MAC sublayer entity removes the PCI from the MAC frame and passes the resulting MAC-SDU to the LLC sublayer.

CSMA/CD MAC FRAME FORMAT

The protocol specification for the CSMA/CD MAC sublayer defines the format of the MAC frame exchanged between MAC sublayer entities in source and destination stations. Box 19.1 shows the format of the CSMA/CD MAC frame and describes its fields.

BOX 19.1 CSMA/CD (Ethernet) MAC frame.

Preamble	Start Frame Delimiter	Dest. MAC Address	Source MAC Address	Length	LLC Data	Pad	Frame Check Sequence
7 octets	1 octet	2 or 6 octets	2 or 6 octets	2 octets	0 – *n* octets	0 – *p* octets	4 octets

- **Preamble.** A sequence of 56 bits with alternating 1 and 0 values used for synchronization.

- **Start Frame Delimiter.** A sequence of 8 bits with the bit configuration 10101011 that indicates the beginning of the MAC frame.

- **Station Addresses.** A *Destination MAC Address* field followed by a *Source MAC Address* field. The Destination MAC Address field identifies the station or stations to receive the MAC frame. The Source MAC Address field identifies the station that originated the frame. Address fields can be either 16 or 48 bits in length, although the great majority of Ethernet implementations use 48-bit addresses. (The MAC addressing mechanism is described in Chapter 18.) The destination MAC address field can specify either an individual address or a group address. A group destination MAC address is called a *multicast-group address*. The group destination MAC address value of all 1 bits refers to all stations on the LAN data link and is called the *broadcast address*.

- **Length.** A 2-octet field that indicates the length of the LLC Data field that follows.

- **LLC Data.** Contains the data unit that is passed from the LLC sublayer entity in the source station and is to be delivered to the LLC sublayer entity in the destination station or stations.

- **Pad.** Octets used to bring a short frame up to the minimum allowable size. Each MAC frame must contain some minimum number of octets, which is determined by the characteristics of the Physical layer. If a MAC frame being assembled for transmission does not have the requisite number of octets, a Pad field is added to bring it up to the minimum length.

- **Frame Check Sequence.** Contains a cyclical redundancy check (CRC) value used for error checking. When the source station assembles a MAC frame, it performs a CRC calculation on the bits in the MAC frame. The specific algorithm used is described in the IEEE and ISO documentation and always results in a 32-bit value. The source station stores this value in the Frame Check Sequence (FCS) field and then transmits the MAC frame. When the destination station receives the MAC frame, it performs the identical CRC calculation. If the calculated value does not match the value in the FCS field, the destination station assumes a transmission error has occurred and discards the MAC frame.

MAC PROTOCOL OPERATION

The CSMA/CD form of medium access control is one of a class of protocols that uses random access or contention techniques to solve the problem of "who goes next" in a system where all stations share a common multiaccess transmission medium. The following sections explain the operation of the IEEE 802.3/ISO 8802-3 variation of the CSMA/CD form of access control and describe how it evolved.

The ALOHA System

One of the earliest of the contention techniques was used in an experimental packet radio broadcasting system called ALOHA, developed at the University of Hawaii in the early 1970s. The protocol used by the ALOHA system is a *free-for-all* technique. When a station has a frame to transmit, it does so. It then waits for a period of time equal to twice the *propagation delay*, which is the length of time it takes a frame to travel between two stations furthest apart in the network. Twice the propagation delay is called the *slot time*. (On an Ethernet LAN, the maximum distance between stations is 2800 meters, giving a slot time of 51.2 microseconds.)

If two stations attempt to transmit frames at the same time, the two transmissions interfere, creating a condition called a *collision*. When collisions occur, frames are damaged. Receiving stations detect collisions through a collision detection mechanism and ignore MAC frames damaged through collisions. Both stations then attempt to retransmit. This protocol is simple but inefficient during high channel utilization. The maximum utilization of the transmission medium with the pure ALOHA protocol is less than 18 percent.

Carrier Sense Multiple Access

With the ALOHA protocol, collisions often occur when a station begins transmitting a frame while another station is already transmitting. A protocol that evolved from the pure ALOHA protocol added the technique of *carrier sensing* to form the *carrier sense multiple access (CSMA)* protocol. With CSMA, a source station first listens to the transmission medium before sending (carrier sense). If the medium is busy, the station waits, thus avoiding a collision. The station sends a frame only when the medium is quiet.

Even with the CSMA technique, two or more stations can listen at exactly the same time, transmit simultaneously, and still cause a collision. When frame transmission times are long compared to the propagation time, a significant portion of channel capacity can be lost due to collisions because each station transmits its entire frame before it discovers that a collision has occurred.

Collision Detection

The final refinement to the CSMA technique is to add the *collision detection (CD)* function, resulting in *CSMA/CD*. In addition to listening to the transmission system before transmitting, a source station continues to listen during the time the frame is being sent. If two or more stations have begun transmitting within a sufficiently short time interval, a collision occurs quickly. When this happens, the transmitting stations immediately detect the collision, cease transmitting data, and all send out a short *jamming signal*. The jamming signal ensures that all stations on the network detect the collision. Any station that has been transmitting then stops transmitting, waits for a time, and, if the carrier is free, transmits its frame again.

Deference Process

The process of monitoring the status of the transmission medium and determining when to begin retransmission is called the *deference process*. If all stations waited the same length of time before checking the carrier and restarting transmission, then another collision would inevitably occur. The deference process avoids this. In performing the deference function, each station generates a random number that determines the length of time it must wait before testing the carrier. This time period is known as the station's *backoff delay*.

Backoff delay is calculated in multiples of slot time. Each station generates a random number that falls within a specified range of values. It then waits that number of slot times before attempting retransmission. The smaller the range of values from which the random number is selected, the greater the likelihood that two stations will select the same number and have another collision. However, if the range of numbers is large, all the stations may wait for several slot times before any station transmits, causing transmission time to be wasted.

Truncated Binary Exponential Backoff

To achieve a balance between these two considerations, the CSMA/CD deference process uses an approach called *truncated binary exponential backoff*. The range of numbers (r) is defined as $0 < r < 2^k$, where k reflects the number of transmission attempts the station has made. For the first attempt the range is 0 to 1; for the second attempt, 0 to 3; for the third, 0 to 7 and so on. If repeated collisions occur, the range continues to expand until k reaches 10 (with r ranging from 0 to 1023), after which the value for k stays at 10. If a station is unsuccessful in transmitting after 16 attempts, the MAC sublayer entity reports an *excessive collisions* error condition.

Binary exponential backoff results in minimum delays before retransmission when traffic on the LAN is light. When traffic is high, repeated collisions cause the range of numbers to increase, thus lessening the chance of further collisions. Of course, when the traffic is extremely high, repeated collisions can still begin to cause excessive collisions error conditions to be generated. However, the CSMA/CD technique, combined with a deference process using truncated binary exponential backoff, results in high utilization, better than 90 percent in many cases.

CSMA/CD ARCHITECTURAL MODEL

The CSMA/CD standard defines the overall architectural model shown in Fig. 19.2. In conformance with the overall IEEE/ISO/ANSI LAN architecture, the Data Link layer is

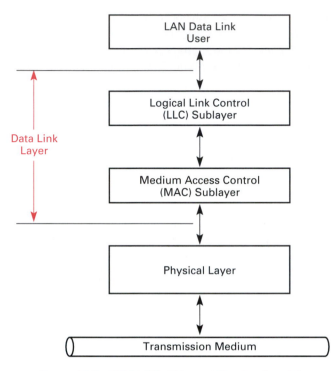

Figure 19.2   CSMA/CD (Ethernet) functional model.

divided into the Logical Link Control (LLC) sublayer and the Medium Access Control (MAC) sublayer.

MAC Sublayer Specifications

The MAC sublayer provides services to a MAC sublayer user. This is normally a Logical Link Control (LLC) sublayer entity. (The LLC sublayer standard is described in Chapter 18.) The MAC sublayer specifications define the CSMA/CD medium access control protocol used to manage access to the transmission medium, which we described earlier.

Physical Layer Specifications

The specifications in the CSMA/CD standard for the Physical layer concern such issues as the physical characteristics of the transmission medium (typically an electrical wire or cable, although fiber optics or wireless transmission is used in some implementations) and the mechanical connection from the station to the transmission medium. These specifications address physical specifications, including plug dimensions, the number of pins in the plug, and the placement of the pins. They also address electrical issues, such as the voltage levels of the signals that flow on the wire, and functional issues, such as the meaning of a particular voltage level on a given wire.

Physical Layer Architectural Model

The CSMA/CD standard defines the Physical layer architectural model shown in Fig. 19.3. The following are descriptions of each Physical layer component and interface shown in the model.

The Physical Signaling Sublayer

The *Physical Signaling (PLS)* sublayer provides services to the MAC sublayer. The PLS sublayer in a source station is responsible for encoding the data passed down from the MAC sublayer in a transmitting station. The data encoding function is responsible for translating the bits being transmitted into the proper electrical signals then broadcast over the transmission medium.

The bits are encoded using the Manchester encoding scheme, illustrated in Fig. 19.4. As described in Chapter 8, with Manchester encoding, the signal state changes at roughly the midpoint of each bit time. The signal for a 1 bit changes from low to high, and the signal for a 0 bit changes from high to low. This type of signaling allows data and clocking signals to be combined, since the destination station can use the state change that occurs during each bit time for synchronization purposes.

The PLS sublayer in a destination station is responsible for decoding the signal it receives. The decoding function translates received signals into an appropriate bit stream and passes the resulting data up to the MAC sublayer. The PLS sublayer is also responsible for listening to the transmission medium, notifying the MAC sublayer whether the carrier is free or busy, and detecting collisions.

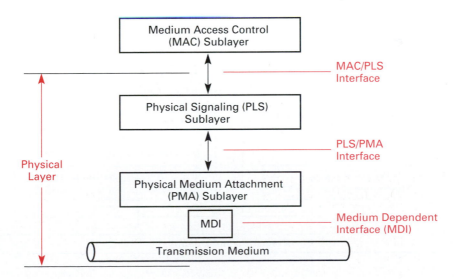

Figure 19.3 CSMA/CD (Ethernet) Physical layer architectural model.

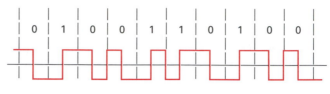

Figure 19.4   Manchester encoding.

The Physical Medium Attachment Sublayer

The *Physical Medium Attachment (PMA)* sublayer provides services to the PLS sub-layer. It performs a translation function between the PLS sublayer and the transmission medium itself and defines the characteristics of a particular type of transmission medium. The CSMA/CD standard allows the PLS and PMA sublayers to be implemented in the same device or in separate devices, as shown in Fig. 19.5. A device implementing both the PLS and PMA sublayers is attached directly to the transmission medium. In such a device, the PLS-PMA interface can be implemented in any desired way within the station itself.

The CSMA/CD standard anticipates that in many implementations the station will be located a short distance away from the transmission medium, which is often installed behind a wall or above a ceiling. So the CSMA/CD standard allows the PMA sublayer to be

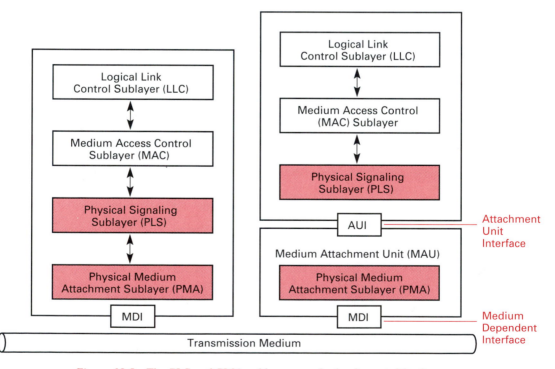

Figure 19.5   The PLS and PMA sublayers can be implemented in the same device or in different devices.

implemented in a separate device called a *Medium Attachment Unit (MAU)*. The MAU described in the standard is often called a *transceiver* in an implementation of the standard.

An MAU provides the physical and electrical interface between a cable segment and a CSMA/CD station. The MAU handles all functions that depend on the specific transmission medium being used. By having an MAU separate from the station itself, the same station can be used with different transmission media simply by changing the MAU.

Attachment Unit Interface

When a separate MAU is used to implement the PMA sublayer, the PLS-PMA interface consists of an interface called the *Attachment Unit Interface (AUI)*. The AUI defines the cable and the connectors used to connect the MAU to the device implementing the PLS sublayer. The AUI also specifies the characteristics of the signals exchanged across the interface. The cable that connects the device implementing the PLS sublayer to an MAU is called an *AUI cable*. The AUI cable is called a *transceiver cable* in many Ethernet implementations.

Medium Dependent Interface

The interface between the PMA sublayer and the transmission medium (the PMA-Medium interface) is an interface called the *Medium Dependent Interface (MDI)*. The MDI for a particular form of transmission medium defines the characteristics of *cable segments* (sometimes called the *trunk cable*), *connectors* for joining cable segments and connecting cable segments to equipment, and *terminators* used at the ends of cable segments. Although the transmission medium ordinarily consists of a physical cable, such as coaxial cable, twisted-pair cable, or fiber-optic cable, it can also consist of a microwave link or another wireless link in some Ethernet implementations.

CSMA/CD TRANSMISSION MEDIA

The CSMA/CD standard defines several different medium specifications, and more are being added to the standard over time. A local area network vendor decides which of the medium specifications to support in a given Ethernet implementation.

The CSMA/CD standard includes medium specifications for many different types of transmission media, each of which has a different set of specifications for the Physical Medium Attachment sublayer. Local area network vendors often develop and market Ethernet products that use other medium specifications in anticipation of future standardization. The following are some of the types of Ethernet transmission media commonly used today:

- Baseband signaling over 50-ohm coaxial cable, approximately 10 mm thick (often called *Standard Ethernet* or *Thick Ethernet* cable).

- Baseband signaling over 50-ohm coaxial cable, approximately 5 mm thick (often called *Thin Ethernet* or *ThinNet* cable.

- Broadband signaling over 75-ohm CATV coaxial cable.

- Baseband signaling over unshielded twisted-pair telephone wiring.
- Baseband signaling over fiber-optic cable.
- Baseband signaling using microwave transmission.

Media standards are designed to encompass signaling rates from 1 Mbps to 20 Mbps. All devices attached to a given LAN data link must operate at a single signaling rate. However, stations and MAUs may be designed to operate at more than one possible rate and may provide the ability to be set manually to a specific rate when attached to a particular LAN data link.

Although the standard allows for a range of signaling rates, virtually all Ethernet implementations of the CSMA/CD standard employ a signaling rate of 10 Mbps. However, work is being done on new medium specifications, often referred to as *Fast Ethernet*, that allow for a data rate of 100 Mbps.

The following sections describe some commonly used Ethernet transmission media. However, the transmission media described here should not be considered an exhaustive list. The IEEE and ISO are working on standards for many forms of transmission media, and the most current IEEE 802.3 and ISO 8802-3 standards documents should be consulted to see what new transmission media have been included in the standard since this was written.

10BASE5—STANDARD ETHERNET

The oldest of the CSMA/CD medium specifications is based on the *Ethernet Version 2 Specification* developed by DEC, Intel, and Xerox. This medium specification defines baseband transmission using coaxial cable supporting a data rate of 10 Mbps. Cable segments may be up to 500 meters in length. The data rate (10 Mbps), the transmission technique (BASEband), and maximum cable segment length (500 meters) are combined to give a shorthand medium specification name of *10BASE5*. With the 10BASE5 medium specification, the original, thick (10 mm) form of 50-ohm coaxial cable is used. This type of cable is often referred to as *thick Ethernet* or *Standard Ethernet* cable.

Electrical characteristics are defined for the Medium Attachment Unit and for its interface to a cable segment. Electrical, mechanical, and physical characteristics are also defined for the coaxial cable and the connectors and terminators used with it. Environmental specifications related to safety, electromagnetic environment, temperature and humidity, and regulatory requirements are also included in the standard.

10BASE5 Configurations

With the 10BASE5 specification, repeaters can be used to create longer cable runs and to build tree-structured configurations. A sample 10BASE5 configuration using repeaters is shown in Fig. 19.6.

According to the 10BASE5 specification, a cable segment with stations attached is called a *coax cable segment* or *multiaccess cable segment*. A cable segment used simply

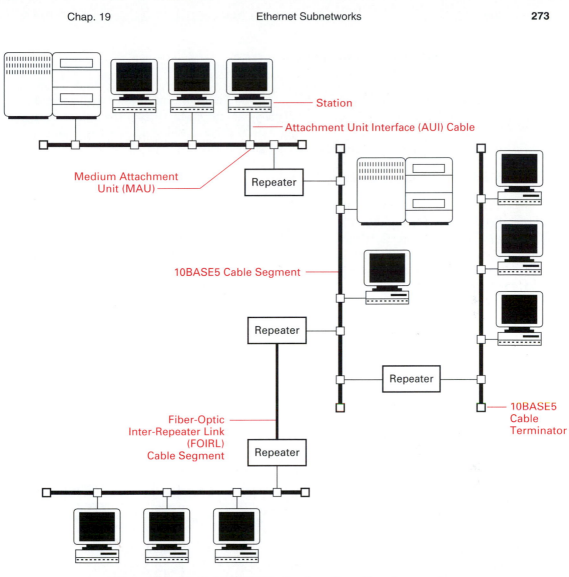

Figure 19.6   Typical 10BASE5 network configuration using repeaters.

to connect two repeaters that does not have stations attached is called a *point-to-point link cable segment*, or an *interrepeater link (IRL)* cable segment.

An interrepeater link cable segment implemented using fiber optics, called a Fiber-Optic Inter-Repeater Link (FOIRL) can be up to 1000 meters in length. Of the five cable segments that can lie in the path between two stations, only three can be coax cable segments; the other two must be point-to-point link cable segments. A particular CSMA/CD data link must be configured so there is never more than one physical path between any two stations.

10BASE5 Medium Attachment Unit

The 10BASE5 medium specification describes the use of a separate Medium Attachment Unit (MAU) to attach a station to a cable segment. The MAU is most often implemented in a device called a *transceiver* clamped directly onto the coaxial cable. The transceiver has a contact that pierces the thick Ethernet coaxial cable shielding and makes appropriate contact with both the shielding and the central conductor.

Maximum Distance between Stations

There can be up to five cable segments, and thus up to four repeaters, in the path between any two stations. The attachment unit interface (AUI) cable connecting a station to its MAU can be up to 50 meters in length. The 10BASE5 medium specification allows for up to 1500 meters of coax cable segments, up to 1000 meters of interrepeater link, and up to six AUI cables connecting stations or repeaters to MAUs. This allows the total distance between two stations to be up to 2800 meters. Figure 19.7 shows an example of an

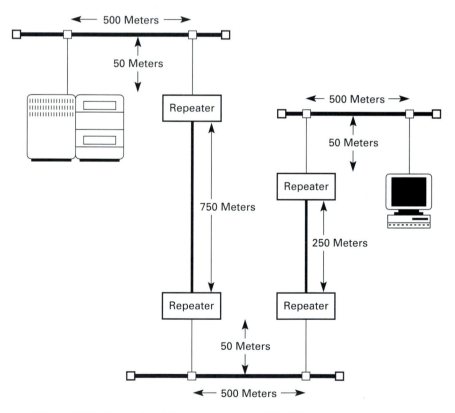

Figure 19.7 Example of implementing the full 2800-meter maximum span between two Ethernet stations.

Ethernet configuration that implements the 2800-meter maximum cable span between two stations.

10BASE5 Collision Detection

Collisions are detected when the signal level on the cable equals or exceeds the combined signal level of two transmitters. As a signal travels along the cable, it gradually attenuates, or weakens. If the signal is allowed to weaken too much, when it combines with the signal from another transmitter the combined signal might not be recognized as a collision.

Figure 19.8 illustrates worst-case collision detection on a CSMA/CD data link that uses 10BASE5 cable segments. Assume that stations 1 and 2 have the maximum allowable distance between them. Station 1 begins transmitting, and just before its signal reaches station 2, station 2 also begins transmitting. The collision occurs near station 2, causing a signal that must travel back the full length of the data link to reach station 1. The MAC frame station 1 is transmitting must be large enough to ensure that station 1 is still transmitting when it detects the collision with station 2's transmission. Otherwise, it will assume that its MAC frame got through without a collision. The maximum allowable distance between stations of 2800 meters results in the minimum size of 46 octets the CSMA/CD standard recommends for the LLC Data and Pad fields in the MAC frame.

The maximum time it takes to detect a collision is twice the propagation time for the maximum cable length defined in the specification. This represents the time it takes station 1's signal to reach the far end plus the time it takes the collision signal to travel the length of the LAN data link to reach station 1.

Another collision detection problem can arise if stations are not spaced properly. Signal reflection may give a false collision indication. To avoid this, the 10BASE5 standard specifies that Medium Attachment Units must be located in such a way that the distance between them is a multiple of 2.5 meters, and that no more than 100 stations can be attached to any one 500-meter cable segment. The cable jacket on Standard Ethernet cable generally has markings at 2.5-meter intervals to facilitate the placement of Medium Attachment Units at the proper intervals.

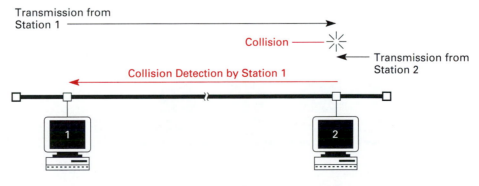

Figure 19.8   Worst-case 10BASE5 collision detection.

10BASE2—THIN ETHERNET

The 10BASE2 medium specification is similar to the 10BASE5 specification. The main difference is that a less expensive, thinner (5 mm) 50-ohm coaxial cable is used. With this specification, baseband transmission is used with the same data rate as the 10BASE5 specification—10 Mbps. With 10BASE2, the maximum cable segment length is 185 meters, and up to 30 stations are supported per cable segment. As with the 10BASE5 specification, longer cable spans and tree structures can be created using repeaters.

The 10BASE2 specification allows lower-cost Ethernet implementations to be constructed, and the 10BASE2 specification is often used in personal computer Ethernet implementations. In most implementations of the 10BASE2 medium specification, the transmission medium is brought directly to the network interface card (NIC), and no separate Medium Attachment Unit is used. The 10BASE2 standard, however, does not specifically preclude the use of a separate Medium Attachment Unit.

A standard T-type BNC connector is typically used to attach two cable segments directly to the NIC, allowing stations to be connected together in a daisy-chain fashion, as shown in Fig. 19.9. The final station in a daisy chain must have a cable terminator attached to the T connector. Station spacing is not critical with the 10BASE2 specification, but the minimum amount of cable that should separate two stations is .5 meters.

Devices called *multiport repeaters* are often used with 10BASE2 configurations. An individual station, or a daisy chain of multiple stations, is connected to each port of the multiport repeater in a star configuration, as shown in Fig. 19.10. Multiport repeaters are sometimes called *hubs*. Hubs and switches that allow stations to be switched from one LAN cable segment to another are also available for Ethernet LANs. The functions of hubs and switches are discussed in Chapter 9.

10BASE-T—TWISTED PAIR

The 10BASE-T medium specification is similar to 10BASE5 and 10BASE2 With 10BASE-T, ordinary twisted-pair telephone cabling is used instead of coaxial cable. With this specification, baseband transmission is used with a 10-Mbps data rate, making signaling on a 10BASE-T cable segment compatible with signaling on 10BASE5 and 10BASE2 cable segments.

With 10BASE-T, each station is generally connected using a single length of cable to a device called a *hub*. A hub generally supports a number of stations in a star configura-

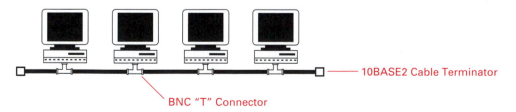

Figure 19.9 10BASE2 daisy chain configuration.

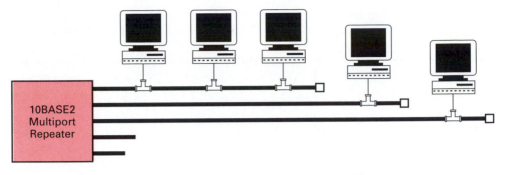

Figure 19.10   10BASE2 star configuration using a multiport repeater.

tion, in a similar manner as a 10BASE2 multiport repeater configuration (see Fig. 19.11). A single port on a 10BASE-T hub connects to only one station. Up to 100 meters of cabling can be used to connect a station to its hub. 10BASE-T stations are not ordinarily daisy chained as in a 10BASE2 configuration. However, equipment is marketed that allows daisy chain configurations to be used with twisted-pair cabling.

The type of connector most often used with 10BASE-T cabling is the *RJ-45 modular connector*. The RJ-45 modular connector is similar to the standard RJ-11 modular connector commonly used in telephone wiring but allows for up to eight conductors rather than six.

10BASE-T hubs can be interconnected to form larger LANs using 10BASE-T, 10BASE2, or 10BASE5 cable segments, depending on the implementation. Adapters are also available that allow stations with existing 10BASE5 AUI interfaces or 10BASE2 connectors to be connected to a 10BASE-T hub.

FOIRL—FIBER OPTIC

The medium specification for a *Fiber-Optic Inter-Repeater Link (FOIRL)* cable segment is a special-purpose medium specification that defines a data rate of 10 Mbps using baseband signaling over a fiber-optic cable. An FOIRL cable segment is used to implement a relatively long-distance, point-to-point connection between two repeaters. FOIRL cable

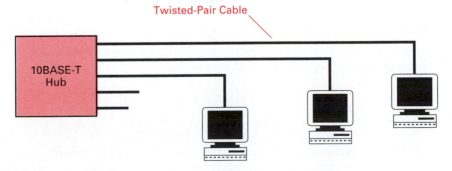

Figure 19.11   10BASE-T star configuration using a hub.

segments can be up to 1000 meters in length, thus allowing longer distances to be spanned between repeaters than can be spanned using a coaxial cable link.

10BROAD36— BROADBAND

A less commonly used CSMA/CD medium specification than 10BASE5, 10BASE2, or 10BASE-T uses broadband transmission over the inexpensive 75-ohm coaxial cable typically used to carry cable television signals. With the 10BROAD36 specification, the maximum length of a cable segment is 1800 meters. The head end can be at the end of a single cable segment, or it can be the root of a branching tree. Thus, the maximum cable span between any two stations is 3600 meters.

ETHERNET NETWORK CONFIGURATIONS

Standard Ethernet cable segments conforming to the 10BASE5 medium specification are often used in practice to form the basis of a high-quality backbone in an Ethernet LAN. This is because Standard Ethernet cable segments can be longer than thin Ethernet and twisted-pair cable segments and are more resistant to noise. However, it is more common today, especially in personal computer LANs, for individual stations to be connected to the LAN using the lower-cost thin Ethernet coaxial cable or twisted-pair cable.

Ethernet network interface cards are available that support multiple medium specifications. For example, NICs are widely available that have an MAU cable connector for an external transceiver and also an internal MAU. The internal MAU may terminate in both an RJ-45 connector for twisted-pair cable and a BNC connector for thin Ethernet cable. Such a NIC could be used with Standard Ethernet, thin Ethernet, or twisted-pair cabling.

The 10BASE5, 10BASE2, or 10BASE-T medium specifications all use the same data rate and the same collision detection scheme. Thus, Standard Ethernet, thin Ethernet, and twisted-pair cable segments can be combined using the repeaters and hubs available from a number of different vendors. A possible combination is shown in Fig. 19.12, in which a Standard Ethernet cable segment is used as a backbone for a number of thin Ethernet and twisted-pair cable segments.

A guideline to follow in creating such combinations is that a thin Ethernet or twisted-pair cable segment should not be used between two Standard Ethernet cable segments. This is because thin Ethernet and twisted-pair cable is not as resistant to noise as Standard Ethernet cable, and a cable segment used as a backbone should be at least as resistant to noise as the cable segments it connects.

ISOCHRONOUS ETHERNET

At the time of writing, work is being done in IEEE Project 802 on the 802.9 *Isochronous Ethernet* specification. Isochronous Ethernet is designed to provide for integrated voice and data transmission over a LAN. The approach used is to multiplex bit streams of digital

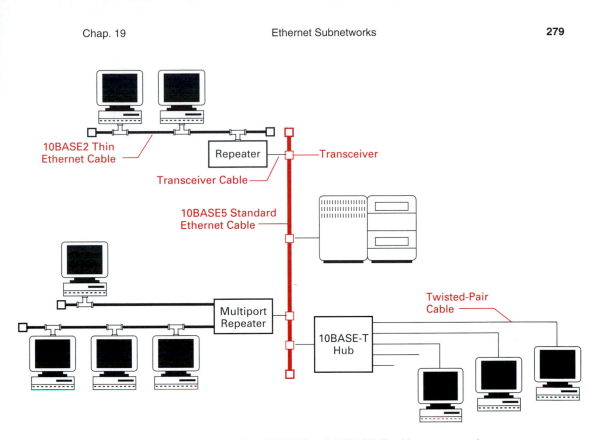

Figure 19.12   Interconnecting 10BASE2 and 10BASE-T cable segments using a 10BASE5 backbone.

data over the transmission medium. It does this by carrying both Ethernet and ISDN transmissions over the same wiring. (See Chapter 13 for a discussion of ISDN.) Isochronous Ethernet uses 10BASE-T wiring in a point-to-point configuration.

The specification defines different channel types for carrying different types of data. A 10-Mbps packet service channel is defined for providing Ethernet data transmission. ISDN channels are used for carrying video and audio transmission. A typical ISDN configuration would have 96 "B" channels of 64 Kbps and one "D" channel of 16 Kbps.

Isochronous Ethernet uses the 4b/5b code conversion and subsequent signal encoding defined for use with FDDI. (See Chapter 22.) With 4b/5b encoding, each 4-bit half octet is converted to a 5-bit value prior to transmission.

The FDDI 4b/5b code is shown in Fig. 19.13. The 5-bit data values used to represent the 4-bit symbols were chosen so there are never more than three consecutive 0-bits. An additional 8 symbols are used for control purposes. Other possible 5-bit values are invalid. With 4b/5b signaling there are never more than three bit times without a transition, making it easy to synchronize the sender and receiver.

The increased efficiency of the FDDI form of transmission allows the Ethernet equipment to support the higher data rate required for the combined Ethernet and ISDN

Code Group	Symbol	Interpretation
Data		
11110	0	hex 0
01001	1	hex 1
10100	2	hex 2
10101	3	hex 3
01010	4	hex 4
01011	5	hex 5
01110	6	hex 6
01111	7	hex 7
10010	8	hex 8
10011	9	hex 9
10110	A	hex A
10111	B	hex B
11010	C	hex C
11011	D	hex D
11100	E	hex E
11101	F	hex F
Control		
00000	Q	Quiet
11111	I	Idle
00100	H	Halt
11000	J	Start Delimiter (1st symbol)
10001	K	Start Delimiter (2nd symbol)
01101	T	Ending Delimiter
00111	R	Reset
11001	S	Set

Figure 19.13   FDDI 4b/5b symbol encoding.

transmission. For example, in the configuration described previously supporting 96 ISDN B channels and one D channel, a total data rate of 16.16 Mbps would be required.

FAST ETHERNET

Work is also in progress on the development of specifications for Fast Ethernet LAN technology that supports a data rate of 100Mbps. Although, at the time of writing, standards have not been finalized for Fast Ethernet, some vendors have already begun shipping 100-Mbps Ethernet NICs and network infrastructure equipment.

At the time of writing, there are two different Fast Ethernet specifications under consideration for standardization:

- **100BASE-T.** The IEEE 802.30 100BASE-T standard couples the CSMA/CD MAC protocols with a 100 Mbps Physical layer based on the FDDI Physical Layer Medium Dependent (PMD) sublayer.
- **100VG-AnyLAN.** The IEEE 802.12 100VG-AnyLAN standard defines its own MAC and Physical layer protocols, but supports both Ethernet and Token Ring frame formats.

BOX 19.2   Fast Ethernet goals.

- 100 Mbps data rate
- Up to 100 meters from a station to a hub
- Support for CSMA/CD frame format
- Use of voice-grade twisted-pair (EIA 568) wiring, with RJ-45 connectors
- FCC class B emissions

Both approaches are being developed to meet the same set of goals, which are listed in Box 19.2. The following sections further describe these two approaches under development for Fast Ethernet.

100BASE-T

The architectural model for 100BASE-T is shown in Fig. 19.14. The MAC sublayer uses the standard CSMA/CD MAC specification. The use of the CSMA/CD MAC transmission parameters leads to a constraint on the maximum distance between two stations when the data rate is increased to 100 Mbps. In order to be able to detect collisions quickly enough, the physical span of the network is limited to 250 meters or less rather than the 2500 meters supported by a conventional Ethernet network.

The Convergence sublayer provides the functions necessary to couple the CSMA/CD access method with the signaling scheme used in the Physical Layer Medium Dependent (PMD) sublayer, which is based on the FDDI specification. A key factor in this is mapping

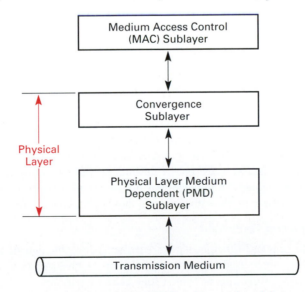

Figure 19.14   100BASE-T architectural model.

the continuous signaling system used by FDDI to the start-stop system used with CSMA/CD.

The PMD sublayer defines medium specifications. 100BASE-T includes two medium specifications based on the PMD sublayer in FDDI. One specification is for twisted-pair wiring and the other for fiber-optic cable. The twisted-pair wiring can be either data-grade (category 5) unshielded twisted pair or shielded twisted pair.

An additional medium specification, referred to as 4T+, is also being developed. 4T+ uses four pairs of voice-grade (category 3) unshielded twisted-pair wiring, the same type of wiring used with 10BASE-T.

Signaling Techniques

With the FDDI-based medium specifications used with 100BASE-T, data transmission uses FDDI 4b/5b encoding. If the transmission medium is fiber-optic cable, bits are converted to and from electrical signals using NRZI encoding. If the transmission medium is twisted-pair, the 5-bit segments are scrambled and encoded using a scheme called *Multi-Level Transmission-3 (MLT-3)*. MLT-3 uses three signal levels. A logical low value (0 bit) is sent using the intermediate signal level. A logical high value (1 bit) is sent alternately using the low signal level and the high signal level.

With 4T+, data is sent using an encoding scheme called *8B6T*. With 8B6T encoding, each 8 bit-value is converted to three ternary digits, which are transmitted as three 25-Mhz signals in parallel across three wire pairs. The fourth wire pair is used for collision detection.

100VG-AnyLAN

The 100VG-AnyLAN specification provides for 100 Mbps data transmission using a hub-oriented star topology, where each station is attached to the hub by a point-to-point link. Stations can be located up to 100 meters from the hub. 100VG-AnyLAN supports both Ethernet and Token Ring frame formats. It is designed to use four pairs of voice-grade (category 3) unshielded twisted-pair wiring as the transmission medium (10BASE-T wiring).

Demand Priority Access Method

100VG-AnyLAN uses a Demand Priority access method to control transmission of frames. With this scheme, when a station has a frame to transmit, it sends a request to the hub. As part of the request, it indicates whether the request is a normal or a high-priority request. If the data link is idle, the hub acknowledges the request, and the station transmits the frame to the hub. The hub then functions as a switch, transmitting the frame to the destination station based on the destination address in the frame. If the hub receives more than one request simultaneously, it services a high-priority request first. If there are multiple requests with the same priority, they are serviced in turn.

Signaling Technique

With standard Ethernet 10BASE-T transmission, one pair of wires is used to transmit and another pair is used to listen for collisions. 100VG-AnyLAN uses a form of signaling called *Quartet Signaling*, in which four pairs of wire are used simultaneously either to transmit or to receive. The use of the Demand Priority access method eliminates the need for collision detection. Data encoding involves dividing the data into five-bit segments, or *quintets*. Quintets are scrambled, and then encoded using 5b/6b NRZ encoding. The six-bit values transmitted all contain at least two 0 bits and two 1 bits. With this type of encoding, transmission includes twice the number of bits per cycle as the standard Ethernet Manchester encoding. With the more efficient transmission, each wire pair supports a data rate of 25 Mbps.

Transmission Media

In addition to being used with voice-grade, unshielded, twisted-pair wiring, 100VG-AnyLAN includes medium specifications for using data-grade (category 5) twisted-pair wiring or fiber-optic cable. With data-grade twisted-pair, stations can be up to 150 meters from the hub. With fiber-optic cable, they can be up to 2000 meters away.

ETHERNET VERSION 2 SPECIFICATION

This section describes the original Ethernet Version 2 specification on which the CSMA/CD standard was based. Some older LANs are based on this specification rather than on the newer CSMA/CD standard.

Today's modern Ethernet standard had its beginning in 1972, when the Palo Alto Research Center of Xerox Corporation (Xerox PARC) began developing a local area network system called *Experimental Ethernet*. Later, Digital Equipment Corporation, Intel, and Xerox worked together to jointly define and publish a revised and improved *Ethernet Specification*. This was further refined in Version 2 of the specification. The work done on Ethernet Version 2 contributed substantially to the IEEE/ISO CSMA/CD standard. The *Ethernet Version 2 Specification*, and the name *Ethernet*, were made publicly available, and any local area networking product vendor is free to produce Ethernet LAN equipment conforming to either the CSMA/CD standard or to the *Ethernet Version 2 Specification*. By far the majority of the Ethernet equipment manufactured today conforms to the IEEE/ISO CSMA/CD standard. Some older Ethernet equipment still in use may conform to the Ethernet Version 2 Specification. The older Ethernet Version 2 Specification is very close to the CSMA/CD standard and differs from it mainly in the use made of one of the fields in the MAC frame.

Protocol Specification

Like today's LANs based on the CSMA/CD standard, an Ethernet Version 2 LAN data link uses building blocks of individual coaxial cable segments to which one or more stations is attached in a bus- or tree-structured topology. The only form of coaxial cable described in the *Ethernet Version 2 Specification* is Standard Ethernet cable. This is the 10-mm, 50-ohm coaxial cable defined in the 10BASE5 medium specification of the CSMA/CD standard.

The *Ethernet Version 2 Specification* specifies a single protocol to carry out the procedures the IEEE/ISO LAN standards specify in the protocols for the Logical Link Control and Medium Access Control sublayers. The protocol defines only a connectionless Data Link layer service equivalent to that provided by Type 1 operation defined in the IEEE/ISO Logical Link Control sublayer standard. The Ethernet Version 2 protocol also defines procedures equivalent to those defined by the CSMA/CD Medium Access Control sublayer standard for controlling access to the transmission medium and for detecting and recovering from collisions.

Frame Format

Box 19.3 compares the format of the MAC frame format described by the CSMA/CD standard with the Ethernet Version 2 frame and describes the fields in the Ethernet Version 2 MAC frame.

BOX 19.3   Ethernet Version 2 MAC frame.

Preamble	Start Frame Delimiter	Dest. MAC Address	Source MAC Address	Length	LLC Data	⟩⟩	Pad	Frame Check Sequence
7 octets	1 octet	2 or 6 octets	2 or 6 octets	2 octets	0 – n octets		0 – p octets	4 octets

CSMA/CD (Ethernet) Frame Format

Preamble	Dest. Address	Source Address	Type	LLC Data	⟩⟩	Frame Check Sequence
8 octets	2 or 6 octets	2 or 6 octets	2 octets	0 – n octets		4 octets

Ethernet Version 2 Frame Format

- **Preamble.** Eight octets used to provide synchronization and to mark the start of a frame. The same bit pattern is used for the Ethernet Version 2 Preamble field as for the CSMA/CD Preamble and Start Frame Delimiter fields.

- **Address Fields.** A *Destination MAC Address* field followed by a *MAC Source Address* field. A destination address can reference an individual station or a group of stations, and globally administered or locally administered addresses can be used. Xerox Corporation provides vendors of Ethernet Version 2 products with blocks of addresses to use in assigning unique addresses to individual network interface cards (NICs).

- **Type.** A Type value used in place of the Length field of the CSMA/CD MAC frame. The Type field is meaningful to the higher layers and is ordinarily used to identify a Network layer protocol.

- **Information.** Contains the packet passed to the Data Link layer by the Ethernet data link user. The Ethernet Version 2 Specification defines a minimum frame size of 72 octets and a maximum frame size of 1526 octets, including all header and trailer fields. This is equivalent to the recommended 46–1500 octet limitation of the LLC Data plus Pad fields described in the CSMA/CD standard. If the data to be sent is smaller or larger, it is the responsibility of the Ethernet data link user to pad it or to break it into multiple packets.

- **Frame Check Sequence (FCS).** A CRC value used for error checking in the same manner as for the CSMA/CD standard.

Interoperation of Ethernet Version 2 and CSMA/CD Stations

The Ethernet Version 2 Specification and the IEEE/ISO CSMA/CD standard are quite similar. However the difference in frame formats is enough to make a NIC that conforms to only one specification incompatible with one that conforms only to the other specification. There are techniques, however, that LAN vendors have employed to allow devices of the two types to coexist on the same LAN data link.

To permit interoperation, a NIC designed to handle both the CSMA/CD standard and the Ethernet Version 2 specification normally transmits IEEE/ISO CSMA/CD frames and accepts incoming frames in either the CSMA/CD or Ethernet Version 2 format. When a NIC receives an IEEE/ISO CSMA/CD frame from another station, it replies to that station with CSMA/CD frames; when it receives an Ethernet Version 2 frame, it replies to that station with Ethernet Version 2 frames.

A NIC distinguishes between an Ethernet Version 2 frame and an IEEE/ISO CSMA/CD frame by examining the two-octet Length field, which corresponds to the Type field in an Ethernet Version 2 frame. Because of the maximum frame size restriction, the Length field value in a CSMA/CD frame must contain a value that falls within the range of 3 to 1500. Therefore, if the length field value falls within the range of 3 to 1500, the frame is a CSMA/CD frame; if the length field value falls outside of this range, it is an Ethernet Version 2 frame.

SUMMARY

The IEEE/ISO Carrier Sense Multiple Access with Collision Detection (CSMA/CD) standard is based on the Ethernet Version 2 technology. CSMA/CD, or Ethernet, medium access control technology implements a multiaccess data link that uses a bus- or tree-structured network topology in which all stations receive all transmissions within a period of time determined by the propagation delay of the network.

The CSMA/CD form of medium access control uses a contention technique to determine which station transmits next. Each station that has a frame to send listens to the transmission medium and transmits when the medium is free. If two or more stations transmit simultaneously, a collision results. A station detecting a collision stops transmitting and sends out a jamming signal to ensure that other stations also detect the collision. The station then uses a deference process based on a binary exponential backoff procedure to wait for a period of time before retransmitting.

The CSMA/CD architectural model divides the Physical layer into a Physical Signaling (PLS) sublayer and a Physical Medium Attachment (PMA) sublayer. Both sublayers can be implemented in the station, or a separate Medium Attachment Unit (MAU), located a short distance from the station, can be used to implement the PMA sublayer. The CSMA/CD standard also documents Physical layer specifications for a repeater that can be used to interconnect two or more cable segments.

Medium specifications for the CSMA/CD standard supporting a 10-Mbps transmission speed include 10BASE5 for standard Ethernet coaxial cable, 10BASE2 for thin Ethernet coaxial cable, 10BASE-T for twisted-pair cable, FOIRL for fiber-optic interrepeater link cable segments, and 10BROAD36 for broadband transmission over CATV-type coaxial cable. Work is underway on a number of specifications that allow Ethernet technology to support 100 Mbps transmission.

Chapter 20 describes the Token Ring form of medium access control technology. The Token Ring medium access control method uses a token-passing technique to implement ring-structured LAN data links using point-to-point cable segments.

Chapter **20**

Token Ring Subnetworks

This chapter describes the Token Ring medium access control method defined in the IEEE 802.5 and ISO 8802-5 standards. The Token Ring standard defines a LAN data link technology in which stations are connected to one another in a *ring* structure using a series of point-to-point physical circuits. Each station is connected both to the next station and to the previous station to form a physical ring around which data circulates. The logical structure of a simple Token Ring network is shown in Fig. 20.1.

   A Token Ring LAN implements a multiaccess form of data link, in which all stations on the LAN data link eventually receive the transmissions of all other stations. All MAC frames are repeated all the way around the ring and reach every station on the LAN. Each station is responsible for interpreting the destination MAC address contained in a frame and for copying those frames addressed to it.

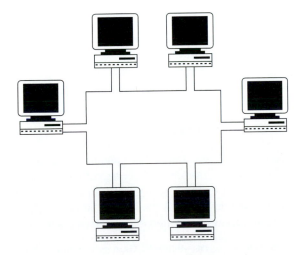

Figure 20.1   Token Ring LAN basic topology.

MAC SUBLAYER PROTOCOL SPECIFICATION

The data unit the MAC sublayer receives from the LLC sublayer is the *medium-access-control-service-data-unit (MAC-SDU)*. The MAC-SDU contains the LLC-PDU that the two LLC sublayer entities are exchanging.

MAC Sublayer Functions

During MAC frame transmission, the Medium Access Control sublayer entities in all stations on the ring perform the following functions:

- **Source Station MAC Sublayer Functions.** The MAC sublayer in a source station accepts each LLC-PDU from the LLC sublayer entity in the form of a MAC-SDU. A data encapsulation function in the source MAC sublayer entity adds protocol-control-information (PCI) to the MAC-SDU to form a *medium-access-control-protocol-data-unit (MAC-PDU)* or *MAC frame*. The MAC sublayer then uses the services of the Physical layer to transmit the MAC frame to the next station on the ring.

- **Receiving Station MAC Sublayer Functions.** The MAC sublayer in a receiving station uses the Physical layer to receive MAC frames from the previous station on the ring. It interprets the destination MAC address in each frame it receives and copies only frames addressed to that station. For each frame it copies, the MAC sublayer entity removes the PCI from the MAC frame and passes the resulting MAC-SDU to the LLC sublayer. The MAC sublayer in a receiving station also interprets the source address in each MAC frame it receives to identify frames it originally placed onto the ring. When a receiving station identifies one of its own frames, it does not repeat that frame, thus removing it from the ring. A receiving station repeats all other MAC frames, whether it copied them or not, to the next station on the ring.

MAC FRAME FORMAT

The protocol specification for the Token Ring MAC sublayer defines the format of the MAC frame exchanged between MAC sublayer entities in source and destination stations. Box 20.1 shows the format of the Token Ring MAC frame and describes its fields.

Because the Frame Status field is outside the scope of the FCS bits, the ACrr bits are included twice in this octet to provide a redundancy check to help in detecting transmission errors in this octet.

MAC Sublayer Control Frames

As discussed earlier, a MAC frame can contain either an LLC-PDU passed from Logical Link Control or control information generated by the Medium Access Control sublayer. The following is a list of the MAC control frames defined by the standard. The control frame mnemonic and the value of the control bit (ZZZZZZ) portion of the frame control field are shown in parentheses following each frame's name.

- **Claim Token (CL_TK—000011).** Used by a station to become the active monitor when no active monitor is present on the ring.

BOX 20.1   Token Ring MAC frame.

Start Frame Delimiter	Access Control	Frame Control	Dest. MAC Address	Source MAC Address	Information	Frame Check Sequence	End Frame Delimiter	Frame Status
1 octet	1 octet	1 octet	2 or 6 octets	2 or 6 octets	0 – n octets	4 octets	1 octet	1 octet

Start-of-Frame Sequence | FCS Coverage | End-of-Frame Sequence

- **Start Frame Delimiter.** An octet containing a unique signal pattern that identifies the start of a frame. The Token Ring medium access control method uses differential Manchester encoding, which allows for signal values that do not correspond to either a 0 or a 1 bit. These are called the nondata J signal and the nondata K signal. The use of nondata signals ensures that no data sequence will ever be mistaken for a delimiter. The signal configuration for a Start Frame Delimiter field is JK0JK000. The differential Manchester encoding scheme is described in Chapter 8.

- **Access Control.** A field used to control the operation of the MAC protocol. The Access Control field bits are interpreted as PPPTMRRR:

  — **PPP.** *Priority* bits containing a value from 0 through 7 indicating the transmission priority of the frame or token.
  — **T.** A *token* bit containing a 0 in a token and a 1 in a MAC frame.
  — **M.** A *monitor* bit set to 1 by the active monitor to detect and avoid an endlessly circulating frame or a persistent high-priority token.
  — **RRR.** *Reservation* bits set to a value from 0 through 7 by a station that has frames to send to request that the token be issued at the specified priority.

- **Frame Control.** Identifies the type of frame and, for certain control frames, the particular function to be performed. The Frame Control field bits are interpreted as FFZZZZZZ:

  — **FF.** *Frame type* bits containing 00 if the frame is a control frame generated by the MAC sublayer or 01 if the frame contains an LLC-PDU. Bit values of 10 and 11 indicate an undefined format and are reserved for future use.
  — **ZZZZZZ.** *Control bits* interpreted differently in MAC frames containing LLC-PDUs and in MAC control frames. In a MAC frame that contains an LLC-PDU, the bits are interpreted as rrrYYY. The YYY bits contain the same value as specified in the priority parameter passed with the LLC-PDU to the MAC sublayer in the source station. For a MAC control frame, the control bits indicate the MAC control frame type. MAC control frames are described later in this chapter.

- **Station Addresses.** A *Destination MAC Address* field and a *Source MAC Address* field. The Destination MAC Address field identifies the station or stations to receive the MAC frame. The Source MAC Address field identifies the source station. Address fields can be either 16 bits or 48 bits in length. (The MAC addressing mechanism is described in Chapter 18.) The destination address can specify either an individual station or a group of stations.

- **Information.** Contains either an LLC-PDU passed from the Logical Link Control sublayer or control information supplied by the Medium Access Control sublayer.

(Continued)

BOX 20.1   *(Continued)*

- **Frame Check Sequence (FCS).** A cyclical redundancy check (CRC) value used for error checking. When the sending station assembles a frame, it performs a CRC calculation on the bits in the frame. The specific algorithm used is described in the IEEE/ISO Token Ring standard. The source station stores the calculated value in the Frame Check Sequence field and then transmits the frame. When a receiving station receives the frame, it performs an identical CRC calculation and compares the result with the value in the Frame Check Sequence field. If the two values do not match, the receiving station assumes a transmission error has occurred and discards the corrupted frame.

- **End Frame Delimiter.** A value that identifies the first octet of the end-of-frame sequence. The End Frame Delimiter bits are interpreted as JK1JK1IE:

  — **JK1JK1.** Bits that identify this octet as the ending delimiter and contain a unique combination of data and nondata signals.
  — **I.** An *intermediate frame* bit set to 0 if this is the last or only frame the station is transmitting or 1 if more frames follow this one.
  — **E.** An *error* bit set to 1 by a station that detects an error in frame reception so subsequent stations know this frame has been damaged by a transmission error.

- **Frame Status.** The final octet of the frame. The bits of the Frame Status field are interpreted as ACrrACrr:

  — **A.** An *address recognized* bit set by a station recognizing the frame as being addressed to it.
  — **C.** A *packet copied* set by a station copying the packet contained in the frame.
  — **rr.** Bits reserved for future use.

- **Duplicate Address Test (DAT—000000).** Used when a station is added to the ring to ensure that its address is unique.

- **Active Monitor Present (AMP—000101).** Used to notify all stations that an active monitor is present.

- **Standby Monitor Present (SMP—000110).** Used to notify all stations that a standby monitor is present.

- **Beacon (BCN—000010).** Sent when a serious ring failure occurs, to help identify the location of the failure.

- **Purge (PRG—000100).** Sent by the active monitor after claiming the token or to reinitialize the ring.

Abort Sequence

In addition to tokens and MAC frames, a special frame format called the *abort sequence* is used to prematurely terminate the transmission of a frame. Figure 20.2 shows the format of the abort sequence.

Start Frame Delimiter	End Frame Delimiter
1 octet	1 octet

Figure 20.2   Abort sequence.

MAC PROTOCOL OPERATION

During the operation of the Token Ring MAC protocol, data units are passed from one station to the next, in a single direction, in physical sequence around the ring. Each station transmits the data unit to the next station, acting as a repeater. Data units that flow from station to station around the ring consist of tokens and MAC frames. MAC frames are of two types:

- Frames that contain LLC-PDUs passed down from the LLC sublayer.
- Control frames generated by the MAC sublayer to control network operation.

The right to transmit frames is controlled by a token, which is passed from one station to the next around the ring.

A station sends a frame by waiting for the token to arrive. It then transforms the token to form a start-of-frame sequence. The station next attaches the remainder of the frame to the start-of-frame sequence to create a complete MAC frame and then transmits the MAC frame to the next station on the ring. A station that has MAC frames to send starts a timer and can then send frames either until it has no more frames to send or until the timer expires.

MAC frames travel from station to station around the ring. Each station that receives a frame checks the destination address in it to see if it should copy that frame. Whether or not a station copies a MAC frame, it sends the frame to the next station. When a frame returns to the station that originally sent it, that station removes the frame from the ring and sends a token to the next station. Figure 20.3 illustrates this procedure.

Notice that a new token is issued only after a frame has made its way all the way around the ring to the station that originated it. This means that only frames from one station can be outstanding on the ring at any given time.

Since a frame travels to all stations and then returns to the sending station, it is possible for destination stations to set control bits in the frame as they pass it on to the next station, indicating whether or not the frame was processed and whether any errors were detected. Three control bits have been defined for these purposes:

- **Address Recognized.** The destination station identified this frame as being addressed to it.
- **Packet Copied.** The destination station passed a copy of the frame up to the Logical Link Control sublayer for processing.
- **Error.** An error condition was detected. This bit can be set by any station on the ring, not only by a station that has copied the frame.

Different combinations of the Address Recognized and Packet Copied bits allow the source station to differentiate among various circumstances. Possible circumstances are as follows:

- The frame was copied by one or more destination stations.
- The destination station recognized the frame as being addressed to it, but was not able to copy it.
- The destination station either did not recognize the frame or is nonexistent or inactive.

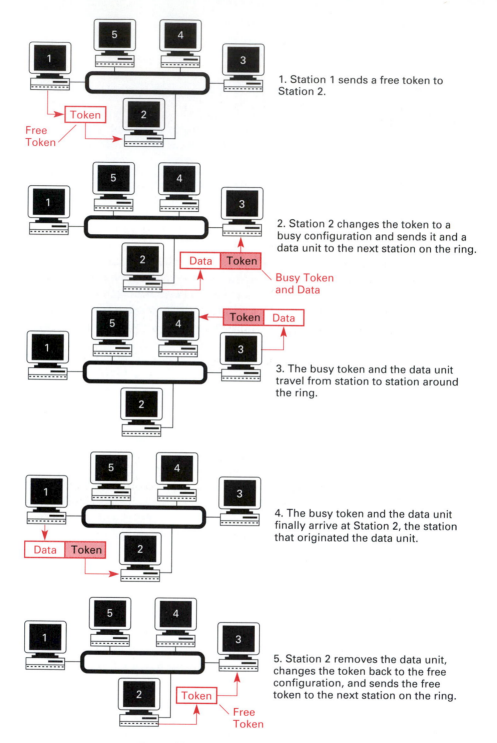

1. Station 1 sends a free token to Station 2.

2. Station 2 changes the token to a busy configuration and sends it and a data unit to the next station on the ring.

3. The busy token and the data unit travel from station to station around the ring.

4. The busy token and the data unit finally arrive at Station 2, the station that originated the data unit.

5. Station 2 removes the data unit, changes the token back to the free configuration, and sends the free token to the next station on the ring.

Figure 20.3   Token Ring protocol operation.

Fault Management

There are two error conditions that can seriously impact the operation of a Token Ring network: the loss of the token or an endlessly circulating frame. The approach taken to detecting and correcting these conditions is to have one of the stations on the network functions as an *active monitor*.

Active Monitor Functions

The station designated as the active monitor continuously monitors the network. If a predetermined period of time elapses with no token being detected, the monitor assumes that the token has been lost and issues a new token.

To check for a endlessly circulating frame, the monitor sets a Monitor bit in each frame it receives. If a frame returns to the active monitor station with the Monitor bit still set, the monitor knows the source station failed to remove the frame from the network. The active monitor removes the frame by changing the start-of-frame sequence into a new token, discarding the remainder of the frame, and starting the new token circulating. Two situations can cause an endlessly circulating frame. A transmission problem may have damaged the frame so that the source station does not recognize it as its own, or the source station may have failed.

All other stations on the network act as *passive monitors;* they monitor the operation of the active monitor. If for some reason the active monitor fails, the passive monitors use a contention resolution procedure to determine which station should take over the role of active monitor.

Bypassing a Failed Station

When a station fails, it may no longer be able to transmit data units, thus causing the ring to be broken. The approach used to deal with this is to provide a *bypass switch* as part of each station. If a station fails, the bypass switch can be closed, either manually or automatically, removing the station from the ring and allowing data units to again circulate around the ring.

Most Token Ring implementations use a physical-star wiring configuration, which makes physical failures in the ring simple to correct. Figure 20.4 illustrates the use of star wiring and bypass switches. With star wiring, each device is attached to a centrally located access unit, which contains the bypass switches. If a failure occurs in a device, or a disruption occurs in the cable attaching the device, the bypass switch is closed, and the ring remains unbroken.

Notice that the logical topology of the network is still a ring and not a star, since the central access unit does not have the intelligence to act as a network station. It is simply a passive wiring concentrator. However, by having a portion of the wiring centrally located, it is much easier to attach new devices or to identify and isolate faults.

Optional Priority Scheme

Token ring access control can be operated on either a nonpriority or a priority basis. When the optional priority scheme is not implemented, a station can send frames when-

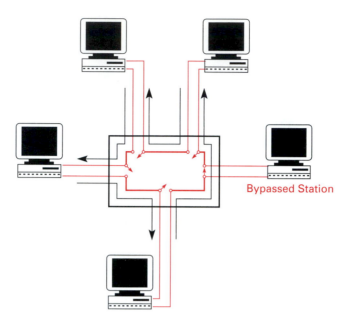

Figure 20.4   Star wiring and bypass switches.

ever it receives a token. When the *priority* scheme is implemented, three bits in each frame are used to represent its priority. A token also has a priority value. When a station receives a token, it compares the priority value in the token against the priority of any frames it has to transmit. If a frame's priority is equal to or higher than the token priority, the station transmits that frame. If the frame's priority value is lower than that of the token, the station does not transmit that frame.

Each frame also contains three *reservation* bits. If a station has a frame to transmit that has a priority greater than 0, when it receives and retransmits a frame, it checks the reservation bits in the frame. If the reservation bits are not already set to a higher value, it sets them to the priority value of the frame it has waiting to send. When the original sending station removes the frame and generates a token, it checks the reservation bits. If the priority of the reservation bits is higher than the current token priority, it sets the token priority to the higher value. When a station raises the token's priority value, it saves the previous lower value of the token's priority and is responsible for eventually restoring the token priority to the original lower value. This allows higher priority frames to be sent first.

TOKEN RING ARCHITECTURAL MODEL

The IEEE/ISO Token Ring standard defines the architectural model shown in Fig. 20.5. In conformance with the IEEE/ISO/ANSI LAN architecture, the Token Ring architectural model defines a Logical Link Control sublayer, a Medium Access Control sublayer, and a Phys-

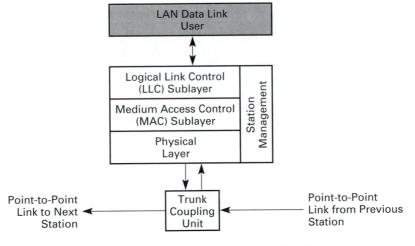

Figure 20.5   Token Ring architectural model.

ical layer. A Token Ring network interface card (NIC) is attached to the transmission medium using a *trunk coupling unit*. The trunk coupling unit has two point-to-point links attached to it: one leading to the next station in the ring and the other leading to the previous station in the ring.

PHYSICAL LAYER SPECIFICATIONS

The Physical layer specifications for the Token Ring form of medium access control include a specification for the interface between the MAC sublayer and the Physical layer. The standard also documents functional specifications for the Physical layer and includes medium specifications.

Data Encoding

The Physical layer is responsible for encoding data received from the MAC sublayer. The Token Ring standard uses differential Manchester encoding. As with Manchester encoding, differential Manchester encoding always has a transition in the middle of a bit time, which allows the encoded data to be self-clocking. The differential Manchester encoding system used with the Token Ring standard is illustrated in Fig. 20.6. A signal that has a

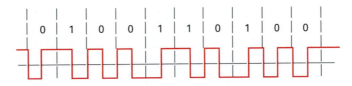

Figure 20.6   Differential Manchester encoding.

| 0 | 1 | K | 1 | 1 | J | 1 | 1 | 0 | 0 |

Figure 20.7   J and K code violations.

transition at the beginning of a bit time is interpreted as a 0 bit; a signal that has no transition at the beginning of a bit time is considered a 1 bit.

If there is no transition at the midpoint of a bit signal, this is considered a *code violation*. There are two types of code violations, called J and K. A J violation consists of a bit time in which there is no transition at the start of the bit time and also no transition at the midpoint. A K violation consists of a bit time in which there is a transition at the start but none in the middle. These two types of code violations, illustrated in Fig. 20.7, are used in the starting and ending frame delimiters to distinguish the delimiters from data.

Station Attachment Specification

The physical model defined by the Token Ring standard for station attachment is shown in Fig. 20.8. The transmission medium is implemented in the form of *trunk cable* segments that connect stations to form the physical and logical ring. A *trunk coupling unit (TCU)* is used to connect each station to an incoming and outgoing trunk cable segment. The station itself is connected to the trunk coupling unit via a cable called the *medium interface cable*. The medium interface cable itself can consist of multiple segments of cable connected together using a *medium interface connector (MIC)*. The medium interface cable is shielded and contains two balanced, 150-ohm twisted pairs.

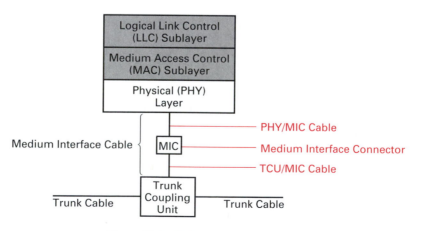

Figure 20.8   Token Ring physical model.

Medium Specifications

The Token Ring standard defines functional, electrical, and mechanical characteristics for baseband transmission using 150-ohm shielded, twisted-pair cable. With this form of transmission medium, data rates of 1 Mbps or 4 Mbps can be supported. A variation of the standard that has also been implemented allows for a transmission rate of 16 Mbps over shielded twisted-pair cable. Some LAN vendors also offer implementations of both the 4-Mbps and 16-Mbps variations of the Token Ring standard that run over unshielded twisted-pair cable, although these are not described in the version of the Token Ring standard current at the time of writing.

SUMMARY

The Token Ring standard defines a multiaccess form of data link that uses a ring-structured network topology. Stations are connected to one another using point-to-point cable segments to form a ring, and stations pass frames from one station to the next so that all stations eventually receive all frames that are transmitted.

With the Token Ring access control method, a data unit, called the token, is passed from one station to the next around a physical ring. When a station receives the token, it is allowed to transmit MAC frames for a specified time. The station that originates a frame is responsible for removing that frame from the ring after it has circulated all the way around and then sending a token to the next station. Each station that receives a frame can set bits in the frame that indicate whether the destination MAC address was recognized, the frame was copied, or an error was detected. Different priorities can be assigned to frames. The priority value associated with the token then determines when different frames can be transmitted.

A station designated as the active monitor is responsible for detecting and recovering from the loss of the token or a persistently busy token. Stations designated as passive monitors monitor the active monitor station and take over its functions if it fails.

The Token Ring standard defines a medium specification for shielded, 150-ohm twisted-pair cable, although unshielded twisted-pair cable is used in many implementations of the standard. Data rates of 1, 4, and 16 Mbps can be supported.

Chapter 21 examines the Token Bus form of LAN data link subnetwork that uses token passing in a bus- or tree-structured configuration.

Chapter **21**

Token Bus and ARCnet Subnetworks

The Token Bus LAN standard is documented in the IEEE 802.4 and ISO 8802-4 international standards. A Token Bus LAN uses token passing in conjunction with a network that has a bus- or tree-structured topology. A Token Bus LAN can be described as a combination of a *logical ring* with a *physical bus or tree*. This is illustrated in Fig. 21.1.

A Token Bus LAN implements a multiaccess form of data link in which all stations on the LAN receive the transmissions of all other stations. All MAC frames broadcast over the transmission medium reach every station, and each station is responsible for interpreting the destination MAC address contained in a frame and for accepting frames addressed to it.

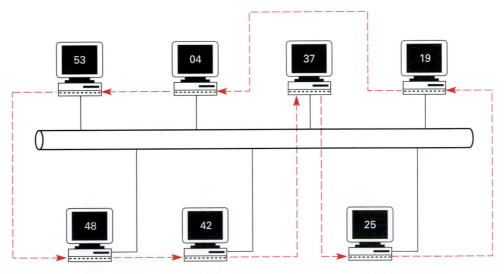

Figure 21.1   Token Bus network topology—logical ring on a physical bus.

MAC SUBLAYER PROTOCOL SPECIFICATION

The Medium Access Control sublayer protocol specifies procedures that perform the following functions:

- **Interface to the LLC Sublayer.** In a sending station, the MAC sublayer must receive LLC-PDUs from the LLC sublayer and prepare them for transmission. On the receiving side, the MAC sublayer must receive frames that have been transmitted across the network and pass the LLC-PDUs in them up to the LLC sublayer.

- **Token Handling.** This includes passing the token from one station to the next, recognizing a token when it is received, and optionally, providing for the prioritization of data units.

- **Ring Maintenance.** The logical ring the stations form must be initialized when the network is powered up, then modified as stations are added or deleted.

- **Fault Detection and Recovery.** Possible faults include multiple tokens, lost tokens, token pass failures, stations with inoperative receivers, and duplicate station addresses. These must be detected, and where possible, corrected.

- **Sending and Receiving Data.** In a source station, MAC frames are passed from the MAC sublayer to the Physical layer for transmission across the network; in a destination station, MAC frames must be received by the MAC sublayer from the Physical layer. These functions include adding and removing the control information necessary to form MAC frames in the format described in the Token Bus standard.

MAC FRAME FORMAT

The protocol specification for the Token Bus MAC sublayer defines the format of the MAC frame exchanged between MAC sublayer entities in source and destination stations. Box 21.1 shows the format of the Token Bus MAC frame and describes its fields.

Control Frames

The MAC sublayer generates its own control frames, which are transmitted across the network and used to control the operation of the MAC sublayer protocol. These control frames are in addition to the frames used to transmit the LLC-PDUs passed down from the LLC sublayer. With control frames, no information is exchanged with the LLC sublayer, either in the sending or the receiving station, and the LLC sublayer is not aware of the control frames the MAC sublayer transmits over the LAN.

Control frames are used for token passing and ring maintenance functions. Listed below are the control frames defined in the Token Bus standard. The binary control field value is included in parentheses after the name of each frame.

- **Claim_token (00000000).** Used to initiate token-passing operations when a network is initialized or when the token is lost.

- **Solicit_successor_1 (00000001).** Used to invite new stations to be added to the network. Invited stations are those whose addresses are between the holder of the token and its current successor.

BOX 21.1   Token Bus MAC frame format.

Preamble	Start Frame Delimiter	Frame Control	Dest. MAC Address	Source MAC Address	Information	Frame Check Sequence	Frame End Delimiter
	1 octet	2 octets	2 or 6 octets	2 or 6 octets	0 – n octets	4 octets	1 octet

- **Preamble.** A sequence of octets used by the receiving station for synchronization. The length of this field and its contents vary with the modulation method and the data rate used in the particular implementation of the standard.

- **Start Frame Delimiter.** An octet containing a signaling pattern always distinguishable from data. (For example, with Manchester encoding, this might be an octet containing one or more bit times in which no transition takes place.) Manchester encoding is described in Chapter 8.

- **Frame Control.** An octet that identifies the type of frame being sent. Possible types are LLC data frames, token control frames, MAC management data frames, and special-purpose data frames.

- **Station Addresses.** A *Destination MAC Address* field followed by a *Source MAC Address* field. The destination address identifies the station or stations to receive the MAC frame. The source address identifies the sending station. Address fields can be either 16 bits or 48 bits in length. (The MAC addressing mechanism is described in Chapter 18.) The destination MAC address field can specify either an individual station or a group of stations.

- **Information.** Contains an LLC-PDU, token control data, management data, or special-purpose data, as indicated by the frame control field. The Information field can be 0 octets in length for some types of MAC frames.

- **Frame Check Sequence.** A cyclic redundancy check (CRC) value used for error checking. When the sending station assembles a frame, it performs a CRC calculation on the bits in the frame. The specific algorithm used is described in the IEEE/ISO Token Bus standard. The sending station stores this value in the Frame Check Sequence field and then transmits the frame. When the receiving station receives the frame, it performs an identical CRC calculation and compares the results with the value in the Frame Check Sequence field. If the two values do not match, the receiving station assumes that a transmission error has occurred and discards the frame.

- **End Frame Delimiter.** An octet containing a signaling value always distinguishable from data. It marks the end of the frame and also identifies the position of the Frame Check Sequence field.

- **Solicit_successor_2 (00000010).** Used to invite new stations to be added to the network. Invited stations are those whose addresses are not between the holder of the token and its current successor.

- **Who_follows (00000011).** Used when a successor station does not respond to being passed the token. Based on the response to this frame, the station sending the token acquires a new successor.

- **Resolve_contention (00000100).** Used when multiple stations respond to a Solicit_successor frame.

- **Token (00001000).** The holder of the Token is the station allowed to transmit.
- **Set_successor (00001100).** Used in response to a Who_follows frame or a Solicit_successor frame to supply the address of the new successor station.

MAC PROTOCOL OPERATION

With the Token Bus approach to medium access control, access to the transmission medium is determined by possession of a special data unit called the *token*, which is passed from station to station.

When a station receives the token, it is allowed to transmit data units until a maximum amount of time has been reached. It then transmits the token to the next station. If a station that receives the token has no data units to transmit, it passes the token immediately to the next station.

Network stations are physically attached to the transmission medium in a *bus* or *tree* topology. However, the token, as indicated by the dashed line in Fig. 21.1, follows a *logical ring* around the network. The token is passed from one station to the next based on descending order of MAC addresses. When the station with the lowest MAC address value is reached, the token passes back to the station with the highest MAC address.

Token Addressing

Because the physical topology of a Token Bus LAN takes the form of a bus or tree, the token and all other frames are sent in a broadcast fashion and are received by all stations on the network. Every frame, including the token, contains a destination MAC address field that identifies the station or stations to receive it. Each station then accepts and processes only frames addressed to it. A station passes the token by changing the destination MAC address field in the token to that of the next logical station in the ring before it transmits the token.

Since a station transmits only when it has received the token, two stations can never transmit at the same time and collisions cannot occur. Because there can be no collisions, there is no minimum length requirement for frames, and the token can be a very short data unit. It contains only the control information required for proper processing.

Optional Priority Scheme

The Token Bus standard allows each MAC frame to be assigned to one of four classes of service: 6, 4, 2, and 0, with 6 being the highest-priority service class. The priority parameter value included by the LLC sublayer when an LLC-PDU is passed to the MAC sublayer specifies the class of service to assign to the MAC frame. If an odd priority value is specified, the value is mapped to the service class one lower than the specified priority value.

When the optional priority scheme is not implemented, the MAC sublayer treats all MAC frames as if they are assigned to service class 6, no matter what priority value is assigned to them. When the optional priority scheme is implemented, the MAC sublayer stores LLC-PDUs it receives from the LLC sublayer in four queues according to the service

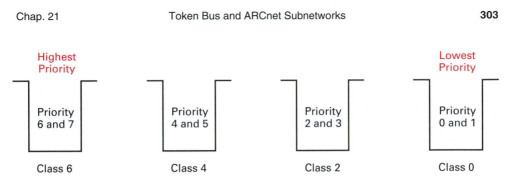

Figure 21.2   Token Bus priority values and service classes.

class to which each LLC-PDU is assigned (see Fig. 21.2). LLC-PDUs held in the queue for service class 6 are treated as though the priority system were not in operation. A station that receives the token is always allowed to transmit LLC-PDUs in service class 6 until its timer expires.

Target Token Rotation Times

When the priority scheme is implemented, each of the three lower-priority service classes has a *target token rotation time* assigned to it, with higher-priority classes assigned longer target token rotation times than the lower-priority classes. Each station sets three rotation timers to the three target rotation time values each time it transmits the token. These timers all begin to count down as soon as the token begins to circulate around the ring (see Fig. 21.3).

Suppose a station has transmitted all the LLC-PDUs assigned to service class 6 that it has queued up. It then examines the rotation timer for service class 4 to see if that time limit has expired. If the timer for service class 4 has not yet expired, the station is able to transmit any LLC-PDUs it might have queued up in service class 4. It transmits these either

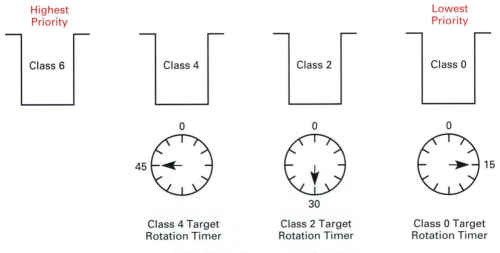

Figure 21.3   Token Bus target rotation timers.

until it has no more service class 4 LLC-PDUs or until the rotation timer assigned to service class 4 expires. If the station transmits all the LLC-PDUs assigned to service class 4, and the timer for service class 4 has still not expired, the station checks the timer for service class 2, and if that timer has not yet expired, it transmits any available LLC-PDUs from that queue. The station then moves down to service class 0 if the timer for service class 2 has not yet expired.

Priority Algorithm Intent

The priority algorithm is designed so that transmission capacity is assigned to the highest-priority LLC-PDUs as long as there are LLC-PDUs assigned to service class 6 available for transmission by any station on the network. Lower-priority LLC-PDUs are sent only when there is sufficient capacity available for them. If many stations have LLC-PDUs in service class 6 to transmit, it is likely that by the time a station finally receives the token, all of its rotation timers will already have expired. The station will then be allowed to transmit only LLC-PDUs assigned to service class 6. On the other hand, if traffic on the network is light, a station may receive the token before any of its rotation timers have expired, and the chances are better that lower-priority LLC-PDUs will be transmitted.

Ring Maintenance

In order to control the operation of the logical ring, each station must know the address of its *predecessor*, the station from which it received the token, and its *successor*, the station to which it transmits the token. When a Token Bus network is initialized, or when it is reestablished following a major failure, each station must establish its predecessor and successor station addresses. As stations are added to or deleted from the network, stations update their predecessor and successor values accordingly.

Adding a Station to the Ring

In order to allow for additions to the ring, each station must periodically provide an opportunity for new stations to be added to the ring. To do this, a station that has received the token transmits a special control frame, called a Solicit_successor frame, that contains the station's own MAC address and the MAC address of its current successor. Any station on the network with an address that falls within the range of these two MAC addresses can request that it be added to the ring.

Ring maintenance procedures are designed so new stations are added to the ring only when traffic on the network is relatively light. A station consults a timer, called the *ring maintenance rotation timer*, before transmitting a Solicit_successor frame. If the current value of the ring maintenance rotation timer is greater than the maximum ring maintenance rotation time, the station does not transmit a Solicit_successor frame for that rotation of the token.

After a station holding the token transmits a Solicit_successor frame, it waits a period of time called the *response window* to see if any station responds. The response window is the maximum amount of time it would take a response to reach the transmitting station, and is equal to the *slot time*—twice the end-to-end propagation delay of the network. If the token holder detects no response during the response window, it assumes no new station wishes to be added to the ring.

A station wishing to be added to the ring, and that has an address within the range specified in Solicit_successor frame, responds to that frame. If only one station responds, that station is added to the ring. The station addition process involves the following steps:

1. The token holder changes its successor MAC address to be that of the station being added. The token holder also transmits the token to the station being added.

2. The station being added sets its successor and predecessor MAC addresses appropriately and proceeds to process the token.

3. When the old successor receives a frame from the station just added, it saves that station's MAC address as its new predecessor MAC address.

If more than one new station responds to the Solicit_successor frame, their responses collide and cause a garbled transmission. If the token holder detects a garbled transmission, it uses a contention resolution procedure to determine which station to add. The token holder begins the contention resolution procedure by transmitting a Resolve_contention frame. A station wishing to be added must wait 0, 1, 2, or 3 response windows before responding, depending on the value of its address. If a station detects a response from another station while it is waiting, that station does not respond.

If another conflict occurs, and the token holder again detects a garbled transmission, it sends out another Resolve_contention frame. This time, only stations that responded to the first Resolve_contention frame are allowed to respond. They wait 0, 1, 2, or 3 response windows again based on the values of their addresses. This process continues until a single station responds or a maximum number of retries have been attempted. If the retry maximum is reached, the token holder passes the token on to its successor without adding a station to the ring.

Deleting a Station from the Ring

The process of deleting a station from the ring is simpler than the station addition process. When a station wishes to be deleted, it waits until it receives the token. It then sends a Set_successor frame to its predecessor, notifying it to change its successor address to the successor address of the station being deleted. Now its predecessor will pass the token directly to the deleted station's successor, bypassing the deleted station. When the new successor receives a MAC frame from its new predecessor, it saves that address as its predecessor address.

Fault Management

The Token Bus standard defines how certain error conditions are to be detected and corrected. Among these conditions are the following:

- A station failure that breaks the logical ring.
- The presence of multiple tokens on the ring.
- The loss of the token from the ring.

Station Failure

After a station transmits the token, it listens for a period of time equal to the response window to be sure that its successor station has received the token and is transmitting. If a station detects a transmission within the response window, it assumes that its successor station is operating properly.

If the issuing station does not detect a transmission within the response window period, it assumes that its successor station has not received its transmission. The issuing station then retransmits the token. If the station detects no activity following the second token transmission, the station assumes that its successor station has failed. The station then transmits a Who_follows frame, which asks the station that follows the failed station to identify itself. The station that follows the failed station identifies itself by transmitting a Set_successor frame.

When the issuing station receives the Set_successor frame, it changes its successor station address and passes the token to its new successor station, thus deleting the failed station from the ring. If there is no response to the Who_follows frame, the station sends the Who_follows frame a second time. If no response is received the second time, the issuer transmits a Solicit_successor frame that contains a range of addresses that includes all stations on the LAN.

Responses to the Solicit_successor frame are handled according to the procedure for adding a new station to the ring. The end result is to establish a two-station ring. The process is then repeated to add a third station to the ring, and so on until the entire ring is reestablished. If no response is received to the Solicit_successor frame, the issuer transmits the frame a second time. If no response is received after the second attempt, the issuing station reverts to listening mode.

Multiple Tokens

If a station that has received a token detects a transmission on the network, this indicates that some other station is also holding a token and is currently transmitting. To eliminate a multiple-token condition, the station that received a token and has detected a transmission drops the token and reverts to a receiving state. This reduces the number of token holders to either one or zero. If a station drops the token and there is no other token circulation around the ring, the lost token procedure, described next, starts a new token circulating.

Lost Token

If a station detects a lack of activity on the transmission medium that lasts longer than a predetermined period of time, the station assumes the token has been lost. When this happens, the station transmits a Claim_token frame that invites any station on the ring to claim the token and begin processing. Contending responses to the Claim_token frame are handled in the same way as an addition to the ring. In this way, a single claimant is identified and is issued the token.

There are several conditions that can trigger lost token processing, including failure of the token-holding station and a corrupted token. When the network is being initially powered up, there will be no token. Lost token processing procedures provide the ring initialization necessary to start up the network.

TOKEN BUS ARCHITECTURAL MODEL

The Token Bus standard employs the architectural model shown in Fig. 21.4. In conformance with the overall IEEE/ISO/ANSI LAN architecture, the Data Link layer is divided into the Logical Link Control (LLC) sublayer and the Medium Access Control (MAC) sublayer. The MAC sublayer provides services to a MAC sublayer user, which is normally a Logical Link Control (LLC) sublayer entity. The LLC sublayer standard is described in Chapter 18.

PHYSICAL LAYER SPECIFICATIONS

The Physical layer standards for the Token Bus form of medium access control include a specification for the interface between the MAC sublayer and the Physical layer. The standard also documents functional specifications for the Physical layer and describes different medium specifications. Two of the medium specifications are for baseband coaxial cable transmission, and one is for broadband coaxial cable transmission. A fiber-optic implementation is also described in the standard.

Medium Attachment Physical Model

The Token Bus standard defines a physical model for the way in which a station is attached to the transmission medium. This model is illustrated in Fig. 21.5. The transmission medium itself is called the *trunk cable*, and a *trunk coupling unit* is used to tap into

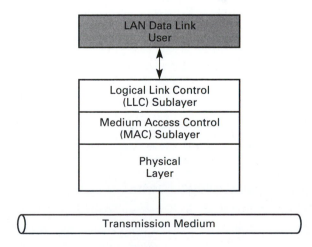

Figure 21.4   Token Bus architectural model.

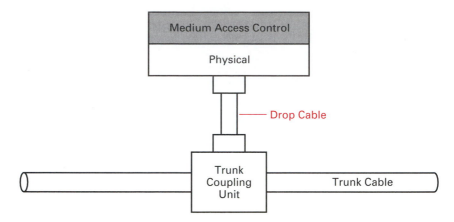

Figure 21.5   Physical model for Token Bus station attachment.

the trunk cable. A *drop cable* is then used to attach the trunk coupling unit to the component in the network interface card that implements the Physical layer.

MEDIUM SPECIFICATIONS

The Token Bus standard defines medium specifications for three different types of transmission. For each transmission type, there is a specification for the Physical layer and a description of the physical transmission medium. Physical layer specifications include detailed descriptions of functional, electrical, and physical characteristics; as well as environmental specifications related to safety, electromagnetic and electrical environment, temperature, humidity, and regulatory requirements. Transmission medium descriptions also specify transmission path delay considerations and in some cases, network sizing considerations.

The three most commonly implemented forms of transmission defined by the standard are:

- **Baseband—Single-channel Phase-continuous FSK.** This is the lowest cost implementation type.
- **Baseband—Single-channel Phase-coherent FSK.** An implementation of this type is typically more expensive than single-channel phase-continuous FSK, but less expensive than a full broadband implementation.
- **Broadband.** This is typically the most expensive of the three types of transmission to implement.

Baseband—Single-Channel Phase-Continuous FSK

The single-channel phase-continuous FSK medium specification uses baseband transmission. *Frequency-shift keying (FSK)* is used as the modulation technique, where the changes in frequency occur continuously (phase-continuous).

Manchester Encoding

This medium specification defines the use of Manchester encoding. With the form of Manchester encoding used with single-channel phase-continuous FSK, a low-high signal combination represents a 1 bit, and a high-low combination represents a 0 bit. The other possible combinations, low-low and high-high, are used to represent nondata bits. These nondata bits are used to identify start and end frame delimiters. By using signals different from data signals, the beginning and end of a frame are always clearly identifiable, and no combination of bits in a frame can be mistaken for a frame delimiter.

Repeater and Jabber-Inhibit Functions

In addition to the basic signal transmission and reception functions, the Physical layer specification for single-channel phase-continuous FSK includes the following functions:

- **Repeater Function.** The repeater function allows a station to act as a repeater only, connecting two cable segments and regenerating the signal as it passes from one segment to the other.
- **Jabber-Inhibit Function.** The jabber-inhibit function allows a station to interrupt a transmission and disable the transmitter if the transmission continues for too long a time.

Transmission Medium and Data Rate

A 75-ohm, CATV-type coaxial cable is used for the trunk cable. Devices are attached to the trunk cable using a very short 35- to 50-ohm drop cable, no more than 35 cm in length. The data rate is 1 Mbps. The carrier frequency ranges from 3.75 MHz to 6.25 MHz.

Baseband—Single-Channel Phase-Coherent FSK

With the single-channel phase-coherent FSK medium specification, baseband transmission is used and the modulation technique is frequency modulation. Here, the frequency varies between two discrete values rather than varying continuously.

Manchester Encoding

The encoding technique used is another variation of Manchester encoding. A low-low combination represents a 1 bit, and a high-high combination a 0 bit. The other combinations, low-high and high-low, are used for nondata bits employed in the frame delimiters. The repeater and jabber-inhibit functions are also supported with this transmission specification.

Transmission Medium and Data Rates

This specification also uses 75-ohm, CATV-type coaxial cable for the trunk cable. Two data rates are supported: 5 Mbps and 10 Mbps. For the 5-Mbps rate, the frequencies used are 5 MHz and 10 MHz. For the 10-Mbps rate, the frequencies are 10 MHz and 20 MHz. A 75-ohm cable is also used for the drop cable and can be up to about 30 meters in length.

Broadband

The broadband medium specification uses broadband transmission over a bus-structured network. Either a single-cable, midsplit, or a dual-cable configuration can be used, although the single-cable configuration is recommended. The modulation technique used is called *multilevel duobinary AM/PSK*. This modulation technique uses amplitude modulation (AM) combined with phase-shift keying (PSK).

Signaling Technique

The signaling technique, which is called *multilevel duobinary*, allows for three distinct amplitude levels. The three levels are symbolically represented as {0}, {2}, and {4}. Nondata bits are represented by the signal value {2}, 0 bits by {0}, and 1 bits by {4}. A scrambler function is also used when there is a long sequence of 0 bits or a long sequence of 1 bits, in which a pseudo-random function is used to convert certain 0 bits to 1 bits and vice-versa. This prevents long sequences of a given bit value from affecting synchronization. On the receiving end, a reverse descrambling function restores the bits to their original values.

Transmission Medium and Data Rates

The transmission medium is standard 75-ohm, CATV coaxial cable. Three data rates are supported: 1 Mbps, 5 Mbps and 10 Mbps. With 1 Mbps, a 1.5-MHz channel bandwidth is required. With 5 Mbps, a 6-MHz channel bandwidth is required. With 10 Mbps, a 12-MHz channel bandwidth is required.

ARCNET PRODUCTS

ARCnet, developed by Datapoint, is a popular form of LAN technology that uses a token bus form of medium access control. However, ARCnet products were first released before the IEEE/ISO Token Bus standard was finalized and do not conform to the standard. ARCnet is a popular, low-cost form of LAN data link, and products that conform to ARCnet specifications are available from a number of vendors. The data rate supported on an ARCnet LAN data link is 2.5 Mbps, although a variation of the ARCnet specification supporting a data rate of 20 Mbps has been developed.

Network Topology

ARCnet uses a bus- or tree-structured network topology, in which all stations on the LAN data link receive the transmissions of all other stations. An ARCnet implementation typically uses RG-62 coaxial cable, in conjunction with hubs or repeaters, to create physical star structures. Twisted-pair cable and fiber-optic cable have been used in some ARCnet implementations.

The ARCnet specification allows up to a maximum of 20,000 feet of cable to lie between the most distant points in the network, and up to about 2,000 feet of cable can be used to connect active hubs or repeaters.

Medium Access Control

A token passing protocol, similar to that defined for Token Bus, is used on an ARCnet LAN data link to determine when stations are allowed to transmit. Token passing is based on station addresses, which range in value from 1 to 255. Station addresses are normally manually set on an ARCnet LAN data link. If a station currently holding the token has data to transmit, it is allowed to send it.

Token Retransmission

When the station finishes sending data, or if it has no data to send, it transmits the token to the station that has the next sequentially higher address. When a station receives the token, it either sends data or passes the token to the next station. In either case, there will be activity on the transmission medium. The station that previously sent the token monitors the transmission medium. If it detects activity within a certain time period, it assumes that the token was successfully received. If there is no activity within this time period, it increments the address used previously and sends the token again. This continues until the token is sent to a station that successfully receives it. The sending station then continues to use this address in subsequent processing as the next station address.

Station Failure

The failure of a station is a condition that causes a station to increment its next station address. When a station fails or is powered down, the preceding station will detect this after it transmits the token. It will then continue transmitting the token until it reaches the next station in sequence. When a station fails to receive a token after a period of time, it triggers a process called *reconfiguration* by generating a noise burst to destroy the token being passed. This causes token passing to stop and the network to become temporarily idle.

Reconfiguration Timeout

All stations in the network monitor the transmission medium. If a period of time equal to the maximum delay between transmissions expires and no transmission is detected, the network goes through a reconfiguration process. Each station waits a period of time based on its station address, with a station having a higher address waiting a shorter period of time. When the time period elapses, the station sends a token to the station with an address that is its own address plus one. If it detects no activity after waiting the appropriate period, it increments the address by one and sends the token again. This continues, with the address wrapping around from 255 to 1 if necessary, until the station detects activity after it has sent the token.

Activity indicates that the token has been successfully received and recognized by another station. The original sending station then saves the address used when the token was successfully transmitted. Each station on the network follows this same procedure, sending the token to each address in sequence, until the token is successfully received. From that point on, stations transmit the token to the saved address.

Triggering Reconfiguration

Several conditions will trigger the reconfiguration process. When the network is initially powered up, the reconfiguration process prepares the network for operation. When a new station is powered up and wants to be added to the network, it transmits a reconfiguration burst. This is a transmission that interferes with any other transmission on the network. The reconfiguration burst is long enough in duration to ensure it will interfere with any data being transmitted and with the token following it. After the token is destroyed through this interference, a reconfiguration timeout occurs and the reconfiguration process takes place. Since the token is sent to each possible address, the new station will be included in the network following the reconfiguration process.

Lost Token

A reconfiguration will also occur if the token is inadvertently destroyed by noise on the network. The sending station interprets the noise as a transmission and does not attempt to retransmit the token. When no further transmission takes place, the stations begin the reconfiguration process.

SUMMARY

The Token Bus standard defines a multiaccess form of data link that uses a bus- or tree-structured network topology. All stations receive all transmissions within a period of time determined by the propagation delay of the network. The right to transmit is granted by passing a special data unit called the token from station to station in a sequence based on station addresses.

With the Token Bus form of medium access control, the token is passed in a logical ring structure from one station to the next. When a station receives the token, it is allowed to transmit for a specified period of time. Different priorities can be assigned to frames, and token rotation timers are used to allow transmission based on priority values. Each station knows the address of its predecessor and successor on the logical ring. When a station is added to or deleted from the LAN, or when the LAN is initialized, stations use control frames to update predecessor and successor addresses. Fault management procedures are defined to detect multiple tokens, the loss of the token, and inactive stations.

The Token Bus Physical layer specifications define three types of transmission: baseband transmission using single-channel phase-continuous FSK, baseband transmission using single-channel phase-coherent FSK, and broadband transmission.

Datapoint's ARCnet products use a token bus form of medium access control that does not conform to the IEEE/ISO Token Bus standard. The data rate supported on a typical ARCnet LAN data link is 2.5 megabits per second.

Chapter 22 describes the Fiber Distributed Data Interface (FDDI) form of medium access control technology. The FDDI medium access control method uses a timed-token passing technique to implement ring-structured LAN data links using a fiber-optic transmission medium.

Chapter 22

FDDI Subnetworks

The *Fiber Distributed Data Interface (FDDI)* standard defines a ring-structured network that uses a token-passing form of medium access control. The FDDI standard specifies the use of full-duplex, point-to-point, fiber-optic physical links to interconnect stations, although implementations based on twisted-pair cable have also been developed. (The variation of the FDDI standard adapted for twisted-pair cable is often called CDDI, for *copper distributed data interface*.) An FDDI LAN operates at a data rate of 100 Mbps. A special data unit called the *token* circulates around the ring, and a station can transmit frames only when it is in possession of the token. Figure 22.1 shows the basic topology of an FDDI LAN data link.

An FDDI LAN implements a multiaccess form of data link in which all stations on the LAN eventually receive the transmissions of all other stations. All MAC frames are repeat-

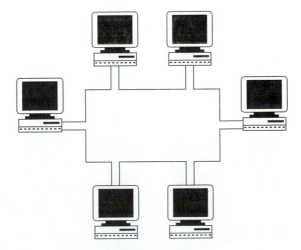

Figure 22.1   FDDI LAN basic topology.

ed all the way around the ring and reach every station on the LAN. Each station is responsible for interpreting the destination MAC address contained in a frame and for copying those frames addressed to it.

FDDI has many similarities with the IEEE/ISO LAN standards described in the previous chapters. However, the FDDI standard was developed by the Accredited Standards Committee (ASC) X3T9.5 of the American National Standards Institute (ANSI). It has been accepted by ISO as an international standard and is also published as ISO 9314.

The FDDI standard is designed to meet requirements for both high-performance individual networks and high-speed connections between networks. It addresses the requirements associated with a variety of different types of local networks, including *backend local networks*, *high-speed local networks*, and *backbone local networks*. The characteristics of these are described in Box 22.1.

MAC SUBLAYER PROTOCOL SPECIFICATION

The general functions performed by the FDDI MAC sublayer are similar to the functions performed by the MAC sublayer in other LAN standards. During MAC frame transmission, the Medium Access Control sublayer entities in all stations on the ring perform the following functions:

- **Source Station MAC Sublayer Functions.** The MAC sublayer in a source station accepts each LLC-PDU from the LLC sublayer. A data encapsulation function in the source MAC sublayer entity adds protocol-control-information (PCI) to the LLC-PDU to form a *medium-access-control-protocol-data-unit (MAC-PDU)* or *MAC frame*. The MAC sublayer then uses the services of the Physical layer to transmit the MAC frame to the next station on the ring.

- **Receiving Station MAC Sublayer Functions.** The MAC sublayer in a receiving station uses the Physical layer to receive MAC frames from the previous station on the ring. It

---

BOX 22.1   Potential uses for FDDI LAN technology.

- **Backend Local Networks.** *Backend local networks* are used to interconnect enterprise computing systems and large data storage devices where there is a need for high-volume data transfer operations. In a backend local network there will typically be a small number of devices to be connected, and they will be close together. This was the original use for which FDDI was intended, but FDDI LANs will probably be used much more extensively for the other two uses, described next.

- **High-Speed Local Networks.** The need for *high-speed local networks* has arisen from the increased use of image and graphics processing devices in the desktop computing environment. The use of graphics and images can increase the amount of data that needs to be transmitted on a network by orders of magnitude. A typical data processing transaction may involve 500 bits, while a document page image may require the transmission of half a million bits or more.

- **Backbone Local Networks.** *Backbone local networks* are used to provide a high-capacity LAN data link that can be used to interconnect other, lower-capacity LANs.

interprets the destination MAC address in each frame it receives and copies only frames addressed to that station. For each frame it copies, the MAC sublayer entity removes the PCI from the MAC frame and passes the resulting LLC-PDU to the LLC sublayer. The MAC sublayer in a receiving station also interprets the source address in each MAC frame it receives to identify frames it originally placed onto the ring. When a receiving station identifies one of its own frames, it does not repeat that frame, thus removing it from the ring. A receiving station repeats all other MAC frames, whether it copied them or not, to the next station on the ring.

MAC FRAME FORMAT

The MAC frame format is described in the FDDI standard using the term *symbol* to refer to a group of four bits. Symbols are encoded in a way that allows both data and nondata values to be represented. The FDDI symbol encoding scheme is described later in this chapter when we discuss Physical layer specifications. Box 22.2 shows the format of the FDDI MAC frame and describes its fields.

Frame Types

The Frame Control field contains bits that indicate a frame's type. The FDDI specification defines eight types of frames:

- **Void Frame.** A data unit considered logically not to be a frame; its contents are ignored.
- **Token.** The token, used to grant permission to transmit.
- **Restricted Token.** The restricted token, used to control transmission in multiframe dialogs.
- **SMT Frames.** Data units sent by station management components to control their operation.
- **MAC Frames.** Data units used to control the operation of the MAC protocol, including the Claim and Beacon frames.
- **LLC Frames.** Data units containing an LLC-PDU passed down from the LLC sublayer.
- **Implementor Frames.** Data units reserved for the implementor.
- **Reserved Frames.** Data units intended for use in future versions of the FDDI standard.

Token Format

A special data unit format, illustrated in Fig. 22.2, is used for the token. A token consists of a Preamble, Start Frame Delimiter, Frame Control field, and End Frame Delimiter.

MAC PROTOCOL OPERATION

The FDDI MAC sublayer uses a timed-token ring access protocol that governs the way in which a MAC sublayer entity gains access to the ring to transmit data. Although FDDI uses a *token ring* form of medium access control, the timed-token ring access protocol used by FDDI is substantially different from the access protocol defined in the IEEE/ISO Token Ring standard and is not compatible with it.

BOX 22.2   FDDI MAC frame format.

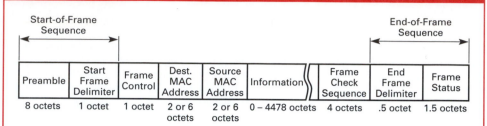

Preamble	Start Frame Delimiter	Frame Control	Dest. MAC Address	Source MAC Address	Information		Frame Check Sequence	End Frame Delimiter	Frame Status
8 octets	1 octet	1 octet	2 or 6 octets	2 or 6 octets	0 – 4478 octets		4 octets	.5 octet	1.5 octets

- **Preamble.** An 8-octet symbol pattern used to synchronize each station's clock with frame transmission.

- **Start Frame Delimiter.** A unique signal pattern, using nondata symbols, that identifies the start of the frame.

- **Frame Control.** Identifies the frame's type. It has the bit format CLFFZZZZ, interpreted as follows:

  — **C.** Identifies this as a synchronous or asynchronous frame.
  — **L.** Specifies whether 16- or 48-bit addresses are used.
  — **FF.** Indicates the frame's type.
  — **ZZZZ.** Provides control information for MAC frames.

- **Station Addresses.** A *Destination MAC Address* field and a *Source MAC Address* field. Station addresses can be either 16 bits or 48 bits in length. A ring may contain a mixture of stations using 16-bit and 48-bit addresses. The destination address can specify an individual address, a group address, or the broadcast address. The source address must identify an individual station. The MAC addressing scheme is described in Chapter 18.

- **Information.** Contains an LLC-PDU passed from the LLC sublayer or control information supplied by the MAC sublayer. FDDI Physical layer specifications limit the maximum length of a frame to 9000 symbols, including the four symbols of the Preamble. This limits the length of the Information field to a maximum of 8956 symbols or 4478 octets.

- **Frame Check Sequence (FCS).** Contains a cyclic redundancy check (CRC) value used for error checking. The value is calculated by the source station based on the contents of the Frame Control, Destination MAC Address, Source MAC Address, and Information fields. A destination station performs the same CRC calculation as the source station. If the calculated CRC value does not match the value in the FCS field, the frame is considered to be corrupted and is discarded.

- **End Frame Delimiter.** Identifies the end of the frame. The ending delimiter for a token consists of two symbols (1 octet). For all other frames, it consists of a single symbol (1/2 octet).

- **Frame Status.** Contains information about the status of a frame, including whether an error was detected, the address was recognized, or the frame was copied. Additional implementation-defined indicators may also be included in this field.

Preamble	Start Frame Delimiter	Frame Control	End Frame Delimiter
8 octets	1 octet	1 octet	1 octet

Figure 22.2   FDDI token format.

The protocol implemented by the FDDI MAC sublayer performs the following functions in supplying its services:

- Ring initialization.
- Providing fair and deterministic access to the transmission medium.
- Address recognition and address filtering.
- Generation and verification of frame check sequence (FCS) fields.
- Frame transmission and reception.
- Frame repeating.
- Frame stripping (removal of frames from the ring).

During operation of the FDDI timed-token ring access control protocol the token is passed from station to station around the ring. When the token arrives at a station, it is passed up to the MAC sublayer entity in that station. A MAC sublayer entity holding the token is allowed to transmit frames. If the MAC sublayer entity has frames to send, it holds the token and transmits as many frames as desired onto the ring until the station either runs out of frames to send or reaches a predefined time limit. The station then transmits the token to the next station on the ring.

After a frame circulates all the way around the ring and returns to the station originating it, that station is responsible for stripping the frame from the ring by not repeating it. As a station repeats each frame around the ring, it sets bits in the Frame Status field of the frame indicating whether the station detected an error in the frame, recognized the address in the frame's destination MAC address field, or copied the frame for processing. The FDDI token-passing procedure is illustrated in Fig. 22.3.

Notice that a station transmits the token immediately after it finishes transmitting frames. This makes it possible for a station to transmit new frames while frames transmitted by other stations are still circulating around other parts of the ring. Thus, there can be multiple frames, from multiple stations, on different segments of the ring at any given time.

Ring Monitoring Functions

All stations on the ring participate in distributed algorithms that monitor the operation of the ring to check for invalid conditions that may require the ring to be reinitialized. An example of an invalid condition is a ring that currently has no token circulating. To detect the absence of a circulating token, each station maintains a *token rotation timer (TRT),* which the station resets each time it receives the token. If the timer expires twice before the station next receives the token, the station assumes the token has been lost and begins the ring initialization procedure.

Other types of incorrect activity can also cause a station to begin the station initialization procedure. A station begins the ring-initialization process by performing a claim token procedure.

Claim Token Procedure

In performing the *claim token* procedure, a station bids for the right to initialize the ring. The station begins the claim token procedure by issuing a continuous stream of control

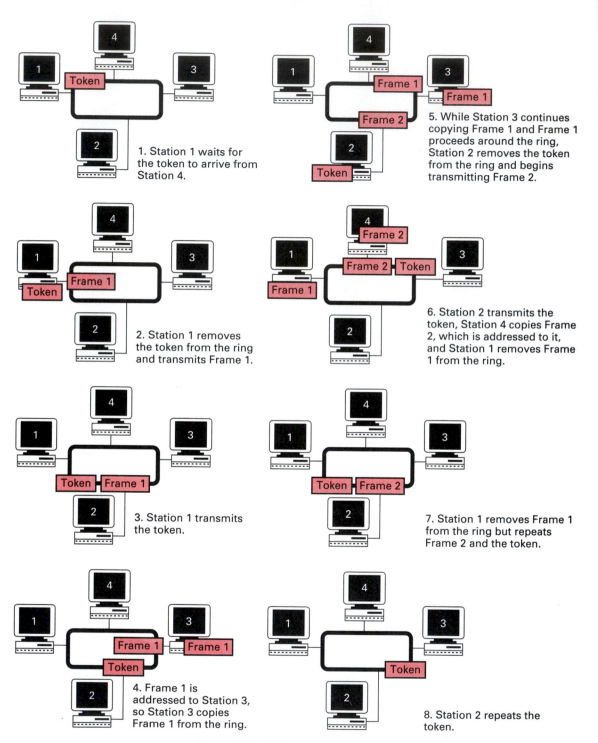

1. Station 1 waits for the token to arrive from Station 4.

2. Station 1 removes the token from the ring and transmits Frame 1.

3. Station 1 transmits the token.

4. Frame 1 is addressed to Station 3, so Station 3 copies Frame 1 from the ring.

5. While Station 3 continues copying Frame 1 and Frame 1 proceeds around the ring, Station 2 removes the token from the ring and begins transmitting Frame 2.

6. Station 2 transmits the token, Station 4 copies Frame 2, which is addressed to it, and Station 1 removes Frame 1 from the ring.

7. Station 1 removes Frame 1 from the ring but repeats Frame 2 and the token.

8. Station 2 repeats the token.

Figure 22.3 FDDI protocol operation.

frames, called Claim frames. Each Claim frame contains a suggested *Target Token Rotation Time (TTRT)* value. If a station sending Claim frames receives a Claim frame from another station, it compares TTRT values. If the station's own TTRT value is lower, it keeps transmitting Claim frames. If the TTRT value in a Claim frame a station receives is lower than its own TTRT value, it passes on the received Claim frame instead of its own. If the values are the same, MAC addresses are used to determine which station takes precedence.

Eventually, the Claim frame with the lowest TTRT value will be passed on by other stations and will return to the station that sent it. At this point the source station recognizes itself as the winner in the claim token procedure. That station has won the right to initialize the ring and continues by performing the ring initialization procedure. As a result of the claim token procedure, all stations now have the TTRT value to be used in subsequent ring operation because all stations have seen the TTRT value in the Claim frame sent by the winning station.

The claim token procedure sounds complex and time consuming, but with a data rate of 100 Mbps, the procedure takes only a millisecond or two to complete, even on a large ring.

Ring Initialization

The station winning the claim token procedure sets its own token rotation timer to the negotiated TTRT and transmits a token onto the ring. Each station that receives the token then sets its own TTRT to the negotiated value and transmits the token to the next station. No frames are transmitted until the token has passed once all the way around the ring. The purpose of the initial token rotation is to align TTRT values and TRT times in all stations on the ring.

Beacon Process

When a serious failure occurs, such as a break in the ring, stations use a *beacon process* to locate the failure. Each station's SMT component can initiate the beacon process. When a station that has been sending Claim frames recognizes that a defined time period has elapsed without the claim token process being resolved, it begins the beacon process by transmitting a continuous stream of Beacon frames. If a station receives a Beacon frame from another station, it stops sending its own Beacon frames and passes on the Beacon frames it has received. Eventually, Beacon frames from the station immediately following the break will be propagated to all stations in the network. Some process external to the MAC sublayer entity must then be invoked to diagnose the problem and to reconfigure the ring to bypass the failure. If during the beacon process a station receives its own Beacon frames, it assumes the ring has been restored and initiates the claim token procedure.

Optional FDDI MAC Protocol Features

The FDDI standard specifies optional mechanisms that implement a capacity allocation scheme. This scheme is designed to support a mixture of stream and burst transmissions and transmissions involving dialogs between pairs of stations.

Synchronous and Asynchronous Frames

Two types of MAC frames are defined by the FDDI standard: *asynchronous* frames and *synchronous* frames. In normal FDDI protocol operation, only asynchronous frames are transmitted. The use of synchronous frames is optional, and an FDDI implementation need not support them.

Each station may be allocated a certain length of time during which it can transmit synchronous frames. This time interval is called its *synchronous allocation (SA)*. The target token rotation time must be large enough to accommodate the sum of all the station synchronous transmission times plus the time it takes for a frame of maximum size to travel around the ring.

Each station keeps track of the time elapsed since it last received the token. When a station next receives the token, it records the elapsed time since the last token was received. The station is then allowed to transmit synchronous frames for its synchronous allocation time. Then, if the elapsed time, as recorded when the token was received, is less than the TTRT, the station is allowed to send asynchronous frames for a time interval equal to that time difference.

All stations having a synchronous allocation are guaranteed an opportunity to transmit synchronous frames, but a station sends asynchronous frames only if time permits. Asynchronous frames can optionally be subdivided using levels of priority that are then used to further prioritize the sending of asynchronous traffic.

Multiframe Dialogs

FDDI provides another optional mechanism for implementing *multiframe dialogs* between pairs of stations. When a station needs to enter into a dialog with another station, it can do so using its asynchronous transmission capacity. After the station transmits the first frame in the dialog, it transmits a *restricted token*. Only the station receiving the first frame is allowed to use the restricted token for transmitting asynchronous frames. The two stations can then exchange data frames and restricted tokens for the duration of the dialog. During this time, other stations are able to send synchronous frames but not asynchronous frames.

FDDI ARCHITECTURAL MODEL

The FDDI specification defines an architectural model describing the organization of the Data Link and Physical layers. This architectural model is illustrated in Fig. 22.4. The components in the architectural model can be divided among those components associated with the Data Link layer, those associated with the Physical layer, and those associated with the station management (SMT) function.

Data Link Layer Components

The Data Link layer is divided into a *Logical Link Control (LLC)* sublayer and a *Medium Access Control (MAC)* sublayer. The FDDI standard does not define the LLC sublayer but permits the use of the IEEE/ISO Logical Link Control standard for this sublayer. The Medi-

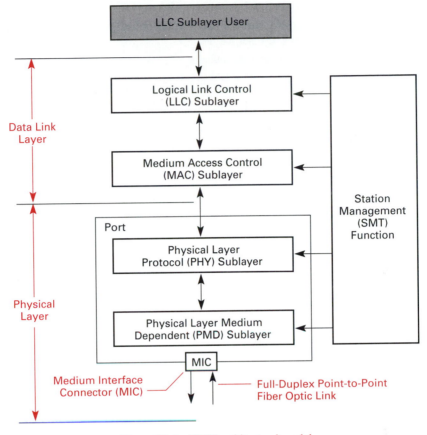

Figure 22.4   FDDI architectural model.

um Access Control sublayer of the Data Link layer is concerned with the protocol used to handle the transmission of tokens and data frames around the ring.

Physical Layer Components

The FDDI Physical layer is divided into a *Physical Layer Protocol (PHY)* sublayer and a *Physical Layer Medium Dependent (PMD)* sublayer. The Physical Layer Protocol (PHY) sublayer is responsible for encoding, transmitting, and decoding data and control information. The Physical Layer Medium Dependent (PMD) sublayer is responsible for sending and receiving signals over a particular physical transmission medium.

Station Management Component

A station has a single *station management (SMT)* component, which is responsible for monitoring the operation of the station and for controlling the various management-oriented attributes of other station components. The SMT component implements the following functions:

- Adding, initializing, and removing stations.
- Managing a station's configuration, its attachment to the FDDI transmission medium, and its connections with other stations.
- Isolating and recovering from faults.

STATION TYPES AND NETWORK TOPOLOGIES

In FDDI terminology, a *station* is an addressable network component capable of generating and receiving frames. Each instance of a PHY sublayer entity and a PMD sublayer entity within a station is called a *port*. A station can implement one or more ports. Each port is attached to the transmission medium through a *Medium Interface Connector (MIC)*.

A station contains one or more MAC sublayer entities, one or more ports, and a single station management (SMT) entity. There are various ways in which stations and other devices can be configured to form an FDDI network, and various types of MICs are defined for attaching a device to the network. We will look next at the station configurations and MIC types defined by the FDDI standard and examine the various types of network topologies that can be formed using the different station configurations.

Dual-Attachment Station

A *dual-attachment station (DAS)* is designed to connect to two separate full-duplex transmission medium segments. A dual-attachment station has one SMT entity, one or more MAC sublayer entities, and exactly two ports. Each of the ports is associated with its own MIC. The architectural model for a dual-attachment station is shown in Fig. 22.5.

Dual-attachment stations are used to form a structure commonly called a *dual ring*, or *trunk ring* structure. The two rings are called the *primary ring* and the *secondary ring*.

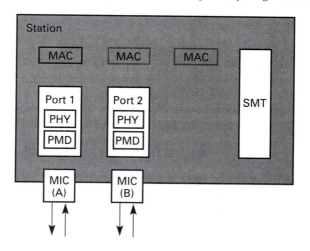

Figure 22.5   FDDI dual-attachment station (DAS) architectural model.

In a dual ring structure, when each MIC is properly connected, two physical and logical rings are formed.

To properly form a dual ring, each dual-attachment station must implement exactly two MICs: one MIC of type A and one MIC of type B. The type A and type B MICs are defined as follows:

- MIC **Type A.** A MIC of type A is defined to be the *input* of the path for the primary ring.
- MIC **Type B.** A MIC of type B is defined to be the *output* of the path for the primary ring.

Figure 22.6 shows a simple FDDI network consisting of four dual-attachment stations. The network is formed by connecting the type A MIC of one station to the type B MIC of the next station with a single transmission medium segment. Since each transmission medium segment is full-duplex, transmissions can flow in both directions simultaneously over each segment, thus forming a dual, counter-rotating ring structure.

FDDI MICs and transmission medium segments are designed to facilitate the connection of MICs in the proper manner. For example, the connectors at the end of transmission medium segments do not allow one type A MIC to be attached to another type A MIC .

The FDDI standard does not specify how the primary and secondary rings are to be used. This is left to the implementors. Normally, the primary ring is used to carry data, and the secondary ring is idle and is used to recover from physical link and station failures. However, it is possible, although not common, for an FDDI implementation to employ both rings simultaneously for data transmission.

Dual-Attachment Concentrator

A *concentrator* is an FDDI device that has more ports than are needed to simply attach the concentrator itself to the FDDI network. The additional ports can be used to attach other stations to the network. A *dual-attachment concentrator (DAC)* is a station that has three or more ports, each associated with its own MIC.

A dual-attachment concentrator is used to create a network topology called a *dual ring of trees*, in which tree structures branch off the dual counter-rotating ring to connect *single-attachment stations* (SASS). (The architecture of a single attachment station is

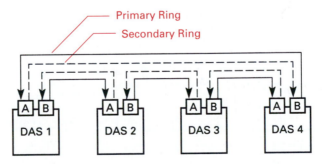

Figure 22.6   Simple ring of dual-attachment stations.

described later in this chapter.) A dual-attachment concentrator implements one MIC of type A, one of type B, and one or more MICs of type M. Each MIC of type M (short for *master*) in a concentrator is attached to a MIC of type S (short for *slave*), implemented in a single-attachment station.

A simple concentrator network—made up of dual-attachment stations, dual-attachment concentrators, and single-attachment stations—is shown in Fig. 22.7.

The numbers next to each station in Fig. 22.7 indicate the path of the token as it travels from station to station around the primary ring. This example assumes that each concentrator implements a MAC sublayer entity and also acts as a station. When a concentrator is also a station, it logically follows any slave stations to which it is attached.

An architectural model of the dual-attachment concentrator is shown in Fig. 22.8. A dual-attachment concentrator can implements zero or more MAC entities. If a device performs a concentrator function only, it implements no MAC entities, and the concentrator will not be the source or the final destination of any frames. In this case, the concentrator is not addressable and is not considered to be a station on the network; it performs a concentrator function only. A concentrator can contain MAC entities, however, and also function as a station.

Single-Attachment Station

A *single-attachment station (SAS)* implements a single MIC of type S. A single-attachment station is typically connected, via a single transmission medium segment, to a concentra-

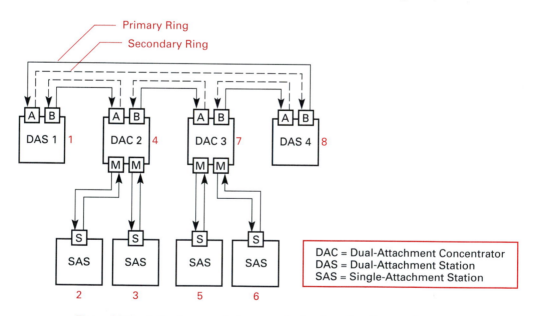

Figure 22.7   A simple concentrator network showing token flow on the primary ring. The numbers next to the stations indicate the sequence in which the MAC sublayer entities receive the token.

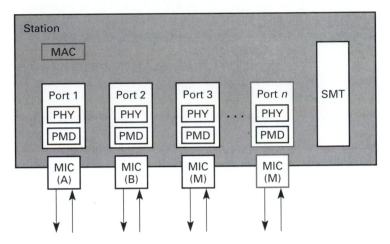

Figure 22.8   FDDI dual-attachment concentrator (DAC) architectural model.

tor implementing a MIC connector of type M. Figure 22.9 shows the architectural model of a single-attachment station. It contains an SMT entity, a MAC sublayer entity, and one port having a MIC of type S.

Single-Attachment Concentrator

A *single-attachment concentrator (SAC)* can be used to create a hierarchy of trees. This configuration is illustrated in Fig. 22.10. The architectural model of the single-attachment concentrator is shown in Fig. 22.11.

Null-Attachment Concentrator

It is also possible to have an FDDI network that consists only of a tree structure with no dual ring. In such a configuration, as shown in Fig. 22.12, the topmost concentrator is a

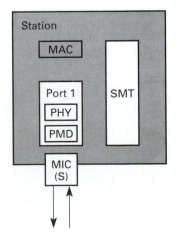

Figure 22.9   FDDI single-attachment station (SAS) architectural model.

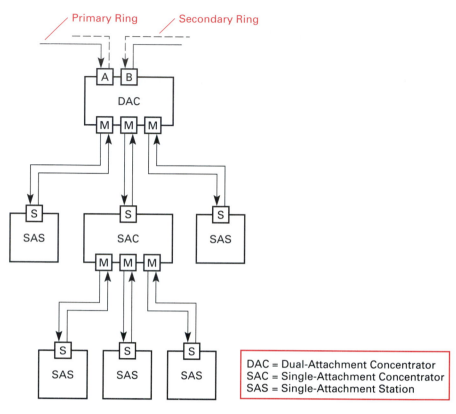

Figure 22.10 Hierarchy of trees.

DAC = Dual-Attachment Concentrator
SAC = Single-Attachment Concentrator
SAS = Single-Attachment Station

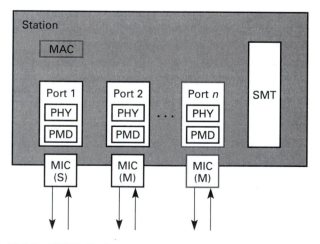

Figure 22.11 FDDI single-attachment concentrator (SAC) architectural model.

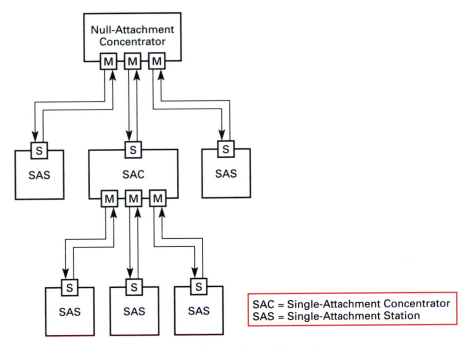

Figure 22.12   Hierarchy of trees using a null-attachment concentrator.

null-attachment concentrator. A null-attachment concentrator has no MICs of type A or B for connection to a dual ring and no MIC of type S to a higher-level concentrator. It contains only MICs of type M for attachment of stations and concentrators at a lower level.

NETWORK RECONFIGURATION

In addition to supporting high data transfer rates, FDDI has been designed to provide a high level of reliability. One way in which it does this is by including the secondary ring as part of the basic network topology. The secondary ring can be used to recover from physical failures of links or stations by allowing the network to be dynamically reconfigured to bypass a failed component.

Physical Link Failures

If a physical link failure occurs, stations can perform procedures to detect the failure and set bypass switches to use the secondary ring to bypass the problem. This is shown in Fig. 22.13. The redundant physical links that implement the secondary ring can be used to bypass the missing physical link, thus reconfiguring the primary ring. The numbers in the diagram show the sequence in which the token flows around the ring both before and after the link failure.

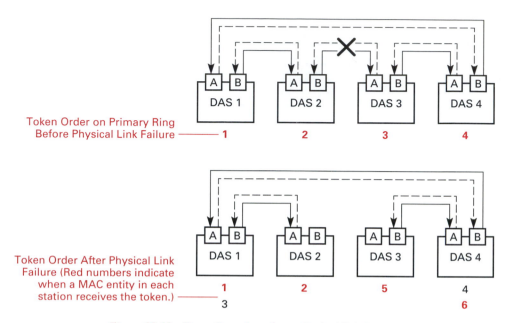

Token Order on Primary Ring
Before Physical Link Failure ——— 1   2   3   4

Token Order After Physical Link
Failure (Red numbers indicate
when a MAC entity in each
station receives the token.) ———   1   2   5   4
3   6

Figure 22.13   Reconfiguration after a physical link failure.

Station Failures

The secondary ring can also be used to bypass a station that either fails or is disconnected from the ring. This is shown in Fig. 22.14. Stations on either side of the physical links to the failed station can reconfigure the network using the secondary ring. Again, numbers show the sequence in which the token flows around the ring both before and after the station failure.

PHYSICAL LAYER SPECIFICATIONS

As we described earlier, the FDDI Physical layer is divided into a Physical Layer Protocol (PHY) sublayer and a Physical Layer Medium Dependent (PMD) sublayer. Each sublayer performs a different set of functions and has its own service definition.

The PHY Sublayer

The *Physical Layer Protocol (PHY)* sublayer performs the following functions:

- Encoding and decoding data and control information.
- Transmitting data received from the MAC sublayer.
- Performing clock synchronization and recovering the data coming in from the PMD sublayer.
- Transmitting and receiving groups of code bits, called *line states,* used to initialize and condition the transmission medium.

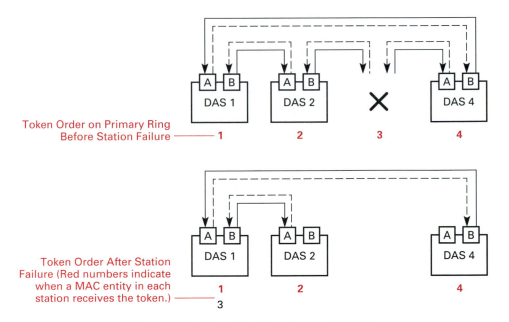

Figure 22.14   Reconfiguration after a station failure.

Code Conversion

A key service provided by the PHY sublayer is the encoding and decoding of data. The encoding system used by FDDI is designed to provide ease of synchronization as well as reliable data transmission. Data and control information is carried on the transmission medium in the form of code bits. A *code bit* is the smallest signaling entity. A *code group* is a consecutive sequence of 5 code bits used to represent a *symbol* on the transmission medium.

A *4b/5b code* is used to convert each 4-bit symbol to a 5-bit value prior to transmission, and to return it to the original 4-bit value after transmission. The FDDI 4b/5b code is shown in Fig. 22.15. The 5-bit data values used to represent the 4-bit symbols were chosen so there are never more than three consecutive 0 bits. With the signaling system used with FDDI , this means there will be no more than three bit times without a transition. An additional 8 symbols are used for control purposes. Other possible 5-bit values are invalid.

PMD Sublayer

The *Physical Layer Medium Dependent (PMD)* sublayer performs the following functions:

- Providing the services required to transport an encoded digital bit stream from one station to the next over a point-to-point transmission medium.
- Defining requirements for the *Medium Interface Connector (MIC)* and the keying of various types of MIC receptacles. The MIC is a fiber-optic connector that connects the fiber-optic transmission medium to the FDDI attachment.

Code Group	Symbol	Interpretation
Data		
11110	0	hex 0
01001	1	hex 1
10100	2	hex 2
10101	3	hex 3
01010	4	hex 4
01011	5	hex 5
01110	6	hex 6
01111	7	hex 7
10010	8	hex 8
10011	9	hex 9
10110	A	hex A
10111	B	hex B
11010	C	hex C
11011	D	hex D
11100	E	hex E
11101	F	hex F
Control		
00000	Q	Quiet
11111	I	Idle
00100	H	Halt
11000	J	Start Delimiter (1st symbol)
10001	K	Start Delimiter (2nd symbol)
01101	T	Ending Delimiter
00111	R	Reset
11001	S	Set

Figure 22.15   FDDI 4b/5b symbol encoding.

- Specifying the characteristics of drivers and receivers, transmission media, connectors, power budgets, and other physical, hardware-related characteristics.

- Determining when an actual signal is being received by a receiver.

The PMD sublayer is responsible for translating the bit stream used by the PHY sublayer to and from signals transmitted over the transmission medium to the next station on the ring. The transmission medium consists of the portion of the physical communication channel to which two or more PMD sublayer entities are connected. Each transmission medium segment implements a full-duplex transmission path.

Medium Specifications

FDDI was designed based on the use of fiber-optic cable as the transmission medium, and there is a medium specification in the standard that defines the characteristics of optical signals and a fiber-optic transmission medium. A second medium specification is under development that addresses the use of twisted-pair wiring as the transmission medium.

This version of FDDI is commonly referred to as *Copper Distributed Data Interface (CDDI),* for the copper wire that replaces the fiber-optic cable.

Fiber-Optic Medium Specification

The medium specification for the use of fiber-optic cable as the transmission medium recommends the use of 62.5/125 multimode fiber-optic cable, although single mode fiber-optic cable can also be used. Connections between stations or between a station and a concentrator can be up to 2000 meters in length.

Following the 4b/5b code conversion, bits are encoded using nonreturn to zero inverted (NRZI) encoding. With NRZI, a 1 bit is represented by a transition in the signal, and a 0 bit by no transition.

CDDI Medium Specification

The medium specification for twisted-pair wiring specifies the use of either data-grade (category 5) unshielded twisted-pair or shielded twisted-pair cable. With unshielded twisted-pair cable, connections between stations or between a station and a concentrator can be up to 50 meters in length; with shielded twisted-pair, connections can be up to 100 meters long.

Following the 4b/5b code conversion, the 5-bit code groups are scrambled and encoded using a form of encoding called *Multi-Level Transmission-3 (MLT-3)*. MLT-3 uses three signal levels. A logical low value (0 bit) is sent using the intermediate signal level. A logical high value (1 bit) is sent alternately using the low signal level and the high signal level. MLT-3 is used to avoid the higher emission levels that sometimes result from supporting high data transmission rates over unshielded twisted-pair cable, so CDDI products will be able to maintain an FCC class B certification.

FDDI II

At the time of writing, an upwardly compatible extension of FDDI, called *FDDI II* is undergoing standardization in ISO. The original FDDI specification is now sometimes called *FDDI I*. The original intent of FDDI technology was to provide a higher-speed alternative to other types of LAN technology, such as Ethernet and Token Ring, for data applications. However, since standardization work on FDDI was begun, there has been an increasing need for integrated networks that carry both data and nondata traffic, such as voice and video.

An FDDI I LAN uses packet-switching technology to carry user data in variable-length frames. As discussed earlier in this chapter FDDI I defines a capacity allocation scheme, using synchronous frames, that can be used to control the amount of time any single station has access to the transmission medium. This mechanism can be used to guarantee a certain minimum sustained data rate to a user, but it does not provide for a uniform data stream between two communicating stations. Packet-switching mechanisms are not well suited for communication applications in which a constant, uniform data stream is required. Circuit-switching technologies are better suited for such applications.

Isochronous Transmission

FDDI II defines additional optional protocol mechanisms that allow an FDDI data link to be used to provide circuit-switched services in addition to packet-switched services. The mode of transmission used to provide circuit-switched services is called *isochronous transmission*. The FDDI II isochronous transmission mechanisms impose a 125-microsecond frame structure on the ring. The frame structure is used to divide the total transmission capacity into a number of discrete channels by allocating regularly repeating time slots to users that require them. These discrete channels are used to provide a virtual circuit between pairs of communicating stations.

Basic and Hybrid Operation

An FDDI II network can operate in either *basic* or *hybrid* mode. In basic mode, the network functions in an identical fashion to an FDDI I network and provides only packet-switching services. In hybrid mode, the capacity of the transmission medium is split between packet switching and circuit switching.

Figure 22.16 illustrates the FDDI II architectural model. A new sublayer structure imposes a *Hybrid Ring Control (HRC)* function between the conventional FDDI Medium Access Control (MAC) sublayer and the Physical layer. The HRC function contains a new *Isochronous Medium Access Control (IMAC)* sublayer and a *Hybrid Multiplexor (HMUX)* function. The IMAC sublayer provides services to a circuit-switched multiplexor component that operates at the level of the LLC sublayer. The HMUX function provides an interface between the Physical layer and the two alternative MAC sublayer functions and divides the transmission capacity into channels that can be split between packet-switching and circuit-switching applications.

Wideband Channels

When an FDDI II network is operating in basic mode, the entire 100 Mbps transmission capacity is used for packet-switching services. When the network is operating in hybrid mode, the transmission capacity is split between a *packet-data channel* and several *wideband channels (WBCS)*. Up to 16 wideband channels can be used that each supports a data rate of 6.144 Mbps. The minimum capacity of the packet-data channel is .768 Mbps. A total of .928 Mbps of channel capacity is devoted to overhead functions, making the total capacity of an FDDI II network operating in hybrid mode 99.072 Mbps.

A wideband channel can be devoted to providing a single virtual circuit between a pair of communicating stations, or the capacity of a single wideband channel can be split to provide lower capacity virtual circuits that can be used by different pairs of communicating stations. Any number of the wideband channels can also be devoted to packet-switching service and can be used to increase the capacity of the packet-data channel. Thus, the capacity of the packet-data channel can grow in 6.144 Mbps increments.

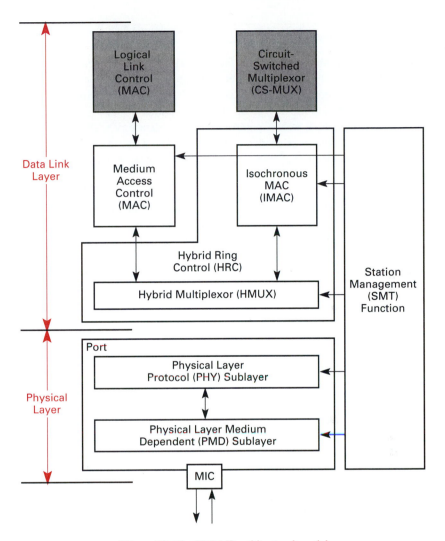

Figure 22.16 FDDI II architectural model.

Future Direction

FDDI II represents a refinement of the shared access technology used in local area networks that allows the LAN to be used for applications better suited to circuit switching. However, the future direction of networking technology to support both data and nondata applications most probably lies in the use of Asynchronous Transfer Mode (ATM) technology, in which any pair of communicating stations is always provided with a high-speed virtual circuit. ATM technology is described in Chapter 15 as a wide area network transmission technology, but ATM will have applications in LANs as well.

SUMMARY

The Fiber Distributed Data Interface (FDDI) standard defines a multiaccess form of data link that uses a ring-structured network topology. Stations are connected to one another using point-to-point fiber-optic cable segments to form a ring, and stations pass frames from one station to the next so all stations eventually receive all frames transmitted.

With the FDDI access control method, a data unit, called the token, is passed from one station to the next around a physical ring. When a station receives the token, it is allowed to transmit MAC frames for a specified time. After a station finishes transmitting frames, it immediately transmits a token granting the next station on the ring the right to transmit frames. Frames from multiple stations can all be circulating at any time around the ring. Each station that receives a frame can set bits in the frame that indicate whether the destination MAC address was recognized, the frame was copied, or an error was detected. The station that originates a frame is responsible for removing that frame from the ring after it has circulated all the way around.

The FDDI standard defines optional procedures for implementing a capacity allocation scheme using synchronous and asynchronous frames and a multiframe dialog mechanism using restricted tokens.

The FDDI standard defines architectural models for various types of stations, including dual-attachment stations, dual-attachment concentrators, single-attachment stations, single-attachment concentrators, and null-attachment concentrators. Stations are connected using full-duplex transmission medium segments that allow dual ring and tree structures to be formed. The dual ring formed by dual-attachment stations and concentrators allow the ring structure to be dynamically reconfigured to recover from station and link failures.

The FDDI standard defines a fiber-optic transmission medium supporting baseband transmission at a 100-Mbps data rate. Some implementations of the standard use twisted-pair cable.

Chapter 23 describes the LocalTalk form of LAN data link defined by AppleTalk, Apple's networking system. LocalTalk uses the Carrier Sense Multiple Access with Collision Avoidance (CSMA/CA) medium access control method to implement bus- or tree-structured LAN data links.

Apple LocalTalk Subnetworks

LocalTalk is the name of the LAN technology included as part of Apple's AppleTalk network architecture. The AppleTalk protocol family does not conform completely to the OSI model or to the IEEE/ISO/ANSI LAN architecture. However, AppleTalk includes protocols that correspond to many of the functions defined by the Data Link and Physical layers of the IEEE/ISO/ANSI LAN architecture. In this chapter, we describe the LAN protocols AppleTalk defines for the Data Link and Physical layers.

The full name of the AppleTalk LAN data link protocol is *LocalTalk Link Access Protocol (LLAP)*. It defines operations associated with the Physical and Data Link layers of the OSI model and performs functions analogous to the protocols used with other LAN technologies. AppleTalk supports the use of Ethernet and Token Ring LAN data links in the Data Link and Physical layers and in an AppleTalk network.

NETWORK CONNECTION

A typical Apple computer includes serial ports that can be used for a variety of purposes, including attaching the computer to a LocalTalk network. The serial port is connected to the network using an inexpensive external connector that interfaces with the LAN transmission medium. LocalTalk Network Interface Cards (NICs) are also available for computing systems other than Apple computers, such as IBM-compatible personal computers and various types of workstations. LocalTalk NICs allow the same external connectors used with Apple computer systems to connect to a LocalTalk LAN data link. A typical small LocalTalk LAN consisting of Apple personal computers, an IBM-compatible personal computer, and a network printer is shown in Fig. 23.1.

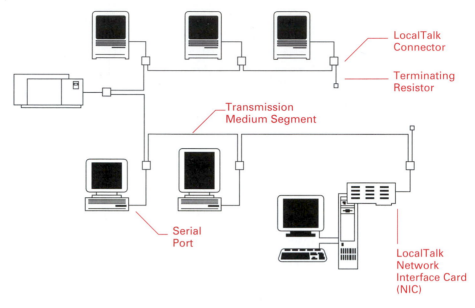

Figure 23.1   LocalTalk LAN data link daisy-chain configuration.

NETWORK TOPOLOGY AND TRANSMISSION MEDIUM

LocalTalk uses a bus- or tree-structured topology using twisted-pair cable as the most commonly used form of transmission medium. Optical fiber is also used with some LocalTalk implementations. The LocalTalk specification defines a data rate of 230.4 Kbps, but some LocalTalk implementations support a higher data rate. LocalTalk is designed to allow up to 32 devices to be attached to a single LocalTalk data link. Larger AppleTalk networks can be constructed using data link interconnection devices.

LocalTalk Connectors

The original form of transmission medium defined for use with LocalTalk data links uses an external connector that attaches to shielded twisted-pair cable segments to create a daisy-chain configuration. These external connectors are often called *LocalTalk connectors*. The maximum total cable length defined by the LocalTalk specification is 300 meters, but each LocalTalk implementation defines its own cable-length limitations.

PhoneNet Connectors

Different external connectors are available from a variety of vendors that use ordinary telephone wiring as a transmission medium. These connectors are sometimes called *PhoneNet* or *PhoneTalk* connectors. Cable length limitations when using external connectors that support unshielded telephone wiring are defined by the vendor supplying the external connectors.

LOCALTALK DATA LINK ADDRESSING

On a LocalTalk LAN data link, each system is identified by a unique 8-bit Data Link address, called a *node ID*. Node IDs are not assigned externally or hard-coded in network devices. Instead, the LocalTalk specification defines a mechanism used to dynamically assign a unique node ID to each system when it is physically attached to a LocalTalk LAN data link.

Node ID Assignment

When a system is activated, a LocalTalk process running in that system makes a "guess" at the system's node ID value by extracting a value from some form of long-term memory, such as nonvolatile RAM or disk, or by generating a random number. It then checks to see if the guessed node ID value is already in use by some other device on the network. LLAP does this by placing its guessed node ID value in an Enquiry control frame it broadcasts to all systems on the data link. If another system is using the guessed node ID value, that system sends back an acknowledgment indicating the guessed node ID value is already in use. The new system then generates a new node ID value and repeats the verification process. If the system receives no acknowledgment to its Enquiry frame, it assumes that its guessed node ID value is unique and accepts that value as the system's permanent node ID value.

LLAP supports connectionless data transfer and does not provide a reliable data transfer service. Therefore, there is no guarantee that all systems will receive an Enquiry frame a station sends. A system broadcasts a series of Enquiry control frames to increase the chances that all systems on the data link will receive it. Mechanisms are provided to recover from situations in which a system inadvertently assigns a nonunique node ID value because of a delay in receiving an acknowledgment to an Enquiry frame.

AppleTalk systems are divided into two classes: *server systems* and *client systems*. Client systems are sometimes referred to as *workstations* in AppleTalk documentation. Each class of system uses a different range of node ID values. Server systems use node ID values that range from 128 to 254; client systems use node ID values that range from 1 to 127. A server system implements more extensive checking in assigning its own node ID value than do client systems. This is because network operation can be disrupted if a system inadvertently acquires a node ID value the same as that of some active server in the network.

LLAP MEDIUM ACCESS CONTROL

The medium access control method used on an LLAP data link is designed for the purpose of transmitting frames across a single AppleTalk LAN data link. Delivery of frames uses a connectionless form of data transfer, and frames are transmitted on a best-efforts basis, with no acknowledgments or retransmissions of corrupted frames.

CSMA/CA

An LLAP data link uses a *Carrier Sense Multiple Access with Collision Avoidance (CSMA/CA)* technique for controlling access to the transmission medium, which we introduced in Chapter 17. With the LocalTalk variation of CSMA/CA medium access control, a transmitting system uses the Physical layer to sense the link and see if it is busy. If the link is busy, the system *defers* (waits until the link becomes idle). Once the transmitting system determines the link is idle, it waits for a period of time called the minimum *interdialog gap (IDG),* which is typically 400 microseconds. If the link continues to be idle for this period, the system waits a further randomly generated length of time. If the link is still idle after the second wait, the system sends its frame.

The use of a random wait period reduces the chances of a collision occurring by making it relatively unlikely that two systems will attempt to transmit at the same time. LLAP does not perform functions to directly detect collisions. A system assumes that a collision has occurred if it does not receive an expected response within 200 microseconds, a period of time called the maximum *interframe gap (IFG).*

When a transmitting system does not receive an expected response, it retransmits the previous frame sent using the same waiting process. The method used to determine the random wait time is based on recent transmission history, using the number of deferrals and number of presumed collisions that have occurred while attempting to send the current frame. As the number of deferrals and collisions increases, the range from which the random number is chosen increases. Thus, when transmission loads are heavy, and there is high contention for the transmission medium, the random wait time is selected from a relatively large range. This has the affect of spreading out over time the attempted transmissions of all the systems contending for access to the transmission medium. If the number of deferrals and collisions is small, the range is also small, so little time is spent waiting.

Transmission Dialogs

LocalTalk defines two types of frame transmission dialogs used on a LocalTalk LAN:

- **Directed Transmission Dialogs.** A *directed transmission dialog* is used when a frame is being sent to a single destination system. The source system waits until the carrier has been idle for both the minimum IDG time and the random wait time. It then sends a Request-to-Send control frame to the intended destination. The destination system returns a Clear-to-Send control frame to the source system if it is able to receive the transmission. If the source system receives a Clear-to-Send frame within the expected response time, it then transmits the Data frame. If the source system does not receive the Clear-to-Send frame within the expected time, the source system assumes that a collision has occurred and repeats the process.

- **Broadcast Transmission Dialogs.** A *broadcast transmission dialog* is used when a source system is sending a frame to all active systems on the network using the broadcast destination address. With a broadcast transmission dialog, the source system waits the minimum IDG time plus a random wait time and then sends out a Request-to-Send control frame with a destination address value of 255. It then waits the maximum IFG time. If the source station receives no transmission during that time, it transmits the Data frame. If the source station detects a transmission during the maximum IFG time, the source system repeats the process.

With either of these forms of transmission dialog, if the source system is unable to transmit the data frame after 32 attempts, the Data Link layer reports a failure condition to the user of the LLAP service.

LLAP FRAME FORMAT

LLAP frames are used to carry user data and are also generated by LLAP itself to control frame transmission. Box 23.1 shows the format of the LLAP frame and describes its fields.

The AppleTalk specifications make a distinction between the *LLAP packet* and the *LLAP frame*. The LLAP packet consists of the station address, Type, and Data fields. The LLAP frame consists of the LLAP packet encapsulated by the Preamble field and a *trailer* that consists of the Frame Check Sequence, Ending Flag, and Abort Sequence fields.*

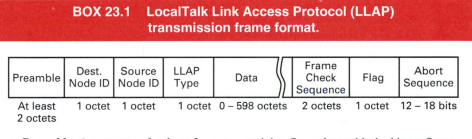

BOX 23.1   LocalTalk Link Access Protocol (LLAP) transmission frame format.

Preamble	Dest. Node ID	Source Node ID	LLAP Type	Data	Frame Check Sequence	Flag	Abort Sequence
At least 2 octets	1 octet	1 octet	1 octet	0 – 598 octets	2 octets	1 octet	12 – 18 bits

- **Preamble.** A sequence of at least 2 octets containing flag values with the bit configuration 01111110.

- **Station Addresses.** A Destination Node ID value and a Source Node ID value that identify the destination and source stations.

- **LLAP Type.** Identifies the frame's type.

- **Data.** Contains 0–600 octets of user data or control information.

- **Frame Check Sequence.** A cyclical redundancy check (CRC) value used for error detection. A CRC value is calculated by the source system based on the contents of the LLAP frame. In the destination system, the CRC value is calculated based on the contents of the received frame. If the calculated value does not match the received value, the frame is discarded as being in error.

- **Flag.** A single flag octet containing the bit configuration 01111110.

- **Abort Sequence.** A sequence of 12–18 1 bits.

---

* This is an unfortunate choice of terminology, since most authorities use the term *packet* to refer to the data unit exchanged by the layer above the Data Link layer, which is carried in the LLAP frame's Data field.

PHYSICAL LAYER SPECIFICATIONS

The LocalTalk Physical layer specification describes the functions of bit encoding/decoding, signal transmission/reception, and carrier sensing. The encoding method specified is called *FM-0*. With FM-0, there is always a transition at the beginning of each bit time. For a zero bit, there is also a transition in the middle of the bit time; for a one bit, there is no transition in the middle. Signal transmission is differential, balanced-voltage and is based on the EIA-422 signaling standard. The Physical layer carrier sensing function provides an indication to the Data Link layer of whether or not a transmission is in progress on the transmission medium.

ETHERTALK AND TOKENTALK LINK ACCESS PROTOCOLS

In addition to LocalTalk, the data link protocol defined in the AppleTalk specification, the AppleTalk protocol family supports the use of the IEEE/ISO CSMA/CD (Ethernet) and Token Ring protocols in the Data Link and Physical layers.

Ethernet support is provided through the *EtherTalk Link Access Protocol (ELAP),* and Token Ring support is provided through the *TokenTalk Link Access Protocol (TLAP).* In both cases, standard IEEE/ISO Logical Link Control (LLC) interfaces and data formats are used. Only the connectionless type 1 LLC service is used.

ELAP and TLAP Frame Formats

Figure 23.2 shows the frame formats used with EtherTalk and TokenTalk. They are the same as those defined in the IEEE/ISO Logical Link Control, CSMA/CD, and Token Ring standards. AppleTalk specifies the use of the IEEE/ISO Subnetwork Access Protocol (SNAP). Therefore, the DSAP and SSAP fields in the LLC header always carry the hexadecimal value 'AA'. A SNAP Identifier value of hex '080007809B' identifies the higher-level protocol as the AppleTalk Datagram Delivery Protocol (DDP), the AppleTalk Network layer protocol.

AppleTalk Address Resolution Protocol (AARP)

As we have seen, each system on an AppleTalk data link is identified by a unique 8-bit node ID value. In order to send data using CSMA/CD or Token Ring frames, however, the destination address and source address values contained in the CSMA/CD or Token Ring frame must contain station address values as defined by the IEEE/ISO standards. CSMA/CD and Token Ring NICs employed on AppleTalk networks use 48-bit universal addressing and have globally unique station addresses assigned to them. Therefore, a translation function is required to convert between 48-bit station addresses and the 8-bit node ID values used on a LocalTalk data link. This translation function is performed by the *AppleTalk Address Resolution Protocol (AARP).*

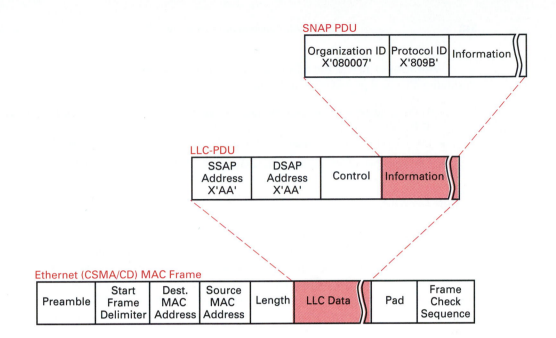

EtherTalk Frame Format

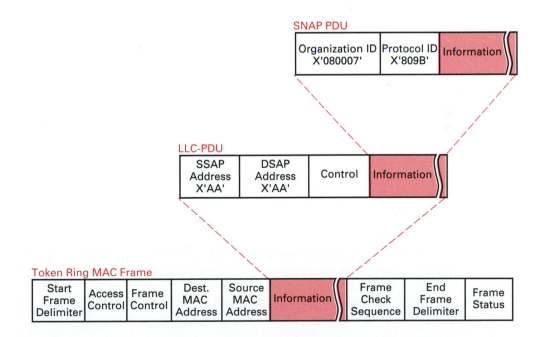

TokenTalk Frame Format

Figure 23.2 EtherTalk and TokenTalk frame formats.

With respect to the EtherTalk and TokenTalk protocols, the AppleTalk Address Resolution Protocol provides the following services:

- Translating between AppleTalk node ID values and CSMA/CD or Token Ring station addresses.
- Dynamically assigning a unique node ID value to a system when it is activated.
- Checking that a frame received has a destination node ID value addressed to the receiving system.

Broadcast Addresses

When an EtherTalk or TokenTalk system needs to send a frame to all systems on the network using the AppleTalk broadcast address, it translates the AppleTalk broadcast address into an appropriate group destination address. The broadcast group address is not used by EtherTalk or TokenTalk. Instead, an AppleTalk-defined group address is used that refers only to the AppleTalk stations on the LAN. When an AppleTalk system is activated, it must register itself as part of the AppleTalk broadcast group. This allows the AppleTalk protocols to operate correctly when the EtherTalk or TokenTalk protocols are used on a LAN on which traffic conforming to other protocols also exists.

SUMMARY

The LAN data link protocol defined by Apple's AppleTalk protocol family is the LocalTalk Link Access Protocol (LLAP). LocalTalk implements a multiaccess form of data link in which stations are attached, using LocalTalk connectors, in a bus- or tree-structured configuration using twisted-pair cable. A data rate of 230.4 Kbps is supported. A LocalTalk station dynamically chooses an 8-bit node ID value for use as a station address when the station is powered on and attached to the data link.

A LocalTalk LAN data link uses a carrier sense multiple access with collision avoidance (CSMA/CA) form of medium access control. With CSMA/CA, a station that has a frame to transmit listens to the carrier and transmits when it determines the medium is available. Stations use a deference process to reduce the likelihood of two stations transmitting at the same time. Stations retransmit frames when they determine that frames have been damaged by collisions. Collisions are assumed when expected responses to transmitted frames are not received.

The AppleTalk protocol family also supports the use of Ethernet LAN data links through the EtherTalk Link Access Protocol (ELAP) and the use of Token Ring LAN data links through the TokenTalk Link Access Protocol (TLAP).

Chapter 24 discusses technology that allows LAN equipment to communicate over relatively short distances using wireless transmission.

Wireless LAN Subnetworks

The local area network technologies described in the previous chapters all rely on a physical wire or cable to interconnect the various devices on the LAN. LAN vendors also employ various data transmission technologies that allow computers to be interconnected in a LAN using wireless transmission media.

At the time of writing, there are no widely accepted standards for wireless LAN interconnection, and each vendor has typically implemented a unique form of wireless signal transmission. This means that one vendor's wireless LAN equipment cannot easily be combined with another vendor's equipment in the same LAN without using specially designed bridges or routers.

The IEEE is currently working on standards for wireless LANs in its IEEE 802.11 committee. The IEEE 802.11 committee is developing standards for two wireless LAN technologies: transmission using infrared signals and transmission using radio signals.

INFRARED SIGNALING

Infrared signals are propagated on a line-of-sight basis and cannot penetrate walls, floors, or partitions. Two forms of infrared signaling can be used to implement a wireless LAN: direct infrared and diffuse infrared.

Direct Infrared

With *direct infrared* signaling, infrared signals are concentrated in a narrow beam. The receiver and transmitter must be pointed directly at one another for transmission to take place.

Diffuse Infrared

With *diffuse infrared* signaling, sending devices transmit infrared signals that flood the entire room and bounce off walls and ceilings. Receivers anywhere in the room can then receive the signal. Transceivers can be positioned anywhere within the room as long as they can transmit and receive signals without obstruction.

RADIO SIGNALING

Radio signaling can also be used to implement wireless LANs. Most radio-based LAN products use one of two forms of radio transmission: *narrowband* transmission and *spread-spectrum* transmission.

Narrowband Transmission

With *narrowband transmission*, a relatively small bandwidth is used with signals occupying a specific portion of the spectrum licensed specifically for this type of purpose by the FCC. Since the portion of the spectrum used is reserved for the particular licensed use, it is somewhat protected from interference by other sources of radio signals.

Spread Spectrum

With *spread-spectrum transmission*, a wider bandwidth is used with signals occupying an unlicensed portion of the spectrum. With spread-spectrum transmission, there is more likelihood of interference from other sources, such as paging facilities, security systems, and other radio networks.

The following two methods can be used to overcome the interference inherent in spread-spectrum transmission:

- **Direct Sequencing.** With *direct sequencing,* the bandwidth is divided into a small number of wide channels. A signal sent across a channel is encoded in such a way as to be easily distinguished from background noise.
- **Frequency Hopping.** With *frequency hopping,* the bandwidth is divided into a large number of small channels. A transmission switches from using one channel to another in a pre-determined pseudo-random pattern. If interference is encountered on one channel, data can be retransmitted over a different channel. By using different patterns, multiple users can transmit at the same time without interfering with one another.

WIRELESS LAN ARCHITECTURAL APPROACHES

There are two major architectural approaches that vendors have taken with respect to wireless LAN data transmission: the *peer-to-peer* approach and the *hub* approach. These two approaches can be applied to LANs that use either radio or infrared signals for data transmission. The two architectural approaches are illustrated in Fig. 24.1 and are briefly described below:

- **Peer-to-Peer Approach.** With *peer-to-peer* wireless LANS, each station sends signals directly to and receives signals directly from every other station on the LAN.
- **Hub Approach.** With a wireless LAN that uses a *hub* configuration, all stations send signals to a central hub. The hub then retransmits the signals to all the stations on the LAN.

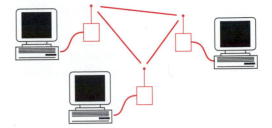

Peer-to-Peer Wireless LAN

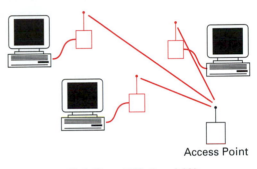

Access Point

Figure 24.1   Wireless LAN architecture.   Hub-Based Wireless LAN

With this approach a station receives signals only from the hub and not directly from individual stations. The central hub, sometimes called an *access point,* acts as a repeater, thus possibly extending the range of the LAN beyond what might be possible using a peer-to-peer approach.

WIRELESS LAN MEDIUM ACCESS CONTROL

As with other forms of LAN technology, wireless LANs typically use the IEEE 802.2 Logical Link Control standard to specify the services that the LAN provides to users. And, also like other LAN technologies, a wireless LAN must be based on a medium access control specification that defines the type of transmission medium used and the method used to control how individual stations access the transmission medium. The following sections describe the two models for medium access control under consideration by the IEEE 802.11 committee.

Centralized Control

With the centralized control model for medium access control, if a station has data to transmit, it sends a Request-to-Send command to a device performing the role of the *central controller*. The central controller then sends back a Permission-to-Send response, and the station then transmits its data. If multiple stations send Request-to-Send commands at approximately the same time, the central controller sends Permission-to-Send responses to each station in turn.

The centralized control model can be applied to both hub-based LANs and peer-to-peer LANs. With a hub-based LAN, the hub or access point plays the role of the central controller. With a peer-to-peer LAN, one of the stations must be designated as the central controller.

Collision Avoidance

With the collision avoidance approach to medium access control, when a source station has data to send, it sends a Ready-to-Send command to the destination station. The Ready-to-Send command indicates the amount of data the source station has to transmit.

After the destination station receives the Ready-to-Send command, it sends a Clear-to-Send response to the source station. The Clear-to-Send response indicates the amount of data the destination station is ready to receive. The source station then sends that amount of data. After the destination station has received all expected data, it transmits an acknowledgment to the source station.

With the collision avoidance approach, all stations on the LAN receive all the commands and responses transmitted. Stations not involved in a particular exchange between a source and a destination station must refrain from accessing the transmission medium from the time they receive the Clear-to-Send response until they receive the Acknowledgment.

Each station implements a timer used to detect that data may have been lost because of a signal collision. If a station does not receive an expected response within some predefined period of time, the station waits a random amount of time and attempts retransmission.

INTERCONNECTING WIRELESS LANS WITH WIRED NETWORKS

We discuss data link subnetwork interconnection in depth in Chapter 10. However, some words are appropriate here to point out some of the special characteristics of network interconnection when wireless LAN equipment is involved.

Most wireless LAN products use a standard Ethernet frame format. This makes it relatively easy to design equipment, such as NICs, bridges, and routers, to interconnect wireless LAN equipment with wired networks. Network interconnection equipment must be designed specifically for connecting a particular vendor's wireless LAN equipment with a particular standard form of wired LAN technology.

In a hub-based wireless LAN, one of the access points typically serves as a point of interconnection between the wireless LAN and a wired network. Some types of access points act as bridges, and others act as routers.

Mobile Devices

Some wireless LANs also support the use of mobile computing devices. A mobile system can be moved around within an area defined by the maximum range of the wireless LAN. It may also be possible to move a system from one wireless LAN to another. In order to do this it may be necessary to make changes to directory services and routing information as a system moves from one LAN to another.

Wireless Ethernet LANs

Most wireless LANs do not use the same form of collision detection used with Ethernet LANs because stations may not be able to receive at the same time they are transmitting and thus may not be able to directly detect collisions. However, at least one vendor has designed an Ethernet-compatible line of wireless LAN equipment that directly implements the Ethernet CSMA/CD medium access control method using radio transmission. This equipment supports a 10-Mbps data rate and is more compatible with conventional Ethernet LAN equipment than many other wireless LAN products.

SUMMARY

The IEEE is working on standards for wireless LANs using two technologies: transmission using infrared signals, which can use either direct infrared or diffuse infrared signaling, and transmission using radio signals, which can employ either narrowband transmission or spread-spectrum transmission.

Vendors have taken two major architectural approaches with respect to wireless LAN data transmission. With the peer-to-peer approach, each station sends signals directly to and receives signals directly from every other station on the LAN. With the hub approach, all stations send signals to a central hub, and the hub retransmits the signals to other stations. The central hub acts as a repeater, thus possibly extending the range of the LAN.

Most wireless LAN products use a standard Ethernet frame format, which makes it relatively easy to design NICs, bridges, and routers to interconnect wireless LAN equipment with wired networks.

Chapter 25 describes metropolitan area network (MAN) technology, which uses transmission techniques similar to those used on LANs to bridge the gap between local area networks and wide area networks in some environments.

Metropolitan Area Network Subnetworks

A *metropolitan area network (MAN)* spans a range greater than that of a local area network but less than that spanned by many wide area network data links. A typical metropolitan area network might support a range large enough to encompass the metropolitan area of a large city. MAN technology has much in common with LAN technology, so we conclude our discussion of LAN technology with a discussion of an international standard for metropolitan area networks.

THE IEEE 802.6 MAN STANDARD

In addition to defining standards for local area networks, IEEE Project 802 has defined the IEEE 802.6 standard for metropolitan area networks. This standard defines technology intended to be used for a network spanning a range of up to several hundred kilometers. Networks using this technology can be interconnected with bridges or routers to provide service over even larger geographic areas.

The technology the IEEE 802.6 standard defines is based on a medium access control technology called *Distributed Queue Dual Bus (DQDB)*. Like the IEEE Project 802 LAN standards covered in the previous chapters, the IEEE 802.6 DQDB standard is based on the use of a shared transmission medium and defines standards for the Medium Access Control (MAC) sublayer and the Physical layer of the IEEE/ISO/ANSI LAN architecture. The IEEE 802.6 standard allows the use of the IEEE 802.2 type 1 connectionless service in the Logical Link Control sublayer in the same manner as the MAC sublayer standards for LANs. As we will discuss later in this chapter, the technology defined by the DQDB standard can also be used to implement WAN data links that can span very long distances.

The IEEE 802.6 DQDB standard supports the use of the same 48-bit or 16-bit MAC sublayer station addresses used on LANs. The standard also includes an alternative 60-bit station address specification.

TRANSMISSION MEDIUM AND DATA RATES

The DQDB standard assumes that stations are interconnected using a fiber-optic transmission medium and support data rates in the range of 1.544 Mbps to 155 Mbps. The initial DQDB Physical layer specification is for DS3 transmission, which specifies a data rate of 45 Mbps. Other transmission systems referenced in the IEEE 802.6 standard support data rates of 35, 140, and 155 Mbps.

DISTRIBUTED QUEUE DUAL BUS ARCHITECTURE

On a DQDB network, stations are interconnected, using fiber-optic cable, to form two buses, each of which carries data in the opposite direction. Data is carried from station to station on each of the buses in the form of 53-octet cells called *slots*. The data units carried in DQDB slots are similar to the cells used in Asynchronous Transfer Mode (ATM) transmission. (See Chapter 15 for a discussion of ATM.)

Some stations on the network must generate empty slots that flow from station to station through the network. Each station then places data into empty slots passing by. Another station on the network removes slots from the network. The protocol governing how slots are used to carry data is discussed later in this chapter.

Each station on the network has access to both buses and is able to send and receive data using the slots flowing on both of them. On a given bus, a station transmits only to stations downstream of it on that bus. By using both buses, a station can send data to and receive data from any other station on the network. The DQDB standard supports the use of two different network topologies: an open bus topology and a looped bus topology.

Open Bus Topology

Figure 25.1 illustrates a network that implements the *open bus* topology. With the open bus topology, the slots on bus A are generated by node 1 and removed by node 5. Slots

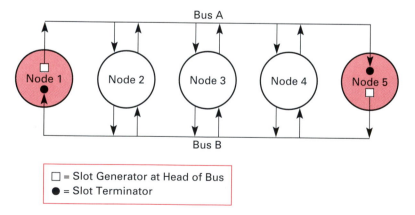

Figure 25.1   Distributed Queue Dual Bus (DQDB) open bus topology.

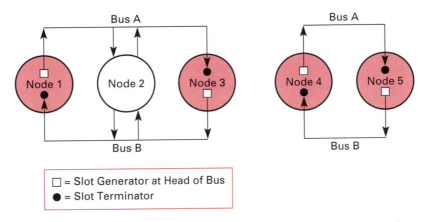

Figure 25.2　Reconfiguring an open bus DQDB network after a break in the transmission medium.

for bus B are generated by node 5 and removed by node 1. If node 3 has data to transmit to Node 5, it places the data into empty slots flowing on bus A; if it has data for node 2, it uses slots flowing on bus B.

Figure 25.2 shows how the network from Fig. 25.1 would be reconfigured if a break in the LAN cabling occurred between node 3 and node 4. Reconfiguration after a break in an open bus network results in two separate networks.

Looped Bus Topology

Figure 25.3 shows a DQDB network conforming to the *looped bus* topology. In this type of network, slots for both buses are generated and removed by the same node. Figure 25.4 shows how the network in Fig. 25.3 is reconfigured if a break in the transmission medium occurs. With the looped bus topology, a single network results from the reconfiguration process, and all the stations are still able to communicate with one another after the break.

DQDB SERVICE DEFINITION

Three types of service have been specified in the service definition for the DQDB standard:

- **Connectionless data service.** Provides support for LLC type 1 connectionless data communication.
- **Connection-oriented data service.** Provides support for a form of permanent virtual circuit. A connection is established between the source and the destination, but there is no guaranteed arrival rate.
- **Isochronous service.** Provides transmission with a guaranteed regular arrival rate. The isochronous service is suitable for sound and video transmission.

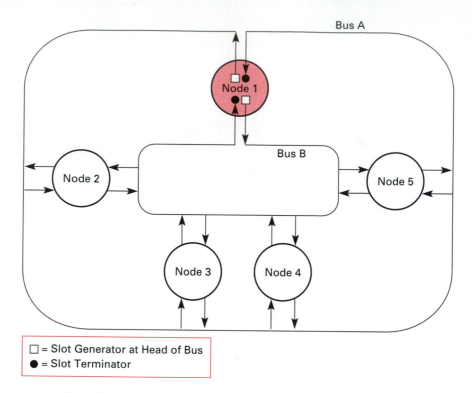

Figure 25.3   Distributed Queue Dual Bus (DQDB) looped bus topology.

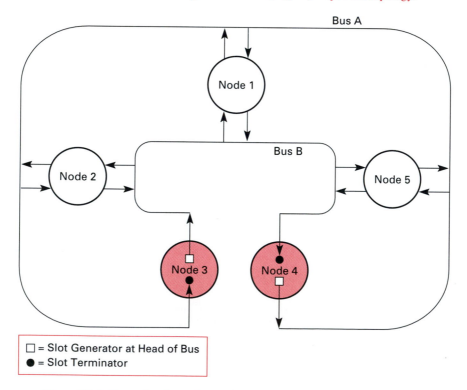

Figure 25.4   Reconfiguring a looped bus DQDB network after a break in the transmission medium.

At the time of writing, only the connectionless data service and the isochronous service have been fully defined. The connection-oriented data service is still under development.

DQDB SLOT FORMATS

As we discussed earlier, DQDB uses a series of 53-octet slots that flow over the transmission medium from one station to another. Box 25.1 describes the basic slot format used with DQDB.

DQDB MAC PROTOCOL SPECIFICATION

During the operation of the DQDB MAC protocol, a station with data to transmit places it into empty slots flowing over one of the buses interconnecting the stations. The DQDB standard defines two types of slots: *prearbitrated (PA)* slots and *queued-arbitrated (QA)* slots. The standard defines two separate access control methods for the two types of slots: PA access control and QA access control.

PA Access Control

PA access control is used to carry isochronous data in PA slots. The head-of-bus function generates PA slots at appropriate intervals to provide channels of defined bandwidth. PA slots carry a virtual channel identifier (VCI) that identifies a particular channel. An isochronous connection transmits by placing its data in the PA slots associated with a particular virtual channel. If an isochronous connection does not require the entire capacity of the virtual channel, the virtual channel might be shared by multiple isochronous connections. Each connection uses a specified portion of all the slots allocated to a channel.

QA Access Control

QA access control is used to implement the connectionless data service using QA slots. Access to QA slots operates using a distributed reservation system. When a node has data to transmit, it sends out a reservation request on each bus. Data is always transmitted downstream, but reservation requests are sent upstream.

A station sends a reservation request by setting bits in the first octet of an empty slot that passes by. Each node keeps track of reservation requests it has received from nodes downstream of that node. The reservation requests tell a sending station when it is that station's turn to transmit. Box 25.2 illustrates the basic operation of the reservation system.

Each node keeps a reservation request counter for each bus. A node uses this counter to keep track of reservation requests that flow by while it is waiting to transmit. The use of priority levels in the DQDB reservation system is under definition. To implement different priority levels, reservation request counts would have to be kept separately for each priority level.

BOX 25.1   DQDB slot format.

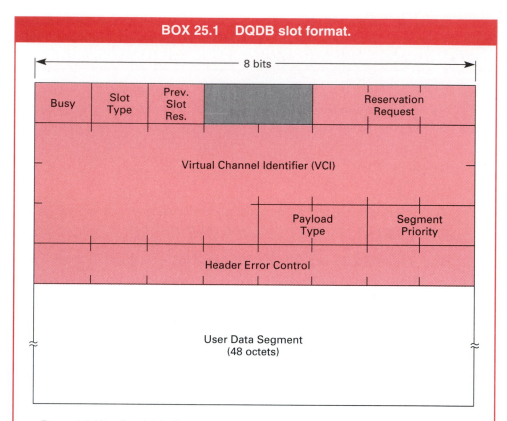

- **Busy.** A 1-bit value that indicates whether the slot contains data or is free.

- **Slot Type.** Indicates whether this is a QA or PA slot.

- **Previous Slot Reserved.** Indicates whether the previous slot can be cleared. The use of this field is under study.

- **Reservation Request.** A 3-bit value used to indicate a reservation request. The three bits allow for three priority levels.

- **Virtual Channel Identifier (VCI).** Identifies the logical connection, or virtual channel, for which this slot is being used. For QA slots, this field contains a value of all ones.

- **Payload Type.** Identifies the type of data being transmitted. The use of this field is under study.

- **Segment Priority.** Reserved for future use with multiport bridges.

- **Header Error Control.** Contains a value used for error checking and correction of the slot header.

- **User Data Segment.** Contains user data.

BOX 25.2   Distributed Queue Dual Bus (DQDB) distributed reservation system.

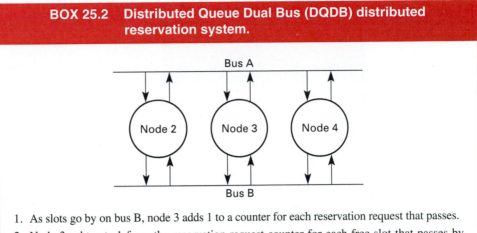

1. As slots go by on bus B, node 3 adds 1 to a counter for each reservation request that passes.

2. Node 3 subtracts 1 from the reservation request counter for each free slot that passes by on bus A. A free slot is a slot that has not had its busy bit set.

3. When node 3 has data to transmit on node 4, it sets the reservation bits in the first slot that arrives on bus B that does not have its reservation bits already set. Node 3 checks the current reservation request count from bus B. When that number of free slots have passed by on bus A, node 3 uses the next free slot on bus A to transmit its data.

TRANSFER OF LLC-PDUS

DQDB provides the service of transmitting LLC-PDUs contained within MAC frames. These frames, in turn, are carried in the slots the MAC sublayer transmits from one station to another.

A MAC sublayer entity accepts an LLC-PDU from the LLC sublayer and forms an initial MAC frame by adding a MAC header, any required padding, a CRC value, and a MAC trailer to the LLC-PDU. The MAC frame is then broken into a series of 44-octet segments for transmission. A 2-octet header and a 2-octet trailer are added to each segment to form a 48-octet User Data Segment. Each User Data Segment is carried within the 48-octet Information field of a QA slot. This process is illustrated in Fig. 25.5.

After the destination station has received all the slots containing a particular MAC frame, it reassembles the MAC frame and performs a CRC check on the entire frame. If the CRC check indicates the data has not been corrupted, the destination station extracts the LLC-PDU from the MAC frame and passes it up to the LLC sublayer. Box 25.3 describes the data formats used in this process.

Identification of the destination station is based on the destination address value contained in the MAC header. Since QA slots are used, the VCI field will always contain all 1s and is not usable as a way of identifying the destination associated with a particular virtual circuit. Because of this, data contained in DQDB QA slots cannot be switched at the slot, or cell, level. In order for MAC frames to be sent from one DQDB network to another, the entire frame must be reassembled and processed as a unit using a bridge, router, or frame-level switch.

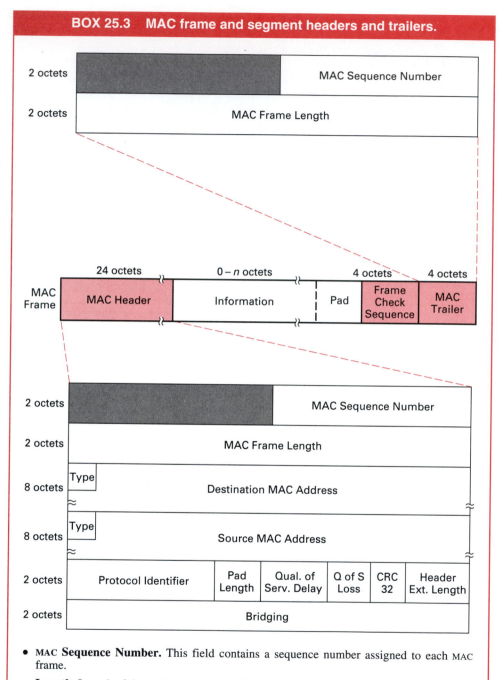

BOX 25.3 MAC frame and segment headers and trailers.

- MAC **Sequence Number.** This field contains a sequence number assigned to each MAC frame.
- **Length.** Length of the entire MAC frame. This is used for buffer allocation.

BOX 25.3 *(Continued)*

- **Destination Address.** Contains a 16-, 48- or 60-bit destination address. The Type subfield indicates the format of the address.

- **Source Address.** Contain a 16-, 48- or 60-bit source address. The Type subfield indicates the format of the address.

- **Protocol Identifier.** Indicates the user of the MAC service, which can be LLC or a locally defined protocol.

- **PAD Length.** Indicates the number of octets of padding added to the Information field to make it a multiple of 4 octets.

- **Quality of Service Delay.** Indicates the requested quality of service relative to delay.

- **Quality of Service Loss.** Currently reserved. May be used for congestion control at bridges.

- **CRC 32 Indicator.** Indicates whether a 32-bit CRC value is included in the MAC frame.

- **Header Extension Length.** Indicates whether a header extension is used to carry additional control information, and if so, its length.

- **Bridging.** Reserved for future use with MAC-level bridging.

Segment Header and Trailer Formats

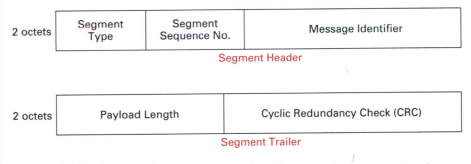

- **Segment Type.** A 2-bit field indicating whether this segment is the beginning of a MAC frame, the middle, the end, or an entire MAC frame.

- **Segment Sequence Number.** A 4-bit field used for a MAC frame contained in multiple segments. This field contains the MAC sequence number. The number is incremented by 1 for each succeeding segment, thus indicating the sequence of the segments. It is used to ensure all segments of a MAC frame are received.

- **Message Identifier.** A 10-bit field containing a value that uniquely identifies a particular MAC frame.

- **Payload Length.** A 6-bit field indicating the number of octets of data from the MAC frame included in the segment.

- **CRC.** A 10-bit cyclic redundancy check value used to check this segment, including the segment header and trailer.

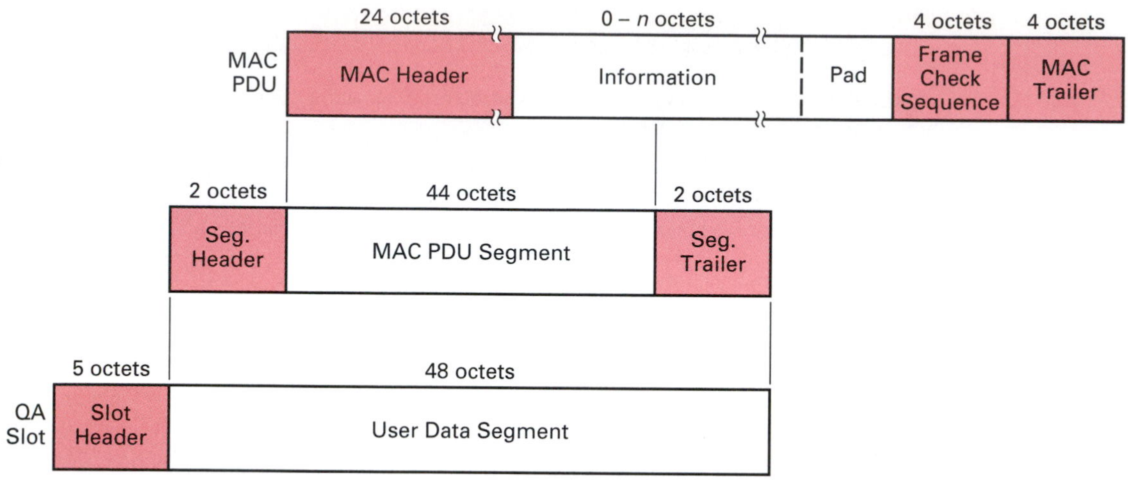

Figure 25.5   Transmitting an LLC-PDU as a series of segments.

SWITCHED MULTI-MEGABIT DATA SERVICE

As we introduced earlier, the DQDB technology is intended for the relatively short-distance communication required to support data transmission within the metropolitan area of a large city. However, the DQDB transmission technology is now also being used in a telecommunications service offering, called *Switched Multi-Megabit Data Service (SMDS)*. A number of common carriers provide SMDS facilities that can be used to implement high-speed WAN data links of any desired length. An SMDS data link is designed to carry data over long distances at speeds comparable to the speed of LANs.

SMDS Access Classes

SMDS defines a connectionless data transfer service that can be used to carry data at different data rates. Each SMDS user is assigned an *access class* that determines the maximum rate of data transmission that can be used over an extended interval. Box 25.4 lists access classes commonly implemented in SMDS networks.

SMDS Addressing

Each physical interface to an SMDS network is assigned one or more ten-digit addresses. The subscriber to the SMDS service can then assign different addresses, as desired, to the different systems or other devices using the SMDS service for data transmission.

Group addressing is available with SMDS that allows a device to send data to up to 128 different destinations in a single transmission. SMDS group addressing provides a function similar to multicasting on a LAN.

BOX 25.4　SMDS access classes.	
Access Class	**Sustained Data Rate**
1	4 Mbps
2	10 Mbps
3	16 Mbps
4	25 Mbps
5	34 Mbps

SUMMARY

A metropolitan area network (MAN) is intended to span a range greater than that of a LAN but less than that of a WAN, such as a range large enough to encompass the metropolitan area of a large city. IEEE Project 802 has defined the IEEE 802.6 MAN standard, which is based on Distributed Queue Dual Bus (DQDB) technology. The DQDB standard assumes that transmission takes place over a fiber-optic transmission medium to support data rates in the range of from 1.544 Mbps to 155 Mbps.

The DQDB transmission medium forms two buses, each of which carries data in the opposite direction. Data is carried in the form of 53-octet cells called slots. There are two types of slots: prearbitrated (PA) slots and queued-arbitrated (QA) slots, and a separate access control method is defined for each type of slot.

The three types of service specified in the DQDB service definition are connectionless data service that provides support for LLC type 1 connectionless transmission, connection-oriented data service that provides support for a form of permanent virtual circuit, and isochronous service that provides transmission with a guaranteed regular arrival rate.

Although the DQDB technology was originally intended for relatively short-distance communication, DQDB transmission technology is also used to provide Switched Multimegabit Data Service (SMDS) WAN data links. An SMDS data link is designed to carry data over long distances at speeds comparable to the speed of LANs.

PART **V**

Appendices

Appendix  A

Standards Organizations

A number of organizations around the world are actively involved in developing standards and architectures for data communications and computer networking. Four important standards organizations for the computer networking industries are ISO, IEEE, ANSI, and ITU-T, all of which we discuss in this appendix. Other important standards organizations and standards terminology are also briefly described.

INTERNATIONAL ORGANIZATION FOR STANDARDIZATION (ISO)

A prominent standards organization is the *International Organization for Standardization (ISO)*, the largest standards organization in the world. ISO produces large numbers of standards on nearly every subject, from humane animal traps to screw threads. It is also the dominant information technology standardization organization in the world. The members of ISO are individual national standards organizations; only national positions—positions representing an entire country—are discussed in ISO. The ISO member organization from the United States is the American National Standards Institute (ANSI); every major industrialized country has a similar standards organization that represents its national interests in ISO. ISO technical meetings take place at various locations around the world.

ISO Organizational Structure

The Secretariat of ISO, located in Geneva, Switzerland, is the organization charged with running the day-to-day affairs of ISO, including keeping track of its numerous technical committees (TCs) and publishing the standards the technical committees produce. The technical committees—which not only create the standards but also determine what standards to produce—are composed of thousands of volunteers from computer manufacturers, suppliers of communication products, major computer users, governments, and consulting organizations.

To participate, these delegates operate under the aegis of the national body. For example, a delegate from the United States not only brings technical expertise to the committee but also represents his or her sponsoring organization (ANSI, described later) and the United States itself. A TC is ordinarily divided into subcommittees (SCs) and working groups (WGs), which write the standards. The standards then receive the approval of the technical committee as a whole before they finally become accepted as international standards.

International Electrotechnical Commission

Closely associated with ISO is the *International Electrotechnical Commission (IEC)*. IEC has a role similar to that of ISO but is restricted to electrical and electronic matters. There is an agreement between ISO and IEC to ensure that their work does not overlap. In the field of communications standards, IEC's role is limited to Physical layer aspects, such as electrical safety.

Joint Technical Committee 1

ISO and IEC have recently merged their Technical Committees working on information technology into a single organization, called ISO/IEC Joint Technical Committee 1 (JTC1), to ensure and improve continued close cooperation.

JTC1 is the ISO/IEC technical committee that oversees a particularly important framework for a computer network architecture called the *Reference Model for Open Systems Interconnection* or the *OSI model* for short. JTC1 is also publishing a comprehensive set of standards for the various functional layers defined by the OSI model. The OSI model is described in Chapter 2 and discussed further in Appendix B.

The ISO Standardization Process

There are four major steps in the standardization process. A standard begins its journey through the standardization process as a *working document*. After the working group or subcommittee agrees that the working document should be developed into an international standard, it becomes a *committee draft*, at which time ISO/IEC assigns a unique number to it. At this stage, the standard is referred to with the letters "CD," such as ISO CD 12345. (A committee draft was formerly called a *draft proposal* and was abbreviated DP.)

After the subcommittee or working group agrees that the standard is close to being accepted as an international standard, it is given *draft international standard* status and is referred to using its number and the letters DIS, such as ISO DIS 12345.

A standard may go through multiple revisions at both the committee draft and draft international standard phases. A standard that has made it all the way through the standardization process and has been accepted by ISO is called an *international standard* and is referred to only by its number, such as ISO 12345.

ISO also sometimes produces documents called *technical reports* when support cannot be obtained for the publication of a standard, when a subject is still under technical development, or when a technical committee has collected information of a different kind from that normally published as a standard. The identification number of a technical report is preceded by the letters TR, such as ISO TR 12345.

Amendments

ISO also produces amendments to international standards as changes are required. Like the international standards themselves, amendments go through four phases. An amendment to an international standard begins as a *working draft* and then progresses to a *committee draft amendment (CDAM),* goes on to become a *draft amendment (DAM),* and finally becomes an *amendment (AM)* when it is approved. Generally, amendments are eventually incorporated into the text of their associated standards after the amendment is accepted. Amendments were formerly called *Addenda (ADs),* draft amendments were called *Draft Addenda (DADs),* and committee draft amendments were *proposed draft addenda (PDADs).*

Sources for ISO Standards

ISO/IEC standards documents and technical reports can be obtained in the United States from ANSI, Inc., 1430 Broadway, New York, NY 10018. Global Engineering Documents, 2805 McGaw Avenue, Ervine, CA 92714, telephone (800) 854-7179 also stocks copies of ISO standards.

INTERNATIONAL TELECOMMUNICATION UNION-TELECOMMUNICATIONS (ITU-T)

The *International Telecommunication Union (ITU)* has existed since around the early 1900s and is the leading organization involved in the development of standards relating to telephone and other telecommunications services. The ITU is a body of the United Nations, and the delegation to the ITU from the United States is the Department of State. In other countries, the ITU delegation is often the governmentally controlled Postal, Telephone, and Telegraph (PTT) organization.

The Telecommunications sector of the ITU (ITU-T) publishes important standards relating to computer networking. ITU-T standards for the information technology standards were formerly known as CCITT standards for the *International Telegraph and Telephone Consultative Committee*, the old name for ITU-T.

ITU-T Areas of Standardization

The ITU-T deals with standards for interconnecting the world's telephone networks and for the signaling systems used by modems in sending computer data over telephone lines. The ITU-T calls the standards it produces *recommendations,* such as Recommendation X.25 and Recommendation X.400. It was a natural outgrowth of the data aspects of telephone service that ITU-T should become involved in information system standards, particularly those directly related to public data networks. In the last decade, ITU-T has also been involved in a major effort to define standards for a worldwide *Integrated Services Digital Network (ISDN)* for providing unified public voice and data communication services.

ITU-T Organizational Structure

The principal contributors to ITU are individuals representing the public and private telecommunications organizations, although nonvoting memberships are also open to industrial organizations. The ITU maintains a secretariat in Geneva, where most of the meetings take place. However, representation is international. As with ISO, all of the technical contribution comes from individual volunteers drawn primarily from telephone companies and other companies that supply telecommunications products and services. Again, membership is limited to national body representation—it is the State Department, not U.S. common carriers, that represents the U.S. national position.

ITU Publication Process

ITU recommendations are published at four-year intervals, with the color of the covers changed with each new edition. Although the recommendations are newly published every four years, each new version represents evolutionary change from the previous version; many of the recommendations change little from one version of the recommendations to another. Each set of ITU recommendations is published in the form of a series of volumes, each of which is divided into separately bound *fascicles*. Each fascicle can be ordered separately.

ISO/IEC/ITU-T Cooperation

ISO, IEC, and ITU-T cooperate quite closely. ISO and ITU-T, in particular, have a strong interest in aligning their standards and thus try not to duplicate work between them. (Unfortunately, duplication of effort still sometimes occurs.) Standards of mutual interest typically are developed in one organization and then published by both. For example, the OSI model was developed principally by a subcommittee of ISO and is documented in ISO 7498; ITU-T also publishes the OSI model as Recommendation X.200. Similarly, ITU-T has developed Recommendation X.400, which standardizes electronic mail facilities. Recommendation X.400 has been adopted by ISO, which publishes it as ISO 10021. The technical people participating in committees of ISO are very often the same people on ITU-T committees, and the technical development activities associated with information systems standardization are often undertaken jointly by ISO and ITU-T.

Sources for ITU-T Standards

ITU-T recommendations can be obtained from the United States Department of Commerce, National Technical Information Service, 5285 Port Royal Road, Springfield, VA 22161. They can also be obtained from Global Engineering Documents, whose address was given previously.

INSTITUTE OF ELECTRICAL AND ELECTRONICS ENGINEERS (IEEE)

The *Institute of Electrical and Electronics Engineers (IEEE)* is a professional society whose members are individual engineers rather than companies. The IEEE operates under ANSI guidelines when it develops standards and ordinarily concentrates on product standards.

The IEEE Computer Society Local Network Committee (Project 802) has focused on standards related to local area networks, and has produced a set of LAN standards. The IEEE LAN standards have been accepted by ISO as international standards and are published by ISO as well as by IEEE. ANSI standards for local area networks also conform to the IEEE Project 802 LAN architecture. The IEEE Project 802 standards are described in detail in Part III.

AMERICAN NATIONAL STANDARDS INSTITUTE (ANSI)

Virtually every country in the world has a national standards organization responsible for publishing standards to guide that nation's industries. In the United States, this organization is the *American National Standards Institute (ANSI)*. ANSI is a nonprofit organization that writes the rules for standards bodies to follow and publishes standards produced under its rules of consensus. ANSI accredits standards committees to write standards in areas of their expertise. The major accredited standards committees (ASCs) in the information technology arena are:

- **JTC1 TAG.** This is the U.S. *technical advisory group (TAG)* for the ISO/IEC JTC1. This group provides U.S. positions on JTC1 standards and is the single interface to ISO/IEC JTC1 in the United States.

- **ASC X3.** This committee produces approximately 90 percent of the standards for U.S. information technology and provides the technical expertise for a majority of U.S. technical advisory groups to the subcommittees and working groups in ISO/IEC JTC1. A subcommittee of ANSI X3 is responsible for standardizing the Fiber Distributed Data Interface (FDDI) LAN data link technology.

- **ASC T1.** This group is the voluntary standards-making body for the U.S. telecommunications industry and sets U.S. national telecommunications standards. T1 helps the State Department with ITU-T positions.

- **ASC X12.** This group is responsible for standards relating to electronic data interchange (EDI) in the United States. It acts to set national positions for the United Nations EDIFACT group, which is establishing EDI standards worldwide.

ANSI has a small secretariat located in New York City whose function is organizational and administrative rather than technical. ANSI is not a government organization; it is funded by its members and through the sale of standards.

National standards organizations from other countries include:

- **France.** Association Française de Normalisation (AFNOR).
- **United Kingdom.** British Standards Institute (BSI).
- **Canada.** Canadian Standards Association (CSA).

- **Germany.** Deutsches Institut für Normung e.V. (DIN).
- **Japan.** Japanese Industrial Standards Committee (JISC).

These standards organizations have the same general role and organization as ANSI and provide a discussion forum for individuals. Some of those individuals then participate in international meetings and represent the agreed views of their countries. It is the national bodies that vote in the formal approval process for standards.

OTHER STANDARDS ORGANIZATIONS

There are a number of other organizations that participate in information systems standardization. The following sections provide brief descriptions of some of the more prominent ones.

Open Systems Foundation (OSF)

OSF is a nonprofit organization established by a number of computer manufacturers to develop a common foundation for open computing. It is not directly concerned with standards but rather with the development of an agreed collection of software around a UNIX-like operating system kernel. OSF has its own permanent technical staff and depends on the participation of its members. Particularly important in the NAS environment is the Distributed Computing Environment (DCE) that OSF has defined.

European Computer Manufacturers Association (ECMA)

ECMA was originally formed by a group of European companies. Since then, its membership has grown to become international and includes representatives from such organizations as IBM, Digital, AT&T, British Telecom, and Toshiba. ECMA is considered a regional standards organization and develops information technology standards for the European region. ECMA standards are often forwarded to ISO/IEC JTC1 for development as international standards. Such cooperation between organizations can result in a faster standards development process, since consensus has already been demonstrated. ECMA has a small secretariat in Geneva, and its members meet in various places throughout Europe.

Comité Européen de Normalisation (CEN) and Comité Européen de Normalisation dans le domain Electrique (CENELEC)

CEN and its associated organization CENELEC have a relationship similar to that between ISO and IEC. They are concerned with the adoption of standards by the countries of the European Economic Community (EEC) and other European countries. Standards adopted by CEN/CENELEC are called European Norms (ENs) and are binding for procurement purposes on the CEN's member countries. CEN normally does not develop its own standards but instead relies heavily on standards developed by other organizations, especially ISO. Where there is no ISO or IEC standard, however, CEN will develop its own standard and forward it to ISO for development as an international standard.

National Institute for Science and Technology (NIST)

NIST (formerly known as the National Bureau of Standards) is a U.S. government organization. ISO standards often cover broad ranges of function and allow many choices to be made by individual implementors. The NIST has taken a leadership role in creating *profiles* that define preferred groups of choices from among the many options documented in ISO standards. Initially this was done in an informal workshop that developed *implementors' agreements*. As the importance of these profiles has increased and other organizations have started similar work internationally, the NIST workshop has become more formally organized. NIST is one of the three major international contributors to the development of Internationally Standardized Profiles (ISPs), which are the profiles formally ratified by ISO.

European Workshop on Open Systems (EWOS)

EWOS has the same role in Europe as the NIST workshop has in the United States. EWOS was started primarily by members of SPAG (see below) to ensure that Europe had a voice in the development of profiles. It also serves as the technical committee to support the technical activity of CEN. EWOS and NIST work closely together to achieve and maintain harmonization of their profiles. EWOS is located in Brussels.

Promotion of OSI/Asia and Oceania Workshop (POSI/AOW)

AOW is another organization that contributes to the international adoption of profiles. POSI is a Japanese organization concerned with promoting the adoption of ISO standards for the OSI model, while AOW is an open workshop that includes Australia and other Pacific countries as well as Japan.

Corporation for Open Systems (COS)

COS was initiated as a consortium of computer manufacturers and others to encourage the adoption of ISO information systems standards. It has initially directed its efforts toward the development of testing procedures to allow vendors to demonstrate conformance to ISO standards. COS operates as a nonprofit organization funded by its members. It does not produce standards nor does it contribute to the development of standards. COS is located in McLean, VA.

Standards Promotion and Application Group (SPAG)

SPAG was initially a private consortium of European companies, set up with objectives similar to those of the COS. Like COS, it has now directed its efforts primarily toward the development of testing procedures, and it cooperates closely with COS in that regard. Membership in SPAG is now open, and many U.S. companies are members.

Electrical Industries Association (EIA)

EIA is an association of companies involved in electrical and related industries. EIA undertakes some standardization projects and operates in that capacity as an accredited organization (AO) under the rules of consensus standards formulated by ANSI. The standards developed by the EIA are concerned primarily with physical communication interfaces and electrical signaling. A well-known EIA standard is RS-232-D, which documents the way in which a terminal or computer is attached to a modem.

Conference of European PTTS (CEPT)

CEPT was established by the European PTTs primarily to develop technical standards that could be used in Europe prior to the development of corresponding ITU-T standards. With the establishment of ETSI (see below), CEPT remains a closed forum concerned mainly with marketing and lobbying.

European Telecommunications Standards Institute (ETSI)

ETSI was established by the European Economic Commission to formalize many of the activities formerly undertaken by CEPT. Membership is open to suppliers of telecommunications equipment and services, PTTs, and other industrial organizations, with formal voting on a national basis. ETSI develops European telecommunications standards (ETSS). Some of these are intended as a basis for the provision of services and as a foundation for ITU-T work, while others are oriented toward permission to connect testing for the attachment of equipment to public networks. ETSI is based in Sophie Antipolis, France. It has its own permanent technical staff and depends on the participation of its members.

X/Open

X/Open was set up by European computer manufacturers to develop a consistent UNIX-like suite of application programming interfaces to permit application portability. Membership is open and worldwide.

ADDITIONAL STANDARDS TERMINOLOGY

A number of additional terms making up the alphabet soup of information technology standardization are defined below:

- **Manufacturing Automation Protocol (MAP).** A project started in the United States by General Motors to develop a single standard for communication between devices in a factory automation environment. Its work has been based on U.S. national and ISO standards and also defines additional standards specific to factory automation applications.

- **Technical and Office Protocols (TOP).** A complementary project to MAP started by Boeing to extend the applicability of MAP into other environments, such as office information systems and computer-aided design.

- **Government Open Systems Interconnection Profile (GOSIP).** A name for procurement-oriented standard profiles specifying how ISO standards will be used for U.S. government computing. The acronym GOSIP has been adopted by other countries to describe their own government procurement specifications.

- **European Procurement Handbook for Open Systems (EPHOS).** A project similar to GOSIP for government computing throughout Europe.

- **Open Distributed Processing (ODP).** A project started within ISO to develop standards for a heterogeneous distributed computing environment. It is defining an overall reference model for distributed computing that goes beyond the OSI model.

- **POSIX.** A standard developed by IEEE under its Project 1003 that defines a UNIX-like interface to basic operating system functions to provide for application portability.

Appendix  B

The OSI Reference Model

During the time that today's network architectures and communication protocols were being developed, an ambitious project was underway in ISO to develop a single international standard set of communication protocols that could be used in a communication network. By 1984, ISO had defined the *Reference Model for Open Systems Interconnection (OSI model),* a generalized model of system interconnection described in international standard ISO 7498 and in ITU-T Recommendation X.200.

PURPOSE OF THE OSI MODEL

The OSI model is designed to provide a common basis for the coordination of standards development for the purpose of interconnecting *open systems.* The term *open* in this context means systems open to one another by virtue of their mutual use of applicable standards.

The OSI model describes how machines can communicate with one another in a standardized and highly flexible way by defining the functional layers that should be incorporated into each communicating machine. The OSI model does not define the networking software itself, nor does it define detailed standards for that software; it simply defines the broad categories of function each layer should perform.

THE OSI NETWORK ARCHITECTURE

ISO has also developed a comprehensive set of standards for the various layers of the OSI model. These standards together make up the *OSI architecture* for computer networking.

The standards making up the OSI architecture are not today widely implemented in commercial products for computer networking, nor does it appear that they will be widely implemented in the forseeable future. However, the OSI model is still important. Many of the concepts and terminology associated with the OSI model have become generally accepted as a basis for discussing and describing network architectures. The layering structure of the OSI model is also often used in categorizing the various communication protocols in common use today and in comparing one network architecture with another.

The remainder of this appendix introduces the seven functional layers defined by the OSI model.

OSI MODEL FUNCTIONAL LAYERS

The OSI model defines the seven functional layers shown in Fig. B.1. Each layer performs a different set of functions, and the intent was to make each layer as independent as possible from all the others. The following sections briefly describe each of the seven layers of the OSI model, working from the bottom up.

| Application Layer |
| Presentation Layer |
| Session Layer |
| Transport Layer |
| Network Layer |
| Data Link Layer |
| Physical Layer |

Figure B.1   OSI model functional layers.

The Physical Layer

The *Physical* layer is responsible for the actual transmission of a bit stream across a physical circuit. It allows signals, such as electrical signals, optical signals, or radio signals, to be exchanged among communicating machines. The Physical layer, shown in Fig. B.2, typically consists of hardware permanently installed in the communicating devices. The Physical layer also addresses the cables, connectors, modems, and other devices used to permit machines to communicate physically.

Physical layer mechanisms in each of the communicating machines typically control the generation and detection of signals interpreted as 0 bits and 1 bits. The Physical

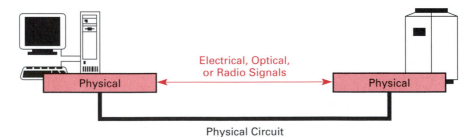

Figure B.2   The Physical layer is concerned with sending and receiving signals over a communications medium.

layer does not assign any significance to the bits. For example, it is not concerned with how many bits make up each unit of data, nor is it concerned with the meaning of the data being transmitted. In the Physical layer, the sender simply transmits a signal and the receiver detects it.

The Data Link Layer

The *Data Link* layer is responsible for providing data transmission over a single connection from one system to another. Control mechanisms in the Data Link layer handle the transmission of data units, often called *frames*, over a physical circuit. Functions operating in the Data Link layer allow data to be transmitted, in a relatively error-free fashion, over a sometimes error-prone physical circuit (see Fig. B.3). This layer is concerned with how bits are grouped into frames and performs synchronization functions with respect to failures occurring in the Physical layer. The Data Link layer implements error-detection mechanisms that identify transmission errors. With some types of data links, the Data Link layer may also perform procedures for flow control, frame sequencing, and recovering from transmission errors.

Figure B.3 The Data Link layer is responsible for the transmission of data units over a physical circuit.

The Network Layer

The *Network* layer is concerned with making routing decisions and with relaying data from one device to another through the network. The OSI model classifies each system in the network as one of two types: *end systems* act as the source or the final destination of data, and *intermediate systems* perform routing and relaying functions (see Fig. B.4).

The facilities provided by the Network layer supply a service that higher layers employ for moving data units, often called *packets*, from one end system to another, where the packets may flow through any number of intermediate systems. End systems generally implement all seven layers of the OSI model, allowing application programs to exchange information with each other. It is possible for intermediate systems performing *only* routing and relaying functions to implement only the bottom three layers of the OSI model.

In a complex network, the path between any two systems may at one instant be via a number of data links. The application programs running in two end systems that wish to

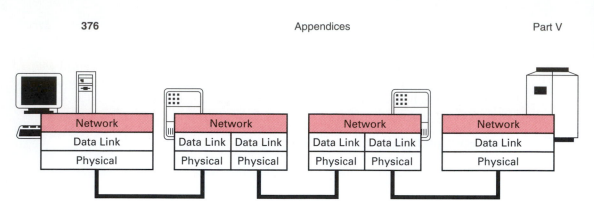

Figure B.4   The Network layer allows communication across multiple data links.

communicate should not need to be concerned with the route packets take nor with how many data links they must cross. The Network layer functions operating in end systems and in intermediate systems together handle these routing and relaying functions.

Whereas the Data Link layer provides for the transmission of frames between *adjacent* systems across a single data link, the Network layer provides for the much more complex task of transmitting packets between *any* two end systems in the network, regardless of how many data links may need to be traversed.

The Transport Layer

The *Transport* layer builds on the services of the Network layer and the layers below it to form the uppermost layer of a reliable end-to-end *data transport service*. The Transport layer hides from the higher layers all the details concerning the actual moving of packets and frames from one computer to another. The Network layer shields network users from the complexities of network operation.

The lowest three layers of the OSI model implement a common physical network that many machines can share independently of one another, just as many independent users share the postal service. It is possible for the postal service to occasionally lose a letter. To detect the loss of a letter, two users of the postal service might apply their own end-to-end controls, such as sequentially numbering their letters. The functions performed in the Transport layer can include similar end-to-end integrity controls to recover from lost, out-of-sequence, or duplicate messages.

Transport layer functions handle addressing of the processes, such as application programs, that use the network for communication. The Transport layer can also control the rate at which messages flow through the network to prevent and control congestion. Whereas the Network layer is concerned with the interface between network systems and operates in end systems and intermediate systems, the Transport layer provides an end-to-end service that programs can use for moving data back and forth between them.

The Transport layer is the lowest layer required *only* in the computers running the programs that use the network for communication (see Fig. B.5). The Transport layer need not be implemented in intermediate systems that perform only routing and relaying functions.

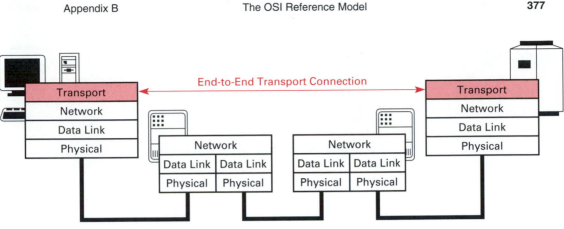

Figure B.5   The Transport layer is the lowest layer required only in the communicating end systems.

The Session Layer

There is a fundamental difference in orientation between the bottom four layers and the top three. The bottom four layers are concerned more with the network itself and provide a general data transport service useful to any application. The top three layers are more concerned with services oriented to the application programs themselves (see Fig. B.6).

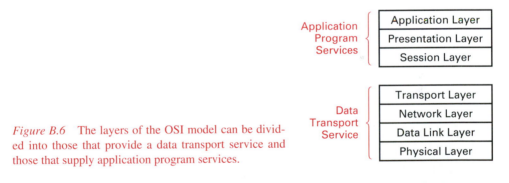

Figure B.6   The layers of the OSI model can be divided into those that provide a data transport service and those that supply application program services.

The *Session* layer is the lowest of the layers associated with the application programs. It is responsible for organizing the dialog between two application programs and for managing the data exchanges between them. To do this, the Session layer imposes a structure on the interaction between two communicating programs (see Fig. B.7).

The Session layer defines three types of dialogs: two-way simultaneous interaction, where both programs can send and receive concurrently; two-way alternate interaction, where the programs take turns sending and receiving; and one-way interaction, where one program sends and the other only receives. In addition to organizing the dialog, the Session layer services include establishing synchronization points within the dialog, allowing a dialog to be interrupted, and resuming a dialog from a synchronization point.

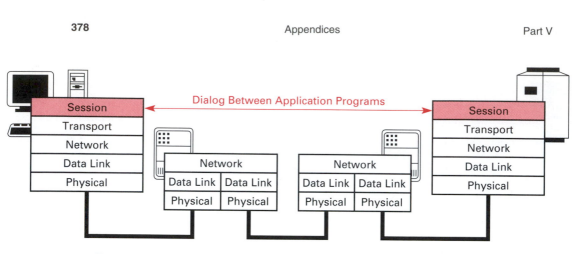

Figure B.7   The Session layer organizes the dialog between two application processes.

The Presentation Layer

The five layers below the *Presentation* layer are all concerned with the orderly movement of a stream of bits from one program to another. The Presentation layer is the lowest layer interested in the *meaning* of those bits. It deals with preserving the *information content* of data transmitted over the network (see Fig. B.8).

The Presentation layer is concerned with three types of *data syntax* that can be used for describing and representing data:

- **Abstract Syntax.** An *abstract syntax* consists of a formal definition of the information content of the data two programs exchange. An abstract syntax is concerned only with information content and not with how that information content is represented in a computer or how it is encoded for transmission. For example, an abstract syntax might define a data type called AccountNumber, values of which consist of integers. ISO 8824 *Abstract Syntax Notation One (ASN.1)* defines an international standard notation often used in practice to define abstract syntaxes in information technology standards.

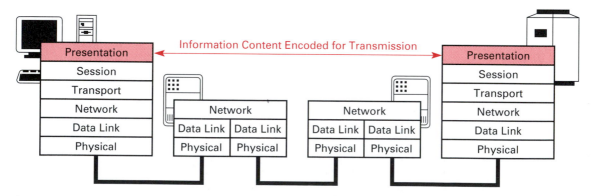

Figure B.8   The Presentation layer is responsible for preserving the information content of the data transmitted over the network.

- **Transfer Syntax.** A *transfer syntax* defines how the information content of data is encoded for transmission over the network. A value of the AccountNumber type might be transferred over the network using some form of encoding scheme that identifies the value as being of the AccountNumber type, specifies that it consists of an integer, and encodes that integer's value using a minimum number of bits.

- **Local Concrete Syntax.** A *local concrete syntax* defines how the information content of data is actually represented in a computing system. Two communicating systems might use different local concrete syntaxes. For example, one system might represent the integers in an account number in the form of a binary number using 2's complement notation; another system might use a string of decimal digits. The OSI model is not concerned with the local concrete syntax, and programs are free to represent data internally in any desired way.

The OSI model defines two major functions for the Presentation layer. First, the Presentation layer in the two communicating systems must negotiate a common transfer syntax to be used to transfer the messages defined by a particular abstract syntax. Second, the Presentation layer must ensure that one system does not need to care what local concrete syntax the other system is using. If the local concrete syntaxes in the two communicating systems are different, an implementation of the Presentation layer is responsible for transforming from the local concrete syntax to the transfer syntax in the sending system and from the transfer syntax to the local concrete syntax in the receiving system.

If both computers are running C programs in personal computers that use Intel microprocessors, the Presentation layer has little to do, since both programs use the same local concrete syntax. However, if a Pascal program running in a VAX is communicating with a FORTRAN program running in an IBM mainframe, the Presentation layer becomes more important. The FORTRAN program may represent an integer in decimal using a variable-length field; the Pascal program may represent an integer in binary using a 32-bit word. The Presentation layer performs the necessary conversions that allow each program to work with data in its own preferred format without having to be aware of the data formats that its partner uses.

The Application Layer

The topmost layer, the one user processes plug into, is the *Application* layer (see Fig. B.9). The Application layer is concerned with high-level functions that provide support to the application programs using the network for communication. The Application layer provides a means for application programs to access the system interconnection facilities to exchange information. It provides all functions related to communication between systems not provided by the lower layers.

The Application layer provides a means for application programs to exchange information with each other. Communication services provided by the Application layer hide the complexity of the layers below from the communicating programs. As far as the Application layer is concerned, a program running in one computer sends a message, and a program running in some other computer receives it. The Application layer is not concerned with any of the details concerning how the message gets from the source computer to the destination computer.

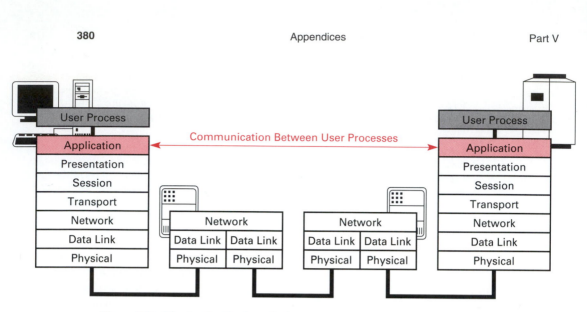

Figure B.9   The Application layer is the topmost layer into which user process-es plug.

The Application layer is more open ended than the layers below. Due to the wide variety of applications that will ultimately use networks for communication, many standards for the Application layer have been developed, and many new ones will eventually be required.

OSI CONCEPTS

Many information technology standards for computer networking are based on the OSI model and use much of the terminology that ISO has adopted in documenting communication services and protocols. In order to understand the wide variety of standards important to enterprise networking, it is useful to understand some of the concepts underlying the OSI model.

The OSI model is concerned with the interconnection of systems—the way in which they exchange information—and not the internal functions performed by a given system. In OSI terminology, a system is defined as follows:

> A *system* is a set of one or more computers, the associated software, peripherals, terminals, human operators, physical processes, transfer means, etc., that forms an autonomous whole capable of performing information processing and/or information transfer.

The OSI model provides a generalized view of a layered architecture. With the broad definition given for a system, the architecture can apply to a very simple system, such as a point-to-point connection between two computers, or to a very complex system, such as the interconnection of two entire computer networks.

Entities and Service Access Points

The notions of entities and service access points are important to understanding how interactions take place between layers in communicating systems.

- **Entity.** An active element within a layer. Two communicating entities within the same layer, but in different network systems, are called *peer entities*. Entities in the Application layer are called *Application entities*, entities in the Presentation layer are called *Presentation entities*, and so on. A particular layer provides services to entities running in the layer above.

- **Service-Access-Point (SAP).** The point at which the services of a layer are provided. Each layer defines service-access-points at which entities in the layer above request the services of that layer. Each service-access-point has a *SAP address*, by which the particular entity employing a layer service can be differentiated from all other entities that might also be able to concurrently use that layer service.

Abstract Interfaces

The OSI model defines an interface between any two pairs of adjacent layers in the same system. At any point in the architecture, layer n can be viewed as a *service provider*, and layer $n + 1$ can be viewed as the *service requester* or *service user* (see Fig. B.10). An entity in layer n provides a set of services to entities running in layer $n + 1$ via layer n's service-access-point. The set of services provided by layer n defines the *abstract interface* between layer n and layer $n + 1$.

An abstract interface describes the semantics of the interactions that can occur between two architectural layers. An abstract interface does not specify implementation details, nor does it describe the syntax that must be used to implement the interface. The interactions between two adjacent layers are described only in terms of an abstract set of services that layer n provides to layer $n + 1$.

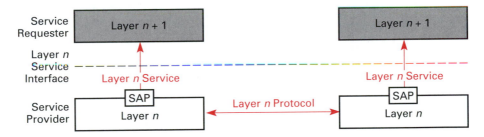

Figure B.10   A service provider provides a defined set of services to a service requester via a service-access-point (SAP). The set of services provided by layer n defines an abstract interface between layer n and layer $n + 1$.

Concrete Interfaces

In addition to abstract interfaces, *concrete interfaces* are also important at some points in the architecture, especially in the Physical layer and at points where application programming interfaces (APIS) must be specified. A concrete interface might describe a point in the architecture at which a physical connector is used, for example, to connect a device to a cable. A concrete interface might provide electrical and mechanical specifications for the cables and connectors that must be used to properly implement the architecture. A concrete interface might also define an application programming interface a programmer must adhere to in writing programs to request the services of a layer.

Services and Protocols

The ISO standards for the OSI model define for each layer a single service definition and one or more protocol specifications. A *service definition* defines the specific services a layer provides to the layer above it. A service definition specifically *does not* say anything about how those services are to be provided. A *protocol specification* describes the formats of the data units exchanged and specifies the procedures a layer must perform in exchanging those data units in providing the services of that layer.

The relationship between the services Layer n provides and the protocol governing its operation are shown in Fig. B.11. As shown here, the layer n protocol uses the services of layer $n - 1$ to provide a defined set of services to layer $n + 1$ above it.

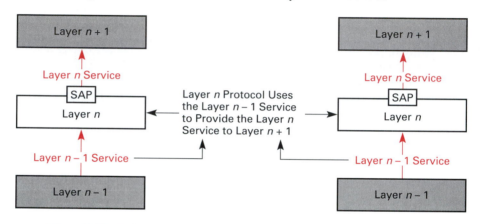

Figure B.11   Relationship between a layer's service definition and its protocol specification.

Some layer services are intended to be used to transmit units of data from a layer entity in one system to a peer layer entity in another system. A layer does this by issuing a data transfer request to the layer below and passing the data unit to be transferred as a parameter of the request. Data units passed from a service requester to a service provider are called *service-data-units (SDUs)*.

The name of the SDU passed from a layer to the layer below begins with the name of the layer to which the SDU is passed. For example, the SDUs passed from the Transport layer to the Network layer are called *network-service-data-units (NSDUs)*, the SDUs passed from the Network layer to the Data Link layer are called *data-link-service-data-units (DLSDUs)*, and so on.

Protocol Specifications

Another principle of the OSI model is that when two network systems are communicating with one another, an entity in each layer in the first system communicates with its peer entity in the second system using a *protocol*. Figure B.12 illustrates protocols operating in each of the seven layers of the OSI model.

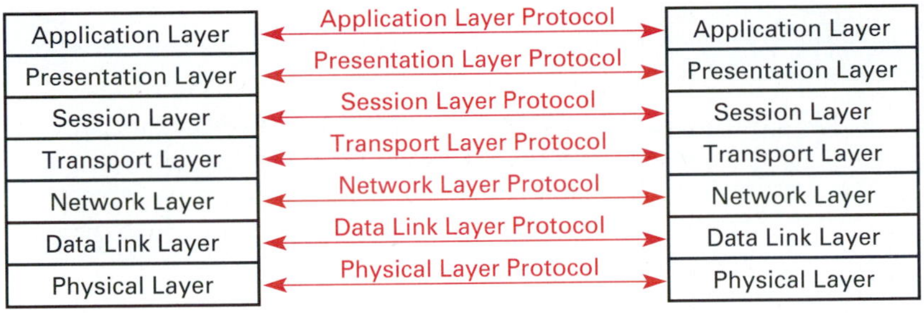

Figure B.12   A separate protocol controls the operation of each layer in the OSI model.

A protocol specification for layer n defines the following:

- The formats of the data units exchanged between peer layer n entities.

- The interactions that occur between peer layer n entities in exchanging data units.

- The way in which layer n and layer $n + 1$ interact in exchanging the service requests and responses defined in the service definition for layer n.

- The way in which the layer n and layer $n - 1$ interact in exchanging the service requests and responses defined in the service definition for layer $n - 1$.

Protocol-Data-Units

Data units sent from a layer entity in one system to a peer layer entity in another system are called *protocol-data-units (PDUs)*. PDUs appear to flow from a layer $n + 1$ entity in the sending system to a layer $n + 1$ entity in the receiving system using the layer $n + 1$ protocol. From this perspective, functions performed in layer n and below are hidden from layer $n + 1$.

Protocol Control Information

A layer constructs a protocol-data-unit from the service-data-unit passed down from the layer above by adding *protocol-control-information (PCI)* to it (see Fig. B.13). Some of the information making up the protocol information may be passed down from layer $n + 1$ to layer n in the form of service request parameters. The PCI is used to control the operation of the protocol in a particular layer. Protocol-control-information is carried in the form of a header (and, in the case of the Data Link layer, also a trailer) added to the SDU.

Segmentation and Blocking

In some cases, a layer might implement a *segmentation* facility in which a single SDU is used to create a number of individual PDUs. It is also possible for a layer to implement a *blocking* facility that allows multiple SDUs to be grouped together and transported across the network in a single PDU.

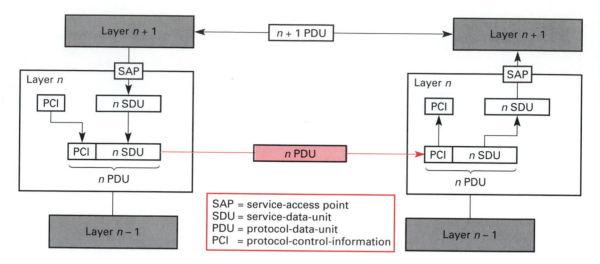

Figure B.13   A layer entity in one machine accepts a service-data-unit (SDU) from the layer above via its service-access-point (SAP). The layer entity then adds protocol-control-information (PCI) to the SDU to create a protocol-data-unit (PDU) and sends that PDU to its peer layer entity in another machine.

Generated PDUs

A layer *n* entity can also itself generate PDUs apart from the PDUs it creates from the SDUs it receives from layer *n* + 1. Such generated PDUs are typically transmitted between peer layer *n* entities to control the operation of the layer *n* protocol. The layer *n* + 1 service requester is not directly aware of the existence of these PDUs.

Appendix C

The IEEE/ISO/ANSI LAN Architecture

The IEEE has undertaken a major role in local area network standards development. IEEE Project 802 has defined a flexible architecture oriented specifically to the standardization of local area network data link technology. The approach the IEEE has taken in developing its LAN architecture is in conformance with the OSI model. However, IEEE Project 802 addresses only the lowest two layers of the OSI model, the Physical and Data Link layers.

The IEEE Project 802 LAN architecture has subsequently been accepted by ISO and ANSI to form the underlying basis for their own LAN standardization efforts. In this book, we refer to the architecture that began its development in IEEE Project 802 as the IEEE/ISO/ANSI LAN architecture.

FUNCTIONAL LAYERS

Figure C.1 illustrates the relationships between the OSI model and the LAN architecture that underlies IEEE, ISO, and ANSI standards for local area networks. In the IEEE/ISO/ANSI LAN architecture, the Data Link layer is divided into two sublayers: the *Logical Link Control (LLC)* sublayer and the *Medium Access Control (MAC)* sublayer.

DATA LINK LAYER FUNCTIONS

Box C.1 lists some of the general functions that the OSI model defines for the Data Link layer.

LOGICAL LINK CONTROL SUBLAYER

The Logical Link Control sublayer is responsible for medium-independent data link functions. It allows a LAN data link user to access the services of a local area network data link without having to be concerned with the form of medium access control or physical trans-

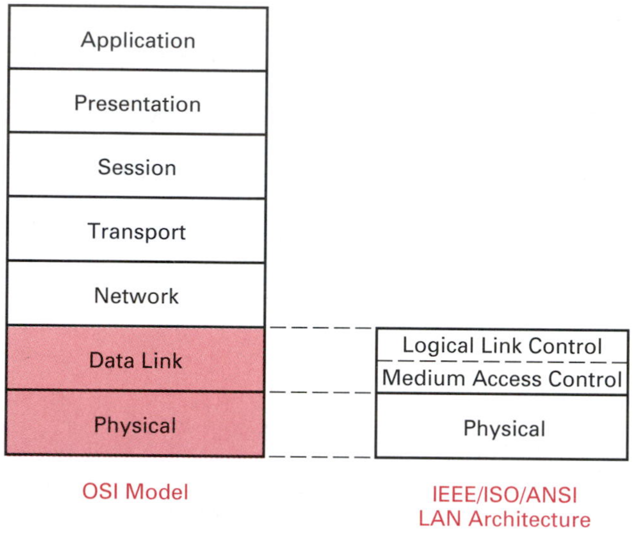

Figure C.1   Comparing the layers of the OSI model with the layers and sub-layers of the IEEE/ISO/ANSI LAN architecture.

BOX C.1   OSI model Data Link layer functions.

- **Data Link Connection Establishment and Release.** Dynamically establishes, for a connection-oriented Data Link service, a logical data link connection between two users of the Data Link service (typically Network layer entities), and releases the connection when it is no longer required. These functions are not provided for a connectionless Data Link service, in which connections are not used.

- **Service-Data-Units.** Defines the service-data-unit (SDU) passed down from the user of the Data Link layer service to a Data Link layer entity in the sending system and up from a Data Link layer entity to the user of the Data Link layer service in the receiving system.

- **Framing.** Creates a single protocol-data-unit (PDU) from each SDU passed from a user of the Data Link layer service, marks the beginning and the end of the PDU when sending, and determines the beginning and ending of PDUs when receiving. The term *frame* is often used as an informal name for the PDU exchanged between peer Data Link layer entities.

- **Data Transfer.** Transfers frames over a physical circuit, extracts the SDU from each frame by removing the protocol-control-information (PCI), and passes SDUs up to the user of the Data Link layer service in the receiving system.

- **Frame Synchronization.** Establishes and maintains synchronization between the sending system and the receiving system. This means the receiving system must be capable of determining where each frame begins and ends.

- **Frame Sequencing.** Uses sequence numbers, for a connection-oriented Data Link service, to ensure that frames are delivered in the same order in which they were transmitted. Frame sequencing does not apply to a connectionless Data Link layer service.

BOX C.1   *(Continued)*

- **Error Detection.** Detects transmission errors, frame format errors, and procedural errors on the data link connection using redundant bits carried in the PCI in the frame.
- **Error Recovery.** Recovers from errors detected on data links using connection-oriented operation. Error recovery does not apply to a connectionless Data Link service.
- **Identification and Parameter Exchange.** Performs a set of identification and parameter exchange functions, typically prior to the exchange of frames carrying user data. Some types of Data Link services allow parameter values to be negotiated.
- **Flow Control.** Controls the rate at which a user of a connection-oriented Data Link layer service receives frames to prevent a user of the Data Link layer service from being overloaded. Flow control does not apply to a connectionless Data Link service.
- **Physical Layer Services.** Uses the services of the Physical layer to transmit and receive data and to control the operation of the physical transmission medium.
- **Network Management.** Monitors and controls the operation of the Data Link layer. Management functions might include setting Data Link layer protocol operating characteristics, enabling and disabling data link connections, monitoring the status of enabled connections, and performing loopback tests for verifying correct operation of the data link.

mission medium used. The LLC sublayer is shared by a variety of different medium access control technologies, many of which are described in the chapters in Part IV. The LLC sublayer presents a common interface to the LAN data link user.

LLC-PDUs

The data unit that LLC sublayer entities exchange is called the *logical-link-control-protocol-data-unit (LLC-PDU)*. As shown in Fig. C.2, the LLC sublayer adds protocol-control-information (PCI) in the form of a header to each message it receives from the LAN data link user to create an LLC-PDU.

LLC Service-Access-Points

The user of a LAN data link requests data transmission services through a *service-access-point (SAP)* into the LLC sublayer. It is possible for an implementation of Logical Link Control in a system to allow more than one user to concurrently access the services of the LAN data link. Each does so through a separate SAP with a different SAP identifier (see Fig. C.3).

MEDIUM ACCESS CONTROL SUBLAYER

A local area network typically supports multiple devices that all contend for access to a single physical transmission medium. The Medium Access Control sublayer provides services to a user of the MAC sublayer service, which is typically the LLC sublayer.

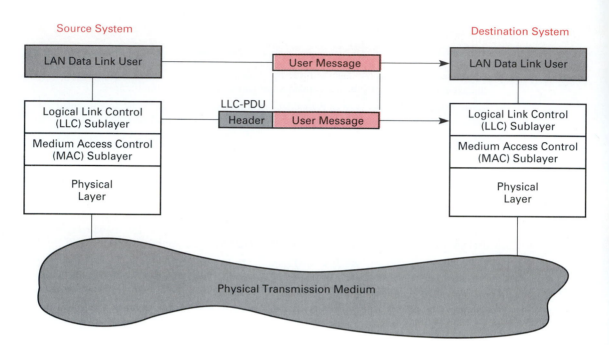

Figure C.2 Relationship between the LAN data link user message and the LLC-PDU.

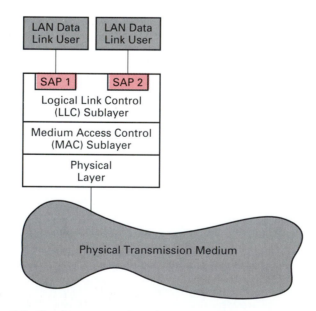

Figure C.3 Service-access-points (SAPs) provide points of access into the LLC sublayer.

The data unit that MAC sublayer entities exchange is called the *medium-access-control-protocol-data-unit (MAC-PDU)*. The MAC-PDU is often called a *MAC frame*. The purpose of the MAC frame is to carry the LLC-PDU across a specific type of physical transmission medium from one network device to another.

Figure C.4 illustrates the relationship between the LLC sublayer, the MAC sublayer, and the PDUs associated with them. The MAC sublayer adds PCI in the form of a header and a trailer to each LLC-PDU that it receives from the LLC sublayer to create a MAC-PDU (MAC frame).

The standards defining the functions of the MAC sublayer are primarily concerned with the rules that must be followed for network devices to be able to share access to a common transmission medium. The MAC sublayer performs a framing function that adds header and trailer information to each MAC frame sent. The header and trailer contain information necessary to identify the beginning and end of a frame, specify the source and destination of a message, synchronize the sender and receiver, and provide for error detection.

PHYSICAL LAYER

The lowest layer in the IEEE/ISO/ANSI LAN architecture corresponds directly to the Physical layer of the OSI model. It provides services to a user of the Physical layer, which is typically the MAC sublayer. Box C.2 lists some of the functions that the OSI model defines for

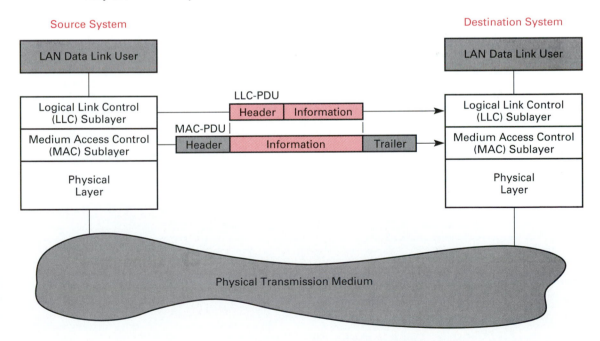

Figure C.4   Relationship between the LLC-PDU and the MAC-PDU.

the Physical layer. The PDUs exchanged by the Physical layer consist of signals that represent the individual bits making up a MAC frame.

The Physical layer is concerned with the physical transmission of signals across a transmission medium. This layer defines procedures for establishing physical connections to the transmission medium and for transmitting and receiving signals over it. Physical layer specifications also include descriptions of the types of cabling, plugs, and connectors to be used and the characteristics of the signals exchanged.

BOX C.2   OSI model Physical layer functions.

- **Circuit Establishment and Release.** Allows a physical circuit to be dynamically established when it is required and released when the circuit is no longer needed. This function is typically used for a circuit implemented by a temporary facility, such as a dial-up line in the telephone network. It is typically not used with local area networks that use dedicated cabling.

- **Bit Synchronization.** Establishes synchronization in a receiving device with a stream of bits coming in and clocks data in from the communication circuit at the correct rate.

- **Service-Data-Units.** Defines the service-data-unit (SDU) passed down from a user of the Physical layer in the sending device and up from the Physical layer to its user in the receiving device. A Physical layer SDU typically consists of a signal representing a single bit.

- **Data Transfer and Sequencing.** Allows electrical signals to be exchanged over the circuit connecting two communicating devices and allows bits to be accepted by the receiving device in the same order in which they are delivered by the sending device.

- **Fault Condition Notification.** Notifies the Physical layer user when fault conditions occur.

- **Network Management.** Controls and monitors the operation of functions operating in the Physical layer. Network management functions include setting the operating characteristics of the communication link, activating and deactivating physical circuits, monitoring the status of physical links, and performing diagnostic procedures, such as loopback tests.

- **Medium Specific Control Functions.** Provides control functions for specific forms of transmission media, such as encoding/decoding, carrier sensing, collision detection, collision announcement, and detection of illegal cabling topologies.

Glossary

AARP. AppleTalk Address Resolution Protocol.

ABSTRACT INTERFACE. An interface describing the interactions that can occur between two layers of an architecture. An abstract interface does not specify implementation details, nor does it describe any coding syntax that must be used to implement the interface.

ABSTRACT SYNTAX NOTATION ONE (ASN.1). An international standard data description notation that allows the format and meaning of data structures to be defined without specifying how those data structures are represented in a computer or how they are encoded for transmission through a network.

ACCESS CONTROL METHOD. Mechanism by which communicating systems manage their access to a physical transmission medium.

ACCESS UNIT. See *Concentrator.*

ACCREDITED STANDARDS COMMITTEE (ASC). A committee of the American National Standards Institute (ANSI) that develops standards later adopted and published by ANSI. Members of sub-committee X3T9.5 of the Accredited Standards Committee for Information Processing Systems developed the Fiber Distributed Data Interface (FDDI) local area network standard. See *American National Standards Institute.*

ACKNOWLEDGED CONNECTIONLESS LLC SERVICE. A service of the Logical Link Control sublayer in the IEEE/ISO/ANSI LAN architecture in which LLC-SDUS are acknowledged but no connection is established between LLC entities.

ADDRESS RESOLUTION PROTOCOL (ARP). In TCP/IP, a Network layer protocol that helps a source end system deliver data to a destination system on the same LAN data link. ARP can also be used by an end system to determine the physical hardware address of a router.

AEP. AppleTalk Echo Protocol.

AMERICAN NATIONAL STANDARDS INSTITUTE (ANSI). The national standards organization for the United States. ANSI is a nonprofit organization that writes the rules for standards bodies to follow and publishes standards produced under its rules of consensus. ANSI accredits standards committees to write standards in areas of their expertise.

ANSI. American National Standards Institute.

API. Application Programming Interface.

APPLETALK. Apple Computer's networking scheme, integrated into most Apple system software, that allows Apple computing systems to participate in peer-to-peer computer networks and to also access the services of AppleTalk servers. AppleTalk hardware and software is available for non-Apple equipment from third-party vendors.

APPLETALK ADDRESS RESOLUTION PROTOCOL (AARP). In AppleTalk, a Network layer protocol that helps a source end system to deliver data to a destination system on the same subnetwork. AARP can also be used by an end system to determine the physical hardware address of a router.

APPLETALK ECHO PROTOCOL (AEP). In AppleTalk, a Transport layer protocol that provides a system reachability test function.

APPLETALK TRANSACTION PROTOCOL (ATP). In AppleTalk, a Transport layer protocol that provides a reliable, connection-oriented, sequenced data transfer service.

APPLICATION LAYER. Layer seven and the topmost layer of the OSI model. The Application layer provides a means for application programs to access the system interconnection facilities to exchange information. Communication services provided by the Application layer hide the complexity of the layers below from the communicating programs.

APPLICATION PROGRAMMING INTERFACE (API). A specification defining how an application program invokes a defined set of services.

APPLICATION SERVER. A network system that implements software that allows other systems to request the services of application programs running on the application server.

APPN. Advanced Peer-to-Peer Networking. See *Systems Network Architecture.*

ARCNET. A relatively low-speed form of LAN data link technology (2.5 megabits per second), developed by Datapoint, in which all systems are attached to a common coaxial cable. ARCnet uses a token bus form of medium access control in which a system transmits only when it has the token.

ARP. Address Resolution Protocol.

ARPA. See *Defense Advanced Research Projects Agency.*

ARPANET. An early packet-switching network, funded by the Defense Advanced Research Projects Agency (DARPA) that led to the development of the Internet. See *Internet.*

ASC. Accredited Standards Committee.

ASN.1. Abstract Syntax Notation One.

ASYNCHRONOUS TRANSFER MODE (ATM). A form of very fast packet switching in which data is carried in fixed-length units called *cells*. Each cell is 53 octets in length, with 5 octets used as a header in each cell. ATM employs mechanisms that can be used to set up virtual circuits between users, in which a pair of communicating users appear to have a dedicated circuit between them.

ASYNCHRONOUS TRANSMISSION. A form of transmission using start and stop bits to control transmission in which a single character is transmitted in each data unit.

ATM. Asynchronous Transfer Mode.

ATP. AppleTalk Transaction Protocol.

AUTONOMOUS SYSTEM. In TCP/IP, a collection of end systems (hosts) and routers administered by a single authority.

BACKBONE LOCAL AREA NETWORK. A central local area network used to interconnect two or more other local area networks. Connection to the backbone LAN can be made using a repeater, bridge, router, or gateway, depending on the types of networks being interconnected.

BACKOFF DELAY. The length of time that a station on a network that employs the CSMA/CD (Ethernet) form of medium access control must wait before attempting to retransmit a frame after detecting a collision. See also *Deference process*.

BANDWIDTH. Term used to specify the capacity of a communication channel that refers to the difference between the highest and the lowest frequencies carried over the channel. The higher the bandwidth, the more information can be carried.

BASEBAND TRANSMISSION. A form of transmission in which data signals are carried over the physical communication medium in the form of discrete pulses of electricity or light.

BAUD. A measurement of the signaling speed of a channel that refers to the number of times in each second the line condition changes. Bauds are equal to bits per second only if each change in line condition represents a single bit.

BELLMAN-FORD ROUTING ALGORITHM. See *Distance-vector routing algorithm*.

BGP. Border Gateway Protocol.

BINARY EXPONENTIAL BACKOFF. Technique used with the CSMA/CD (Ethernet) form of medium access control in which the backoff delay becomes longer each time the station detects a successive collision. See also *Backoff delay*.

B-ISDN. Broadband ISDN.

BLOCKING FUNCTION. In the OSI model, a function performed by a layer or sublayer entity that transmits two or more service-data-units (SDUs) in the form of a single protocol-data-unit (PDU).

BORDER GATEWAY PROTOCOL (BGP). In TCP/IP, a Network layer routing protocol that allows routers to communicate between autonomous systems. See also *Exterior Gateway Protocol*.

BRIDGE. A device operating at the level of the Medium Access Control sublayer used to interconnect two or more LAN data links that use either the same or different forms of medium access control. Sometimes called a *Filtering bridge*.

BROADBAND ISDN. A high-speed form of integrated services digital network, representing a probable future direction of the telephone industry, that uses optical fiber transmission. See *Integrated services digital network* and *SONET*.

BROADBAND TRANSMISSION. A form of transmission in which the signals employed are continuous and nondiscrete and in which data is carried in the form of modulated electromagnetic waves.

BROADCAST ADDRESS. A station address containing all 1 bits that addresses all the stations attached to a LAN data link.

BROUTER. A network interconnection device that combines the functions of a router and a bridge. A brouter routes the data traffic associated with certain protocols and bridges all other data traffic. See *Bridge* and *Router*.

BUS TOPOLOGY. A network structure in which each system is directly attached to a common communication channel.

CABLING SYSTEM. A system of cable segments, cable connectors, and attachment units used to physically interconnect the stations on a LAN data link. In some cases, cable segments in a LAN are replaced with some form of wireless communication, such as radio, microwave, or infrared signaling.

CARRIER SENSE MULTIPLE ACCESS WITH COLLISION AVOIDANCE (CSMA/CA). A form of medium access control in which each system "listens" to the carrier while each transmission is in progress. After the transmission ends, each system waits for a specified period of time different for each system. If no other system has started transmitting by the time a particular system's waiting time has elapsed, it may begin sending.

CARRIER SENSE MULTIPLE ACCESS WITH COLLISION DETECTION (CSMA/CD). The Ethernet form of LAN data link technology, defined by ISO 802.3 and ISO 8802-3. Also refers to a generic means of medium access control in which stations transmit on a bus- or tree-structured transmission medium whenever the transmission medium is available and retransmit when collisions occur.

CCB. Command control block.

CCITT. International Telegraph and Telephone Consultative Committee. Now known as the Telecommunications sector of the International Telecommunication Union (ITU).

CDDI. Copper Distributed Data Interface.

CLASS I LLC. A Logical Link Control sublayer implementation that provides only the connectionless LLC service (type 1 LLC operation). See *Connectionless LLC service.*

CLASS II LLC. A Logical Link Control sublayer implementation that provides the connectionless LLC service (type 1 LLC operation) and the connection-oriented LLC service (type 2 LLC operation). See *Connectionless LLC service* and *Connection-oriented LLC service.*

CLASS III LLC. A Logical Link Control sublayer implementation that provides the connectionless LLC service (type 1 LLC operation) and the acknowledged connectionless LLC service (type 3 LLC operation). See *Connectionless LLC service* and *Acknowledged connectionless LLC service.*

CLASS IV LLC. A Logical Link Control sublayer implementation that provides the connectionless LLC service (type 1 LLC operation), the connection-oriented LLC service (type 2 LLC operation), and the acknowledged connectionless LLC service (type 3 LLC operation). See *Connectionless LLC service*, *Connection-oriented LLC service*, and *Acknowledged connectionless LLC service.*

CLIENT. In client/server computing, an application component that makes a request for a service of some other application component operating in the role of a server. See *Client/server computing.*

CLIENT/SERVER COMPUTING. A form of distributed computing in which application components operating in the role of clients request the services of other application components operating in the role of servers. Client and server components can run on the same computing system or on different computing systems connected by a network.

CMIP. Common Management Information Protocol.

CMIP OVER TCP/IP (CMOT). A specification that describes how the international standard Common Management Information Protocol (CMIP) can be used to manage a TCP/IP network. See *Common Management Information Protocol* and *Simple Network Management Protocol.*

CMOT. See *CMIP over TCP/IP.*

COAX CABLE SEGMENT. A transmission medium segment in a local area network that conforms to the IEEE/ISO CSMA/CD (Ethernet) standard to which stations are attached.

COAXIAL CABLE. An electrical cable that contains a central copper conductor, surrounded by insulating material, and then surrounded by an outer tubular conductor that consists of braided wire mesh or a solid sleeve. A protective, nonconducting sheath ordinarily protects the outer conductor.

COLLISION. A condition on the transmission medium that occurs with the CSMA/CD (Ethernet) form of medium access control when two or more stations transmit signals concurrently.

COMMAND. A logical-link-control-protocol-data-unit (LLC-PDU) sent by an LLC sublayer entity initiating a data transfer operation. See also *Response.*

COMMAND CONTROL BLOCK (CCB). A control block used to request the functions defined by the Direct Interface for IBM local area networking products. See *Direct Interface*.

COMMON CARRIER. A company in the United States that furnishes communication services to the general public.

COMMON MANAGEMENT INFORMATION PROTOCOL (CMIP). A protocol used for network management being standardized by the International Organization for Standardization (ISO).

COMMUNICATION CHANNEL. A logical medium in a communication system over which data is transmitted.

CONCENTRATOR. Local area network equipment that allows multiple network devices to be connected to the LAN cabling system through a central point. Sometimes called a *hub*.

CONCRETE INTERFACE. A specification that defines an application programming interface (API) or electrical and mechanical specifications for cables and connectors.

CONFIRMED SERVICE. A service provided by a layer or sublayer entity in which the service requester is informed by the distant peer layer or sublayer entity of the success or failure of the service request.

CONFIRM SERVICE PRIMITIVE. A service primitive issued by a service provider to notify the higher-level layer service requester of the results of one or more *request* service primitives that the service requester previously issued. See also *Indication service primitive*, *Request service primitive*, and *Response service primitive*.

CONNECTIONLESS LLC SERVICE. An unreliable data transfer service provided by the IEEE 802.2/ISO 8802-2 Logical Link Control sublayer in which there is no need to establish a prior association between the source and destination system before data transmission can take place. Each LLC-PDU sent using the connectionless LLC service is processed independently of any other LLC-PDU. No sequence checking is done to ensure that LLC-PDUs are received in the same sequence in which they were sent, and the receiving system sends no acknowledgment that it has received an LLC-PDU.

CONNECTIONLESS SERVICE. In the OSI model, a service provided by any layer or sublayer entity in which each data unit sent is sent and processed independently of any other data units. No sequence checking is done to ensure that data units are received in the same sequence in which they were sent, and the receiving station sends no acknowledgment that it has received a data unit. No flow control or error recovery is provided. A connectionless service is often called a *Datagram* service.

CONNECTION-ORIENTED LLC SERVICE. A reliable data transfer service provided by the IEEE 802.2/ISO 8802-2 Logical Link Control sublayer in which delivery of LLC-PDUs is guaranteed as long as an LLC connection is maintained between a source LLC service-access-point and a destination LLC service-access-point. With the connection-oriented LLC service, a connection between the source and the destination LLC sublayer entities must be established before data transfer can begin, the connection must be maintained while data transfer proceeds, and the connection can be terminated when data transfer is no longer required.

CONNECTION-ORIENTED SERVICE. In the OSI model, a service provided by any layer or sublayer entity in which the delivery of data units is guaranteed as long as the connection is maintained between a source service-access-point and a destination service-access-point.

CONNECTION-ORIENTED TRANSPORT PROTOCOL (ISO 8073). In the OSI architecture and in DECnet/OSI, a Transport layer protocol that provides a reliable, sequenced data transport service.

COPPER DISTRIBUTED DATA INTERFACE (CDDI). A variation of the Fiber Distributed Data Interface (FDDI) standard adapted for twisted-pair cable. See *Fiber Distributed Data Interface*.

CSMA/CA. Carrier Sense Multiple Access with Collision Avoidance.

CSMA/CD. Carrier Sense Multiple Access with Collision Detection.

DAC. Dual-attachment concentrator.

DARPA. Defense Advanced Research Projects Agency.

DATAGRAM. An informal name for the data unit exchanged during the operation of a connectionless data delivery protocol.

DATAGRAM DELIVERY PROTOCOL (DDP). In AppleTalk, a Network layer protocol that provides an unreliable, connectionless datagram delivery service.

DATAGRAM SERVICE. See *Connectionless service*.

DATA LINK LAYER. The second layer of the OSI model. The Data Link layer is responsible for providing data transmission over a single link from one system to another. Control mechanisms in the Data Link layer handle the transmission of data units, often called frames, over a physical circuit. Functions operating in the Data Link layer allow data to be transmitted, in a relatively error-free fashion, over a sometimes error-prone physical circuit. This layer is concerned with how bits are grouped into frames and implements error-detection mechanisms that identify transmission errors. With some types of data links, the Data Link layer may also perform procedures for flow control, frame sequencing, and recovering from transmission errors.

DCE. Distributed Computing Environment.

DDP. Datagram Delivery Protocol.

DECNET. A term used by Digital Equipment Corporation to refer to its own line of networking products that conform to the Digital Network Architecture (DNA).

DECNET/OSI. A term used to refer to DECnet products that conform to Phase V, the most recent phase, of the Digital Network Architecture (DNA). A major characteristic of DECnet/OSI products is that they implement the major protocols published by ISO to support the OSI model.

DECNET PHASE IV. A term used to refer to DECnet products that conform to Phase IV of the Digital Network Architecture (DNA). The most current phase of DNA is Phase V. See also *DECnet/OSI*.

DECNET PHASE V. See *DECnet/OSI*.

DEFENSE ADVANCED RESEARCH PROJECTS AGENCY (DARPA). Agency of the U.S. government that funded the development of the ARPANET, the network that led to the development of the Internet. See *Internet*.

DEFERENCE PROCESS. On a CSMA/CD (Ethernet) LAN data link, the process of monitoring the status of the transmission medium and determining when to begin retransmission. See also *Backoff delay*.

DESTINATION MAC ADDRESS. Address identifying the station or stations on a LAN data link to which a MAC frame is being sent. See also *MAC address* and *Station*.

DESTINATION-SERVICE-ACCESS-POINT ADDRESS. See *DSAP address*.

DIFFERENTIAL MANCHESTER ENCODING. A form of Manchester encoding in which a transition occurs during each bit time, as with conventional Manchester encoding, but in which the interpretation of the transition from positive to negative or from negative to positive depends on whether the previous bit time represented a 0 or a 1.

DIGITAL NETWORK ARCHITECTURE (DNA). Digital Equipment Corporation's proprietary network architecture, which has passed through a series of phases. The most current phase of DNA is DNA Phase V. See also *DECnet*, *DECnet Phase IV*, and *DECnet/OSI*.

DIGITAL ROUTING PROTOCOL (DRP). In DECnet Phase IV, a Network layer protocol that uses a distributed adaptive routing algorithm that implements hierarchical routing in which a large network can be divided into areas.

DIRECT INTERFACE. An IBM application programming interface (API), based on a control block called a Command Control Block (CCB), that allows a program to directly request Medium Access Control sublayer services.

DISK SERVER. A network system that implements software that allows other network systems to share the disk server's disk units.

DISTANCE-VECTOR ROUTING ALGORITHM. A form of routing algorithm, sometimes called a *Bellman-Ford* algorithm, in which each router learns about the network topology by exchanging routing information packets with its neighbor routers. See also *Link-state routing algorithm*.

DISTRIBUTED COMPUTING ENVIRONMENT (DCE). A specification for distributed computing, developed by the Open Software Foundation (OSF). The DCE includes interfaces for a Remote Procedure Call Service for program-to-program communication, a Threads Service for controlling multitasking activities, a Directory Service for handling naming functions, a Distributed File Service for managing remote file access facilities, a Distributed Time Service for handling date and time-of-day requests, and a Security Services for performing authorization and authentication functions.

DISTRIBUTED QUEUE DUAL BUS (DQDB). A protocol used in a form of Metropolitan Area Network (MAN) technology that can be used to provide LAN-like services over a wider geographic area. DQDB provides a service similar to that defined by IEEE 802.2/ISO 8802-2 Logical Link Control.

DLC INTERFACE. An application programming interface (API), defined for IBM local area network products, through which an application program can directly invoke the services of the Logical Link Control sublayer.

DNA. Digital Network Architecture.

DNS. Domain Name System.

DOMAIN NAME SYSTEM (DNS). In TCP/IP, a directory service that can be used to maintain the mappings between names and internet addresses in a limited number of places in the network rather than at the location of each system.

DOTTED-DECIMAL NOTATION. A form of notation typically used in the TCP/IP environment to represent 32-bit internet addresses in the form of four decimal numbers, separated by periods, with each number representing the decimal value of one octet of the address.

DQDB. Distributed Queue Dual Bus.

DROP CABLE. Used with some forms of LAN data link technology to attach the network interface card (NIC) to the transmission medium.

DRP. Digital Routing Protocol.

DSAP ADDRESS. In the IEEE/ISO/ANSI LAN architecture, an address that identifies the LLC sublayer user, or users, to receive the LLC-PDU. The destination service-access-point address can be either an *individual* address, which identifies a single SAP; or it can be a *group* address, which identifies a set of SAPs. See also *SSAP address*.

DUAL-ATTACHMENT CONCENTRATOR (DAC). On a Fiber Distributed Data Interface (FDDI) LAN data link, a device with three or more medium interface connectors (MICs). One of the MICs is of type A, one is of type B, and one or more are of type M. The type A and B MICs are used to connect the concentrator to the dual ring and the type M MICs are used to connect other single-attachment stations having MICs of type S to the concentrator. See *Medium interface connector*, *MIC type A*, *MIC type B*, *MIC type M*, *MIC type S*, and *Single-attachment station*.

DUAL-ATTACHMENT STATION (DAS). On a Fiber Distributed Data Interface (FDDI) LAN data link, a station with two medium interface connectors (MICs) that allow the station to be attached to two separate full-duplex transmission medium segments used to implement a dual ring structure. See *Medium interface connector*.

DUAL-CABLE BROADBAND. A broadband network configuration in which each device is attached to two cables. One cable is used to send and the other to receive. See *Broadband transmission*.

ECHO PROTOCOL. In NetWare and in the Xerox Network System, a Transport layer protocol that allows an end system to verify the existence of a route between one end system and another end system in the network.

EGP. Exterior Gateway Protocol.

ELAP. EtherTalk Link Access Protocol.

ENCAPSULATION FACILITY. A network interconnection facility that allows two systems that conform to a given network architecture to communicate using a network that conforms to some other network architecture. See also *Tunnel* and *Portal*.

ENDING DELIMITER. A field in a MAC frame that identifies the end of the information field and the beginning of the first octet of the frame check sequence (FCS) field.

END SYSTEM. A device in a communication system that serves as the source or final destination of data. See also *Intermediate system*.

END SYSTEM TO INTERMEDIATE SYSTEM ROUTING EXCHANGE PROTOCOL (ISO 9542). In the OSI architecture and in DECnet/OSI, a Network layer protocol that allows an end system to exchange messages with a router for the purposes of automatically configuring an end system into an OSI network. ISO 9542 allows an end system to be connected to an OSI network without requiring manual network management intervention.

ENTERPRISE NETWORK. A computer network, often called an *internet*, designed to serve the needs of an entire enterprise. An enterprise network is typically constructed of individual local area network data links interconnected using network interconnection devices and wide area network data links.

ENTITY. In the OSI model, an active element within a layer. A particular layer provides services to entities running in the layer above.

EQUIPMENT ROOM. In the EIA cable plant architecture, those physical places at which cables are physically terminated.

ERROR PROTOCOL. In NetWare and in the Xerox Network System, a Transport layer protocol that provides for detecting and reporting on errors between an end system and a router to which the end system is directly attached.

ES-IS PROTOCOL. End System to Intermediate System Routing Exchange Protocol (ISO 9542).

ETHERNET. A form of LAN data link that implements the IEEE 802.3/ISO 8802-3 CSMA/CD standard. On an Ethernet LAN data link, stations are attached to a common transmission facility, such as a coaxial cable or twisted-pair cable, and a station typically attempts to transmit whenever it has data to send. See *CSMA/CD*.

ETHERNET CABLE. Informal name for the 50-ohm, 10-mm coaxial cable specified in the IEEE/ISO CSMA/CD (Ethernet) 10BASE5 medium specification. Often called *thick Ethernet* cable to distinguish it from the 5-mm coaxial cable specified by the 10BASE2 medium specification.

ETHERNET VERSION 2. A form of LAN data link technology, developed by Digital Equipment Corporation, Xerox, and Intel, that served as the basis for the IEEE/ISO CSMA/CD (Ethernet) standard.

ETHERTALK LINK ACCESS PROTOCOL (ELAP). In AppleTalk, the data link protocol that provides Ethernet LAN support. Standard IEEE/ISO Logical Link Control (LLC) interfaces and data formats are used to provide the connectionless Type 1 LLC service.

EXTENDED LAN. A network that consists of two or more separate LAN data links, using either the same or different forms of medium access control, interconnected using bridges. See also *Bridge*.

EXTERIOR GATEWAY PROTOCOL (EGP). In TCP/IP, a Network layer routing protocol used by routers that must communicate with routers in other autonomous systems. See also *Border Gateway Protocol*.

FAST ETHERNET. Term used to describe the standards being developed to define a 100-Mbps version of the CSMA/CD (Ethernet) standard.

FCS. Frame Check Sequence.

FDDI. Fiber Distributed Data Interface.

FIBER DISTRIBUTED DATA INTERFACE (FDDI). A form of local area network, developed by members of subcommittee X3T9.5 of ANSI, in which systems are connected to one another using point-to-point fiber-optic cable segments to form a ring topology. An FDDI data link supports a data rate of 100 Mbps.

FIBER-OPTIC CABLE. A cable that contains one or more thin cylinders of glass, each of which is called a *core*. Each core is surrounded by a concentric cylinder of glass called the *cladding*, which has a different refractive index than the core. The core of a fiber-optic cable carries signals in the form of a modulated light beam.

FIBER-OPTIC INTER-REPEATER LINK (FOIRL). A CSMA/CD (Ethernet) medium specification for a fiber-optic inter-repeater link cable segment. An FOIRL cable segment is used to implement a relatively long-distance, point-to-point connection between two repeaters. FOIRL cable segments can be up to 1000 meters in length, thus allowing longer distances to be spanned between repeaters than can be spanned using a coaxial cable segment.

FILE SERVER. A network system that implements software allowing other network systems to share the data files stored on the file server's disk units.

FILE TRANSFER PROTOCOL (FTP). In TCP/IP, a user-oriented Application service that allows the user to transfer files in both directions between the local system and a remote system. FTP uses the reliability controls provided by the TCP transport protocol to ensure that data is transferred reliably and that a transferred file is an exact copy of the original.

FILTERING BRIDGE. See *Bridge*.

4b/5b CODE. In the Fiber Distributed Data Interface (FDDI) specification, the scheme used to encode data for transmission in which 5-bit symbols correspond to 4-bit binary data values.

FRAME. An informal name for the protocol-data-unit (PDU) exchanged between peer Data Link layer entities or between peer Medium Access Control sublayer entities.

FRAME CHECK SEQUENCE (FCS). The field in a MAC frame used to implement an error detection mechanism and contains the results of a cyclical redundancy check (CRC) calculation performed on the bits contained in the frame.

FRAME RELAY. A data network that provides services similar to those provided by X.25 packet-switching networks. In a Frame Relay network, routing decisions are made in the Data Link layer rather than in the Network layer. Frame Relay networks support a variety of transmission speeds, but the target speed is generally in the neighborhood of the speeds supported by T1 facilities.

FRAME STATUS FIELD. A field in a MAC frame, used with some forms of medium access control, that contains information such as whether an error was detected, the address was recognized, or the frame was copied.

FTP. File Transfer Protocol.

GATEWAY. A device that operates at the level of the OSI model Application layer, used to interconnect networks that may have entirely different architectures. Different protocols can be used at any of the functional layers, with the gateway converting from one set of protocols to another. In some TCP/IP literature, the term gateway is sometimes used to refer to a device that performs the function of a router in a TCP/IP network. See *Router*.

GLOBALLY-ADMINISTERED MAC ADDRESSING. A form of LAN station addressing in which MAC addresses are 48 bits in length and whose values are globally unique. Address values are set by the organization that manufactures the network interface card (NIC). A manufacturer applies to the IEEE for a unique block of addresses and assigns to each NIC that it manufactures a unique MAC address from its assigned block. Sometimes called *Universal addressing*.

GROUP ADDRESS. A MAC address, whose first bit has the value 1, that identifies a particular group of stations.

GUARANTEED DELIVERY SERVICE. In the OSI model, a service provided by a layer or sublayer in which delivery is not explicitly confirmed but is guaranteed by the service provider.

HDLC. High-level Data Link Control.

HIGH-LEVEL DATA LINK CONTROL (HDLC). An international standard, bit-oriented, wide area network protocol that operates at the level of the OSI model Data Link layer.

HOST. In TCP/IP, a term used to refer to any end system attached to a TCP/IP network.

HUB. See *Concentrator*.

ICMP. Internet Control Message Protocol.

IDP. Internetwork Datagram Protocol.

IEEE. Institute of Electrical and Electronics Engineers.

I-FORMAT LLC-PDU. See *Information LLC-PDU*.

INDICATION SERVICE PRIMITIVE. In the OSI model, a service primitive issued by the lower-level service provider to notify a higher-level service requester that a significant event has occurred. See also *Confirm service primitive*, *Request service primitive*, and *Response service primitive*.

INDIVIDUAL ADDRESS. A MAC address, whose first bit has the value 0, that identifies a single station.

INFORMATION LLC-PDU. The primary function of an Information LLC-PDU (I-format LLC-PDU) is to carry user data. However, I-format LLC-PDUs sometimes also perform control functions. See *Logical-link-control-protocol-data-unit*.

INSTITUTE OF ELECTRICAL AND ELECTRONICS ENGINEERS (IEEE). A professional society whose members are individual engineers. The IEEE operates under ANSI guidelines when it develops standards. The IEEE Computer Society Local Network Committee (Project 802) has focused on standards related to local area networks and has produced a set of LAN standards that have been accepted by ISO as international standards.

INTEGRATED SERVICES DIGITAL NETWORK (ISDN). A public telecommunications network—typically administered by a common carrier or another telecommunications provider—that supplies end-to-end digital telecommunications services that can be used for both voice and nonvoice purposes.

INTERMEDIATE SYSTEM. A device in a communication system that may lie between two end systems and is concerned with performing routing and relaying functions. See also *End system*.

INTERMEDIATE SYSTEM TO INTERMEDIATE SYSTEM INTRA-DOMAIN ROUTING EXCHANGE PROTOCOL (ISO 10589). In the OSI architecture and in DECnet/OSI, a Network layer routing protocol that implements a link-state routing algorithm for automatically calculating optimum routes for relaying traffic from one router to another through an OSI network.

INTERNATIONAL ORGANIZATION FOR STANDARDIZATION (ISO). The dominant information technology standardization organization whose individual members consist of individual national standards organizations. The ISO member organization from the United States is the American National Standards Institute (ANSI). See also *American National Standards Institute*.

INTERNATIONAL TELECOMMUNICATION UNION-TELECOMMUNICATIONS (ITU-T). The leading organization involved in the development of standards relating to telephone and other telecommunications services. The ITU-T is the Telecommunications sector of the International Telecommunication Union, a body of the United Nations. (ITU-T standards for the information technology industry were formerly referred to using the old name International Telegraph and Telephone Consultative Committee (CCITT).)

INTERNET (1). Term used to refer to an enterprise network typically constructed using individual LAN data links interconnected using network interconnection devices and wide area network data links. In TCP/IP, a collection of individual hosts and data links interconnected using routers. Spelled with a lowercase i.

INTERNET (2). The world's largest TCP/IP network, which interconnects thousands of networks containing millions of computers in universities, national laboratories, and commercial organizations. Sometimes called the *Worldwide Internet*.

INTERNET CONTROL MESSAGE PROTOCOL (ICMP). In TCP/IP, a Network layer protocol that allows end systems to report on error conditions and to provide information about unexpected circumstances.

INTERNET PROTOCOL (IP). In TCP/IP, a connectionless Network layer protocol that provides a best-efforts datagram delivery service.

INTERNETWORK. See *Internet (1)*.

INTERNETWORK DATAGRAM PROTOCOL (IDP). In the Xerox Network System, a Network layer protocol that provides an unreliable, connectionless, datagram delivery service.

INTERNETWORK PACKET EXCHANGE (IPX) PROTOCOL. In NetWare, a Network layer protocol that provides an unreliable, connectionless, datagram delivery service.

IP. Internet Protocol.

IPX. Internetwork Packet Exchange protocol.

ISDN. Integrated Services Digital Network.

IS-IS PROTOCOL. Intermediate System to Intermediate System Intra-Domain Routing Exchange Protocol (ISO 10589).

ISO. International Organization for Standardization.

ISO 8073. See *Connection-Oriented Transport Protocol.*

ISO 8473. See *Protocol for Providing the Connectionless-Mode Network Service.*

ISO 8878. See *Use of X.25 to Provide the OSI Connection-Mode Network Service.*

ISO 9542. See *End System to Intermediate System Routing Exchange Protocol.*

ISO 10589. See *Intermediate System to Intermediate System Intra-Domain Routing Exchange Protocol.*

ITU. International Telecommunication Union.

ITU-T. Telecommunications sector of the International Telecommunications Union.

ITU-T RECOMMENDATION X.25. See *X.25.*

JAMMING SIGNAL. In the CSMA/CD (Ethernet) form of LAN data link technology, the signal that a station transmits when it detects a collision condition on the transmission medium. The jamming signal is sent to ensure that all stations know that a collision has occurred.

KERBEROS. An encryption-based security system that provides mutual authentication between a client component and a server component in a distributed computing environment. Kerberos also provides authorization services that can be used to control which clients are authorized to access which servers.

LAN. Local area network.

LAN DATA LINK. A multiaccess communication facility that consists of two or more devices connected using local area network technology.

LAN MANAGER. A family of network operating system software for personal computers codeveloped by Microsoft and IBM and marketed by Microsoft.

LAN SERVER. A family of network operating system software for personal computers codeveloped by Microsoft and IBM and marketed by IBM.

LAN STATION. See *Station.*

LAN SWITCH. A network interconnection device used to allow the network interface card in a computing device to be connected to one of multiple LAN transmission medium segments.

LANTASTIC. A family of network operating system software for personal computers marketed by Artisoft.

LINK-STATE ROUTING ALGORITHM. A form of distributed adaptive routing algorithm in which each router knows the complete topology of the network in terms of the existence of all other routers and the links between them. Each router broadcasts information about the routers to which it is directly attached and the status of the data links between them. A router constructs a map of the network from this information, consisting of a graph with routers as systems and links as edges. Routers are then able to calculate routes from this graph using the Dijkstra shortest-path algorithm. See also *Distance-vector routing algorithm.*

LLAP. LocalTalk Link Access Protocol.

LLC. Logical Link Control.

LLC-PDU. Logical-link-control-protocol-data-unit.

LLC-SDU. Logical-link-control-service-data-unit.

LOCAL AREA NETWORK (LAN). A term used to refer to a form of data link technology used to implement a high-speed, relatively short-distance form of computer communication. The term is also used to refer to a computer network constructed using LAN data link technology.

LOCALLY-ADMINISTERED MAC ADDRESSING. A form of LAN station addressing, in which MAC addresses are either 16 bits or 48 bits in length. With locally-administered addressing, the organization installing the network is responsible for assigning a unique MAC address to each network station. This is often done with DIP switches on the NIC, or it might be done using a software function. See *MAC address* and *Globally-administered MAC addressing*.

LOCALTALK. A low-speed form of LAN data link technology—part of Apple Computer's AppleTalk networking scheme—that uses a carrier sense multiple access with collision avoidance (CSMA/CA) form of medium access control. See also *AppleTalk* and *Carrier sense multiple access with collision avoidance*.

LOCALTALK CONNECTOR. A device used to connect a LocalTalk NIC to the original form of transmission medium defined by Apple for use with LocalTalk data links. See *LocalTalk* and *PhoneNet connector*.

LOCALTALK LINK ACCESS PROTOCOL (LLAP). The AppleTalk protocol that defines operations associated with LocalTalk LAN data links. See *LocalTalk* and *AppleTalk*.

LOGICAL LINK CONTROL (LLC) SUBLAYER. A sublayer of the Data Link layer, defined by IEEE 802.2 and ISO 8802-2, responsible for medium-independent data link functions. It allows the layer entity above to access the services of a LAN data link without regard to what form of physical transmission medium is used. In the context of the OSI model, the LLC sublayer provides services to the Network layer.

LOGICAL-LINK-CONTROL-PROTOCOL-DATA-UNIT (LLC-PDU). The data unit exchanged between peer Logical Link Control sublayer entities.

LOGICAL-LINK-CONTROL-SERVICE-DATA-UNIT (LLC-SDU). The data unit that a LAN data link user passes to the Logical Link Control sublayer when requesting a data transfer service.

MAC. Medium Access Control.

MAC ADDRESS. In the Medium Access Control sublayer of the IEEE/ISO/ANSI LAN architecture, a value that uniquely identifies an individual station that implements a single point of physical attachment to a LAN data link. Each station attached to a LAN data link must have a unique MAC address on that LAN data link. Sometimes called the *Station address*.

MAC FRAME. Informal name for the medium-access-control-protocol-data-unit (MAC-PDU). See also *Frame*.

MAC-PDU. Medium-access-control-protocol-data-unit.

MAC-SDU. Medium-access-control-service-data-unit.

MAIL APPLICATION PROGRAMMING INTERFACE (MAPI). An application programming interface (API) for electronic messaging developed by Microsoft.

MAN. Metropolitan Area Network.

MANAGEMENT INFORMATION BASE (MIB). In the ISO Common Management Information Protocol (CMIP), a repository, or database, that defines all the objects that can be managed in a network. Portions of the MIB are distributed among all the devices in the network—such as end systems, routers, terminal servers, etc.—that need to be managed.

MANCHESTER ENCODING. A form of data encoding in which each bit time that represents a data bit has a transition in the middle of the bit time.

MANUFACTURING AUTOMATION PROTOCOL (MAP). A group formed under the leadership of General Motors to address the networking needs of factory automation applications. See also *Technical and Office Protocols (TOP)*.

MAP. Manufacturing Automation Protocol.

MAPI. Mail Application Programming Interface.

MBPS. Megabits per second.

MEDIUM ACCESS CONTROL ADDRESS. See *MAC address*.

MEDIUM ACCESS CONTROL (MAC) SUBLAYER. A sublayer of the Data Link layer, defined by the IEEE/ISO/ANSI LAN architecture, concerned with how access to the physical transmission medium is managed. The MAC sublayer provides services to the Logical Link Control (LLC) sublayer.

MEDIUM-ACCESS-CONTROL-PROTOCOL-DATA-UNIT (MAC-PDU). The data unit exchanged between peer Medium Access Control (MAC) sublayer entities. Sometimes referred to by the informal name *MAC frame*.

MEDIUM-ACCESS-CONTROL-SERVICE-DATA-UNIT (MAC-SDU). The data unit that a user of the Medium Access Control (MAC) sublayer service passes to the MAC sublayer when requesting a data transfer service.

MEDIUM ATTACHMENT UNIT. Optional component defined in the IEEE/ISO CSMA/CD (Ethernet) standard that handles all functions dependent on the transmission medium being used. When used, it is often implemented in a device called a *Transceiver*.

MEDIUM INTERFACE CABLE. Used with some forms of LAN data link technology to attach the network interface card (NIC) to the transmission medium.

MEDIUM INTERFACE CONNECTOR (MIC). On a Fiber Distributed Data Interface (FDDI) LAN data link, the physical connector that allows a port on a station to be connected to a full duplex transmission medium segment. See *MIC type A*, *MIC type B*, *MIC type M*, and *MIC type S*.

MEDIUM SPECIFICATION. The part of a local area network standard that defines for a particular type of transmission medium the physical and electrical characteristics of the transmission medium and the method by which a station is attached to the transmission medium.

METROPOLITAN AREA NETWORK (MAN). A form of networking technology, related to LAN technology, that spans distances up to about 20 or 30 miles. Metropolitan area networks are sometimes used to bridge the gap between wide area networks and local area networks.

MIB. Management Information Base.

MIC. Medium interface connector. See *MIC type A*, *MIC type B*, *MIC type M*, and *MIC type S*.

MIC TYPE A. In a Fiber Distributed Data Interface (FDDI) station or concentrator, a medium interface connector that is the *input* of the path for the primary ring. See *Medium interface connector*.

MIC TYPE B. In a Fiber Distributed Data Interface (FDDI) station or concentrator, a medium interface connector that is the *output* of the path for the primary ring. See *Medium interface connector*.

MIC TYPE M. In a Fiber Distributed Data Interface (FDDI) concentrator, a medium interface connector used to connect the concentrator to a cable segment that leads to a MIC of type S, which is generally in a lower-level single-attachment station or concentrator. See *Medium interface connector*, *MIC type S*, *Single-attachment concentrator*, *Single-attachment station*.

MIC TYPE S. In a Fiber Distributed Data Interface (FDDI) single-attachment station or concentrator, a medium interface connector used to connect the station or concentrator to a cable segment that leads to a MIC of type M, which is generally in a higher-level concentrator. See *Medium interface connector, MIC type M, Single-attachment concentrator, Single-attachment station.*

MID-SPLIT BROADBAND. A broadband network configuration in which the cable bandwidth is divided into two channels, each using a different range of frequencies. One channel is used to transmit signals and the other is used to receive.

MODEM. A device that implements *modulator-demodulator* functions to convert between digital data and analog signals.

MODULATION TECHNIQUE. Signaling technique in which a data signal is superimposed on a carrier signal by varying the carrier signal's amplitude, frequency, or phase.

MULTILEVEL DUOBINARY SIGNALING. A signaling system used in networks that conform to the IEEE/ISO Token Bus standard that allows for three distinct amplitude levels symbolically represented as {0}, {2}, and {4}. Nondata bits are represented by the signal value {2}, 0 bits by {0}, and 1 bits by {4}.

MULTIPORT REPEATER. A repeater in a network that conforms to the IEEE/ISO CSMA/CD (Ethernet) standard to which individual local area network stations are attached, each with its own cable segment.

NAC. Null-attachment concentrator.

NAME BINDING PROTOCOL (NBP). In AppleTalk, a Transport layer protocol that provides a directory service in which names can be assigned to objects, such as application programs and services available over the network. The service translates between names and the network addresses of the systems associated with those names.

NAMED PIPES. An application programming interface for interprocess communication, jointly developed by IBM and Microsoft, in which a data structure called a *named pipe* is referenced by function calls to send data between a pair of communicating processes.

NBP. Name Binding Protocol.

NCB. Network Control Block.

NCP. NetWare Core Protocol.

NETBEUI. A name sometimes used to refer to the Transport layer protocol used in conjunction with NetBIOS. See *NetBIOS.*

NETBIOS. An application programming interface (API) and Transport layer protocol, developed by IBM and Microsoft for use in the personal computer networking environment. The NetBIOS protocol operates in the OSI model Transport layer and provides data delivery services to application programs and higher-level protocols. The NetBIOS Transport protocol is sometimes called NetBEUI after the program module that first implemented it. NetBIOS has become a de facto Transport layer standard for personal computer LAN communication, and NetBIOS services are provided by a wide variety of different networking software subsystems.

NETWARE. A family of network operating system software for personal computers marketed by Novell.

NETWARE CORE PROTOCOL (NCP). In NetWare, a Transport layer protocol that handles all client requests for services from a server and allows users to access NetWare application-level services.

NETWARE LOADABLE MODULE (NLM). In NetWare, an extension added to the base NetWare software that runs in a NetWare server.

NETWORK ARCHITECTURE. A comprehensive plan and a set of rules that governs the design and operation of the hardware and software components used to create computer networks. Network architectures define sets of communication protocols that govern how communication takes place.

NETWORK-AWARE APPLICATION. An application program that explicitly invokes network communication services.

NETWORK CONTROL BLOCK (NCB). The control block used to implement the NetBIOS application programming interface. See *NetBIOS*.

NETWORK FILE SYSTEM (NFS). In TCP/IP, an application service that provides authorized users with access to files located on remote systems. System administrators generally designate one or more systems in the network as NFS servers that make certain designated directories on their disk storage devices available to other systems. A user accesses an NFS-mounted directory in the same manner as accessing a directory on a local disk.

NETWORK INFORMATION CENTER (NIC). Organization responsible for administration of the Internet. See *Internet (2)*.

NETWORKING SOFTWARE. Software that implements high-level networking functions that end users employ for doing useful work. In the personal computer environment, networking software is often implemented in subsystems called network operating systems.

NETWORK INTERFACE CARD (NIC). A circuit board installed in a computing device used to attach the device to a network. A NIC performs the hardware functions required to provide a computing device with physical communication capabilities.

NETWORK LAYER. Layer three of the OSI model. The Network layer is concerned with making routing decisions and relaying data from one system to another through the network. The facilities provided by the Network layer supply a service that higher layers employ for moving data units, often called *packets*, from one end system to another, where the packets may flow through any number of intermediate systems.

NETWORK OPERATING SYSTEM. A software product, typically used in the personal computer environment, that provides high-level networking functions to users and application programs.

NETWORK-PROTOCOL-DATA-UNIT (NPDU). The data unit exchanged by peer Network layer entities.

NETWORK SERVICE PROTOCOL (NSP). In DECnet Phase IV, a Transport layer protocol that provides a reliable, sequenced, connection-oriented, end-to-end data delivery service.

NETWORK-TRANSPARENT APPLICATION. An application program not specifically designed to take advantage of networking facilities.

NFS. Network File System.

NIC. Network interface card or, in the Internet, the Network Information Center.

NLM. NetWare Loadable Module.

NONCONFIRMED SERVICE. In the OSI model, a service provided by a layer or sublayer entity in which the service requester is not informed of the success or failure of the service request. With such a service, any required error handling must be provided by higher-level layers.

NOVELL NETWARE. See *NetWare*.

NPDU. Network-protocol-data-unit.

NSP. Network Services Protocol.

NULL-ATTACHMENT CONCENTRATOR (NAC). On a Fiber Distributed Data Interface (FDDI) LAN data link, a concentrator that contains only medium interface connectors (MICs) of type S for connection to single-attachment stations. See *Medium interface connector*, *MIC type S*, and *Single-attachment station*.

100BASE-X. See *Fast Ethernet*.

OPEN SHORTEST PATH FIRST (OSPF) PROTOCOL. In TCP/IP, a Network layer routing protocol that operates within a single autonomous system and implements a link-state routing algorithm.

OPEN SOFTWARE FOUNDATION (OSF). A nonprofit organization established by a number of computer manufacturers to develop a common foundation for open systems computing.

OSF. Open Software Foundation.

OSF DCE. See *Distributed Computing Environment*.

OSI. Open systems interconnection.

OSI MODEL. The seven-layer *Reference Model for Open Systems Interconnection*, developed by members of the International Organization for Standardization (ISO) and documented in ISO 7498, that provides a common basis for the coordination of standards development for the purpose of systems interconnection.

OSPF. Open Shortest Path First.

PACKET. Informal name for the network protocol-data-unit (NPDU).

PACKET EXCHANGE PROTOCOL (PEP). In the Xerox Network System, a Transport layer protocol that provides application programs with an unreliable, connectionless, end-to-end data transport service.

PACKET SWITCHING. A Network layer mechanism in which data is routed and relayed through the network in units called *packets*. Each packet carries its own addressing information and is typically handled by the network independently of other packets.

PARALLEL PORT. A communication device in a computer system that allows data to be transmitted and received an octet at a time with a separate circuit used for each bit.

PARALLEL PORT NETWORK INTERFACE CARD (NIC). An external NIC that attaches to a computing system's parallel port. Such a NIC allows a notebook PC that has limited expansion capability to be connected to a conventional LAN data link in the same manner as a desktop computer.

PATHWORKS. A family of network operating system software for personal computers marketed by Digital Equipment Corporation.

PCI. Protocol-control-information.

PCMCIA. Personal Computer Memory Card International Association.

PCMCIA NETWORK INTERFACE CARD (NIC). An external NIC that attaches to a computing system's Personal Computer Memory Card International Association (PCMCIA) expansion slot. PCMCIA slots are often used on notebook personal computers to allow credit-card sized peripherals to be attached to the personal computer.

PC NETWORK—BASEBAND. An IBM LAN data link hardware product line that implements a CSMA/CD form of medium access control using baseband transmission.

PC NETWORK—BROADBAND. An IBM LAN data link hardware product line that implements a CSMA/CD form of medium access control method using broadband transmission.

PDU. Protocol-data-unit.

PEER-TO-PEER PROTOCOLS. See *Protocol*.

PEP. Packet Exchange Protocol.

PHONENET CONNECTOR. A connector used to connect a LocalTalk network interface card (NIC) to a LocalTalk LAN data link implemented using twisted-pair telephone wiring. Sometimes called a *PhoneTalk connector*. See also *LocalTalk connector*.

PHYSICAL LAYER. Layer one of the OSI model. The *Physical* layer is responsible for the transmission of signals, such as electrical signals, optical signals, or radio signals, between communicating machines. Physical layer mechanisms in each of the communicating machines typically control the generation and detection of signals interpreted as 0 bits and 1 bits.

PING. In TCP/IP, an Application service that can be used to test for connectivity between any two systems in the network.

POINT-TO-POINT LINK CABLE SEGMENT. A transmission medium segment in a local area network that conforms to the IEEE/ISO CSMA/CD (Ethernet) standard that serves only to link two repeaters and to which no stations are attached.

POINT-TO-POINT PROTOCOL (PPP). An adaptation of HDLC that grew out of work done by the Internet Engineering Task Force and that improves on HDLC by adding the Network layer protocol identification mechanism required for enterprise networking. The Point-to-Point protocol allows a point-to-point connection to be established between two network devices that allows frames associated with multiple Network layer protocols to flow over data links without interfering with one another.

PORT. A communication device in a computer system that can be used to transmit and receive data. A data structure in a network software subsystem used to control data transmission activities.

PORTAL. Term used to refer to each end of an encapsulation facility. Two portals can be viewed as implementing a tunnel that transports messages through a network conforming to a foreign network architecture. See *Encapsulation facility*.

POSTAL, TELEGRAPH, AND TELEPHONE ADMINISTRATION (PTT). A public organization in many countries that provides communications services to the general public in a similar manner to a common carrier in the United States.

PPP. Point-to-Point Protocol.

PREAMBLE. A field used with some forms of medium access control that precedes the start frame delimiter field of the MAC frame and is used for synchronization purposes.

PREDECESSOR STATION. In a network that conforms to the IEEE/ISO Token Bus standard, the station on the network having the next higher MAC address from which a station receives frames.

PRESENTATION LAYER. Layer six of the OSI model. The Presentation layer is the lowest layer interested in the *meaning* of the streams of bits exchanged between communicating programs and deals with preserving the *information content* of data transmitted over the network. The Presentation layer in the two communicating systems negotiates a common syntax for transferring the messages exchanged by two communicating programs and ensures that one system does not need to care what form of internal data representation the other system is using.

PRIMITIVE. See *Service primitive*.

PRINT SERVER. A network system that implements software allowing other network systems to share the print server's printers.

PROJECT 802. A committee of the IEEE responsible for the development of an architecture and standards for local area networking. IEEE Project 802 LAN standards have been accepted as international standards by ISO.

PROPAGATION TIME. The length of time it takes a MAC frame to travel between two stations.

PROTOCOL. A set of rules or conventions that define the formats of data units handled by a particular layer or sublayer entity and the data flows that take place in exchanging data units between peer layer or sublayer entities.

PROTOCOL-CONTROL-INFORMATION (PCI). Control information, taking the form of a header and sometimes also a trailer, that a layer or sublayer entity attaches to the data in a service-data-unit to create one or more protocol-data-units.

PROTOCOL-DATA-UNIT (PDU). The data unit that a layer or sublayer entity transmits across the network to a peer layer or sublayer entity.

PROTOCOL FOR PROVIDING THE CONNECTIONLESS-MODE NETWORK SERVICE (ISO 8473). In the OSI architecture and in DECnet/OSI, a Network layer protocol, often called the ISO Internet protocol, that provides an unreliable, datagram data delivery service.

PTT. Postal, Telegraph, and Telephone Administration.

RARP. Reverse Address Resolution Protocol.

REDIRECTOR. A software function in networking software that intercepts all I/O function calls and checks to see if the call applies to a resource under the control of a server rather than to a local resource. The redirector handles the network communication required to handle I/O requests for access to remote resources.

REMOTE PROCEDURE CALL (RPC) FACILITY. A facility for interprocess communication in which an application program issues function and procedure calls by name to program modules that may reside in other network systems. Arguments and results are automatically transmitted through the network transparently to the application program.

REPEATER. A device that operates at the level of the Physical layer and is used to relay signals between two or more cable segments that implement a bus- or tree-structured LAN data link.

REQUEST FOR COMMENTS (RFC). Documentation of the operation of the protocols making up the TCP/IP protocol suite. RFCs are available in machine-readable form on the Internet or in hard-copy form from the Internet Network Information Center (NIC).

REQUEST SERVICE PRIMITIVE. In the OSI model, a service primitive issued by a service requester to request that a particular service be performed by a lower-level layer and to pass parameters needed to fully specify the requested service. See also *Confirm service primitive*, *Indication service primitive*, and *Response service primitive*.

RESPONSE. A logical-link-control-protocol-data-unit (LLC-PDU) sent by an LLC sublayer entity in reply to a command. See also *Command*.

RESPONSE SERVICE PRIMITIVE. In the OSI model, a service primitive issued by the higher-level service requester to acknowledge or complete some procedure previously invoked by the lower-level service provider through an *indication* service primitive. See also *Confirm service primitive*, *Indication service primitive*, and *Request service primitive*.

REVERSE ADDRESS RESOLUTION PROTOCOL (RARP). In TCP/IP, a Network layer protocol that allows an end system that does not yet have its network address to obtain it. RARP is typically used to support workstations and intelligent terminals that do not have their own disk storage.

RFC. Request for Comments.

RING TOPOLOGY. A network configuration in which the cabling forms a loop, with a simple, point-to-point connection attaching each system to the next around the ring. Each system acts as a repeater for all signals it receives and retransmits them to the next system in the ring at their original signal strength.

RIP. Routing Information Protocol.

RLOGIN. In TCP/IP, an Application service that allows a user at a UNIX system to log into some other UNIX system. See also *Telnet*.

ROUTER. A network device that sends and receives Network protocol-data-units (packets) and relays packets from one device to another through the network. Sometimes called an *intermediate system*. In TCP/IP literature, a router is sometimes called a *gateway*.

ROUTING INFORMATION PROTOCOL (RIP). In TCP/IP, in NetWare, and in the Xerox Network system, a Network layer routing protocol that allows routers to communicate with one another for the purposes of determining routes and for relaying user traffic from one router to another through the network.

ROUTING TABLE MAINTENANCE PROTOCOL (RTMP). In AppleTalk, a Transport layer routing protocol that allows routers to communicate with one another for the purposes of determining routes and for relaying user traffic from one router to another through the network.

RPC. Remote procedure call.

RSH. In TCP/IP, an Application service that allows the user to issue, at the local system, a command to request an operating system function or to request the execution of an application program on some other system in the network.

RS-232-D. An EIA standard for asynchronous data communication. See also *Asynchronous transmission*.

RTMP. Routing Table Maintenance Protocol.

SAC. Single-attachment concentrator.

SAP. Service-access-point or Service Advertising Protocol.

SAP ADDRESS. In the OSI model, a value representing a point of access into a layer. In the Logical Link Control sublayer of the IEEE/ISO/ANSI LAN architecture, a value that represents a particular mechanism, process, or protocol requesting LLC sublayer services. Each mechanism, process, or protocol concurrently using the services of the LLC sublayer in a given station must use a different SAP address.

SAS. Single-attachment station.

SDU. Service-data-unit.

SEGMENTATION FUNCTION. In the OSI model, a function performed by a layer or sublayer entity that creates two or more protocol-data-units from a single service-data-unit.

SEQUENCED PACKET EXCHANGE (SPX) PROTOCOL. In NetWare, a Transport layer protocol that provides application programs with a reliable, sequenced, connection-oriented data transport service.

SEQUENCED PACKET PROTOCOL (SPP). In the Xerox Network System, a Transport layer protocol that provides application programs with a reliable, sequenced, connection-oriented data transport service.

SERIAL PORT. A communication device in a computer system that allows data to be transmitted and received a single bit at a time.

SERVER. A computing system in a network that runs software that provides services to other computing systems. In client/server computing, an application component that provides a service for one or more other application components operating in the role of clients. See *Client* and *Client/server computing*.

SERVER MESSAGE BLOCK (SMB). A term that refers to an API that application programs use to request high-level application services and also to a protocol for providing those services. The SMB services and protocol were originally developed for networking software that operated in the MS-DOS environment. Many newer networking software subsystems for the OS/2, Windows, and Windows/NT environments continue to support the SMB interface and protocol.

SERVICE-ACCESS-POINT (SAP). In the OSI model, the point at which the services of a layer are provided. Each service-access-point has a SAP address, by which the particular entity employing a layer service can be differentiated from all other entities that might also be able to use that layer service. In the IEEE/ISO/ANSI LAN architecture, the Logical Link Control sublayer implements service-access-points that identify each user of the LAN data link in a particular station.

SERVICE-ACCESS-POINT ADDRESS. See *Service-access-point* and *SAP address*.

SERVICE ADVERTISING PROTOCOL (SAP). In NetWare, a Transport layer broadcast protocol that NetWare servers employ to inform NetWare clients of the available services.

SERVICE-DATA-UNIT (SDU). In the OSI model, the data unit that a layer or sublayer entity passes down to the adjacent layer or sublayer below it in requesting a data transmission service.

SERVICE PRIMITIVE. In the OSI model, a description of the semantics (not coding syntax) of one element of a layer or sublayer service. A particular service primitive can be issued by a service requester to a service provider or by a service provider to a service requester.

SERVICE PROVIDER. In the OSI model, a layer or sublayer entity that provides a service to an adjacent layer or sublayer entity above it.

SERVICE REQUESTER. In the OSI model, a layer or sublayer entity that requests a service of an adjacent layer or sublayer entity below it.

SESSION LAYER. Layer five of the OSI model. The Session layer is responsible for organizing the dialog between two communicating programs and for managing the data exchanges between them. It imposes a structure on the interaction between two communicating programs and defines three types of dialogs: two-way simultaneous interaction, where both programs can send and receive concurrently; two-way alternate interaction, where the programs take turns sending and receiving; and one-way interaction, where one program sends and the other only receives. In addition to organizing the dialog, Session layer services include establishing synchronization points within the dialog, allowing a dialog to be interrupted, and resuming a dialog from a synchronization point.

S-FORMAT LLC-PDU. See *Supervisory LLC-PDU*.

SIMPLE MAIL TRANSFER PROTOCOL (SMTP). In TCP/IP, an Application protocol used for the transfer of electronic mail messages. SMTP is designed to be used by electronic mail software that provides the user with access to messaging facilities.

SIMPLE NETWORK MANAGEMENT PROTOCOL (SNMP). In TCP/IP, an application protocol that defines the formats of network management messages and the rules by which the messages are exchanged.

SINGLE-ATTACHMENT CONCENTRATOR (SAC). On a Fiber Distributed Data Interface (FDDI) LAN data link, a device with two or more medium interface connectors (MICs). One of the MICs is of type S for connection to a concentrator, and one or more MICs are of type M for connection to single-attachment stations. See *Medium interface connector*, *MIC type S*, *MIC type M*, and *Single-attachment station*.

SINGLE-ATTACHMENT STATION (SAS). On a Fiber Distributed Data Interface (FDDI) LAN data link, a station with a single medium interface connector (MIC) of type S. A single-attachment station is typically connected, via a single transmission medium segment, to a concentrator implementing a MIC of type M. See *Medium interface connector*, *MIC type M*, and *MIC type S*.

SLOT TIME. The length of time it takes for a signal to travel the maximum allowable distance from one end of the network to the other and back again.

SMB. Server Message Block.

SMDS. Switched Multi-Megabit Data Service.

SMTP. Simple Mail Transfer Protocol.

SNA. Systems Network Architecture.

SNAP. Subnetwork Access Protocol.

SNAP LLC-PDU. Subnetwork-access-protocol-logical-link-control-protocol-data-unit.

SNAP PDU. See *SNAP LLC-PDU*.

SNMP. Simple Network Management Protocol.

SOCKETS INTERFACE. A networking application programming interface initially developed for the variation of the UNIX operating system developed by the University of California at Berkeley (BSD UNIX). By using the Sockets interface, two application programs, one running in the local system and another running in the remote system, can communicate with one another in a standardized manner.

SONET. Physical layer communication facilities, using fiber optics, on which broadband ISDN services are based. OC-1 SONET provides a 51-Mbps data rate, OC-3 SONET provides a 155-Mbps data rate, OC-12 SONET provides a 622-Mbps data rate, and OC-48 SONET provides a 2.4-Gbps data rate.

SOURCE MAC ADDRESS. Address identifying the station that originated a MAC frame. See also *MAC address* and *Station*.

SOURCE ROUTING BRIDGE. A bridge used to form an extended LAN consisting of a structure in which there can be more than one path between any two LAN stations. With source routing bridges, each station is expected to know the route over which to send each data unit. If a station does not know the route, or if a previously known route is no longer active, the station sends out route discovery data units over the bridges and then determines from the responses that come back the appropriate route to use. Source routing bridges are typically used only with Token Ring LAN data links. See *Extended LAN* and *Transparent bridge*.

SOURCE-SERVICE-ACCESS-POINT (SSAP). A service-access-point that identifies the originator of a data unit. See *Service-access-point*.

SPANNING TREE. A graph structure that includes all the bridges and stations on an extended LAN but in which there is never more than one active path connecting any two stations. See *Bridge*, *Transparent bridge*, and *Extended LAN*.

SPANNING TREE BRIDGE. See *Transparent bridge*.

SPP. Sequenced Packet Protocol.

SPX. Sequenced Packet Exchange protocol.

SSAP ADDRESS. In the IEEE/ISO/ANSI LAN architecture, an address that identifies the service-access-point (SAP) responsible for originating the LLC-PDU.

START FRAME DELIMITER. A MAC frame field that contains a particular bit pattern and indicates the beginning of a frame.

STAR TOPOLOGY. A network configuration in which there is a central point to which a group of systems are directly connected. With the star topology, all transmissions from one system to another pass through the central point, which may consist of a device that plays a role in managing and controlling communication.

START-STOP TRANSMISSION. See *Asynchronous transmission.*

STATION. A collection of hardware, firmware, and software that appears to other stations as a single functional and addressable unit on a LAN data link. A station implements a single physical point of connection to the transmission medium. A station is a collection of one or more hardware and/or software components that performs the functions of the LLC sublayer, the MAC sublayer, and the Physical layer.

STATION ADDRESS. See *MAC address.*

STATION MANAGEMENT. A function defined by some forms of medium access control responsible for control functions, such as resetting a MAC sublayer entity and specifying values for constants used in the network.

SUBNET. In TCP/IP, the use of a single network identifier in multiple networks. When using subnetting, some of the high-order bits in the host identifier portion of the address are used to identify individual subnets. A value called a *subnet mask* is used by each system to identify how the internet address bits should be interpreted in a particular network.

SUBNETWORK. A collection of systems attached to a single virtual transmission medium so that each system in the subnetwork is one "hop" from any other system on that subnetwork. A *hop* is defined as a traversal from one system to another across a single data link, as viewed from the perspective of software operating in the OSI Network layer.

SUBNETWORK ACCESS PROTOCOL (SNAP). A protocol, defined by IEEE, that implements a mechanism for distinguishing LLC-PDUs carrying packets associated with one Network layer protocol from LLC-PDUs carrying packets associated with some other Network layer protocol.

SUBNETWORK-ACCESS-PROTOCOL-LOGICAL-LINK-CONTROL-PROTOCOL-DATA-UNIT (SNAP LLC-PDU). Data unit, sometimes called a SNAP PDU, exchanged by peer entities implementing the IEEE Subnetwork Access Protocol. SNAP LLC-PDUs carry SSAP and DSAP address values of hexadecimal 'AA'. See *Subnetwork Access Protocol.*

SUBVECTOR. In IBM Token-Ring Network MAC control frames, a field, formatted with a 1- or 3-octet length field followed by data, carried within a vector in the frame Information field. See *Vector.*

SUCCESSOR STATION. In a network that conforms to the IEEE/ISO Token Bus standard, the station with the next lower MAC address to which a station transmits data units.

SUPERVISORY LLC-PDU. Supervisory LLC-PDUs (S-format LLC-PDUs) are used to carry information necessary to control the operation of the LLC sublayer protocol. See *Logical-link-control-protocol-data-unit.*

SWITCH. See *LAN switch.*

SWITCHED MULTI-MEGABIT DATA SERVICE (SMDS). A high-speed wide area network packet-switching service built on top of broadband ISDN services to provide services similar to an X.25 network.

SYSTEM. Any computing device attached to a network that implements one or more stations for communicating with other systems. In the OSI model, a set of one or more computers, the associated software, peripherals, terminals, human operators, physical processes, transfer means, etc., that forms an autonomous whole capable of performing information processing and/or information transfer.

SYSTEMS NETWORK ARCHITECTURE (SNA). IBM's own proprietary network architecture, widely used in the IBM large-system environment. Many networks built using IBM equipment and software conform to SNA specifications. SNA defines specifications for constructing the hardware and software components that make up an SNA network and include definitions of the formats of data units and the protocols that govern how data units flow over the network. SNA defines two forms of networking: *SNA subarea networking and Advanced Peer-to-Peer Networking (APPN)*.

T1. A digital telecommunication facility, available from telecommunications providers, that supports a bit rate of 1.544 Mbps.

T3. A digital telecommunication facility, available from telecommunications providers, that supports a bit rate of 45 Mbps.

TCP. Transmission Control Protocol.

TCP/IP. Transmission Control Protocol/Internet Protocol.

TECHNICAL AND OFFICE PROTOCOLS (TOP). A group, sponsored by the Boeing Company, whose purpose is to address the networking needs of engineering and general office applications. See also *Manufacturing Automation Protocol*.

TELNET. In TCP/IP, an Application service that allows a user at the local system to log into any type of remote TCP/IP system. See also *Rlogin*.

10BASE5. Shorthand notation for an IEEE/ISO CSMA/CD (Ethernet) medium specification in which the data rate is 10 Mbps, the transmission technique is baseband, and the maximum cable segment length is 500 meters. 10BASE5 is the CSMA/CD medium specification based on the original Ethernet Version 2 specification and specifies the use of 50-ohm, 10-mm coaxial cable often called *Ethernet cable* or *thick Ethernet cable*.

10BASE-T. Shorthand notation for an IEEE/ISO CSMA/CD (Ethernet) medium specification in which the data rate is 10 Mbps, the transmission technique is baseband, and the maximum cable segment length is 100 meters. 10BASE-T is the CSMA/CD medium specification that specifies the use of twisted-pair cable.

10BASE2. Shorthand notation for an IEEE/ISO CSMA/CD (Ethernet) medium specification in which the data rate is 10 Mbps, the transmission technique is baseband, and the maximum cable segment length is 185 meters. 10BASE2 is the CSMA/CD medium specification that specifies the use of 50-ohm, 5-mm coaxial cable, sometimes called *ThinWire* or *ThinNet* cable.

10BROAD36. Shorthand notation for an IEEE/ISO CSMA/CD (Ethernet) medium specification in which the data rate is 10 Mbps, the transmission technique is broadband, and the maximum cable segment length is 3600 meters. 10BROAD36 is the CSMA/CD medium specification that specifies the use of 75-ohm coaxial cable typically used to carry cable television signals.

TFTP. Trivial File Transfer Protocol.

THICK ETHERNET CABLE. See *Ethernet cable*.

ThinWire Cable. Informal name for the 50-ohm, 5-mm coaxial cable specified in the IEEE/ISO CSMA/CD (Ethernet) 10BASE2 medium specification.

Time-Sequence Diagram. A graphical form of documentation used in ISO standard service definitions that describes the sequence in which service primitives are issued.

TLAP. TokenTalk Link Access Protocol.

TLI. Transport Layer Interface.

Token. A special data unit, used with Token Bus, Token Ring, and FDDI LAN data links, passed from station to station to control access to the transmission medium. Only a station that possesses the token is allowed to transmit MAC frames.

Token Bus. A LAN data link technology, defined by IEEE 802.4 and ISO 8802-4, in which systems are connected to a common transmission medium in a similar manner to an Ethernet LAN. A system is allowed to transmit only when it has a special data unit, called the *token*, passed from one system to another.

Token Ring. A LAN data link technology, defined by IEEE 802.5 and ISO 8802-5, in which systems are connected to one another using point-to-point twisted-pair cable segments to form a ring structure. A system is allowed to transmit only when it has the token, which is passed from one system to another around the ring.

Token-Ring Network. The name of IBM's implementation of the IEEE/ISO Token Ring standard.

TokenTalk Link Access Protocol (TLAP). In AppleTalk, the data link protocol that provides Token Ring LAN support. Standard IEEE/ISO Logical Link Control (LLC) interfaces and data formats are used to provide the connectionless type 1 LLC service.

TOP. Technical and Office Protocols.

Topology. Characteristic of a communication network that concerns both the *physical* configuration of the cabling used to interconnect communicating systems and the *logical* way in which systems view the structure of the network. See *Bus topology*, *Ring topology*, and *Star topology*.

Transceiver. Device that implements the medium attachment unit component defined by the IEEE/ISO CSMA/CD (Ethernet) standard used to attach a station to the transmission medium.

Transmission Control Protocol (TCP). In TCP/IP, a connection-oriented Transport layer protocol that provides for reliable, sequenced, stream data delivery.

Transmission Control Protocol/Internet Protocol (TCP/IP). A set of communication protocols that grew out of a research project that was funded by the United States Department of Defense. The TCP/IP networking scheme implements a peer-to-peer client/server architecture. Any computing system in the network can run TCP/IP server software and can provide services to any other computing system that runs complementary TCP/IP client software.

Transmission Medium. The cable or other physical circuit used to interconnect systems in a network.

Transmission Technique. The type of signaling used to exchange information over a physical transmission medium. See also *Baseband transmission* and *Broadband transmission*.

Transparent Bridge. A bridge used to form an extended LAN consisting of a tree structure in which only one active path connects any two stations in the extended LAN. Stations on the interconnected LANs are not aware of the presence of transparent bridges. Transparent bridges learn appropriate routes for messages by observing transmissions that take place on the LANs to which they are connected and forward messages that they receive to the opposite network when required. See *Extended LAN* and *Source routing bridge*.

TRANSPORT LAYER. Layer four of the OSI model. The Transport layer is the lowest layer required only in two communicating end systems. The Transport layer forms the uppermost layer of a reliable end-to-end data transport service and hides from the higher layers all the details concerning the actual moving of streams of bits from one computer to another. The functions performed in the Transport layer include end-to-end integrity controls used to recover from lost, out-of-sequence, or duplicate messages.

TRANSPORT LAYER INTERFACE (TLI). A networking application programming interface (API) that was originally defined for use with AT&T System V UNIX and is now implemented by a variety of networking software subsystems, especially in the TCP/IP environment.

TRIVIAL FILE TRANSFER PROTOCOL (TFTP). In TCP/IP, a simple file transfer service that implements its own reliability controls and can run on top of any type of transport service. UDP is used by most TFTP implementations. The end-to-end reliability controls that TFTP implements take the form of a message sequencing system, timeouts, and retransmissions to ensure that files are transferred intact. TFTP is generally used only by system software that performs such functions as downline loading of program code; it is not intended to be employed directly by end users.

TRUNK CABLE. Used in some forms of medium access control to refer to a transmission medium cable segment.

TRUNK COUPLING UNIT. Used with some forms of medium access control to connect a station to the transmission medium.

TUNNEL. Term used in reference to an encapsulation facility. An encapsulation facility can be viewed as two portals that implement a tunnel that transports messages through a network conforming to a foreign network architecture. See *Encapsulation facility.*

TWISTED-PAIR CABLE. A cable that contains one or more pairs of insulated copper conductors twisted around one another to provide a degree of protection from electrical interference.

TYPE 1 LLC OPERATION. Form of Logical Link Control sublayer protocol operation that provides the connectionless LLC service. See *Connectionless LLC service.*

TYPE 2 LLC OPERATION. Form of Logical Link Control sublayer protocol operation that provides the connection-oriented LLC service. See *Connection-oriented LLC service.*

TYPE 3 LLC OPERATION. Form of Logical Link Control sublayer protocol operation that provides the acknowledged connectionless LLC service. See *Acknowledged connectionless LLC service.*

UDP. User Datagram Protocol.

U-FORMAT LLC-PDU. See *Unnumbered LLC-PDU.*

UNIVERSAL ADDRESSING. See *Globally-administered MAC addressing.*

UNNUMBERED LLC-PDU. Logical-link-control-protocol-data-units sometimes used to carry data and are sometimes used for special functions, such as performing initialization procedures and invoking diagnostic sequences. See *Logical-link-control-protocol-data-unit.*

USE OF X.25 TO PROVIDE THE OSI CONNECTION-MODE NETWORK SERVICE (ISO 8878). In the OSI architecture and in DECnet/OSI, a Network layer protocol that provides the OSI connection-oriented Network service.

USER DATAGRAM PROTOCOL (UDP). In TCP/IP, a Transport layer protocol that provides a best-efforts, connectionless datagram delivery service.

VECTOR. In IBM Token-Ring Network MAC control frames, a frame Information field formatted with a 2-octet length field followed by data. See also *Subvector.*

VENDOR INDEPENDENT MESSAGING (VIM). An application programming interface (API) for electronic messaging jointly developed by Lotus, Novell, Apple, and Borland.

VIM. Vendor Independent Messaging.

VINES. A family of network operating system software marketed by Banyan Systems.

VistaLAN/1. A family of LAN products, available from Allen-Bradley, that uses a token bus form of medium access control. VistaLAN/1 products use broadband transmission over a bus- or tree-structured network.

WAN. Wide area network.

WIDE AREA NETWORK (WAN). Networks that tie together computing devices widely separated geographically.

WIRELESS TRANSMISSION. Form of data communication in which infrared or radio signals are used to exchange information without requiring devices to be physically interconnected using cabling.

WIRING CLOSET. A room or cabinet that serves as a central point from which cables lead to individual local area network stations. See also *Equipment room*.

WORLDWIDE INTERNET. See *Internet (2)*.

XEROX NETWORK SYSTEM (XNS). A network architecture for internetworking, defined by Xerox, that allows for the interconnection of individual Ethernet LAN data links and for connecting Ethernet LANs with packet-switched public data networks. The XNS architecture has been published by Xerox and has been made generally available to the public. The XNS architecture is one of the earliest of the published architectures for internetworking, and a number of local area network vendors have adopted forms of the XNS protocols for use in their own products.

XNS. Xerox Network System.

X.25. An international standard, documented in ITU-T Recommendation X.25, that defines the interface between a computing device and a packet-switched data network (PSDN).

X WINDOW SYSTEM. A set of distributed graphical presentation services that implement a windowing system on a graphics display. The X Window System implements a client/server relationship between an application program (the client) and the windowing software in a workstation or terminal that controls a window on the graphical display (the server). The client and server can be running in different computing systems or in the same computing system.

ZERO-SLOT LAN. A form of computer networking in which communication is generally accomplished using software that accesses a computer system's serial or parallel ports. Zero-slot LAN software often provides facilities similar to those provided in a conventional local area network.

Index

*Page numbers in bold refer to terms in the glossary.